A Blessed Rage for Order

A Blessed Rage for Order

DECONSTRUCTION, EVOLUTION, AND CHAOS

Alexander J. Argyros

Ann Arbor

THE UNIVERSITY OF MICHIGAN PRESS

Library of Congress Cataloging-in-Publication Data

Argyros, Alex.
    A blessed rage for order : deconstruction, evolution, and chaos /
Alexander J. Argyros.
        p.   cm.
    Includes bibliographical references (p.   ) and index.
    ISBN 0-472-10221-4 (alk. paper)
    1. Deconstruction. 2. Cosmology. 3. Evolution. 4. Change.
5. Culture—Philosophy.   I. Title.
    B809.6.A74   1991
    149—dc20   91-36053
                                                                CIP

A CIP catalogue record for this book is available from the British Library.

Oh! Blessed rage for order, pale Ramon,
The maker's rage to order words of the sea,
Words of the fragrant portals, dimly-starred,
And of ourselves and of our origins,
In ghostlier demarcations, keener sounds.
                            Wallace Stevens

Acknowledgments

The academy should be a place where ideas are born, communicated, and criticized. Sadly, all too often the protocols of academic institutions dictate that this ideal be put on the back burner. I am fortunate to have been part of a rare exception, a noble experiment in interdisciplinary research and teaching instituted by the University of Texas at Dallas and nurtured by Dean Robert W. Corrigan of the School of Arts and Humanities. Under the wise leadership of Dean Corrigan, an exciting group of scholars, thinkers, and artists has been reexamining the traditional academic disciplines with a view toward discovering their deep unity. I have been spoiled on the rich broth of intellectual stimulation and aesthetic delight offered by UT-D, and for that I am deeply grateful.

I also wish to thank a number of my muses. Frederick Turner has been my teacher, reader, colleague, and friend. I dedicate this book to him. Much of the credit for the fundamental ideas structuring my work belongs to J. T. Fraser, possibly the most innovative living philosopher and certainly one of the most ignored. Finally, the ideas of Gretchen Sween and David Lever are always on my mind and find frequent expression throughout this book.

Three chapters have been previously published and are reprinted here with permission: "Deconstructive Politics" appeared as "Prescriptive Deconstruction" in *Critical Texts* 6, no. 1 (1989); "Collapsing the Literary Function" appeared as "Learning from the Stock Market: Literature as Cultural Investment" in *Mosaic* 22, no. 3 (1989); and "Temporal Asymmetry Reconsidered" appeared as "Towards a View of Time as Depth" in *Diogenes* 151 (1990).

In addition, I am indebted to James Gleick for his permission to use the bifurcation diagram from *Chaos*, to Thomas Weissert for his version of the Lorenz attractor, and to Christopher Parr for the phase space diagram of a real-world pendulum.

I would also like to thank the readers of University of Michigan Press for their productive criticism, Paisley Livingston for his support and his valuable suggestions, Gretchen Sween for her assistance in proofreading the manuscript, and the editors of the University of Michigan Press for their professionalism, vision, and unflagging enthusiasm.

Contents

Introduction

The success of deconstruction as an academic paradigm has been nothing short of spectacular. Although there are many sorts of explanations for this phenomenon, I would like to consider three: the metaphysical, the constructivist, and the natural classical.

The metaphysical explanation: Derrida's success is simply the result of the fact that deconstruction embodies a number of absolute and eternal truths about the nature of reality, the mind, language, culture, knowledge, time, etc.

The constructivist explanation: Derrida's power as a writer is a purely contingent event, depending exclusively on the conditions for philosophical or literary success generated by institutional, historical, or political accidents, conditions that Derrida himself might have helped to constitute.

The natural classical explanation: Although there are certainly many contingent cultural pressures on what may count as a good rhetorical performance, our evolution into human beings has deposited what Frederick Turner (1985) calls "natural classical" predispositions whose respect is an important, although not a sufficient, condition for such success. According to this hypothesis, deconstruction may work because it exploits rhetorical strategies whose basis is a relatively noncontingent, cross-cultural propensity to organize the world in certain ways. For example, a natural classical perspective might lend itself to the following analysis of Derrida's rhetoric. Derrida's strength stems largely from his ability to weave apocalyptic declarations into rousing narratives about the end of philosophy. Therefore, Derrida responds to the needs met by prophets in other cultures. Like all prophets, Derrida is first of all a teller of terrifying stories. His work is a magnificent narrative, what Lyotard (1984) calls a "grand narrative," the oracular story of the death of philosophy. In other words, as opposed to an analysis of deconstruction that would emphasize the sociohistorical conditions for its acceptability as an interpretative paradigm, the natural classical view contends that Derrida's defense of radical contingency has flourished not because of its announced program but because it has ingeniously, though perhaps unwittingly, tapped into an ancient natural classical form, the apocalyptic epic.

Although the metaphysical hypothesis poses a number of obstreperous problems for deconstruction, problems such as the paradox of universal contingency (Is it universally true that there are no universal truths?), I take it as fairly well settled that metaphysical explanations in general are inadequate to the complexity of human cognition. Not so well settled are the relative merits of the constructivist and natural classical views. In fact, I think it unfortunate that the natural classical position, which suggests that a rhetorical or aesthetic performance increases its chances of success if it avails itself of the resources of our genetic-cultural codes, tends to be ignored by the constructivist-dominated language games of much contemporary critical theory. This book is an attempt to redress this situation by presenting an alternative to the deconstructive worldview, an alternative whose basic premise is that the natural world, as revealed by the natural sciences, channels human interpretations of both culture and nature as much as human interpretations of culture and nature are channeled by sociohistorical pressures.

By defining the traditional subjects of philosophy, such as ontology, epistemology, axiology, ethics, and aesthetics, exclusively as the products of cultural forces (history, ideology, institutions, etc.), deconstruction, and all antifoundationalisms, must bracket the entirety of the natural world, including that part of it comprising the nonmind-like components of human beings. The deconstructive version of Cartesianism usually maintains that while the world outside of human culture exists, it has absolutely no say in what constitutes truth, meaning, evidence, knowledge, or beauty for human beings. The central theme of this book is that although socio-institutional contexts certainly have a large voice in constituting the world of human beings, theirs is not the only voice. The kind of dualism that postulates an unbreachable gap between human culture and prehuman nature must be replaced by a systemic view of human culture situating it within a larger natural framework. For deconstructionists, any dialogue with nature can only be a disguised monologue. The natural classical position defended in this book hopes to continue the good work of Turner's *Natural Classicism* with an appeal for humility in the face of the possibility that human beings cannot create the entirety of their world.

Although the central theme of this book is that deconstructive dualism should be replaced by a systemic view of the relations between human culture to its natural environment, such concerns are addressed in the context of a commitment to reexamining the notion of value. For essential reasons, antifoundationalisms such as deconstruction inevitably argue themselves into the corner of radical axiological relativism. Perhaps the quintessential deconstructive statement is Barbara Johnson's, who, in her introduction to her translation of Derrida's *La dissémination*, says:

> Copernicus can be said to have written a critique of the Ptolemaic conception of the universe. But the idea that the earth goes around the sun is not an improvement of the idea that the sun goes around the earth. It is a shift in perspective that literally makes the ground move. (Derrida 1981a, xv)

Johnson's Kuhnian (1970) formulation is necessitated by the ubiquitous deconstructive and postmodern phobia of the notion of value. What Johnson cannot say is that one theory is *better* than another except insofar as the meaning of better has been determined by specific, and radically contingent, socio-institutional contexts. Opposed to such a typically deconstructive stance, this book argues that not only can we legitimately claim that one theory may be better than another (for example, that Copernicus was closer to the truth than Ptolemy) but that such value judgments may also be gauged by standards that transcend the local and the contingent.

Derrida frequently appeals to the notion of affirmation, usually in relation to his vision of a Nietzschean dance. We must not indulge in nostalgia for lost presence, Derrida argues, rather we must actively affirm a world without origin, telos, or deep meaning. Although I disagree with Derrida on what should be affirmed, I believe that his insistence on affirmation is a valuable insight. Unfortunately, when Derrida tries to affirm something more concrete than a world without nostalgia for presence, as in the case of his essays on apartheid, he stumbles for lack of a theory of value. Derrida is unable to claim that apartheid is worse than European liberalism because there are no concepts in his tool kit to allow him to maintain that anything is better than anything else except insofar as value is provisionally determined by conditional, and eminently deconstructible, local contexts. His call for affirmation, although stirring, is hollow. Ultimately, Derrida has nothing to affirm. That is why he sometimes chastises some of his exuberant acolytes with a reminder that deconstruction is not a program that can succeed.

By definition, deconstruction is endless analysis. In his recent essay on Paul de Man's articles published in the Belgian newspaper *Le Soir* between 1940 and 1942, Derrida (1988a) defends de Man by arguing that the condemnation of the bluntly antisemitic nature of some of these articles has been a simplification of the irreducible complexity of de Man's rhetorical strategies. Instead of hasty conclu zsions, the literary world owes de Man interminable analyses: "We owe it to him and we will owe him still more since what he leaves us is also the gift of an ordeal, the summons to a work of reading, historical interpretation, ethico-political reflection, an interminable analysis" (639).

Deconstruction takes apart that which was thought to be whole, and it introduces specters into that which was imagined to be wholly present. But, having shown that reality is a fabric of traces, it offers no alternative to the metaphysics of presence other than the affirmation of the continuous need to deconstruct it. What Derrida cannot conceive of is that metaphysics may not be inevitable and eternal and, consequently, that the more pernicious manifestations of logocentrism may, in fact, be correctable. Deconstruction is powerless to entertain the possibility that certain baneful components of metaphysics are historical moments and nothing more—that is, that metaphysics may itself not be metaphysical through and through—because such a position requires a minimal concept of progress. Simply, one must be prepared to argue that the sclerotic parts of metaphysics should be replaced by more appropriate and productive existential, epistemological, ontological, aesthetic, social, political, and institutional systems. By defining deconstruction as an interminable contestation of metaphysics, a body of analyses whose very axioms decree that it cannot succeed in effecting substantive change, Derrida implicitly assumes the impossibility of progress and, simultaneously, the untranscendable need for local, somewhat terrorist, deconstructive interventions. Metaphysics is Derrida's Vietnam. By presupposing that he can never win the war, he both legitimizes his work and relegates it to a textual DMZ.

A recurring theme of this book is that a theoretical paradigm cannot be undermined by criticism or analysis alone. Criticism may be a necessary first step, a kind of philosophical or ideological pica-dor, but it must be followed by a model that is presented as more valuable than the one being deconstructed. In other words, the suc-cessful contestation of any paradigm must actively proclaim the pos-sibility of progress: the model it proposes must be assumed to be superior to the one it is criticizing on some scale of value. Without an alternate hypothesis about the nature of the object being decon-structed, deconstruction is powerless to make the most elementary of distinctions, such as, for example, the one Scholes (1985) percep-tively adduces.

> From the perspective of deconstruction, there is nothing upon which we can ground an argument for evolutionary biology as opposed to fundamentalist creationism, since both are dis-courses, with their blindness and their insights, and neither one can be said to be more or less accurate than the other, there being no pathway open from the text to the world. (99)

My sense of deception over the emptiness of Derrida's positions stems, in the main, from a growing realization that all that decon-struction can do is devise ever more ingenious strategies to announce that the emperor is naked. And, despite the fact that Derrida's hier-atic style makes such demystification seem like a gesture of world-historical importance, it does little to suggest an alternative to emper-ors, clothed or naked. If we are to replace the emperor with something better, we must believe, and deeply, that better alternatives are pos-sible. And it is of little help to retreat to the safety of axiological relativism, claiming, for example, that value is always the product of local interpretative communities. I do not see how someone could care deeply about values that he or she knows to be purely contin-gent. Even Rorty (1989) must arm his ironist with one cross-cultural universal value, that the infliction of pain is evil, if he is to mount a coherent political argument. And if this slight wedge is thrust into the Pandora's box of noncontingencies, it is sobering to imagine what else might fly out.

This book argues that the only nonmetaphysical way around the impasse generated by the apotheosis of textuality is through a kind of foundationalism based on a view of the universe as a communicative, dynamical, and evolving system. In pursuit of this goal, the book is organized into three parts.

Part 1 is an essentially deconstructive gesture inasmuch as it contests deconstruction in a space defined by deconstruction's own rules. While it attempts to interlace a reportorial account of some of the major themes of deconstruction with analyses signaling their weaknesses, part 1 respects the protocols of deconstruction by refraining from any effort to suggest an alternate theoretical viewpoint from which the inadequacies of deconstruction might be corrected.

The book's second and third parts step outside the conceptual framework of deconstruction in an attempt to replace criticism by affirmation. Consequently, parts 2 and 3 propose the outlines of an alternative to both metaphysical closure and deconstructive demystification. The basic premise of part 2 is that the universe we live in, which includes both the natural and the social worlds, is best described by a hierarchical evolutionary model. Recent developments in a congeries of different disciplines, ranging from high-energy physics to biogenetic anthropology, suggest the contours of a stunningly beautiful model of cosmic evolution. Rather than a flat web of traces, the universe appears to be a marvelously complex, and frequently tangled, dynamical hierarchical, system. With such a systemic view of the universe serving as a foundation, part 2 attempts to postulate an evolutionary ontology, epistemology, and aesthetics.

Part 3 focuses on the emerging science of chaos, arguing that the most robust and complex things in the universe, including human beings and their theories, works of art, and social structures, are best understood neither as Platonic essences nor as random processes, but as chaotic systems. Chaos might be in a position to render outdated the old distinctions between necessity and chance, or between metaphysics and dissemination, replacing them with a dynamical theory that encompasses both local unpredictability and global order. Insofar as chaos theory contributes to reversing the dominant contemporary understanding of the relation between order and freedom, a position that basically equates order with the police and freedom with undecidability, it promises a new ontological and epistemological paradigm.

Part 3 interprets this new paradigm to suggest a number of possible philosophical consequences. Chaos is a scientific theory that rejects scientific reductionism. As a result, it can serve to begin healing the four-hundred-year-old schism between science and the humanities. In addition, chaos may allow us to reaffirm such battered concepts as universality, identity, meaning, truth, and beauty. It traces the dim shape of a postmodern religion, one that situates the ineradicable human rage for totalization and transcendence within the purview of the most powerful explanatory models available to contemporary science. And chaos might offer the basis for a new understanding of art that respects both the reasonable demands of scientifically oriented skeptics and the artist's need to inhabit the chimeras of the imagination.

But perhaps most significantly, chaos theory and an evolutionary epistemology may provide the theoretical framework necessary to rehabilitate the concept of progress, a concept that is almost universally dismissed in today's academic marketplace. Only orthodox Marxism has the courage to define progress; unfortunately it gets its science, history, and human nature wrong. Except for Marxism, the intellectual world is inhabited by various kinds of textualisms, relativisms, constructivisms, and antifoundationalisms whose axiomatic rejection of the idea of progress makes them, in my view, at best politically marginal and at worst ideologically reactionary. The chaotic evolutionary perspective offered by this book rejects both the Derridian "always already" and the constructivist notion of radical, unhierarchical discontinuity, preferring a view of the natural and social worlds that situates them in a softly teleological and endlessly innovative continuum. Plato and Darwin, Aristotle and Hubble, Derrida and Prigogine, Laplace and Crutchfield, these are some of the names whose dance may seem slow and structured by Derridian standards, wild by those of New Critical sobriety, but wise and delightfully eccentric by the only standards that matter in the end, the standards whose respect and transgression pushed some unimaginably simple subatomic particles to organize themselves into human beings.

1

Deconstructive Indeterminacy

Deconstruction is a philosophical system whose basic premise is that, underneath its appearance of stability, the world is governed by an unmasterable web of traces. The purpose of deconstruction is to demystify metaphysical structures by demonstrating their arbitrary and abyssal grounds. Part 1 explores the implications of deconstructive indeterminacy for such concepts as time, subjectivity, language, politics, science, and literature. The theme of these explorations is that while deconstruction does a credible job of dismantling metaphysical objects, it is incapable of providing alternatives. Since it is essentially a negative methodology, when deconstruction is called upon to address concrete issues, such as political ones, its penchant for eliding commitment and its resistance to postulating scales of value render it ineffectual at best and reactionary at worst.

Chapter 1

The Baseless Fabric

It is for us, in the Occident, the culture of common sense that is marked by a powerful scientifico-philosophic tradition, metaphysics, technics, the opposition of subject/object, and precisely a certain organization of the throw (*jet*). Through several differentiated relays, this culture goes back at least to Plato, where the repression of Democritus perhaps leaves the trace of a very large symptom.

—Jacques Derrida, "My Chances"

In direct opposition to Aristotle were the Greek atomists, such as Democritus, who taught that the world is nothing but atoms moving in a void. All structures and forms were regarded as merely different arrangements of atoms, and all change and process were thought of as due to the rearrangements of atoms alone. To the atomist, the universe is a machine in which each component atom moves entirely under the action of the blind forces produced by its neighbors. According to this scheme there are no final causes, no overall plan or end-state towards which things evolve. Teleology is dismissed as mystical. The only causes that bring about change are those produced by the shape and movement of other atoms.

—Paul Davies, *The Cosmic Blueprint*

Perhaps the most serious shortcoming of deconstruction is its inability to propose a positive agenda for either critical, aesthetic, or political action. In an interview in *Art Papers* (Derrida 1986c), Derrida explains why, during a symposium on deconstruction, he was disturbed by the suggestion that his was a philosophy of political liberation: "As far as I can see what this name deconstruction covers, deconstruction is not a movement which one day can arrive at an accomplishment, something which can be achieved—there is no success for deconstruction, there is no goal which we have a hope of reaching, there is no *telos* for deconstruction" (34). That is both deconstruction's strength and its weakness. There is no success for deconstruction because of Derrida's deep-seated belief that what he calls the logocentric or metaphysical tradition is not merely a moment in history that can be surpassed, but a structural component of experience. Derrida's world is largely Sisyphean, a perpetual struggle against the oppressive tendency of metaphysical thought to essentialize Being.[1] Deconstruction does not propose alternatives, it does not imagine a world that is better than the one we live in. On the contrary, it assumes that such an agenda must be, at least in part, ontotheological, and consequently, its self-imposed mission is to neutralize or destabilize the rigid binary oppositions that define the metaphysics of progress. Were Platonism to simply fall from grace, were it to become uninteresting as a way to conceptualize the world, deconstruction would reach its completion and its exhaustion. Without confidence in the residual nostalgia for the Word, Derrida could have no grounds for his belief that the decentering tinkering of deconstruction is an endless enterprise.

As Richard Rorty (1984) claims, it is likely that metaphysics, at least the kind of metaphysics upon which Derrida bases his project of ateleological reinscription, is in fact fast becoming an outmoded model of Being. However, the possible demise of metaphysics does not necessarily imply, as many contemporary theorists believe, that we are entering an era of rampant postmodern simulation. Although this chapter is mainly concerned with deconstruction, I think it might be useful to introduce my analysis of Derrida's guiding presuppositions by distinguishing between the deconstructive and postmodern views of metaphysics.

Postmodernism, as described by such authors as Lyotard, Baudrillard, Jameson, and Hassan, appears to be an extension of deconstruction. In fact, with its emphasis on media, communication, cybernetics, and technology, postmodernism could easily be viewed as an electronic version of the largely philosophical enterprise of deconstruction. This view is, I believe, in the main false. The crucial distinction between deconstruction and postmodernism is that while the former maintains that any surpassing of metaphysics is a naive kind of "liberation philosophy," the latter argues that our culture has already been so penetrated by a regime of simulation that any recourse to logocentric principles, even as that which must be resisted, is a pure chimera. As Jean Baudrillard argues, in postmodern culture, reality has lapsed into indeterminacy: "Today, the entire system is fluctuating in indeterminacy, all of reality absorbed by the hyperreality of the code and of simulation. It is now a principle of simulation, and not of reality, that regulates social life. The finalities have disappeared; we are now engendered by models. There is no longer such a thing as ideology; there are only simulacra" (Fekete 1984, 56). Postmodernism postulates that a completely deconstructed world, a condition that Derrida repeatedly argues is impossible, is already at hand.

Deconstruction differs from postmodernisn, then, in its insistence that metaphysics still determines the conceptual framework through which our culture constitutes its central ontological, epistemological, and ethical positions. Whereas deconstruction sees metaphysics as a recalcitrant illusion, postmodernism considers metaphysics as simply one more simulation engendered by a culture that has turned totally counterfeit. However, as long as this difference is respected, it is clear that deconstruction and postmodernism make common cause in their affirmation that Being is without an ultimate foundation. The core gesture of deconstruction is the demonstration that the binary oppositions structuring Western philosophical thought are, in fact, haunted by undecidable or indeterminate traces that refuse resolution into an either/or structure. Postmodernism simply takes the tension out of deconstruction, stating that there is nothing left to deconstruct. Therefore, both deconstruction and postmodernism believe that the essence of reality is nonessence: what metaphysics has defined as identity is, in fact, according to deconstruction, a reification of indeterminacy and, according to postmodernism, a simulacrum that the "code" has rendered parodic.

The key issue, then, is indeterminacy. In its various manifestations, indeterminacy is the theme uniting many contemporary critical and philosophical positions, especially the deconstructive and postmodern worldviews. It should be noted, however, that, for Derrida, indeterminacy does not mean that concepts are not determined contextually. In fact, Derrida has repeatedly asserted the importance of historical and institutional forces in determining, or reifying, meaning. However, the backbone of deconstruction is the idea that the historical contexts that determine meaning are themselves indeterminate. Deconstruction does not describe the world as an undifferentiated fog of semiotic fragments, but as an indeterminate web of metaphysical determinations.

Consequently, in order to frame the critique of deconstruction that constitutes the first part of this book (and, since postmodernism is, I believe, simply deconstruction without anything left to deconstruct, postmodernism will be implicitly critiqued as well), it would be useful to begin by analyzing the ways in which the notion of indeterminacy has been applied by Derrida to a number of crucial philosophic, linguistic, psychological, and aesthetic concepts. Specifically, I will consider deconstructive indeterminacy as articulated in the following themes or clusters of themes: time and subjectivity, language and semiotics, style, politics, and literature and science.

Chapter 2

Time and Subjectivity

Although Derrida does not write philosophical treatises in which a position is clearly presented, his work does invite reasonable inferences about his posture toward concepts addressed in his typical, indirect style. Two such concepts, time and subjectivity, are a leitmotif throughout Derrida's work. In fact, it would not be unreasonable to claim that Derrida's main agenda is little else than the attempt to deconstruct the Aristotelian notion of time as the succession of now-points and the phenomenological view of transcendental subjectivity.

The closest Derrida has come to an extended discussion of time is in his analysis of Husserl in *Speech and Phenomena* (1973). The aim of this book is the attempt to deconstruct Husserl's (1962) belief in a prepredicative ego having access to the world in a manner best described by the famous phenomenological "principle of principles."

> But enough of such topsy-turvy theories: No theory we can conceive can mislead us in regard to the *principle of all principles: that very primordial dator Intuition is a source of authority (Rechtsquelle) for knowledge, that whatever presents itself in "Intuition" in primordial form* (as it were in its bodily reality), *is simply to be accepted as it gives itself to be, though only within the limits in which it then presents itself.* (Husserl 1969, 83)

In order to muddy the purity of the transcendental ego, Derrida proposes turning Husserl's phenomenology of time consciousness against itself. The punctuality of the present, as envisioned by Husserl, is dialectically related to the concept of presence, simultaneously determining it and determined by it. Consequently, any attempt to shake the foundations of Husserl's Cartesian desire to found

15

an absolutely rigorous and pure first philosophy must pass through the filiation of the spacial concept "presence" to the temporal notion of the present. To this end, Derrida engages in a classic piece of deconstruction, seeking to insinuate an essential core of nonpresence and nonpunctuality into the heart of Husserl's immediately self-intuiting transcendental ego. According to Husserl's logic, although the transcendental ego can generate and interpret signs, it itself cannot contain any of the elements of the sign, specifically the spatial and temporal delay Derrida (1981) will later postulate as constitutive of the functioning of all signs—

> This is why the *a* of *différance* also recalls that spacing is temporization, the detour and postponement by means of which intuition, perception, consummation—in a word, the relationship to the present, the reference to present reality, to a *being*—are always *deferred*. Deferred by virtue of the very principle of difference which holds that an element functions and signifies, takes on or conveys meaning, only by referring to another past or future element in an economy of traces. (1981b, 28–29)

Consequently, if either the structure or the dynamics of the sign could be injected into what Husserl understands as the prepredicative, punctually self-conscious ego, then not only experience of the external world, but even Cartesian immediacy and evidence, would be contaminated by nonexpressivity, nonpresence, or *différance*.

In a chapter entitled "Signs and the Blink of an Eye," Derrida subjects Husserl's theory of phenomenological temporality, as outlined in *The Phenomenology of Internal Time-Consciousness*, to a deconstructive displacement. The present, Derrida argues, is crucial to phenomenology for two chief reasons. First, it guarantees the possibility of a transcendental ego. Second, it is the necessary condition for a punctual origin in general, and, since Derrida has always understood metaphysics or "philosophy" as an edifice built on the concept of an absolute beginning, presence as origin is synonymous with philosophy: "Moreover, within philosophy there is no possible objection concerning this privilege of the present-now; it defines the very element of philosophical thought, it is *evidence* itself, conscious thought itself, it governs every possible concept of truth and sense" (1973, 62). If time is defined as the succession of punctual points, or nows, then the foundation is laid for Husserl's Cartesian enterprise, the establishment of an inviolate transcendental ego whose absolutely certain intuitions can serve as the solid bedrock for philosophy.

As is typical with Derrida's work, his transformative reading of Husserl does not seek to debunk Husserl's arguments with a set of opposing ones. Instead, Derrida attempts to undermine Husserl's position by demonstrating that its premises contaminate it just enough to render it inconsistent with its own requirements of purity. Specifically, Husserl's conception of internal time consciousness has recourse to a transcendental present that contains within itself a retentive trace and a protentive anticipation. Rather than defining time as a succession of pure now-points, Husserl conceives of each of these punctual presents as spread out into a past (whose trace it retains) and a future (whose anticipation it contains). The present, then, is not simple, nor is it simply present. Its power of presentation is contaminated with an irreducible trace of re-presentation.

> One then sees quickly that the presence of the perceived present can appear as such only inasmuch as it is *continuously compounded* with a nonpresence and nonperception, with primary memory and expectation (retention and pretention). These nonperceptions are neither added to, nor do they *occasionally* accompany, the actually perceived now; they are essentially and indispensably involved in its possibility. (Derrida 1973, 64)

For Derrida, then, the present upon which most traditional conceptions of time depend is not a homogeneously simple point, but an amalgamation of presence and re-presentation: "There is a duration to the blink, and it closes the eye. This alterity is in fact the condition for presence, presentation, and thus for *Vorstellung* in general" (65). Since Derrida has always understood time as a succession of instants, the kind of time he is proposing can no longer be called "time" except under erasure: "But what we are calling time must be given a different name—for "time" has always designated a movement conceived in terms of the present, and can mean nothing else" (68). Derrida's point, here, is crucial insofar as it reproduces a gesture typical of deconstruction. Time, Derrida implies, in its filiation to metaphysics, must mean punctuality. It can mean nothing else, since the concept of meaning is itself based on the presence of the present. Deconstruction does not demonstrate the inadequacies of a metaphysical conception of time and then suggest an alternate theory of time that corrects these shortcomings. In fact, deconstruction always renders unto metaphysics what belongs to metaphysics. Rather than enter into a dialectical relationship with what Derrida considers to be the *only* possible concept of time, he introduces a nonconcept, "time" as deferral and temporization, and suggests that instead of competing with the logocentric idea of time, his "archetemporality" is actually its condition of possibility: "Is not the concept of pure solitude—of the monad in the phenomenological sense—*undetermined* by its own origin, by the very condition of its self—presence, that is, by 'time,' to be conceived anew on the basis now of difference within auto-affection, on the basis of identifying identity and nonidentity within the 'sameness' of the *im selben Augenblick*" (68)?

Derrida's notion of time, "time" under erasure, must be understood as nonpresence. In "Freud and the Scene of Writing" he says: "The 'subject' of writing does not exist if we mean by that some sovereign solitude of the author. The subject of writing is a *system* of relations between strata: the Mystic Pad, the psyche, society, the world. Within that scene, on that stage, the punctual simplicity of the classical subject is not to be found" (1978b, 227). Time as *différance*, or as the "scene of writing," is important to Derrida not only in and of itself, but because it gives him access to another seminal philosophical concept that is heavily laden with metaphysical reification: the concept of subjectivity. His analysis of *The Phenomenology of Internal Time-Consciousness* seeks to deconstruct the punctually self-conscious phenomenological subject by attacking its ground, the simplicity of a present moment. In later writings, especially when dealing with Freud, this argument is subsumed under Derrida's concept of primordial delay or *différance*. For example, in "Différance" he explains the importance of Freud for deconstruction: "The two apparently different values of *différance* are tied together in Freudian theory: to differ as discernibility, distinction, separation, diastem, *spacing*; and to defer as detour, relay, reserve, *temporization*" (1982, 18). *Différance*, one of Derrida's key deconstructive concepts, consists of the indissoluble union of two kinds of nonidentity: spatial difference and temporal nonsimultaneity. The temporal component of *différance* is described in "Différance," as it was in "Freud and the Scene of Writing," as a tension between two economies of deferral. One, an economic detour, is Freud's belief that "Under the influence of the ego's instincts of self-preservation, the pleasure principle is replaced by the reality principle. This latter principle does not abandon the intention of ultimately obtaining pleasure, but it nevertheless demands and carries into effect the postponement of satisfaction . . ." (1982, 19). The second kind of delay, first outlined in Derrida's "From Restricted to General Economy: A Hegelianism Without Reserve" (1978), is reprieved in "La Différance" to represent the *différance* of Freud's notion of postponement: "*différance* as the relation to an impossible presence, as expenditure without reserve, as the irreparable loss of presence, the irreversible usage of energy, that is, as the death instinct, and as the entirely other relationship that apparently interrupts every economy" (1982, 19).

Derrida's point is that *différance* understood as primordial delay is analogous to Freud's notion of *Nachträglichkeit*, or aftereffect, a psychological mechanism whereby an event is only experienced after the fact, and then only as a memory. Consciousness, according to Derrida, has an irreducible element of unconsciousness. Derrida's unconscious is not a potential consciousness, but a structure of delay and deferral that refuses to be subsumed into the alternative between presence and absence. Just as in his analysis of Husserl, Derrida seeks to undermine the notion of phenomenological subjectivity through recourse to a kind of time that is neither present nor absent, his reading of Freud unearths a temporality of pure delay, or noncoincidence. Furthermore, refusing the simple division of the subject into conscious and unconscious regions, Derrida wishes to implicate the temporality of the unconscious into what Husserlian phenomenology calls the living present.

> The structure of delay (*Nachträglickeit*) in effect forbids that one make of temporalization (temporization) a simple dialectical complication of the living present as an originary and unceasing synthesis—a synthesis constantly directed back on itself, gathered in on itself and gathering—or retentional traces and protentional openings. The alterity of the "unconscious" makes us concerned not with horizons of modified—past or future—pre-

sents, but with a "past" that has never been present, and which never will be, whose future to come will never be a *production* or a reproduction in the form of presence. (1982, 21)

I have conjoined subjectivity and temporality in this chapter because, for Derrida, their union is not contingent, but structurally necessary. His deconstruction of the present of presence, and his emphasis on temporal delay, on a network of retentive and protentive traces, is guided by his desire to question the Cartesian (or phenomenological) subject. Ultimately, time is important for Derrida insofar as it allows him to claim that the subject is not a pure center of experience, but is itself woven out of a system of differences: "This economic aspect of *différance*, which brings into play a certain not conscious calculation in a field of forces, is inseparable from the more narrowly semiotic aspect of *différance*. It confirms that the subject, and first of all the conscious and speaking subject, depends upon the system of differences and the movement of *différance*, that the subject is constituted only in being divided from itself, in becoming space, in temporizing, in deferral" (1981b, p. 29).

For Derrida the subject is not constitutive but constituted, and time is the medium of its self-alienation. The spectral temporality of *différance* is the insubstantial rock upon which the classic notion of subjectivity is propped: "This movement of *différance* does not arise from a transcendental subject. It produces that subject" (1976, 92). Whether Derrida uses time in his attempt to destabilize the notion of subjectivity, or whether, as in *Of Grammatology*, he employs his deconstructed version of writing—arche-writing—to announce the subject's immanent relation to its own death: "As the subject's relationship to its own death, this becoming is the constitution of subjectivity" (1976, 69), his goals are fundamentally the same. For Derrida, the Cartesian absolute subject depends on an Aristotelian linear temporality to both legitimate itself through self-knowledge and to anchor itself on the presence of external objects in acts of intentionality. If time were shown to be an abyssal fabric of traces, then both the subject and the object are ghosted: "And the original absence of the subject of writing is also the absence of the thing or the referent" (1976, 69). Time as a linear progression of now-instants would guarantee the ultimate determinability of both the subject and the referent. Derrida's deconstructed concept of temporality, one constituted by internal absence, slippage, and death, introduces an uncontrollable element of indeterminacy into the heart of subjectivity and its intentional objects. By deconstructing time, Derrida seeks to undermine what he considers to be the essence of philosophy, the transcendental confidence that the subject and the object can be securely delimited in the presence of the present.

The validity of this position will be one of my major concerns in the following chapters. However, in anticipation of the kinds of arguments to be made there, let me emphasize a fundamental prejudice of Derrida's method. Derrida is essentially a reader and critic of other texts. He has frequently defined his work as the careful, often painstaking, dismembering of the seminal works of what he calls Western Metaphysics. Consequently, Derrida tends not to evaluate concepts as such, since he does not believe that concepts as such exist, but to interrogate their inscription in various kinds of semiotic systems. In other words, he will not offer hypotheses concerning such concepts as time, choosing instead, for programmatic reasons, to restrict himself to deconstructive interpretations of their status in the philosophical systems of others. So much is obvious to any reader of Derrida. What may not be so obvious, because Derrida has made its consideration appear hopelessly unsophisticated, is that, since in the deconstructive theoretical matrix texts are written by human beings, it is meaningless to speculate about the natural world except insofar as it is inscribed in human semiotic webs. In other words, Derrida shares the phenomenological prejudice that the knowable is somehow commensurate with the intentional, that is, with an object as it presents itself to a human knower. Derrida's world may not be the world of books, as some facile readers have claimed, but it is nevertheless a phenomenological prison-house. "There is nothing but the text" means there is nothing meaningful but what has been constructed and distorted by the filter of human culture. Ultimately, deconstruction, like phenomenology, existentialism, and postmodernism, is an anthropocentrism.

Heidegger, to whom Derrida freely and repeatedly acknowledges a huge debt, sums up the phenomenological attitude thus: "language alone brings what is, as something that is, into the Open for the first time. Where there is no language, as in the being of stone, plant, and animal, there is no openness of what is, and consequently no openness either of that which is not and of the empty" (1971, 73).

To my knowledge, except for occasional references to genetics (to be discussed in chapter 6) Derrida has only suggested the possible applicability of his concepts to lower animals once (and even there, parenthetically).[1]

> This is inevitable; one cannot do anything, least of all speak, without determining (in a manner that is not only theoretical, but practical and performative) a context. Such experience is always political because it implies, insofar as it involves determination, a certain type of non-"natural" relationship to others (and this holds as well for what we call "animals," since, without being able to go into it here, what I am saying implies a rather profound transformation of the concept of the "political" along with several others in order to be able to say that man is not the only political animal). (1988b, 136)

Derrida is correct on the political nature of all reality, but, as far as I know, he has never discussed what he claims not to be able to explore in the preceding paragraph, namely the specific manner in which his key concepts, such as arche-writing, dissemination, or the trace, function in the worlds of physics, chemistry, or biology. I suspect that the reason for his silence is that his training as a phenomenologist has resulted in deeply ingrained habits of thought, chief among which is the presupposition that epistemology and ontology are meaningful only within the opening of human intentional experience.

My chief criticism of Derridian deconstruction is that except on a trivial level, that of the truism that we can only know about what we can know about, this phenomenological bracketing of the natural world is epistemologically untenable and ethically dangerous. The reasons for this will, I hope, become increasingly clear. For the moment, I would simply like to observe that Derrida does not consider the possibility that the concept of time could have any meaning except for a constitutive or constituted subject. Again, Heidegger seems to offer a phenomenological precedent: "After all there was a time when man was not. But strictly speaking we cannot say: There was a time when man *was* not. At all *times* man was and is and will be, because time produces itself only insofar as man is. There is no time when man was not, not because man was from eternity and will be for all eternity but because time is not eternity and time fashions itself into a time only as a human, historical being-there" (1974, 84). That, for example, photons, atoms, and nonhuman biological organisms may exist in temporalities that are different from those of human beings is a question that I do not believe either Heidegger or Derrida is in a position to broach.

Différance may be "'older' than the ontological difference or than the truth of Being" (Derrida 1982, 22), yet it too lives in what Heidegger calls "the house of Being." Like other phenomenologists, Derrida refuses commerce with a concept that he considers naive or insane: the meaningfulness of a world that predates and exceeds human consciousness. The antiscientific bent of early Husserl, Heidegger, and, to a large extent, Derrida, stems from their impatience with the supposed referentiality of science. As a phenomenologist, Derrida can accord science no value other than as a semiotic system, that is, a nexus of concepts, ideas, signifiers, etc. The only world in which he is interested is the lived world, the world that, although certainly existing outside of human experience (phenomenologists are not idealists, although Husserl did once speculate that the transcendental ego could survive the possible annihilation of the world), is only accessible as a world given to consciousness. Consequently, Derrida's analysis of time, like his analysis of Being, follows Heidegger's basic idea that whatever the Being of the world outside of human participation is, it is only through human (i.e., natural) language that the Being of beings is disclosed. Time for Derrida is always the human experience of time. That is why it is only to be understood in relation to the idea of subjectivity and to what deconstructionists, following a tradition at least as old as Aristotle, think is nearly synonymous with the human subject—language. Beyond the truism of the following statement by Geoffrey Hartman (1981) lie both the energy and the limitations of deconstruction: "Time is not against language (or vice versa) but coterminous with it: to be in the one is to be in the other" (7).

Chapter 3

Language and Indeterminacy

I do not believe I have ever spoken of "indeterminacy," whether
in regard to "meaning" or anything else.
                                        —Derrida, *Limited, Inc.*

As Rodolphe Gasché points out in "Deconstruction as Criticism"
(1979), although Derrida is by training and inclination a philosopher,
his initial entry into U.S. culture occurred through the mediation of
literature departments. There are historical, political, and institutional reasons for this; however, the result was that deconstruction
was introduced to U.S. academia as a method for doing literary criticism. As such, it had to be tailored to fit the needs and protocols of
academic literary analysis. J. Hillis Miller (Davis and Schleifer [1985])
speculates that, "It has something to do with the role of colleges and
universities and the academy in general in the United States, that has
made America a place where deconstruction has a kind of widespread force in academic life" (87). The now famous Yale school,
which is usually understood to include such critics as J. Hillis Miller,
Paul de Man, Geoffrey Hartman, and perhaps Harold Bloom, has
developed a style of literary criticism borrowing heavily from the
conceptual and philosophical foundations laid by Derrida. Emphasizing rhetoric over reference, *mise en abime* over totalization, intertextuality over closure, dissemination over polysemousness, heterogene-
ity over homogeneity, the Yale critics have made deconstruction a
legitimate and clearly identifiable literary practice. All this is old hat
for most U.S. academics these days, so I won't belabor it. Instead, I
would like to investigate the conditions of its possibility in Derrida's
work. That is, I would like to highlight that part of Derrida's theory

that makes possible the kinds of deconstructive analyses we have come to associate with the Yale school.

To appreciate Derrida's view of language, it is necessary to delineate what deconstruction deconstructs. Although this is a complex issue, I think it is not totally inaccurate to claim that deconstruction is the attempt to undermine philosophy. Despite Derrida's repeated warnings that no concept is ever simple, philosophy appears to be defined (in Derrida's works) by what is presumed to be its guiding telos—the dream of a totally transparent, univocal language. In "White Mythology," among countless other places, Derrida (1982) defines the horizon of philosophy as the desire to reduce language to a rigid set of signifiers whose ultimate fate will be invisibility in the face of the signified: "Univocity is the essence, or better, the *telos* of language. No philosophy, as such, has ever renounced this Aristotelian ideal: This ideal is philosophy" (1982, 247).

According to Derrida, the ideal of an univocal language is "philosophy," "metaphysics," "logocentrism," "phallogocentrism," "ontotheology," etc. Deconstruction, therefore, is simply the dream to disrupt this dream of transparency. It is, of course, curious that deconstruction, a theoretical corpus dedicated to the multiplicity and slipperiness of signification, should be founded as a kind of resistance to what is presumed to be a univocal, identifiable essence. It is, indeed, very curious that Derrida should invoke philosophy as something that has a "self": "Each time that a rhetoric defines metaphor, not only is *a* philosophy implied, but also a conceptual network in which philosophy *itself* has been constituted" (230), or a "heart": "the dream at the heart of philosophy" (268). One cannot help but wonder about the procrustean virtuosity required to prune "philosophy" to such straw man dimensions.

Be that as it may, in contradistinction to this supposed philosophical ideal, Derrida postulates that the essence of language is violence: "To name, to give names that it will on occasion be forbidden to pronounce, such is the originary violence of language which consists in inscribing within a difference, in classifying, in suspending the vocative absolute" (1976, 112). This is an important point that cannot be emphasized enough. Throughout Derrida's work there is an insistence that language is violent in the sense that it is an articulation that disrupts the possibility of pure presence. Of course Derrida does not claim that presence actually precedes language. Far from it, since, according to Derrida, prelinguistic plenitude is, in fact, an illusion generated, retroactively, by that which violates it—language. In creating the plenitude it defers infinitely, language is both a window to presence and a machine incessantly delaying, distancing, and distorting it.

The violence of language is that it both creates and denies the possibility of a punctual, fully self-conscious, presemiotic consciousness. In other words, language is violent because it reverses the hierarchical relation of subject to tool. Rather than being an extension of a fully present consciousness, language is a partially autonomous, partially dead machine generating consciousness as one of its effects. For Derrida, consciousness does not mean—it is, at least in part, meant. Linguistic meaning is not the expression of a self-possessed source, but rather the effect of what Derrida calls the trace, *différance*, arche-writing, etc. Although these terms are not simply synonymous, since they figure in different contexts, the similarity that makes them identifiable as key Derridian "nonconcepts" is that they participate in a nonintentional structure that is the condition of possibility for both signification and phenomenality in general: "*The trace is in fact the absolute origin of sense in general. Which amounts to saying once again that there is no absolute origin of sense in general. The trace is the différance* which opens appearance [*l'apparaître*] and signification" (1977, 65; italics in original). Meaning is a secondary effect of a primal, nonoriginal origin. Meaning, therefore, is a simulacrum of life, neither dead in the way that matter has been understood by "philosophy," nor living as the Cartesian tradition would have the pure ego. The basis of meaning itself has no meaning: "Rather, it is a question of determining the possibility of *meaning* on the basis of a 'formal' organization which in itself has no meaning" (1982, 134).

The meaninglessness at the heart of language and experience stems from a definition of the signifier borrowed from Saussure. According to Saussure, a linguistic signifier is differential and arbitrary. Saussure's insistence that the signifier is differential—"The linguistic signifier . . . is not [in essence] phonic but incorporeal—constituted not by its material substance but the differences that separate its sound-image from all others" (Derrida 1977, 53)—allows Derrida to make two claims. First, since the substance of the voice, its immediate sonic presence, is not constitutive of the meaningfulness of speech, there is no reason in principle to distinguish, as Saussure does, between speech and writing. As is well known, Derrida's deconstruction of Saussure consists in the demonstration that since speech is structured by the same chain of immaterial signifiers as writing, no essential distinction can be made between them. Second, since all language is the product of ghostly differences, and since "difference is never in itself a sensible plenitude" (1977, 53), Derrida is able to claim that meaning can never be stabilized. Signification is differential because the identity of a signifier derives from its relation to all the other signifiers in a lexicon. Furthermore, this relation is not static, a collection of differences that are, as it were, already there, visible in their presence, but a dynamic process, a movement of differentiation that generates differential structures as one of its effects.

> It is not the question of a constituted difference here, but rather, before all determination of the content, of the *pure* movement which produces difference. *The (pure) trace is différance.* It does not depend on any sensible plenitude, audible or visible, phonic or graphic. It is, on the contrary, the condition of such a plenitude. Although it *does not exist,* although it is never a *being-present* outside of all plenitude, its possibility is by rights anterior to all that one calls sign (signifier/signified, content/expression, etc.), concept or operation, motor or sensory. (1977, 62)

The second salient component of Saussure's concept of the sign is that the signifier is arbitrary or unmotivated. By arbitrariness, Saussure means that the linguistic signifier bears no natural or symbolic relation to its signified but is, on the contrary, purely conventional. Unconstrained by the requirements of natural representation, the signifier is free from the demands of mimesis in a sense. It is precisely because the signifier, in general, is differential and arbitrary that Derrida argues that it is impossible to establish a hierarchy between phonic and graphic signifiers on the basis of "naturalness." Furthermore, and more important for Derrida's purposes, is the idea that along with difference, the arbitrariness of the sign dematerializes and de-essentializes the signifying chain. Instituted and differential, signification is, to a large extent, although, Derrida repeats regularly, not totally, liberated from the classical rules of reference. Once the sign has been shown to exist and function outside the laws of representation, it is no longer subject to the system of binary oppositions that serves as a foundation of those laws. Chief among these oppositions is the one between nature and culture. The trace is no more cultural than it is natural. In fact, for Derrida, the very distinction between nature and culture is posterior to, and produced by, the trace: "Thus, as it goes without saying, the trace whereof I speak is not more *natural* (it is not the mark, the natural sign, or the index in the Husserlian sense) than *cultural,* not more physical than psychic, biological than spiritual. It is that starting from which a becoming-unmotivated of the sign, and with it all the ulterior oppositions between *physis* and its other, is possible" (1977, 48).

In order to complete the picture of Derridian semiotics, one more feature of the sign must be addressed. In addition to arbitrariness and difference, Derrida's view of the sign requires the concept of iterability. For a sign to function as a sign, it must be understood to be *this* sign in an infinite number of contexts. A sign is a sign because its identity is not determined by any one of its phenomenal forms. This *word,* this version of the sign *word,* is in no way privileged. For *word* to be a sign, it must be recognizable in other types of print, when hand written, even when misspelled. The point is that a sign is a sign because it has a certain ideality which makes it recognizable "underneath" any of its potential variations. The fundamental Being of a sign includes its potentially infinite repetition in an unspecifiable series of contexts. In other words, the essence of a sign is its iterability.

It might appear that such a definition of the sign runs contrary to Derrida's attempts to use the Saussurian concepts of arbitrariness and difference to undermine traditional notions of representation. After all, once a sign is defined as ideal, it appears to be inviolate. In fact, Derrida's conclusion is the opposite. He argues that since a sign must continue to function outside of any specific context, when cut off from any specific sending or receiving consciousness, and in the possible absence of its referent, its perdurability is, in fact, an index of its disseminatory power. In "Signature Event Context," Derrida explains his deconstruction of the concept of a sign's identity.

Why is this identity paradoxically the division or dissociation from itself which will make of this phonic sign a grapheme? It is because this unity of the signifying form is constituted only by its iterability, by the possibility of being repeated in the absence not only of its referent, which goes without saying, but of a determined signified or current intention of signification, as of every present intention of communication. (1982, 318)

It is precisely because the sign is defined by its iterability that it can, in principle, be severed from a given context and grafted onto others. Therefore, Derrida argues, even the notion of context cannot be used to lend anchorage to the sign's drift. Even though Derrida concedes that, once in a context, the sign's meaning is provisionally determined, and that by definition signs are always in some context or another, he argues that since the context itself is a finite set of signs, it is also iterable. A context is no more immune than a given sign from being lifted and displaced onto other chains of signs. To put the matter in Wittgenstein's terms, Derrida claims that if a context is understood as a set of implicit rules by which to interpret a sign, then there is nothing to prevent the rules themselves from being interpreted according to yet another set of rules. "Can't we imagine," Wittgenstein asks, "a rule determining the application of a rule, and a doubt which it removes—and so on" (1958, 39)? Since a context, like a sign, is a grapheme, an iterable and graftable unit, its identity must not be understood as living presence but, on the contrary, as the empty, infinitely malleable identity of a mindless machine. Therefore, when in *Limited, Inc.* Derrida notes: "Which is to say that from the point of view of semantics, but also of ethics and politics, 'deconstruction' should never lead either to relativism or to any sort of indeterminism" (1988b, 148), what he means is that meanings do not exist in "vague 'indeterminacy,'" but are always determined by relatively stable contexts. However, since these contexts cannot be determined by an absolutely fixed metacontext, they are themselves indeterminate to varying degrees. In short, Derridian indeterminacy stems from the absence of any noncontext-dependent foundation for stabilizing contexts.

The implications of Derrida's deconstructive notion of signification are immensely interesting. Although many of them have been fairly clear from his early work on Husserl, I think that they are nowhere better presented than in a relatively recent essay entitled "My Chances." Originally a paper delivered as the Weigert Lecture at the Forum on Psychiatry and the Humanities, it appeared in a collection of essays entitled *Taking Chances: Derrida, Psychoanalysis, and Literature* (Smith and Kerrigan 1984). Although ostensibly on Freud, the essay is, in fact, mainly concerned with the question of chance and randomness. Derrida's discussion of the concept of chance fleshes out the analysis of iterability and division outlined in "Signature Event Context." Using the term *mark* where previously, in a purely linguistic context, he preferred the term *sign*, Derrida addresses once again the apparent paradox of a deconstructive reading of semiosis which must have recourse to the notion of identity: "The paradox here is the following (I must state it in its broadest generality): to be a mark and to mark its marking effect, a mark must be capable of being *identified*, recognized as the same, being precisely *re-markable* from one context to another" (Smith and Kerrigan 1984, 16). The mark is paradoxical because, by virtue of its definition as an ideal entity maintaining its identity across an endless series of changing contexts, it ultimately has no essential identity.

> The ideal iterability that forms the structure of all marks is that which undoubtedly allows them to be released from any context, to be freed from all determined bonds to its origin, its meaning, or its referent, to emigrate in order to play elsewhere, in whole or in part, another role. I say "in whole or in part" because by means of this essential insignificance the ideality or ideal identity of each mark (which is only a differential function without an ontological basis) can continue to divide itself and to give rise to the proliferation of other ideal identities. This iterability is thus that which allows a mark to be used more than once. It is more than one. It multiplies and divides itself internally. This imprints the capacity for diversion within its very movement. In the destination (*Bestimmung*) there is thus a principle of indetermination, chance, luck, or of destinerring. (16)

"My Chances" is a playful and ironic essay. As such, it wishes both to examine and to serve as an example of the indeterminacy of writing. I think it is useful to emphasize, once again, that contrary to certain popular interpretations of Derrida, indeterminacy does not mean unconstrained free play. Derrida is not arguing here, nor has he ever argued, that deconstruction demonstrates that all meaning, hence all experience, is purely indeterminate. What he does claim is that determinacy is not the fundamental reality of things. If experience is not determinate in its core, then indeterminacy cannot be viewed as a perversion of original purity. Inasmuch as indeterminacy is a logical implication of the structure of the trace, its interventions cannot be predicted or reduced. For Derrida, indeterminacy is not a fallen product of an underlying state of determinacy, but, on the contrary, determinacy is the real, albeit unpredictable, effect of the structure of the mark. Deconstruction does not seek to make the patently false claim that the world of human experience, including, incidentally, the realm of literary criticism, is a random free-for-all. This view of things is the obverse of the paranoid assurance of universal meaningfulness and is just as insane. Derrida's purpose is to argue for the structural necessity for chaos, not for its hegemony.

> Language, however, is only one among those systems of *marks* that claim this curious tendency as their property: they *simultaneously* incline toward increasing the reserves of random, indetermination *as well as* the capacity for coding and overcoding or, in other words, for control and self-regulation. Such competition between randomness and code disrupts the very systematicity of the system while it also, however, regulates the restless, unstable interplay of the system. Whatever its singularity in this respect, the linguistic system of these traces or marks would merely be, it seems to me, just a particular example of the law of destabilization. (Smith and Kerrigan 1984, 2–3)

The concepts of order and chaos constitute the central concern of part 3 of this book, so I will refrain from an extended discussion of their history and implications at this point. However, I would like to make two preliminary comments on the dialectic between randomness and determinacy as it appears in Derrida's work. First, it is indeed surprising that Derrida, whom Geoffrey Hartman has labeled a "boa deconstructor," postulates the possibility of self-regulation or negentropy. Second, although it is certainly possible to argue that Derrida consistently allows a place for order in his various texts, it is nevertheless undeniable that the emphasis of deconstruction has always been on generating a model of experience that focuses on the necessity of effects of randomness. The language that Derrida uses throughout his work makes it clear that he considers order an effect of indeterminacy, not the other way around. In fact, deconstruction has been little else than the concerted effort to undermine logocentric security not by importing a germ of undecidability from the outside, or by a clash of opposing hypotheses, but by seeking to demonstrate that an indeterminate element has always inhabited the body of metaphysics.

Despite the Manichean language of the preceding quotation ("competition between randomness and code"), its conclusion makes it quite clear that Derrida has not abandoned his basic belief that metaphysical stabilities have no ontological basis but are merely the effects of the trace structure or the "law of destabilization." Clearly, however, Derrida's purpose is not to establish an order of precedence. He is not interested in demonstrating that chaos came first, since tha would be as metaphysical a position as one which considers order to be original. Derrida's claim is that an element of indeterminacy has always haunted determination. In other words, the mark/arche-writing/trace structure is *simultaneously* the unoriginal source of order and chaos. It is wrong to ascribe to Derrida the belief that arche-writing is pure chaos and that logocentrism is pure order. Arche-writing is both chaos and order; it is, in Derrida's vocabulary, a double inscription, as much the source of stability as of its simulacrum. However, although the logic of the mark is neither that of order nor randomness, it is nevertheless the case that the recurrent goal of deconstruction is to highlight the effects of indeterminacy on regulation. Over and over again, Derrida asserts that the history of the West is basically synonymous with the hegemony of what he calls the metaphysical tradition.

> It is for us, in the Occident, the culture of common sense that is marked by a powerful scientifico-philosophic tradition, metaphysics, technics, the opposition of subject/object (*sujet/objet*), and precisely a certain organization of the throw (*jet*). Through several differentiated relays, this culture goes back at least to Plato, where the repression of Democritus perhaps leaves the trace of a very large symptom. (Smith and Kerrigan 1984, 24–25)

Therefore, even though Derrida does not claim that the mark is more organized than disseminated, deconstruction is nevertheless a campaign that is mounted against the dominant logocentric organization of experience. "Without being able to take this route today, I will locate only what I have called above a *mark:* in the construction of its concept none of the limits or oppositions that I have just invoked are considered absolutely pertinent or decisive, but rather presuppositions to be deconstructed" (25). Although pertinence is no less original than impertinence, it is nevertheless the case that deconstruction aims, above all, to be impertinent.

In "My Chances," Derrida puns on grammatology, coining the term *programmatology*, a marriage of pragmatics and grammatology. Pragrammatology "should always take the situation of the marks into account; in particular that of utterances, the place of senders and addressees, of framing and of the sociohistorical circumscription, and so forth. It should therefore take account of the problematics of randomness in all fields where it evolves: physics, biology, game theory, and the like" (27–28). It is interesting that Derrida should invoke a number of mathematical and scientific disciplines, implying without the slightest attempt at demonstration that randomness (as he defines it) is an important issue in current scientific research. This assertion is at best problematic, because, if for no other reason, it gives an inaccurate picture of the uses to which randomness is being put in much contemporary scientific thought; but what is truly disturbing is Derrida's theoretical name-dropping. In a typical rhetorical move, Derrida creates allies by simply declaring their compatibility with the deconstructive project. Concentrating on the concepts of order and chaos in particular, and the natural sciences in general, parts 2 and 3 of this book are, in the main, a demonstration of the incompatibility of much contemporary research in science and mathematics with deconstructive principles. For now, however, I simply want to underline Derrida's clear assertion that the mission of pragrammatology is to take randomness into account. For ultimately, even if order and chaos are the *différance* of one another, Derrida has decided that deconstruction must serve as the antidote for the metaphysical tradition's preference for order by emphasizing the chaotic effects of the mark. In some strange way, the mark is closer to chaos than to order.

Derrida never makes this claim, it is simply something that can be inferred from his choice of vocabulary and tone. An analogy here might be helpful. In *Of Grammatology* (1976), Derrida performs the generally familiar two-step process of deconstruction: first he inverts the traditional hierarchical relation between speech and writing, and then he posits that a third term, arche-writing (the logic of the mark) is, in fact, the condition of possibility of the distinction between speech and writing without itself being either one of the concepts it nevertheless generates. During the first wave of deconstruction in U.S. academia, many critics made the mistake of believing that Derrida was simply seeking to rehabilitate writing in the ordinary sense. The following quote makes it quite clear that this was not his purpose, at the same time that it makes it equally clear that the by now universally rejected idea that Derrida is simply a proponent of writing in its historical struggle with speech is not simply wrong.

> I would wish rather to suggest that the alleged derivativeness of writing, however real and massive, was possible only on one condition: that the "original," "natural," etc. language had never existed, never been intact and untouched by writing, that it had itself always been a writing. An arche-writing whose necessity and new concept I wish to indicate and outline here; and which I continue to call writing only because *it essentially communicates with the vulgar concept of writing.* (1976, 56; italics added)

Even though arche-writing is another name for the trace structure that inhabits both speech and writing and serves as their common abyssal origin, Derrida chose to call his "new concept" arche-writing and not arche-speech. Why? Because of an essential communication that unites vulgar writing to the movement of the trace and that allows the former to be the representative of the latter: "Writing is one of the representatives of the trace in general, it is not the trace itself" (1976, 167). To my knowledge, Derrida has never explained why arche-writing, which "can never let itself be reduced to the form of *presence*" (1976, 57) can be said to communicate (It is unclear what communicate connotes here: to resemble, as via metaphor—which, as Derrida points out in "Signature, Event, Concept" is simply another name for communication; to belong to the same conceptual code—but arche-writing is not a concept and is reducible to no code; to be related as genus to species—but arche-writing escapes all logical hierarchies?) with the ordinary concept of writing. Yet, were it not so related, this "thing" which cannot by reduced to the form of presence would be indescribable, a black hole that does not even announce itself though the emission of X-ray radiation.

Let me emphasize that I am not disputing Derrida's right to employ ontic metaphors "sous-rature" for his anti-ontological concept. I am simply arguing that it is significant that the one chosen is writing, not speech. We must conclude that arche-writing does, indeed, communicate in some inexplicable way with writing and, by analogy, that the mark communicates in an equally essential way with chaos. After all, deconstruction, or, in "Taking Chances," pragrammatology, does not seek to take order into account, but, instead, searches for the invasions of indeterminacy into the body of logocentrism. The reason for this is, to return to the analogy and to *Of Grammatology* in general, because the metaphysical tradition has been the systematic repression of arche-writing.

> The latter [the vulgar concept of writing] could not have imposed itself historically except by the dissimulation of the arche-writing, by the desire for a speech displacing its other and its double and working to reduce its difference. If I persist in calling that difference writing, it is because within the work of historical repression, writing was, by its situation, destined to signify the most formidable difference. (1976, 56)

Presumably, Derrida's motivation for emphasizing indeterminacy in "Taking Chances" is similar. Even though the mark is, in principle, no more determined than chaotic, we must assume its essential communication with indeterminacy is both the historical reason for its repression and the imperative Derrida feels to take it into account. That is why the mark, along with arche-writing, the graft, the parergon, the hymen, the woman, etc., are always closer to indeterminacy than to order, more allied to bastardy than to legitimacy, more of the stuff of loss than of profit.

I will conclude this chapter with a discussion of an important, albeit generally ignored, distinction in Derridian semiotics. Roughly speaking, deconstruction understands indeterminacy in two somewhat different ways: indeterminacy created by the logic of the supplement is "microstructural," whereas the indeterminacy of self-reference is "macrostructural." Or, to be more accurate, although in Derridian deconstruction the supplement tends to function microstructurally, a special instance of supplementarity, self-reference, produces indeterminacy in macrostructural ways.

The citability and graftability of the mark is the microstructure of deconstructive indeterminacy. Whenever Derrida seeks to contest the demesne of presence, it is always with some concept that both inhabits the particular manifestation of presence under consideration and is itself structured by the indeterminacy of the mark. Examples of this strategy are arche-writing, gram, *différance,* mark, text, incision, spacing, dissemination, and *écart.* Needless to say, these various concepts are not simply synonymous because they are employed in relation to different historical, textual, and rhetorical strategies. Yet they have enough of a family resemblance to make them unmistakable examples of Derrida's painstaking efforts to demonstrate that an irreducible element of undecidability inheres to any logocentric concept.

The term *microstructure* implies that Derrida's undecidables are not presumed to be accidents or imports from the outside, but are part of the deepest interior of the metaphysical notion being deconstructed. They are, as it were, the fine grain that both holds metaphysical concepts together and destabilizes them. The dynamic logic of Derridian microstructural indeterminacy is the well-known concept of supplementarity. Since supplementarity and its subset, self-reference, are frequently confused, and in order to clarify the microstructure-macrostructure distinction I am elaborating, I will first address the dynamics of Derrida's notion of microstructural supplementarity before proceeding to distinguish it from self-reference.

The concept of supplementarity was first treated at length by Derrida in *Of Grammatology.* Seeking to describe Rousseau's posture toward writing, Derrida enlists two meanings of the word *supplement:* an inessential addition to an already complete whole, and something that is used to make up for a deficiency or lack in the original. The first meaning encapsulates the traditional view of the relation between nature and art, or between speech and writing. "The supplement adds itself, it is a surplus, a plenitude enriching another plenitude, the *fullest measure* of presence. It cumulates and accumulates presence. It is thus that art, *technè,* image, representation, etc. come as supplements to nature and are rich with this entire cumulating function" (1976, 144–145). The second meaning of supplement describes how the presence of the supposedly self-sufficient original can be supplanted by an interior absence. "But the supplement supplants. It adds only to replace. It intervenes or insinuates itself *in-the-*

place-of; it fills, it is as if one fills a void. If it represents and makes an image, it is by the anterior default of a presence" (145). The supplement is possible only because that which it supplants was never whole to begin with. The supposed original was "always already" a kind of supplement, a network of traces supplanting themselves indefinitely. "Through this sequence of supplements a necessity is announced: that of an infinite chain, ineluctably multiplying the supplementary mediations that produce the sense of the very thing they defer: the mirage of the thing itself, of immediate presence, of originary perception. Immediacy is derived" (157).

The Derridian supplement, therefore, is a substitute that signals the absence of an original. The supplement replaces a lacuna that turns out to be supplementarity "itself." What the metaphysical tradition assumes to exist simply and absolutely, reality or nature, is in fact, and always was, a kind of writing.

> What we have tried to show by following the guiding light of the "dangerous supplement," is that in what one calls the real life of these existences "of flesh and bone," beyond and behind what one believes can be circumscribed as Rousseau's text, there has never been anything but writing; there have never been anything but supplements, substitutive significations which could only come forth in a chain of differential references, the "real" supervening, and being added only while taking on meaning from a trace and from an invocation of the supplement etc. And thus to infinity, for we have read, *in the text*, that the absolute present, Nature, that which words like "real mother" name, have always already escaped, have never existed; that what opens meaning and language is writing as the disappearance of natural presence. (158–59)

The void that the supplement fills is the void of writing, the trace, or the mark. And, since the point of arche-writing is that grafts are in a constant process of division and addition—deleting parts of themselves, sending them to other dismembered marks, receiving in turn unforseen fragments—what the supplement supplements is a network of supplementation.

There are two basic steps to Derrida's articulation of the concept of supplementarity. First, he shows how, in Rousseau's work, writing serves as a supplement in the sense that it is an unwelcome guest in the house of presence. Second, Derrida argues that the need for supplementation arose, in the first place, because the house has an abyss at its center, an abyss that was "always already" an internal supplement. Hence, there is no origin, presence, or nature except as so many effects of the trace. An outside comes to fill a gap that turns out to enjoy a relation to itself that is identical to the relation the supplement bears to what it supplements. In other words, the supplement supplants presence because presence was already a kind of supplement. The outside turns out to be the inside. The periphery has already infected the allegedly pure center. Inasmuch as for Derrida the mark is its own infinite self-supplementation, the reversal wrought by supplementarity is to render a purportedly excisable embarrassment (writing for Rousseau, the pharmakon for Plato, the parergon for Kant, the woman for Heidegger, etc.) into the condition of possibility of a kind of center whose purity was to be preserved by the exclusion of what, it turns out, cannot be excluded because it is the thing itself.

Basically, supplementarity is the dynamic configuration of the internal doubling of the trace discussed earlier. I call the supplement microscopic because, in Derrida's analyses, the notion of arche-writing tends to be demonstrated by recourse to the instability of certain elementary particles (trace, sign, mark, etc.) of a system. This is Derrida as Democritus. As Gayatri Spivak explains in her introduction to her translation of *De La Grammatologie*, "The most that can be said, and Derrida has reminded us to say it anew, is that a certain view of the world, of consciousness, and of language has been accepted as the correct one, and, if the minute particulars of that view are examined, a rather different picture (that is also a no-picture, as we shall see) emerges" (Derrida 1976, xiii). Over and over again, Derrida deconstructs a metaphysical position by poking around in its alleged center in order to unearth some trace of its belonging to the system of writing in general. Writing as arche-writing, *différance*, or grapheme is, at least in part, outside of philosophy.

> To "deconstruct" philosophy, thus, would be to think—in the most faithful, interior way—the structured genealogy of philosophy's concepts, but at the same time to determine—from a certain exterior that is unqualifiable or unnameable by philosophy—what this history has been able to dissimulate or forbid,

> making itself into a history by means of this somewhere moti-
> vated repression. (Derrida 1981b, 6)

This "other" is unthinkable by philosophy because, according to Derrida, philosophy cannot but think, is the thought of, presence, and
the gram is neither present nor absent, but the trace of the metaphysical distinction between presence and absence. Its logic is that
of citability and graftability, consequently, its founding conceptualization must be one of divisibility. Only that which is not a plenum
can be divided, and deconstruction claims that any code can be articulated in an infinite number of ways.

> This interweaving results in each "element"—phoneme or
> grapheme—being constituted on the basis of the trace within it
> of the other elements of the chain or system. This interweaving,
> this textile, is the *text* produced only in the transformation of
> another text. Nothing, neither among the elements nor within
> the system, is anywhere ever simply present or absent. There
> are only, everywhere, differences and traces of traces. (1981, 26)

Clearly, Derrida does not suggest that the gram is literally small.
Since his principle of graftability is general, it can include elements
of any size. A book can be grafted as easily as a word, so it also is a
gram in a sense. This deconstructive posture is microscopic not because of the size of its objects, but because of the kinds of operations
performed on them. The principle underlying this phase of deconstruction is the possibility of cutting and recombining. It is telling, for
example, that the metaphors Derrida chooses to describe this kind
of deconstruction, such as difference, graft, articulation, spacing, bri-
sure, articulation, tend to describe the potential for division. Supplementarity, here, is not so much a question of self-reference but of
intertextuality. The undecidability of the gram stems from its internal
difference, the fact that it supplements itself. Because the trace is the
possibility of reference in general, we must assume that it may also
refer to itself, but the point is that its semiotic dispersion is due more
to its divisibility than to its self-inclusion. "The phenomenon of
chance as well as that of literary fiction, not to mention what I call
writing or the trace in general, do not so much lead up to the indivisi-
bility but to a certain divisibility or internal difference of the so-called

ultimate element (*stoikheion*, trait, letter, seminal mark)" (Smith and Kerrigan 1984, 10). As Derrida argues in "The Factor of Truth," it is precisely because a letter is always divisible that it may always not reach its destination. The generative and disseminatory potential of the mark stem from its ability to divide itself out of any context.

> [T]he identity of the mark is also its difference and its differential relation, varying each time according to context, to the network of other marks. The ideal iterability that forms the structure of all marks is that which undoubtedly allows them to be released from any context, to be freed from all determined bonds to its origin, its meaning, or its referent, to emigrate in order to play elsewhere, in whole or in part, another role. I say "in whole or in part" because by means of this essential insignificance the ideality or ideal identity of each mark (which is only a differential function without an ontological basis) can continue to divide itself and to give rise to the proliferation of other ideal entities. This iterability is thus that which allows a mark to be used more than once. It is more than one. It multiplies and divides itself internally. This imprints the capacity for diversion within its very movement. In the destination (*Bestimmung*) there is thus a principle of indeterminism, chance, luck, or of destinerring. (Smith and Kerrigan 1984, 16)

It is clear, I think, that the basis for indeterminacy here is self-simulation via the principle of division and uncontrollable multiplication. Thus, when in *Of Grammatology*, Derrida uses the idea of supplementarity to deconstruct Rousseau, the supplement he adduces is not macroscopic, writing in the vulgar sense coming to replace speech, but microscopic, writing as internal divisibility endlessly supplanting itself. Ultimately, this kind of supplement is simply a synonym for arche-writing, or, to be fair to Derrida, another addition to the chain of deconstructive concepts he is still fashioning.

As opposed to the microscopic supplement, which creates indeterminacy by fissure and dissemination, self-reference is a kind of supplementarity that generates indeterminacy macroscopically by exploiting the strange effects of self-inclusion. Derrida comments on this phenomenon in *The Post Card*.

What happens when acts or performances (discourse or writing, analysis or description, etc.) are part of the objects they designate? When they can be given as examples of precisely that of which they speak or write? Certainly, one does not gain an auto-reflective transparency, on the contrary. A reckoning is no longer possible, nor is an account, and the borders of the set are then neither closed nor open. Their trait is divided. (1987a, 391)

The principle of graftability is of little help here because, for self-reference to occur, the basic element must be considerably more complex than a potentially primitive mark. Although it is certainly possible to argue that self-referential or self-inclusive acts may be grafted, the reverse is not always true, that is, not all grafts produce effects of undecidability through self-reference. After a mark has been divided past the level of a sentence (or possibly a phrase), it no longer has the referential power needed to designate itself or a part of itself. Self-reference needs a threshold of complexity in order to generate its effects of indeterminacy. A mark such as "this phrase," although certainly self-referential, is pretty straightforward. The bizarre effects of self-reference and self-inclusion only begin to occur when one can create self-including loops, such as that produced by a sentence of the type: "This sentence is false." This, and other versions of the Parmenides paradox, cannot occur at a level simpler than a sentence or a complex phrase ("This sentence, being false . . ."). Simply, self-reference requires a discursive (or, as Gödel demonstrated, a symbolic mathematical) system powerful enough to be capable of referring to itself, a capacity beyond the resources of many marks.

Therefore, we must distinguish between the microstructural supplement and the macrostructural supplementarity generated by self-reference. There are two kinds of microstructural supplementarity, what we could call, following Derrida's lead, vulgar and arche-supplementarity. Vulgar supplementarity is, for example, the need Rousseau feels to add writing (in the vulgar sense) to speech. Arche-supplementarity is the reason he must do this—because speech is itself a kind of internally divided grammatological object. Vulgar supplementarity is a symptom of arche-supplementarity that is itself another name for arche-writing. But the logic of the supplement does not necessarily lead to self-reference. Self-reference can only occur when a semiotic system is sufficiently powerful to be able to represent itself. The prime example of self-referential indeterminism in Derrida's work is the parergon. Briefly, Derrida (1987b) argues that, in Kant's third *Critique,* certain elements that are defined as *parerga,* ornaments or frills [Kant mentions "frames of pictures or the drapery on statues, or the colonnades of palaces" [18]), actually function as supplements in the deconstructive sense. "What constitutes them as *parerga* is not simply their exteriority as a surplus, it is the internal structural link which rivets them to the lack in the interior of the *ergon.* And this lack would be constitutive of the very unity of the *ergon.* Without this lack, the *ergon* would have no need of a *parergon.* The *ergon*'s lack is the lack of a *parergon,* of the garment or the column which nevertheless remains exterior to it" (1987b, 59–60). However, in addition to the parergon's role as supplement, it also functions as agent of self-reference. If a frame delimits something in order to give it identity, then this identity is undermined when the frame contains something of the framed, or vice versa. "What would Kant have said about a frame framing a painting representing a building surrounded by columns (examples of this are numerous), columns in the form of clothed human bodies . . . , the whole frame being placed on the easel of a painter who is himself represented by another painting" (61–63). This rhetorical question might seem a bit forced, a polemical fillip whose importance is mitigated by its contingency, were it not for the fact that such framing is, according to Derrida, precisely what is going on in Kant's third *Critique.* Kant describes aesthetic judgment as excluding analysis of any kind. Yet, in order to make that point, Kant needs to import the philosophical apparatus of the other *Critique.* Consequently, an analysis of aesthetic judgment frames that which the analysis itself claims is nonanalytic. The third critique becomes a kind of work of art, framed by that which it both excludes and necessarily includes. It is a work about aesthetic framing that is, itself, an example of the kind of framing it wishes to define as parergonal. Like a painting that depicts its own margins, Kant's *Critique of Judgment* represents itself as a frame. According to Jonathan Culler, the result of this kind of self-reference is the production of indeterminacy.

Derridian analyses that we have considered in this chapter also exploit potential self-reference, applying Freud's description of

the *Fort/Da* game to Freud's own play with the Pleasure Principle
or Kant's account of *parerga* to his own framing procedures in
the "Analytic of the Beautiful." There is a neatness in the relations that deconstruction's exploitation of self-reference reveals
which must seem similar to the coincidence of being and doing
that Brooks and innumerable critics have sought and valued.
But the relation deconstruction reveals is not the transparency
of the text to itself in an act of reflexive self-description or self-
possession; it is rather an uncanny neatness that generates paradox, a self-reference that ultimately brings out the inability of
any discourse to account for itself and the failure of performative
and constative or doing and being to coincide. (Culler 1982, 201)

Whenever a text refers to itself, even if it is only to indicate all
that the text excludes, then self-referential paradox is possible. This
kind of paradox involves the impossibility of establishing a fixed context, of distinguishing between inside and outside, of performing a
"triage" between discourse and metadiscourse, in short, of separating the included from the excluded. Just as it is impossible to say
whether the *Critique* is *ergon* or *parergon*, work or frame, the paradox
of self-referentiality is that a statement can be both true and false
simultaneously. In other words, self-reference yields undecidability.

In summary, Derridian indeterminacy is of two kinds. The first,
the freeplay of the graft, is microscopic insofar as it tends to follow a
logic of division and dissemination. The marks characteristic of this
category of indeterminacy are stretched between two infinities: the
infinitely small mark and the infinitely large text. However, size is
not what determines their characterization as microscopic, but the
unavoidable potential shared by all graphemes to be spliced onto
other graphemes and to be embedded in alien contexts. A special
kind of supplementarity, self-reference, only occurs when a code has
become complex enough to make assertions about itself. Typically,
for Derrida, this is the effect of a large-scale text, as when Kant's
critique can be viewed as a comment on itself; consequently, it is
macroscopic in nature. Besides his treatment of self-reference in the
texts of others (in addition to "The Parergon," a telling example is his
reading of Freud's *Beyond the Pleasure Principle* in "To Speculate—on
'Freud'"), Derrida has employed the trickiness of self-reflection to
emphasize the problematic relation of his own writing to the themes

it juggles. Much of *The Post Card*, for example, consists of written reflections on the vicissitudes of writing. In one "postcard" (a postcard that is really in a book of philosophy or a work of literature devoted to the fortunes of postcards), he writes: "What I like about post cards is that even if in an envelope, they are made to circulate like an open but illegible letter" (1987a, 12). And "Living On: Border Lines," an essay that consists of two texts placed on top of another, with the lower one appearing to serve as commentary on the top one, ends with the following comments: "Never tell of what you are doing, and, pretending to tell, do something else that immediately crypts, adds, entrenches itself. To speak of writing, of triumph, as *living on*, is to enunciate or denounce the manic fantasy. Not without repeating it, and that goes without saying" (Bloom et al. 1979, 176). Although these examples resemble Derrida's analyses of other authors inasmuch as they avail themselves of the ambiguities and paradoxes of self-references, they differ in one crucial aspect. As we shall see in the next chapter, one of Derrida's major concerns has been to develop a style that is adequate (and, in Derrida's system, simultaneously inadequate) to the concepts he is elaborating. Wishing his style to be neither metaphysical nor chaotic, neither detached nor cloyingly self-aware, neither truthful nor mendacious, Derrida has frequently chosen the potential of self-reference to produce impossible neither/nor choices in order to stake out a space for deconstruction. Although I will criticize Derrida's use of self-reflection to create paradox in a subsequent chapter, I am not oblivious to the potential this strategy has for humor. I would, therefore, like to conclude this chapter with a precious moment from "My Chances," where, in a move worthy of Clamence in Camus's *The Fall*, Derrida makes a confession and then confesses that confessors are not always in complete control of their confessions.

> It would be possible to demonstrate that there is nothing random in the concatenation of my findings. An implacable program takes shape through the contextual necessity that requires cutting solids into certain sequences (stereotomy), intersecting and adjusting subsets, mingling voices and proper names, and accelerating a rhythm that merely gives the *feeling* of randomness to those who do not know the prescription—which, incidentally, is also my case. (Smith and Kerrigan 1984, 14)

Of course, as Clamence knows all too well, there is rhetorical capital to be gained from confessions of inadequacy. Sometimes, however, even the canny deconstructor can be caught unawares, and self-reference really gets out of control—at times like this, instead of creating aporia and abyss, recursive self-reference can begin to generate patterns of exquisitely harmonious order. And, as we shall see in part 3, it can do this starting with practically nothing.

Chapter 4

Style

Spurs, the English translation of *Eperons*, was originally a paper entitled "La question du style" read at Cérisy-la-Salle. It is an essay
concerned with the complex relations among two men, Nietzsche
and Heidegger, and two concepts, style and woman. Derrida's analysis yields a definition of woman that makes of her a recognizable
deconstructive term: "There is no such thing as the essence of woman
because woman averts, she is averted of herself. Out of the depths,
endless and unfathomable, she engulfs and distorts all vestige of
essentiality, of identity, of property" (1978a, 43).

Derrida conjoins the concept of woman to the concept of writing
through an analysis of the implications of the notion of style. The
question of writing is always, according to Derrida, a question of
style. In typical Derridian fashion, *Spurs* multiplies the meanings and
resonances of the word *style* far beyond their normal range. However, I think that the book's real importance lies in its normative
claims concerning the practice of deconstruction. Deconstruction, it
maintains, cannot concern itself with the manipulation of concepts,
it needs to actively cultivate a style that is adequate to deconstruction's theoretical positions. In other words, deconstruction cannot
simply argue the impossibility of metaphysical closure in a sober,
traditionally philosophical style; it must develop stylistic strategies
that make of it an example of the logic of dissemination.

After the original presentation of "La question du style," Derrida responded to a series of questions from the audience. One of his
answers is of particular interest. To Fauzia Assaad-Mikhail's question: "Couldn't one find, in the light of your text, a possibility of
engaging in philosophy in a feminine way?" Derrida answers: "I said,
'the woman (of) Nietzsche', the 'woman Nietzsche': at the moment

when he affirms, when he is, or he loves the affirmative woman, he writes, if only one could say that, 'with a woman's hand.' Did you ask me a personal question? I would like to write, also, like (a) woman. I'm trying . . ." (1973, 299; my translation).

The question of style, therefore, is a bridge between the concepts of self-reflection and self-inclusion. When I was first introduced to deconstruction in graduate school, my major criticism of Derrida and poststructuralism in general revolved around the paradox of asserting truthfully that the truth cannot be asserted. Either the truth of nontruth can be stated, it seemed to me, and then deconstruction is wrong, or it can't, and then it is mute. Although I was admonished for my naïveté by professors who argued that the point of deconstruction is that the binary choice between truth or falsehood is haunted by undecidability, I was still troubled. I still am, but for different reasons.

During the course of his career, Derrida has never stopped attempting to develop a style that is in some way adequate to the theory he has been propounding, that is, a style that can communicate the abyssal nature of the trace. Referring to an essay by Samuel Weber included in *Taking Chances*, its editors argue that there are

> two kinds of deconstruction: the "classical" one, which hopes to preserve for itself an exteriority to the intentions of the text being read, and a more recent or recently prominent one that forfeits this exteriority by allowing itself to become, in Derrida's words, "an example of that of which it speaks or writes." An evolving fascination with the second style of reading can be discerned in the difference between the early "Freud and the Scene of Writing" (1978), with its enthusiastic program for purifying psychoanalysis of its naive reiteration of philosophy, and the present "My Chances." (Smith and Kerrigan 1984, xi)

Although, as with everything in Derrida, there are no clear demarcations between early and late work, especially since some parts of his early books, the end of *Edmund Husserl's* The Origin of Geometry: *An Introduction* (1977) for example, seem to employ a style that exemplifies the complexity of the argument he is proposing, it is clearly in his later works, such as *Spurs, Glas,* and *The Post Card,* that he actively inserts himself into his field by self-consciously refusing the simple choice between text and deconstructive commentary. Perhaps Hartman's description of *Glas* best captures the spirit of the work: "*Glas* raises the spectre of texts so tangled, contaminated, displaced, deceptive that the idea of a single, or original author fades, like virginity itself . . ." (1980, 204). Although, as Jonathan Culler observes, *Glas* is far more traditional in its analyses of Hegel, Genet, and Saussure than many critics have claimed, its division into two columns, one devoted to Hegel, the other to Genet, as well as its mosaic of citations and comments, do establish a stylistics of indeterminacy to some degree. Culler suggests that Derrida's tongue-in-cheek account of his purpose in composing *Glas*, "On veut rendre l'écriture imprenable, bien sûr" is, in fact, an accurate description of the work's effects. "Commentators are indeed tempted to suspect that *Glas*'s doubling is a strategy of evasion, designed to make the writing unmasterably elusive. While reading one column you are reminded that the gist lies elsewhere, in the relation between columns if not in the other column itself" (Culler 1982, 137).

Clearly, there is a difference between discovering self-reflective undecidability in the texts of others and in actively seeking to invent a style of writing commensurate to the rules of deconstruction. As early as in "Différance" Derrida recognizes the need to forge a new style. At the end of the essay, originally a paper read to the Société française de philosophie on January 27, 1968, and subsequently included in *Margins of Philosophy*, Derrida suggests that deconstruction must cleanse itself of nostalgia for lost presence and, somewhat lightheaded in the atmosphere of its newfound freedom, joyously affirm a world without absolute truth. "There will be no unique name, even if it were the name of Being. And we must think this without *nostalgia*, that is, outside of the myth of a purely maternal or paternal language, a lost country of thought. On the contrary, we must *affirm* this, in the sense in which Nietzsche puts affirmation into play, in a certain laughter and a certain step of the dance" (1982, 27). Nietzsche's style, or, as the subtitle of *Spurs* indicates, Nietzsche's styles, will provide a model for a kind of writing that, in the elan of its multiplicity, will fashion a knit stretching between, but never synthesizing, two forms of deconstruction, one a painstaking commentary on Being, the other a bold disruptive break with metaphysics. Neither totally textual exegesis nor totally apocalyptic revolution, deconstruction must negotiate the dangers implicit in each of these strategies in order to develop what Derrida calls a "new writing." "It also goes without saying that the choice between these two forms of deconstruction cannot be simple and unique. A new writing must weave and interlace these two motifs of deconstruction. Which amounts to saying that one must speak several languages and produce several texts at once" (1982, 135).

Needless to say, Derrida's writing has always been a paisley of quotations, erasures, notes, etc. I do, however, believe that the new writing he announces in "The Ends of Man," and which echoes his call for affirmative play, became much more of an active stylistic concern after the first wave of deconstruction had somewhat spent itself. *Spurs* is seminal in this regard. Although there is nothing unusual or unexpected in Derrida's analysis of Nietzsche in *Spurs*, what is of crucial concern is that the essay is simultaneously an analysis of style, the attempt to mount a deconstructive style, and a commentary on the futility of taking one's stylistic adventures too seriously. In the context of the essay, Derrida's apparently sincere confession of his desire to write like a woman clearly means that he would like to write like the affirmative woman/Nietzsche, the woman who, no longer either a symbol for truth or for falsehood, "is recognized and affirmed as an affirmative power, a dissimulatress, an artist, a dionysiac" (1978a, 97).

The prototype for this heady adventure is Nietzsche. "Perhaps truth's abyss as non-truth, propriation as appropriation/a-propriation, the declaration become parodying dissimulation, perhaps this is what Nietzsche is calling the style's form and the no-where of woman" (119–21). This quote economically gathers together the central themes circulating around the Derridian notion of style. Self-commentary bleeding into parody becomes self-parody and indeterminacy. A deconstructive style would be an oscillation between exposition and subversion that vigilantly maintains an awareness of its own implication in the field it confronts. Thus, the dawning of a new era of affirmative deconstruction announced at the beginning of *Spurs*: "The 'question of style' is, as you have no doubt recognized, a quotation. Thus it serves to indicate that what I shall put forth here is already a part of that space which certain readings, in launching a new phase in the process of deconstructive (i.e., affirmative) interpretation, have de-marcated during the last two years [the lecture was presented in July, 1972]" (1978a, 370) is, in fact, wonderfully summarized by Derrida's text in general and in particular by the following direct address to his audience toward the end of the presentation.

> Even if it is not so for its totality, there might yet be certain movements where the text, which already you are beginning to forget, could very well slip quite away. Should this indeed be the case, there would be no measure to its undecipherability. My discourse, though, has been every bit as clear as that "I have forgotten my umbrella" [a fragment found among Nietzsche's papers and used by Derrida to demonstrate the unpredictability of textual grafting]. You might even agree that it contained a certain ballast of rhetorical, pedagogical and persuasive qualities. But suppose anyway that it is cryptic. What if those texts of Nietzsche (such as "I have forgotten my umbrella") and those concepts and words (like "spur" ("*éperon*")) were selected for reasons whose history and code I alone know? What if even I fail to see the transparent reason of such a history and code? (1978a, 135)

Derrida's taunting confession epitomizes the parodic, self-reflexive style that he claims to be attempting to develop and that serves as the agenda for the new phase of deconstruction. It is a style that is neither classically philosophical nor jubilantly antiphilosophical but, like the two columns in *Glas*, the complex commerce between these and other classical binary oppositions.

Although logic is not valued by deconstruction, Derrida's stylistic project is certainly a logical extension of his theoretical positions. In "What is Postmodernism," Lyotard distinguishes between modernism and postmodernism by arguing that whereas modernism "allows the unpresentable to be put forward only as the missing contents; but the form, because of its recognizable consistency, continues to offer to the reader or viewer matter for solace and pleasure" whereas postmodernism "puts forward the unpresentable in presentation itself; that which denies itself the solace of good forms . . . in order to impart a stronger sense of the unpresentable" (Lyotard 1984, 81). While they are classical concepts vulnerable to severe deconstruction, fairness and balance seem to guide Derrida's stylistic agenda. Derrida wishes to write in a style that respects Lyotard's sense of the postmodern as the search for forms that are as radically disturbing as the contents of modernism. Simply, he wishes to respect the abyssal nature of Being by inscribing it in an abyssal style.

Derrida's stylistic strategies appear reasonable, and their neglect would certainly smack of hypocrisy. It would indeed seem appropriate that the deconstruction of Western metaphysics should be attempted in a style that seeks to resist logocentric decorum and linearity. And, although such a position might be subject to criticism on purely deconstructive grounds, for example, in its reproduction of the means/ends or form/content dyads, it is nevertheless an intuitively compelling project.

Nevertheless, I believe that Derrida's stylistic blueprint and experiments are self-serving and ultimately incoherent. Floyd Merrel and Gayatri Spivak agree on what is perhaps the only explicit totalizing thesis of Derridian deconstruction. Merrel argues that the fundamental principle of decontruction is: "All texts are undecidable," and therefore, "no text is non-deconstructible" (1985, 75). In her introduction to her translation of *Of Grammatology*, Spivak maintains that "All texts, whether written in the narrow sense or not, are rehearsing their grammatological structure, self-deconstructing as they constitute themselves" (Derrida 1976, lxxvii). Merrel and Spivak correctly describe the basic axiom underlying all of Derrida's work—that all texts are always already haunted by the undecidability of archewriting.

If all texts are deconstructible, then it follows that no text is *essentially* more or less deconstructible than any other text. For if that were the case, Derrida would have to maintain that metaphysics can, in fact, succeed essentially, not merely provisionally, in providing a secure ground of presence and punctuality. For Derrida, metaphysical success must always be an accident and not an essence. Therefore, all texts must be *in principle* equally deconstructible, although it can be argued that *in fact* some texts resist deconstruction more than others. What is true, in principle, for deconstructed texts must be true, a fortiori, for deconstructing texts. That is, texts which do the work of deconstruction, must also be, in principle, equally deconstructible. To put the matter simply, there appears to be no way that a given text can protect itself from future deconstruction. And if that is the case, then it is unclear what purpose forging a new writing style can serve.

Perhaps I can make my point clearer if Derrida's goal of creating a new style is examined from the perspective of arche-writing. Since, again in principle, all texts are haunted equally by arche-writing, and since arche-writing is not an object that can be presented to consciousness, then by definition it cannot be spread out along a scale that measures its quantity or quality in a given text. In other words, either arche-writing is a metaphysical concept, and can be measured, or it is not and is therefore alien to any continuum of quantity or quality. If the latter is the case, as Derrida clearly intends, then on what grounds does one call for a "new writing"? It cannot be because Derrida envisions a kind of writing that escapes the snares of metaphysics, for this would be the creation of a necessarily illusory escape and, as Derrida has repeatedly asserted, there is no better way to advertise your entrapment within logocentrism than to announce its demise. Even parodic and self-undermining texts cannot escape the temptations of a cult of writing.

> One cannot conclude, in order to outmaneuver the hermeneutic hold, that his is an infinite calculus which, but that it would calculate the undecidable, is similar to that of Leibniz' God. Such a conclusion, in its very attempt to elude the snare, succumbs all the more surely to it. To use parody or the simulacrum as a weapon in the service of truth or castration would be in fact to reconstitute religion, as a Nietzsche cult for example, in the interest of a priesthood of parody interpreters. No, somewhere parody always supposes a naivety withdrawing into an unconscious, a vertiginous non-mastery. Parody supposes a loss of consciousness, for were it to be absolutely calculated, it would become a confession or a law table. . . . Nietzsche might well be a little lost in the web of his text, lost much as a spider who finds he is unequal to the web he has spun. (1978a, 99–101)

And yet, further in the same essay, Derrida accuses a text by Heidegger of remaining "in its pre-critical relation to the signified, in the return to the presence of the spoken word, to a natural language, to perception, visibility, in a word, to consciousness, and its phenomenological system" (113). How then, is it possible to accuse a text of doing the inevitable, or, more to the point, how is it possible to affirm a loss of control without that very affirmation establishing a "pre-critical relation"?

One possible solution to this dilemma is to argue that, although all texts are deconstructible because the underpinning of textuality is the inherently unstable and indeterminate web of arche-writing, some discourses are nevertheless blind to their illusion of logocentric adequacy. Without insight into language's reefs and eddies, such discourses invite deconstructive intervention. To write with the hand of a woman, by way of contrast, would be to write with a style that, in its multiplicity, slipperiness, and malleability, would be appropriate to the spirit of deconstruction. But what, exactly, does it mean to promote a style appropriate to deconstructive discourse? Appropriate to what? Since all texts are, by definition, textual, the only possible answer to this question must be that a "double" writing actively and lucidly produces those effects that other texts generate despite themselves. Affirmative deconstruction does not affirm its self-mastery, nor its total control of indeterminacy, but its inevitable lapses. The only difference between Heidegger and Nietzsche, for example, is that Heidegger thought he could escape metaphysics while Nietzsche knew that one is never totally in nor totally out of metaphysics and chose to affirm the inevitable.

Such lucidity regarding the impossibility of either inhabiting metaphysics or simply leaping clear of its sway is presumably what motivates "affirmative deconstruction," yet it is still not clear what has been affirmed. In general, affirmation is only meaningful in a conceptual system that includes as one of its concepts the idea of progress. In other words, something is affirmed because it is seen as an improvement over some less desirable thing. It is, therefore, difficult to imagine the nature of the scale according to which lucidity is preferable to blindness in the deconstructive worldview. Can a writer inscribe within his or her text the awareness that the text must of necessity be both in and out of metaphysics? If so, and if this is a desirable scriptural strategy, is the scale that determines its desirability absolute, or is it itself also the metaphysical product of arche-writing? Or is lucidity a ruse, a ploy to wrest control and power from a readership convinced that metaphysical power is a horrible imposture?

Like Jean-Baptiste Clamence, Derrida himself warns his audience that confessions of fallibility should not necessarily be accepted at face value. They may be a cleverly constructed stratagem, a set of nets set out to embroil those who have faith in nets, but who think that their faith can be an inoculation against true loss. It is tempting to believe that someone who admits he is lying cannot be lying about that.

As suggested above, there can be no scale of value in the Derridian worldview because texts cannot be more or less deconstructible. To allow for a continuum of deconstructibility implies that those works that are essentially less deconstructible are, in fact, more metaphysically secure. Yet it is the belief of deconstruction that metaphysics has no Being in itself, since it is merely the product of a textual half-light. All metaphysical stability, therefore, is merely the effect of arche-writing. Consequently, any gradation of resistance to deconstruction must postulate not an inherent, pretextual core, which certain texts can possess in various degrees, but, at best, more or less successfully executed metaphysical repression of the trace. The trace itself, not being a "thing" reducible to presence, cannot be placed in any sort of continuum.

If affirmative deconstruction declares the impossibility of effecting the delicate "triage" between success and failure, while nevertheless claiming that "pre-critical" texts are examples of a kind of discourse that "settles comfortably into its own private domain" (1978a, 113), or at least thinks it can; if Derrida's stylistic experiments in such works as *Limited, Inc.*, *Glas*, *Spurs*, or *The Post Card* cannot be more or less deconstructible, yet are clearly presented as superior to other kinds of writing (for example, Husserl's), might the question of style concern less the desire to write with the hand of a Nietzchean woman than the Zarathustrian attempt to write with the raw power of a masterful, all too male hand? In a somewhat similar context, Heidegger suggests that caution is appropriate whenever the will appears to will its own eclipse. "The will—in suffering from this passing [of what is into what was], yet being what it is precisely by virtue of this suffering—remains in its willing captive to the passing. Thus will itself wills passing. It wills the passing of its suffering, and thus wills its own passing" (1968, 93).

In light of Heidegger's comments, it becomes possible to read Spivak's claims differently. What if the real will to power in deconstruction does not reside in its obvious instances of critical control, but during those moments when it revels in loss? What if the undecidability between the two forms of deconstructive desire is itself a ruse? What if Derrida does not believe that the nets of textuality, the cuts of graftability, affect all writers equally? What if he has faith that the hair of the dog that bites us all does offer, after all, a measure of protection to those strong enough to swallow it? In short, what if what I suppose to be the universal ironic reading of Derrida's confession in *Spurs* regarding his desire to write a self-centered text is wrong, and, here of all places, Derrida is saying exactly what he means?

Chapter 5

Deconstructive Politics

"There," Castel said, "I don't agree with you. These little brutes have an air of originality. But at bottom, it's always the same thing."

—Camus, *The Plague*

The object of deconstructive analysis is the constantly renewed resources of metaphysics, a philosophical tradition that Derrida dates from at least Plato. Perhaps the most salient characteristic of Derrida's notion of Western metaphysics is its various "centrisms": logocentrism, phonocentrism, ontocentrism, phallocentrism, androcentrism, etc. All of these concepts share one structural feature—inclusion in a binary opposition with an opposing term. Derrida insists, furthermore, that these pairs of concepts are never in a symmetrical relation. In fact, they are always related to each other in a determined hierarchy.

> All metaphysicians, from Plato to Rousseau, Descartes to Husserl, have proceeded in this way, conceiving good to be before evil, the positive before the negative, the pure before the impure, the simple before the complex, the essential before the accidental, the imitated before the imitation, etc. And this is not just *one* metaphysical gesture among others; it is *the* metaphysical exigency, that which has been the most constant, most profound and potent procedure. (Derrida 1988b, 93)

Perhaps the most pressing imperative of Derrida's work is to destabilize hierarchical, binary oppositions. In fact, the new kind of writing it envisions is, in large part, a measure adopted to disrupt hierarchy and to prevent its reemergence in any but temporary form. In one of the clearest expositions of the goals of deconstruction, Derrida (1981b) outlines his posture toward hierarchy. First, he argues, entrenched hierarchies must be overturned.

> On the one hand, we must traverse a phase of *overturning*. To do justice to this necessity is to recognize that in a classical philosophical opposition we are not dealing with the peaceful coexistence of a *vis-à-vis*, but rather with a violent hierarchy. One of the two terms governs the other (axiologically, logically, etc.) or has the upper hand. To deconstruct the opposition, first of all, is to overturn the hierarchy at a given moment. (1981b, 41)

This phase of deconstruction is indistinguishable from traditional ethical, political, religious, critical, or philosophical discourse. The declaration that the degraded should be honored is simply a polemical position within metaphysics. Derrida recognizes, furthermore, that reversed hierarchies are likely to be identical to their original form, with only the relative positions of terms altered. And, although he claims that hierarchical oppositions will always resurface ("it is the necessity of an interminable analysis: the hierarchy of dual oppositions always reestablishes itself" [1981b, 42]), he nevertheless locates the proper work of deconstruction in the development of a double writing that reinscribes the form of hierarchy within a larger textual field.

> By means of this double, and precisely stratified, dislodged and dislodging, writing, we must also mark the interval between inversion, which brings low what was high, and the irruptive emergence of a new "concept," a concept that can no longer be, and never could be, included in the previous regime. (42)

Ignoring, for the moment, the difficulties inherent in the notion of a double writing as outlined in chapter 4, and, assuming its success, a crucial question nevertheless remains. Although much contemporary critical discourse takes it for granted that hierarchy in general is somehow evil, it is not, I think, clear why this is necessarily the case. Of course, some hierarchies are generally acknowledged in our culture to be repressive, say the hierarchy between whites and blacks in South Africa. But attention to such binary oppositions belongs to the first aspect of deconstruction, and, although Derrida cultivates a double writing, it is clear that he savors and has made a career of affirming that part of deconstruction that seeks to displace the notion of hierarchy onto an indeterminate textual field. "Dissemination *affirms* (I do not say produces or controls) endless substitution, it neither arrests nor controls play" (1981b, 86). The question I am asking, then, does not concern the reversal of a specific hierarchical opposition, but the (always renewed) agenda to disrupt the very concept of hierarchy.

To this question must be appended an even more critical one, that of deconstruction's relation to cultural and political change. At times, Derrida seems to condemn the entirety of Western culture as the systematic but unavoidable repression of arche-writing. When he argues in this way, he tends to view the trace structure as both the internal fault of metaphysics and the opening through which the structure might be shaken. "First consequence, *différance* is not. It is not a present being, however excellent, unique, principle, or transcendent. It governs nothing, reigns over nothing, and nowhere exercises any authority. It is not announced by a capital letter. Not only is there no kingdom of *différance,* but *différance* instigates the subversion of every kingdom" (1982, 21–22). Although *différance* offers the resources for questioning and undermining social structures and institutions, it does not offer an alternative. An alternative would be another kingdom, and Derrida is convinced that metaphysical kingdoms, while unavoidable, are nevertheless evil. In a recent interview, Derrida elaborates on those political implications of deconstruction he had previously outlined in "The Conflict of Faculties" and as a part of *GREPH's Qui a peur de la philosophie?* Responding to a question by Robert Cheatham regarding the frequent condemnation of deconstruction as an "apolitical and passive conceptual instrument in the hands of academic intellectuals reading old texts," (Derrida 1986c, 34), Derrida redefines deconstruction as a kind of inquiry that has no institutional limits. "When I say there is no limit to the text, there is nothing outside the text, the sense I give to this word *text* means that deconstruction has no limits. The attempt to assign limits to deconstruction is precisely what deconstruction deconstructs" (34). Although it began as a kind of intraphilosophical questioning, partly as a response to specific political and historical conditions reigning in Paris around 1968, deconstruction is essentially an interrogation of culture and its institutions (including, of course, philosophy). "I can only repeat what you were just quoting, deconstruction has to do with institutions, with sociopolitical forces" (34). However, Derrida emphasizes that, although deconstruction is primarily an instrument for cultural analysis, it should not be understood as a kind of political liberation philosophy. On the contrary, deconstruction cannot succeed, it can have no success because it has no goal. In short, as he has said many times before, deconstruction contests teleology while seeking to remain ateleological. Immediately following his question concerning the perceived apolitical posture of deconstruction, Cheatham continues with a reference to the colloquium in Chicago mentioned earlier, during which Derrida refused the attribute "man of liberation." Although I have already quoted part of Derrida's response, I will reproduce it in its entirety here because it constitutes one of the clearest expositions of his political position.

> Now to go back to the reference you were just making to the Chicago thing, I have to reconstitute the context—it was a symposium on deconstruction; and I was listening to a paper which was presenting deconstruction as political liberation. When I was improvising in saying "well, I am not a man of liberation" I was not confirming that deconstruction is apolitical, I was criticizing this kind of politics, which [the speaker] is associated with, this ideology of liberation, the liberation of desires, the liberation of man, the philosophy of freedom, which is a very specific kind of philosophy and politics which I think should also be deconstructed no matter what sympathy we have with it. I wasn't saying, I'm not the man of liberation, but I'm the man of servitude; no, I was just joking, I was saying, go slowly, slow down with your liberation. As far as I can see what this name deconstruction covers is not a movement which one day can arrive at an accomplishment, something which can be achieved—there is no success for deconstruction, there is no goal which we have a hope of reaching, there is no *telos* for deconstruction. (34)

Deconstruction, which in the same response was characterized as limitless, is here described as covering a field, specifically the field of interminable and ateleological analysis. As long as teleology is uncritically considered an evil concept, Derrida's response appears to be politically progressive. However, the problem with Derrida's formulation, which is typical of his statements concerning the institutional critiques enabled by deconstruction, is that it is either too abstract or too concrete. Deconstruction is too concrete when it performs just the first step, that is, when it reverses a given hierarchical opposition. Although this kind of deconstruction can be specific enough to attack real political problems, it cannot account for its choice of problems. Furthermore, since it is still intrametaphysical, it can only offer false solutions to the problems it does address. The second phase of deconstruction, that which defines the very form of hierarchy as a metaphysical clamp, is too abstract. Although authentically deconstructive, by definition it can make no distinctions among various hierarchical binary oppositions. Thus, it is powerless to intervene in concrete political situations requiring not just hyperlucid analyses but choices that are only partially defensible. In other words, deconstruction of the second phase cannot erect a hierarchy of hierarchical oppositions. Consequently, even though it may be political, it is indiscriminately so.

In the next section, I will analyze a very concrete example of deconstructive political analysis, Derrida's recent texts on apartheid, but by way of introduction, let me pose the problem in its general form. I am claiming that the very logic of deconstruction cannot admit that certain binary oppositions are less metaphysical than others. It would be difficult to imagine Derrida conceding that some hierarchies are better than others, or that metaphysics may, in some of its manifestations, be a desirable and beneficent conceptual system. Since the very form of hierarchical binary opposition implies that one concept is more valuable and central than its more marginal partner, and since Derrida defines metaphysics as the institution of hierarchical binary oppositions serving to repress the uncontrollably disseminating energy of arche-writing, the work of deconstruction must be to undermine hierarchy whenever it finds it. Furthermore, since the various terms signaling the abyssal microstructure of metaphysical oppositions share at least this—that they designate a structure that can never be the object of a science or the referent of a concept—it is, in principle, impossible for one discourse to be more or less meta-physical than another. In other words, since metaphysics is every-where and dissemination is nowhere, deconstruction can only be the continual demonstration of the inclusion of the former in the field of the latter.

Although I do not accept deconstruction's basic principles, here I would like to attempt to demonstrate that, even if one were to play provisionally by Derrida's rules, deconstruction generates insuper-able problems when it ceases to be a critical activity and attempts to make positive claims. Because deconstruction is basically concerned with demystifying logocentric desires, when it is asked to provide the conceptual basis for specific choices, especially political ones, it must uncritically borrow concepts from the very metaphysical tradition Derrida has indefatigably sought to undermine. Even though I think that the concept of *sous-rature* may be less of a philosophical strategy than an example of Sartrean *mauvaise foi*, these concepts are not used under erasure, but, as far as I can tell, quite sincerely.

Of course, it is possible to argue, as Derrida frequently does, that deconstruction is not a homogenous activity, that it practices any number of different styles and strategies that might appear to be incompatible. Although tempting, this argument is unsatisfying for two reasons. First, Derrida's essays and books all have an unmistak-able family resemblance. Deconstruction may be multiple in principle, but in practice it consistently betrays a clearly identifiable approach, style, and value system. If deconstruction were, in fact, totally pro-tean, then could Jonathan Culler have written a book entitled *On Deconstruction*? Second, if deconstruction can encompass contradic-tory discourse, can its multiplicity be extended to fascist, racist, or misogynist discourse? Is *Mein Kampf* deconstructive? It is certainly deconstructible, but it is hardly a text that Derrida would have writ-ten. My point is, when deconstruction claims to be a tissue of texts, these texts are carefully chosen and systematically exclude other kinds of texts. When, however, some excluded texts intrude into what is purportedly a deconstructive analysis, it is unconvincing to argue that such inclusion merely confirms deconstruction (much as a psychoanalyst can fail to convince any but the converted when, seeking to domesticate substantive criticism, he or she labels it *resis-tance*). At such times, it becomes necessary to refuse bad faith rationalization and to consider the possibility that deconstruction may be a seriously flawed theoretical system.

Perhaps no one sums up the issue I am considering as well as Foucault. For example, in *The Archaeology of Knowledge* (1972) he argues that the search for originary difference typical of deconstruction (although Foucault mentions neither Derrida nor deconstruction explicitly here, as he does elsewhere, there is no mistaking his intentions) is, in fact, dangerous because it denies the validity of historical investigation.

> [W]e must renounce two linked, but opposite themes. The first involves a wish that it should never be possible to assign, in the order of discourse, the irruption of a real event; that beyond any apparent beginning, there is always a secret origin—so secret and so fundamental that it can never be quite grasped in itself. Thus one is led inevitably, through the naivety of chronologies, towards an ever-receding point that is never itself present in history; . . . (1972, 25)

According to Foucault, because deconstruction should logically posit history itself as one more discursive field to be deconstructed, it tends to see textuality as transhistorical. As such, it leaves no room in its conceptual apparatus for the irruption of a new discursive event.

> We must renounce all these themes whose function is to ensure the infinite continuity of discourse and its secret presence to itself in the interplay of a constantly recurring absence. We must be ready to receive every moment of discourse in its sudden irruption. (25)

This kind of attack on Derrida appears elsewhere in Foucault and is frequently found in the work of Marxist or sociohistorical critics such as Butler (1984), Eagleton (1976), Jameson (1981), and Lentricchia (1983) among others. Even Michael Ryan, whose *Marxism and Deconstruction* (1982) seeks to reconcile the two, acknowledges a dilemma inherent in any attempt to posit lines of correspondence between deconstruction and any highly historical discipline. "But I take their [Anglo-American empiricist or positivistic critic of deconstruction] side, especially the side of sociohistorically oriented marxists, to the extent that I think Derrida's emphasis on repetition and difference is lopsided. As Anglo-American literary critics prove, it can itself become a metaphysics" (1982, 36). Ryan's resolution of the problem, although an advance over the kind of uncritical acceptance or rejection of deconstruction practiced by many readers of Derrida, is nevertheless not totally satisfying, and can therefore serve as an instructive example of the recalcitrance of the impasse I am describing.

Ryan argues that the political force of deconstruction lies in its hostility to an absolute or transhistorical truth and in its insistence on a definition of history as the product of an essentially open series of differential relations.

> Giving up first principles and last truths also implies entry into history, renouncing the possibility of transcendence, refusing to conceive of the historical passage as a midpoint between an initial axiom and a conclusive goal of ideal meaning or truth. Derrida's notion of "undecidability" can be interpreted as naming the impossibility of decisive or absolute truth determinations which are not differentially produced, which do not therefore bear the trace of an alterity that transforms the supposed totalizing truth determination into a theoretical fiction that is necessarily incomplete or undecidable. (1982, 62)

In the absence of what Lyotard calls a "grand narrative" or secure teleology, deconstruction proposes the concept of undecidability as a description of the contingent historical effects of truth. The problem with Ryan's solution to the dilemma is that his version of Derrida is indistinguishable from the standard version of Foucault. To argue that the historical importance of deconstruction is that, for Derrida, "History is another name for undecidability as the ever-open possibility of extending an axiomatic system" (Ryan 1982, 21), is to finesse the crucial question: If history is the product of arche-writing, can arche-writing be historical in a nontranscendental way? In other words, although a deconstructive point of view is capable of theorizing history *in general* as a fabric of traces, has it anything to say about the contingencies of history, especially when they involve choices among concrete alternatives? In this chapter, I will argue that Derrida's position on this crucial point is, at best, contradictory. Using two recent essays on South African apartheid, I will demonstrate the difficulty of reconciling deconstruction and ideological analysis.

Deconstructing Apartheid

Originally written for inclusion in the catalogue for an itinerant art exhibition, "Art contre/against Apartheid," which opened in Paris in 1985, "Racism's Last Word," in a slightly different form, appeared in the August, 1985, edition of *Critical Inquiry*. As such, it represents a sample of Derrida's later work. Moreover, it is a text whose focus is the least transcendental of phenomena, an evil which, in Derrida's own words, "cannot be summed up in the principial and abstract iniquity of a system. It is also daily suffering, oppression, poverty, violence, torture inflicted by an arrogant white minority" (1985, 293).

Naturally, Derrida declares himself against apartheid. I certainly do not intend to question the sincerity of Derrida's stand, nor do I wish to impugn its daring. Rather than criticize Derrida's position itself, I will seek to elucidate the conceptual presuppositions that allow him to take it; specifically, I will question whether the deconstructive posture that underlies some of Derrida's arguments is, in fact, the theoretical reason for his opposition to apartheid, or whether a rigorous application of the axiomatic propositions of deconstruction might not produce quite a different set of conclusions.

Derrida begins by focusing on the word *apartheid*. It is a word that Derrida, like most people, hopes will someday be the "name of something finally abolished" (291). Having projected a future when apartheid will have a purely lexical existence, he proceeds to analyze the word itself. According to Derrida, *apartheid* remains untranslated into other tongues. It is refused access into other languages because it is taboo, it names the unnameable. "*APARTHEID:* by itself the word occupies the terrain like a concentration camp. System of partition, barbed wire, crowds of mapped out solitudes" (292). *Apartheid* occupies the terrain of a semantic leper colony because it is a sign for the most flagrant of abstractions: forced separation. Ostracized from the internal space of other languages because it is itself the essence of ostracism, *apartheid* is allowed its distant homeland, Afrikaans, so that it can be circumscribed, surveyed, and perhaps denied. However, the taboo against *apartheid* does not stem simply from its relation to racism. *Apartheid* does not just name separation, "like all racism, it tends to pass segregation off as natural—and as the very law of the origin. Such is the monstrosity of this political idiom" (292).

The word *apartheid*, like its referent, is an instance of culture passing itself off as nature. Consequently, Derrida's analysis can be seen as typically deconstructive, analogous to his earlier efforts to demonstrate that every attempt to define speech as the natural and spontaneous emission of signs is doomed because speech—even as Husserlian interior monologue—is, in its essence, structured as writing is. It is probably true that apartheid works, at least in part, by making the forced separation of the races into a natural (or religious) imperative, however it is precisely to the extent that Derrida's position is correct that he runs into trouble. If it is possible to reduce the thrust of Derrida's various books and articles to one central argument, it would be that all the variants of natural, unmotivated presence are, in fact, structured by internal division, referentiality, multiplicity, delay: arche-writing. Nature is an instituted trace, the natural is not absolutely distinguishable from the perverse, purity is the product of difference. More important than Derrida's descriptions of arche-writing, however, is the attitude he recommends toward the lost presence it embodies. For Derrida, it is never enough to deconstruct presence. Derrida repeatedly argues for the importance of actively forgetting what never was—plenitude, seamless continuity, etc.—and, as a consequence, the importance of affirming dissemination. Perhaps the only ethical absolute in Derrida's early work is the call to a Nietzschean refusal of nostalgia and its concomitant, the joyous affirmation of arche-writing.

> Turned toward the presence, lost or impossible, of the absent origin, [the] structuralist thematic of broken immediateness is thus the sad, *negative,* nostalgic, guilty, Rousseauist aspect of the thought of play of which the Nietzschean *affirmation*—the joyous affirmation of the play of the world and of the innocence of becoming, the affirmation of a world of signs without fault, without truth, without origin, offered to an active interpretation—would be the other side. (1978b, 294)

It is therefore remarkable to read the following in "Racism's Last Word."

Even though it offers the excuses of blood, color, birth—or rather, *because* it uses this naturalist and sometimes creationist discourse—racism always betrays the perversion of a man, the "talking animal." It institutes, declares, writes, inscribes, prescribes. A system of marks, it outlines space in order to assign forced residence or to close off borders. It does not discern, it discriminates. (1985, 292)

It is no surprise that apartheid should be decried for its institutionalized and systematic violence; what is curious is that Derrida should describe apartheid in *these* terms, especially if we compare Derrida's recent political essays with his earlier, more theoretical work. I take such texts as *Of Grammatology, Margins of Philosophy,* and *Writing and Difference* to be programmatic of deconstruction in general, especially since, to my knowledge, Derrida has never repudiated any of his former positions. Such a comparison yields the stunning conclusion that Derrida's description of apartheid (perversion, institution, writing, prescription, a system of marks, etc.) has fundamental similarities to his typical earlier descriptions of arche-writing.

We can identify apartheid with arche-writing for two reasons. First, apartheid bears a formal similarity to arche-writing insofar as arche-writing can be defined as the eccentric space of unmotivated (consequently, implicitly perverse) institutionalization. Second, the violence of apartheid is sanctioned by arche-writing because, as Derrida argues in *Of Grammatology,* arche-writing is the general condition of possibility for particular acts of violence.

Anterior to the possibility of violence in the current and derivative sense, the sense used in "A Writing Lesson," [in Claude Lévi-Strauss, *Tristes Tropiques*] there is, as the space of its possibility, the violence of arche-writing, the violence of difference, of classification, and of the system of appellations. (1976, 110)

For Derrida, empirical violence is the manifestation, at a third remove, of the arche-violence of arche-writing. Arche-writing is the primordial violence of naming or classification through the differential nature of language. A second violence, the law that makes the uttering of the proper name (that is, in Derrida's interpretation, the absence of the propriety of a proper name) taboo, is in fact the disguise of the originary violence. To this second violence, a third violence may accrue, what we call violence in the ordinary sense.

> [A] third violence can *possibly* emerge or not (an empirical possibility) within what is commonly called evil, war, indiscretion, rape; which consists of revealing by effraction the so-called proper name, the originary violence which has severed the proper from its property, its self-sameness. . . . It is on this tertiary level, that of the empirical consciousness, that the common concept of violence (the system of moral law and of transgression) whose possibility remains yet unthought, should no doubt be situated. (1976, 112)

Consequently, if apartheid is "daily suffering, oppression, poverty, violence, torture," it is only because the particular, contingent form of its violence is the expression of two levels of prior violence, the violence of the law and its source, "originary violence," the violence of arche-writing. And, to the extent that Derrida frequently argues that both arche-writing and the law are structural components of experience, he is also describing the conditions of possibility for violence in the empirical sense. This is, of course, unremarkable, considering the evidence we have of the cross-cultural and transhistorical insistence of human violence. What is remarkable, and deeply disturbing, is that, if as Derrida has repeatedly argued, not only the demonstration but the affirmation of arche-writing (*différance*, the trace, etc.) is the goal of deconstruction, then it is difficult to determine the theoretical grounds upon which Derrida would condemn arche-violence and its empirical manifestation, "daily suffering."

Needless to say, there is one glaringly obvious difference between Derrida's descriptions of apartheid and arche-writing. Whereas both function to establish difference by means of infraction and separation, arche-writing is used to affirm the impossibility of any absolute foundation of institutionalized traces, whereas the South African discourse surrounding apartheid seeks to establish its signifieds as natural. In other words, while both arche-writing and apartheid participate in the violence of writing, arche-writing affirms that there is nothing outside the text while apartheid is a political strategy to justify racist separation as a natural or theological imperative. This much is perfectly clear, and it is to Derrida's credit that he seeks to expose the political ruses through which the Pretoria regime attempts to legitimize itself.

My analysis in no way wishes to obscure this crucial distinction. Rather, I am simply following Derrida's call, outlined repeatedly, but perhaps most explicitly in *Positions*, to distinguish between the two stages of deconstruction. The question that motivates this section is whether Derrida's denunciation of apartheid is fully deconstructive— that is, if the logic it employs belongs to the class of texts which perform the second step of deconstruction. I am suggesting that, when Derrida critiques apartheid, his discourse is basically neo-Marxist, exposing the ideology of natural or theological legitimation. As such, it belongs to the first phase of deconstruction, and, according to Derrida, "to remain in this phase is still to operate on the terrain of and from within the deconstructed system" (1981b, 42). The second phase, in which the very choice between law and nature is shown to belong to a general text of which they are both meta-physical reifications, is precisely where apartheid would be shown to be a kind of arche-apartheid — the violent institution of breaches, incisions, nonhomogeneities, and spacing. Consequently, just as Derrida deconstructs an "eternal . . . universal . . . divine or natural writing" (1976, 15) by demonstrating that it is derivative with regard to arche-writing, I am claiming that a deconstruction of apartheid yields the surprising proposition that its subtext is identical to that constituting arche-writing: arbitrary separation and violence.

Perhaps my position would be clearer if we were to imagine that Pretoria read "Racism's Last Word" and was convinced by Derrida's rhetoric. Suppose that South Africa took Derrida at his word and decided that it is in its interests to stop pretending that apartheid is a natural or theological mandate but that it should be affirmed as raw political will to power. A kind of apartheid that has decon-structed its metaphysical trappings would affirm the forced separa-tion of the races without nostalgia for absolute legitimation. Such a posture would be oblivious to the binary opposition between natural and cultural, and so would belong to the class of texts that decon-structive discourse typically affirms.

It should not be forgotten that deconstruction is a philosophy of *difference* and *violence*. Commenting on the *picada* that traverses the territory of the Nambikwara in order to critique Lévi-Strauss's desire that the violence of writing be excluded from primitive cultures, Derrida says

> one should meditate upon all of the following together: writing as the possibility of the road and of difference, the history of writing and the history of the road, of the rupture, of the *via rupta*, of the path that is broken, beaten, *fracta*, of the space of reversibility and of repetition traced by the opening, the divergence from, and the violent spacing, of nature, of the natural, savage, salvage, forest. The *silva* is savage, the *via rupta* is written, discerned, and inscribed violently as difference, as form imposed on the *hylè*, in the forest, in wood as in matter. (1976, 107–8)

Within the context of his own theory, Derrida could legitimately criticize apartheid for its rigidity, but not for the violence of forced separation. But would a more flexible form of human oppression, perhaps one that was in no way constrained by the need to legitimize violence, be less pernicious than the current Pretoria regime?[1] And could it be deconstructed?

It is, of course, highly unlikely that as long as it continues to affirm its right to practice apartheid, South Africa would ever abjure the use of naturalist or theological arguments to found its policies. My point, and my fear, is that its deconstruction would not necessarily dismantle apartheid, but would merely lay bare any claims it makes on the basis of nostalgia or natural rights.

Insofar as the ultimate concern of deconstruction is the unearthing and affirmation of the mechanisms of the originary trace (and not of its "vulgar" embodiments, such as writing or violence in the ordinary sense), it is difficult to see the grounds upon which Derrida could logically condemn "arche-apartheid"—not the attempt to naturalize racism, but racism itself. Clearly, the failure to condemn the system *would* be monstrous. I suspect that it is some intimation of such a paralyzing aporia generated by a deconstructive politics that leads Derrida, who has repeatedly exhorted his readers to dissect the notion of Truth in order to reveal its non-dialectical condition of possibility, to deprecate South African racism in the name of a truth that the exhibition organized by the Association of Artists of the World against Apartheid was in the process of unveiling: "in the truth it [the exhibit] exposes" (1985, 294).

Why, then, is Derrida against apartheid? In the name of what principle does he raise his voice in solidarity with those who denounce the South African regime? Not in the name of humanism, or human rights, which he condemns as part of a European discourse that is complicit in a system that allows, perhaps even needs, racism.

> If this verdict [the 1973 declaration by the General Assembly of the United Nations that apartheid is a "crime against humanity"] continues to have an effect, it is because the customary discourse on man, humanism and human rights, has encountered its effective and as yet unthought limit, the limit of the whole system in which it acquires meaning. (298)

Nor in the name of any recognizable ethics, religion, pragmatism, historical imperative, class conflict, evolutionary adaptation etc. Recently, Derrida has been arguing that his analyses of truth and context do not invalidate the possibility of making decisions based on relatively stable interpretative contexts. For example, he says:

> And that within interpretative contexts (that is, within relations of force that are always differential—for example, socio-political-institutional—but even beyond these determinations) that are relatively stable, sometimes apparently almost unshakable, it should be possible to invoke rules of competence, criteria of discussion and of consensus, good faith, lucidity, rigor, criticism, and pedagogy. (1988b, 146)

But it is still unclear whose rules are to count for the stable background required for such a neopragmatist view of stability. Pretoria also has rules, and the issue under discussion is precisely one that is begged by Derrida's argument: in a political situation in which different sets of language games are competing, what sorts of criteria, or metarules, is it legitimate to invoke so as to be able to adjudicate between radically different fields of relative interpretative stability. How does a German defend his or her resistance to Nazism in the late 1930s?

Ultimately, I think that Derrida assumes that he need not explain his opposition to apartheid, since such opposition goes without saying in just about any Western discourse. That may be so, but it does not help us here, inasmuch as tacit agreements and notions of consensus are every bit as susceptible to deconstruction as are laws burned in stone.

At this point let me anticipate an objection that ideologically oriented supporters of Derrida, such as Michael Ryan, might make. There does appear to be one possible resolution of the dilemma, although it must be emphasized that Derrida does not explicitly defend this position. It could be argued that the system of racial demarcation in South Africa is deplorable because it is a rigid and static ideological system. Since apartheid establishes a series of differences that are not subject to the mobility Derrida traditionally attributes to writing, the fluidity of the Derridian notion of *différance* would therefore be the means by which South African institutionalized racism could be opposed in a manner congruent with deconstructive principles.

This line of thought is consistent with the idea that the restriction of freedom, whether of a people's freedom to choose the nature of its political organization or, more generally, to decide its own future, is inherently evil. The only problem with this position is that it requires a bit of prestidigitation to make it belong to the class of arguments that are compatible with those Derrida himself normally attributes to deconstruction. Let me approach the issue in the following way. Most people, and especially most blacks, would agree that it is incomparably better for a black to live in France, or the U.S., than in South Africa. Furthermore, they would undoubtedly invoke the concept of freedom to support their position. What would deconstruction do with this claim? Derrida himself provides the answer. Apartheid is, in fact, only one of the more visible expressions of a baneful European worldview. "Europe, in the enigmatic process of its globalization and of its paradoxical disappearance, seems to project onto this screen, point by point, the silhouette of its internal war, the bottom line of its profits and losses, the double-bind logic of its national and multi-national interests. Their dialectical evaluation provides only a provisional stasis in a precarious equilibrium, one whose price today is *apartheid*" (1985, 298). Therefore, the binary opposition between racism in South Africa and racism in France (or the West in general) is itself the product of some kind of arche-racism inherent in Western metaphysics. And the proper task of deconstruction is to expose the complicity of European culture with this, its rawest manifestation. Although, as I have tried to outline above, even on its own, Derridian, grounds, this argument is fraught with difficulties, especially when it appears that deconstruction ought to affirm originary violence, let us provisionally accept it. Western metaphysics, then, would have a political arm, one of whose functions is to demarcate people into absolutely impregnable divisions, and deconstruction would be a kind of terrorist liberation philosophy, undermining the repressive system whenever it can.

The problem with this view, besides Derrida's own dismissal of the premise that deconstruction is a theory of liberation, is that its field of concern is limited to the first step of deconstruction, the reversal of oppressive binary oppositions. But, according to Derrida, this is only a provisional gesture whose main purpose is its anticipation of the second, properly deconstructive step: the retranscription of the concepts under consideration and their displacement into a new and mobile fabric. It is easy to see what this means in the area of philosophy, since most of Derrida's work has been the demonstration of this principle. However, it is exceedingly difficult to imagine an effective political application of Derrida's model. If all Derrida can say on the political front is that repression is evil and freedom is good, then how is he different from the legions of fair-minded and generous people who would make the same point based on liberal Christianity, Judaism, or Islam, or just on the humanism Derrida savages for its complicity with apartheid? Derrida, the empathetic human being, can deplore the barbarousness of apartheid, but Derrida, the deconstructionist, can make no meaningful distinctions among political regimes that offer their citizens varying degrees of freedom. To deconstruct apartheid would be to displace the entirety of the Western political edifice, along with those distinctions that are of the utmost importance to oppressed people like South African blacks, onto a terrain that Derrida has never attempted to describe.

Textuality is a compelling concept in the field of letters, but when Derrida seeks to transform it from a tool of destabilization into a principle whereby positive political alternatives might be generated, he is at a loss to suggest concrete ways in which his impressive rhetoric might be embodied. Inasmuch as Europe, in the expanded sense it receives in "Racism's Last Word," is roughly synonymous with Western metaphysics, its deconstruction can, it appears, only yield the ineffable or the inconceivable.

That is why Derrida's solution to this dilemma, although at first rather surprising, especially because of who proposes it, is, in the end, the logical expression of the political crisis of deconstruction. Derrida appeals to a future in which *apartheid* will be the name for the unnameable, and nothing more, by a call to silence in the present.

> Things are not the same with this exhibition. Here the single work is multiple, it crosses all national, cultural, and political frontiers. It neither commemorates nor represents an event. Rather it casts a continuous gaze (paintings are always gazing) at what I propose to name a continent. One may do whatever one wishes with all the senses of that word.
>
> Beyond a continent whose limits they point to, the limits surrounding it or crossing through it, the paintings gaze and call out in silence.
>
> And their silence is just. A discourse would once again compel us to reckon with the present state of force and law. It would draw up contracts, dialecticize itself, let itself be reappropriated again.
>
> This silence calls out unconditionally; it keeps watch on that which is not, on that which is not yet, and on the chance of still remembering some faithful day. (1985, 299)

Any discourse, and, a fortiori, the text of "Racism's Last Word," can be reappropriated because it is, in Derrida's own vocabulary, "always already" the carrier of violence. Derrida must invoke silence, the suspension of discursivity, since the rules for discourse he himself has established do not allow for any meaningful distinctions between the various phenomenal expressions of the originary trace (writing/speech, evil/good, democracy/authoritarianism). And yet, silence is an ancient philosophical and theological concept, a version of absolute presence, uncompromising, unconditional, and impatient with political realities. As such it is now what it has always been—an instance of political evil. A silence that calls out unconditionally is not likely to have much effect on a political regime that would like nothing better than worldwide silence or unconditional, silent watches in the future perfect.

Because it cannot be evaluated in traditional philosophical or scientific ways (since it disputes the kinds of truths these disciplines purport to yield), deconstruction must be judged on the strength of its pragmatic usefulness in attacking specific problems. And in this arena, it is at best incapable of making interesting, or politically viable, observations or distinctions, and, at worst, liable to lay the groundwork for a position that, because it can only imagine two kinds of uniform worlds, one of which is the expression of arche-violence (our world) and one of which is impossible to describe, is in fact politically and culturally impotent. Because deconstruction must affirm a kind of pure *différance* it sees operating everywhere, because in the end pure freedom is indistinguishable from pure slavery, any attempt to insert such concepts as arche-writing into a political context is doomed to serve the interests of stasis and reaction.

The entirety of the dilemma I am describing is inscribed in the following quote from "Différance."

> But I would say that this in itself—the silence [of the graphic difference between *e* and *a* in the signifier *différance*] that functions within only a so-called phonetic writing—quite opportunely conveys or reminds us that, contrary to a very widespread prejudice, there is no phonetic writing. There is no purely and rigorously phonetic writing. (1982, 4–5)

Silence, pyramidal silence, is here likened to all that exceeds phonetic or logocentric writing. This typically Derridian statement is only interesting, I think, because of Derrida's strangely ambivalent conclusion. First he proclaims in his typical Zarathustrian tone that phonetic writing does not exist. Then, in an important addendum, he says that phonetic writing can never be pure or rigorous. Between the two claims there is a world of difference. The first is itself absolute, and its object is a straw man—I know of no contemporary philosopher or linguist who is making serious claims for the existence of a pure phonetic writing. The second can be interpreted (especially if its diacritical difference from the first statement is kept in mind) to make the reasonable claim that phonetic writing functions in a continuum; that, although never pure, it nevertheless exists in varying degrees of purity. Thus, Derrida's first statement suggests, by analogy with mathematics, that infinity does not exist; his second, that although any two integers are equally distant from infinity, it is nevertheless possible to claim that $n + 1$ is greater than n. Were one to deconstruct the second, weaker proposition, the logical result would be a theoretical system unable to distinguish between more or less desirable choices in a world in which absolutes do not exist. In the specific instance under consideration, I think that even if it is the manifestation of arche-writing, *apartheid cannot, and should not, be deconstructed* if one is to be allowed the theoretical room to distinguish between racism in South Africa and, say, racism in France, or, between a world that is violent and one that is less violent. Unless one is willing to reduce history to the choice between inevitable arche-violence and an ineffable future, one must respect these differences, despite their vulgarity. Anything else risks the most monstrous of reappropriations, not that of arche-writing by dialectical idealism, but that of progressive political intervention by well-meaning silence.

Prescriptive Deconstruction

Derrida's essay on apartheid occasioned a somewhat notorious debate in *Critical Inquiry*. The Autumn, 1986, issue carried a response to "Racism's Last Word" by Anne McClintock and Rob Nixon, followed by a rebuttal by Derrida. McClintock and Nixon's article is historical in nature, devoting most of its space to chronicling the adventures of the word *apartheid* since its coinage in 1917. Although McClintock and Nixon's central argument is that Derrida ignores the increasing sheepishness of the Afrikaaner governments of South Africa to call their regime of partition and oppression by the name of *apartheid*, the implicit theoretical critique that informs their essay is, in the main, the one I have outlined above. For example, near the end of their response, they argue for an alternative strategy of political analysis.

> For an analysis of racial representation, at least, this would mean abandoning such favored monoliths of post-structuralism as "logocentrism" and "Western metaphysics," not to mention bulky homogeneities such as "the occidental essence of the historical process" and a "European 'discourse' on the concept of life." Instead one would have to regard with a historical eye the uneven traffic between political interests and an array of cul-

tural discourses—a traffic at times clandestine, at times frank, at times symmetrical, at times conflicting and rivalrous, but at all times intimate. (1986, 154)

In short, McClintock and Nixon feel that the abstractions that structure Derrida's article force a continuity and a family resemblance upon events and discourses that are discontinuous and historically contingent.

Needless to say, Derrida (1986a) takes issue with such an analysis. He clothes his comments in the form of a letter to McClintock and Nixon. Beginning with a tone of light sarcasm—thanking them, for instance, for informing the readership of *Critical Inquiry* of the history of South African state racism—Derrida modulates to pique over their inability to make elementary grammatical distinctions in his text, and ends up in what appears to be genuine vexation, as when he screams, "You have the nerve, for example, to write the following . . ." (1986a, 165).

Derrida's response is understandable. Despite McClintock and Nixon's repeated disclaimers to the effect that Derrida's personal commitment to justice in South Africa is not an issue, there are, nevertheless, numerous suggestions in their essay that Derrida colludes with those forces of liberal capitalism he himself apparently rejects. And, since Derrida has been, over the past decade or so, repeatedly reviled by the Left for his political postures, his sensitivity to this sort of attack is no mystery. In fact, he begins his letter by placing it in the context of other, similar critiques.

We have never met but, after reading your "response," I have a sense of something familiar, as if our paths had often crossed at colloquia or in some other academic place. (1986a, 155)

Unfortunately, despite my empathy for Derrida's difficult position and my admiration for his attempts at political intervention, I cannot avoid the conclusion that his response to McClintock and Nixon's essay only confirms their uneasiness with the political implications of deconstruction. In general, Derrida offers two kinds of rebuttals to McClintock and Nixon. The first is thoroughly unconvincing. Derrida repeatedly claims that their historical analysis of the vagaries of the word *apartheid* is somehow a call to ignore the reality of South African racial policies. If, the argument goes, the South African government has phased out the use of the word, should we stop struggling against it?

> I'm still trying to imagine what I should have written if I had been carefully following your "strategic" advice. Perhaps I should have said: You know, *apartheid* is no longer the right word, even *racism* is no longer the right word because ever since "the development of the bantustan policy," " 'the problem in South Africa is basically not one of race, but of nationalism, which is a world-wide problem. There is White nationalism, and there are several Black nationalisms.' " (1986a, 164)

The sarcastic tone Derrida adopts is an index of how deeply hurt he is by any suggestion that his position is less than progressive. But really, it is awfully misplaced. Nowhere do McClintock and Nixon suggest that we ought to ignore the reality of South African racism simply because the government has decided to phase out the word *apartheid*. Their only point is that the undue emphasis Derrida places on the signifier *apartheid* in "Racism's Last Word" might be of less political import than an analysis of its displacements under various South African governments. Their disgust with the euphemistic transformation of the focus of official South African rhetoric from race to nationality and, more generally, their commitment to the overthrow of the Pretoria regime, are hardly debatable.

Much more interesting is Derrida's second major argument.

> Unfortunately, if I had done that, I would have been quoting you quoting Verwoerd or Vorster, or else at best I would have written a paper on the ideological strategies of state racism in South Africa. But I would not have said the essential thing, to wit: *apartheid*, as a state racism and under the name chosen by the Nationalist party, then in control in South Africa, has been and remains the effective and official practice, still today, in spite of all the denegations and certain softening touches to the facade (which, by the way, I also mentioned). And *apartheid* must be fought as such. (1986a, p. 164)

I can see a generation of graduate students, swamped by the complexities of Derrida's earlier texts, breathing a sigh of relief. No obscurity here. And that, ultimately, is my point. Derrida's response to an attack on the political soundness of "Racism's Last Word" is studded with references to clarity, to factuality, to the referent of rhetoric, to the proper name, all parading openly and not under the protection of *sous-rature*. A few quotations will suffice to demonstrate Derrida's strategy: "No doubt you will agree with me on this point: the better informed, the more lucid, and I dare say, the more competent the fight, the better it will be able to adjust its strategies" (155); "You say 'Derrida is repelled by the word.' No, what I find repulsive is the thing that history has linked to the word" (159); "It's you, and not me, who also seem to be frightened by this word because you propose that we take seriously all the substitutes and pseudonyms, the periphrases and metonymies that the official discourse in Pretoria keeps coming up with: the tireless ruse of propaganda, the indefatigable but vain rhetoric of dissimulation." (159); "It's the thing and the concept they should have retired, and not just the word, if they had wanted to put an end to the 'sinister renown'" (161); and "And if you're going to struggle against this *historical* concept and this *historical* reality, well, then you've got to call a thing by its name" (163).

Derrida's appeal to a series of categories and concepts so alien from those he usually employs is an index of an aporia he is unable to affirm. So when, in response to a question concerning his use of such concepts, Derrida argues that deconstruction has never denied them, only attempted to situate them within their determining contexts, he is being disingenuous.

> I have never "put such concepts as truth, reference, and the stability of interpretive contexts radically into question" if "putting radically into question" means contesting that there *are* and that there *should be* truth, reference, and stable contexts of interpretation. I have—but this is something entirely different—posed questions that I hope are radical concerning the possibility of these things, of these values, of these norms, of this stability (which by essence is always provisional and finite). (1988b, 150)

Although it is certainly true that Derrida has never argued for nontruth, indeed that he has argued for the necessity of truth, his stress has always been on demonstrating and affirming the ineradicable element of undecidability that haunts all determinations of truth. What I am signaling here is not a logical contradiction, but a radical change in tone and emphasis. In the past, Derrida acknowledged truth as a rhetorical strategy in his indefatigable efforts to destabilize it; here he affirms truth, clarity, and reference.

Ultimately, the issue of whether *apartheid* is a legitimate signifier of the political situation in South Africa is trivial. Derrida does not reproach McClintock and Nixon for being bad readers. The burgeoning anger of his response is in direct proportion to the difficulty Derrida faces in the attempt to defend his "method."

As he himself describes it, his method is prescriptive ("If you had paid attention to the context and the mode of my text, you would not have fallen into the enormous blunder that led you to take a *prescriptive* utterance for a *descriptive* [theoretical and constative] one" [158]) and deconstructive ("It is in the interest of one side and the other to represent deconstruction as a turning inward and an enclosure by the limits of language, whereas in fact deconstruction *begins* by deconstructing logocentrism, the linguistics of the word, and this very enclosure itself" [168]). "Racism's Last Word" and "But, beyond . . . ," then, are a new, hybrid genre, prescriptive deconstruction. They are prescriptive insofar as they express a wish, that apartheid be both the last form of state racism and that it remain as a memorial and reminder of the horrors of institutionalized oppression. And they are deconstructive when they make apartheid and logocentrism complicitous and proceed to expose and undermine their collusion.

Unfortunately, prescriptive deconstruction is an oxymoron, and the various difficulties I have been signaling in Derrida's texts result from his attempt to make the union of its constituent terms appear unproblematic. At the end of his response, Derrida angrily reproaches McClintock and Nixon for supposedly misunderstanding the deconstructive notion of "*beyond* the text" and of thereby wishing to impose a kind of academic apartheid, in which deconstructionists are restricted to their benign, apolitical work: "When a 'deconstructionist,' as one says, concerns himself with *apartheid*, even if he is on the 'good' side, his strategy is all wrong, he's getting mixed up with things that are none of his business because he's going '*beyond* the text'!" (1986a, 169). Paradoxically, if we dismiss the irony, Derrida's conclusion is correct not because of his premise, but because of its inverse. As I have attempted to demonstrate, it is precisely *because* deconstruction tends to see everything as text that it is incapable of generating meaningful distinctions. There are times, however, when such distinctions are of the essence. The rhetoric of "always already" or "double inscription" is of little help when a necessarily binary political decision needs to be made. At such times, one must perhaps act on the flimsiest of philosophical grounds. One must make clear and binding choices on bases that are perhaps indefensible before a resourceful skeptic—before the kind of author who writes with a woman's hand in *Spurs*, or with a masterful doubleness in *Glas*.

Derrida accurately assesses the value of "Racism's Last Word" as performative rather than constative. That someone with the reputation of Derrida should write against apartheid is a symbolic act of great power. However, to echo Sartre, one is not a deconstructionist like a rock is a rock. When, in "Racism's Last Word," Derrida attempts a deconstructive analysis of apartheid he only succeeds in arguing himself into a labyrinth of silence. That is, if one subjects his text to the kind of reading Derrida might have performed had he not felt the need to defend his property and his name, "Racism's Last Word" yields two levels. As an attempted deconstruction of apartheid it is a dangerous failure. As a liberal humanist call to action, it could be, I hope, a resounding success. "But, beyond . . ." demonstrates quite elegantly the dilemma of "Racism's Last Word." His political effectiveness challenged, Derrida abandons anything like a recognizable deconstructive reading and, in its stead, offers a defense of his position that relies on such undeconstructed notions as clarity, resistance to dissimulation, facts, and calling things by their names. Derrida's position is a good one. There are times when things should be called by their names, when one should resist dissimulation, when clarity and factuality should be valued. Without a distinction between political rhetoric and some concept of objectivity no meaningful political action is possible. Without pragmatically useful notions of evidence and factuality it is very difficult to decide among competing versions of the past. And without a distinction between a name and what it names, it is impossible to denounce fanciful and self-serving discourses. "But, beyond . . . " demonstrates that, when a deconstructionist accosts political questions, he must abandon the acuteness of his critical perspective—his ability to slice texts into infinitely thin segments and to find at their center a tangled web of ghostly traces—and appeal, instead, to a clarity enabled by a kind of amnesia.

In short, when Derrida writes against apartheid, he does so for precisely those reasons and using precisely those concepts that Derrida the deconstructionist would, in another context, challenge. This is the aporia of deconstruction that no amount of self-righteous sarcasm can dissolve.

The Question of Value

Although Foucault's criticism of deconstruction is, I believe, correct, the reason for Derrida's inability to criticize a political regime without recourse to either silence or concepts that are, by his own definition, metaphysical, is that he nonetheless shares a fundamental presupposition with Foucault. Despite his "deconstruction" of Foucault in "Cogito and the History of Madness," Derrida's epistemology is fundamentally like Foucault's inasmuch as he believes that truth is purely the product of contextual historical, institutional, or economic forces. Given his criticism of foundational theories, Derrida could not possibly maintain a theory of truth based on anything but cultural or historical relativity. Although he argues against relativism, "Which is to say that from the point of view of semantics, but also of ethics and politics, 'deconstruction' should never lead to relativism or any sort of indeterminism" (1988b, 148), what he means is that deconstruction does not believe in purely relative or purely indeterminate determinations of truth. The relative stability that Derrida claims is able to rescue his notion of truth from relativism is simply something like what reader-response theorists call an interpretative context, or what Foucault and other constructivists call an "episteme" or "regime of truth." In other words, since for Derrida truth, like other metaphysical concepts, is the reification of arche-writing, it can have no other basis than a particular historical and cultural nexus of discourses, texts, and institutions. The possibility of transcultural truth, or of nonsociologically determined scientific truth, is alien to Derrida's system.

Consequently, since truth is an effect of historical textuality, no one regime of truth can claim to be superior to another. The concept of superiority, and the value system it implies, must itself be historical; therefore, in the absence of a metahistorical perspective from which to compare different value systems, deconstruction cannot claim that one episteme is more valuable than another. In other words, since truth is immanent to the context generating it, it is by definition impossible for a discourse issuing from the same context to make value statements that aspire to some kind of universality, because such comparison would demand a metaframe, a concept that is quintessentially metaphysical in the deconstructive world-view. This is why deconstruction is rarely willing to raise the question of value, and why Derrida would certainly take issue with any claim that human history can be viewed as progressive or regressive.

Derrida cannot use a deconstructive methodology to argue that South Africa is morally inferior to Europe because he cannot argue that it is meaningful to maintain that one truth-generating frame is comparable to another. And yet, like most of us, he knows that South Africa is evil. This knowledge, which may be prereflective and pre-philosophical, is somehow impervious to the objection that it is merely historical and ideological. Most people in the West would take issue with the argument that the only thing wrong with apartheid is that the Pretoria truth-generating machine is weaker than the European one, just as they would reject the idea that the Holocaust was a monstrous breach of ethics merely because the Nazis lost the war. We would like to argue that the Enlightenment notion of human rights is not just historical whimsy, and that genocide is not abhorrent simply because a certain culture finds it in its interests to make it so. Although the full philosophical exposition of the concept of universal human rights may be quite recent, it does not necessarily follow that it is based on nothing more solid than historical accident, any more than the relatively recent discovery of the genetic code proves that DNA is a cultural invention. As opposed to Richard Rorty's position (1989), I do not believe that it is simply the radical contingency of the liberal democratic context in which I live that allows me to denounce apartheid. I take seriously the deeply held conviction shared by Derrida and myself that political regimes like apartheid are, indeed, evil and suggest that a philosophical attitude unable to account for this intuition except on the grounds of historical contingency must be inadequate.

Chapter 6

Literature and Science

Derrida is as impatient with the idea of literature as he is with the idea of philosophy. According to him, both of these notions have traditionally functioned in a network of representational systems aspiring toward the erasure of the trace by the full presence of the signified. A certain conception of literature, in its desire to isolate the literary text from the fabric of general writing and to elevate it to a position of self-possession, is just as vulnerable to logocentric reappropriation as squarely philosophical discourses.

However, with the implicit disclaimer concerning the dangers of elevating literature to a new transcendental concept, Derrida does acknowledge that literature, especially a number of recent experiments in literary style, does possess deconstructive resources that ought to be exploited. Referring to the work of such authors as Artaud, Bataille, Mallarmé, and Sollers, Derrida argues that a certain kind of literary practice can contest both metaphysical philosophy and the kind of literature it promotes.

> Yes, it is incontestable that certain texts classified as "literary" have seemed to me to operate breaches or infractions at the most advanced points. . . . Why? At least for the reason that induces us to suspect the denomination "literature," and which subjects the concept to belles-lettres, to the arts, to poetry, to rhetoric, and to philosophy. These texts operate, in their very movement, the demonstration and practical deconstruction of the *representation* of what was done with literature, it being well understood that long before these "modern" texts a certain "literary" practice was able to operate against this model, against this representation. (1981b, 69)

Thus, there are two concepts of literature in Derrida's view. One, literature as unity, beauty, and truth, is allied to the pernicious repression characteristic of ontotheology. The other, the literature of play, loss, death, nonproduction, in short, of what Bataille calls a general economy, is prized as a kind of writing that can resist the philosophical domination of the concept of literature. For his part, Derrida claims to write neither literature nor philosophy, but to use whatever resources are at his disposal to attempt the rupture of classical aesthetics: "Thus, to answer your questions, I will say that my texts belong to neither the 'philosophical' register nor to the 'literary' register. Thereby they communicate, or so I hope at least, with other texts that, having operated a certain rupture, can be called 'philosophical' or 'literary' only according to a kind of paleonomy..." (1981b, 71).

In short, Derrida's position on literature differs in no significant way from his position on other texts. Like all writing, literature can be metaphysical, either by reproducing logocentric concepts or by its subsumption into classical aesthetic categories, or it can be an economy of transgression and reappropriation. Derrida does not see literature as a special use of language with capabilities and functions different from those of other kinds of language. In fact, Derrida's theory of arche-writing must postulate literature as merely a particular node in a general text. Consequently, whatever specificity a literary use of language might have would be judged by deconstruction to be a secondary manifestation of its primary belonging to the nonempirical trace structure. For Derrida, aesthetics cannot be an autonomous existential or ontological category. Although he clearly acknowledges the existence and cultural power of concepts such as art and beauty, for Derrida they tend to serve as challenges to deconstructive intervention.

There is ample evidence in Derrida's works that science, or the project of science, is to be understood as participating in the same metaphysics of presence as logocentric philosophy or literature. Derrida repeatedly criticizes the supposed scientism of structuralism, Husserlian phenomenology, and Saussurian linguistics. In fact, one of the most powerful formulations of his key concept of arche-writing emphasizes its diacritical distance from scientific objectivity: "This arche-writing, although its concept is *invoked* by the themes of 'the arbitrariness of the sign' and of difference, cannot and can never be recognized as the *object of a science*. It is that very thing which cannot let itself be reduced to the form of *presence*" (1976, 57). Implicit in Derrida's statement is the equation of science with objectification and presence. In fact, in a passage which dispenses with his usual disclaimer quotation marks around concepts whose use *sous-rature* he does not wish to go unnoticed, Derrida describes the essence of science as a teleology of unequivocality. "There is not scientific sense (*Sinn*) without meaning (*bedeuten*), but it belongs to the essence of science to demand an unequivocality without shadow, the absolute transparency of discourse" (1982, 167).

If science is the dream of transparent presence in the face of a totally delimitable empirical object, then deconstruction, whose task is to demonstrate that the scientific object is, itself, the product of "the *original non-empirical science*" (1973, 5) must be in principle hostile to the various manifestations of the scientific spirit. In other words, if presence is a kind of calculus on the "irreducible void" (1973, 5), and if presence is another name for scientific objectification, then clearly deconstruction must postulate an essential communication between metaphysics and science that requires that science be displaced onto Derrida's bed of graphemic instability.

However, as with literature, Derrida does not confine himself to a single definition of science. In fact, he believes that we are currently witnessing the emergence of a new kind of science hostile to its own "essence." Whereas normal science is essentially a humanistic enterprise dominated by the logocentric concepts of presence and objectivity, Derrida sees in recent developments in biology, genetics, and cybernetics a move away from the teleology of empirical closure and toward a *grammatology*. I cite the following lengthy passage from *Of Grammatology* because what it says, and what it omits, are crucial both to an understanding of Derrida's position towards science and to the thesis that this book will present in part 2.

> To affirm in this way that the concept of writing exceeds and comprehends that of language, presupposes of course a certain definition of language and of writing. If we do not attempt to justify it, we shall be giving in to the movement of inflation we have just mentioned, which has also taken over the word *writ-*

ing, and that not fortuitously. For some time now, as a matter of fact, here and there, by a gesture and for motives that are profoundly necessary, whose degradation is easier to denounce than it is to disclose their origin, one says "language" for action, movement, thought, reflection, consciousness, unconsciousness, experience, affectivity, etc. Now we tend to say "writing" for all that and more: to designate not only the physical gestures of literal pictographic and ideographic inscription, but also the totality of what makes it possible; and also, beyond the signifying face, the signified face itself. And thus we say "writing" for all that gives rise to an inscription in general, whether it is literal or not and even if what it distributes in space is alien to the order of the voice: cinematography, choreography, of course, but also pictorial, musical, sculptural "writing." One might also speak of athletic writing, and with even greater certainty of military or political writing in view of the techniques that govern those domains today. All this to describe not only the system of notation secondarily connected with these activities but the essence and the content of these activities themselves. It is also in this sense that the contemporary biologist speaks of writing and *program* in relation to the most elementary processes of information within the living cell. And, finally, whether it has essential limits or not, the entire field covered by the cybernetic *program* will be the field of writing. If the theory of cybernetics is by itself to oust all metaphysical concepts—including the concepts of soul, of life, of value, of choice, of memory—which until recently served to separate the machine from man, it must conserve the notion of writing, trace, gramme [written mark], or grapheme, until its own historico-metaphysical character is also exposed. Even before being determined as human (with all the distinctive characteristics that have always been attributed to man and the entire system of significations they imply) or nonhuman, the *gramme*—or the *grapheme*—would thus name the element. An element without simplicity. An element, whether it is understood as the medium or as the irreducible atom, of the arche-synthesis in general, of what one must forbid oneself to define within the system of oppositions of metaphysics, of what consequently one should not even call *experience* in general, that is to say the origin of *meaning* in general. (1976, 8–9)

This may be one of the most important passages in Derrida's entire oeuvre. In the last twenty years or so, those who have dared to contest deconstruction have tended to let outrage obscure the fact that their critiques have been too generous to Derrida. Well-meaning attacks on deconstructive relativism, such as those launched by Denis Donahue, Gerald Graff, Frank Lentricchia, and others, have tended to be pragmatic in nature. Although I agree that the cultural effects of deconstruction can be pernicious, and that its pragmatic or performative consequences are ultimately the jury that will adjudicate its value, I fear that such analyses tend to begin by conceding too much to Derrida and then proceed to argue their position with a crippling handicap. Instead of granting Derrida the right to choose the rules by which he will be judged, I think that Derrida's fundamental premises must be questioned if deconstruction's ideological, aesthetic, and philosophical effects are to be challenged in a coherent manner. Specifically, an effective critique of deconstruction must be able to claim that Derrida has erected an ontological and epistemological hypothesis that is, if only partially, in error. This is a delicate point whose full demonstration must await the second part of this book. However, as a kind of introduction, I would like to make a few observations about the long passage cited above.

Derrida's purpose in the passage is to justify the erection of writing as a paradigm for Being in general. In a sense, realizing the reductive potential of designating everything as the nonoriginal product of "originary" arche-writing, Derrida seeks to account for the hegemony of the scriptural metaphor in both his work and in critical theory by suggesting that deconstruction bears a family resemblance to work in various other fields. The deemphasis of phonic substance and of its attendant fealty to the metaphysics of presence is a generalized phenomenon with roots in such varied fields as cinematography, choreography, sculpture, biology, theoretical mathematics, genetics, and cybernetics. Grammatology, therefore, is not simply the imposition of a series of powerful philosophical voices (Heidegger, Nietzsche, Bataille, Derrida, etc.) but a sign of a general cultural shift from an emphasis on the *phone* to a recognition of the irreducibility of inscription. And, to the extent that scientific writing is in the forefront of the attack on phonetic writing, it is also a soldier in the epochal, historical reduction of the dominance of metaphysics. "This enclave [mathematics] is also the place where the practice of scientific language challenges intrinsically and with increasing profundity the ideal of phonetic writing and all its implicit metaphysics (metaphysics *itself*)" (1976, 10).

Punning on the etymological heritage of such terms as program, and using his penchant for infinite caution to warn his readers that even cybernetics will one day reveal its own metaphysical character, Derrida argues that genetics and cybernetics are slowly dismembering the traditional affiliation among the concepts of soul, life, experience, meaning, value, memory, and choice. In short, a kind of humanism that values humanity's position in the universe, that sees the human person as a spiritual being, that gives people responsibility for their choices, and that considers humanity as the locus for the generation of value, is, according to Derrida, currently being menaced by scientific writing. Theoretical mathematics, cybernetics, genetics (the absence of quantum mechanics and relativity is salient here), and deconstruction are part of a historical movement whose program is to perturb classical humanistic values. The worldwide computer, by which I take Derrida to mean not just computer science in particular but information and systems technology in general, which in "Racism's Last Word" is seen as the epitome of European metaphysics, is, in this context, a virus lodging itself in its core and, through a process of rampant simulation and spread, threatening its identity.

That cybernetics should be invoked as a metaphor for grammatology in *Of Grammatology* and, in the form of the worldwide computer, as a metaphor for metaphysics in "Racism's Last Word" is the kind of contradiction that Derrida cannot gleefully appropriate as further corroboration of the doubleness of his work. The difficulties outlined earlier in relation to his attempts to stake a political position on the timbers of deconstruction suggest that there comes a time when, as Derrida himself says, "you've got to call a thing by its name" (1986a, 163). And if, again as Derrida says, "within interpretative contexts (that is, within relations of force that are always differential—for example, sociopolitical-institutional—but even beyond these determinations) that are relatively stable, sometimes apparently almost unshakable, it should be possible to invoke rules of competence, criteria of discussion and of consensus, good faith, lucidity, rigor, criticism and pedagogy" (1988b, 146), then it should be possible to claim that Derrida's indecisiveness in regard to certain scientific concepts is just that—indecisiveness occasioned by his procrustean effort to squeeze modern science into the deconstructive worldview. Or, to put the matter bluntly, if Searle can be wrong— "The answer is simple enough: this definition of the deconstructionist is *false* (that's right: false, not true)" (146)—then so can Derrida.

My feeling is that the position defended in *Of Grammatology* is the essentially deconstructive one whose contradictions are brought to the surface in "Racism's Last Word" under the pressure of an imperative to make a choice and defend a political posture. If deconstruction does, indeed, seek to undermine such concepts as soul, life, value, choice, and memory, then a number of Derrida's appeals—to a just silence that "keeps watch on that which is not, on that which is not yet, and on the chance of still remembering some faithful day," (1985, 299); to the need to respect and remember the referent of language: "No, what I find repulsive is the thing that history has now linked to the word, which is why I propose keeping the word so that the history will not be forgotten" (1986a, 159); to the importance of the exhibit "Art contre/against Apartheid" which is a "new satellite of humanity" (1985, 293); to the morality of an essentially humanistic revulsion with apartheid—are proof that, when it comes to commenting on a pressing political issue, deconstruction is bracketed and the traditional humanistic notions of humanity, choice, memory, and value are resurrected.

Under normal conditions, such as his famous essay, "The Ends of Man," Derrida tends to denounce humanist concepts, yet in specific contexts, which are mostly political ones, he seems to affirm their serviceability. Furthermore, science, specifically cybernetics, is sometimes depicted as a deconstructive tool and at others as a metaphysical weapon. I would like to suggest that this brace of inconsistencies is, in fact, two manifestations of the same problem: Derrida's underestimation of the degree to which modern science in fact confirms a number of Renaissance and Enlightenment ideas about the relationship between humanity and the rest of nature.

In the interests of fairness, I will consider a number of other explanations for Derrida's vacillations on the notion of humanism before commenting on the possibility that recent developments in science may be confirming, not contesting, certain traditional humanistic ideas.

One explanation is intradeconstructive, arguing that, since deconstruction has already posited its own vulnerability to metaphysical co-opting, Derrida's flirtation with humanistic ideas is merely an elegant demonstration of his repeated claim that deconstruction is not a metadiscourse impervious to the pressures of the field it criticizes. This is an unsatisfactory solution because it would admit every possible discourse into the deconstructive fold, making deconstruction meaningless in its generality.

A second explanation would be that Derrida's recourse to humanism is an error, a theoretical mistake that could have been avoided. Derrida himself would not accept such a solution. In fact, one of the more enlightening themes of deconstruction has been that error does not befall an otherwise virginal field from the outside, but must have "always already" figured as a structural feature of that field if it is ever to appear subsequently. If Derrida has made a mistake, it is because this kind of mistake has always haunted deconstruction. In other words, deconstruction has always been a humanism. I think that there is some value in this argument, but, like the first one, it is too general to be interesting. If deconstruction has always contained its other, humanism, as its implicit possibility, then all that is being claimed is what Derrida has said all along, namely that metaphysics is not the opposite of deconstruction, but is intimately related to it as its supplement. As with the first argument, the explanation by inclusion risks confirming the basic premises of deconstruction.

A third solution would argue that Derrida has never denounced humanistic concepts as such but has accepted their efficacy within determined contexts. This solution is unconvincing because it simply moves the ethical responsibility for choosing one's concepts back one step. If deconstruction is the study of the complex mechanisms whereby concepts are contextually stabilized: "I say 'undecidability' rather than 'indeterminacy' because I am interested more in relations of force, in differences of force, in everything that allows, precisely, determinations in given situations to be stabilized through a decision of writing . . . There would be no indecision or *double bind* were it not between *determined* (semantic, ethical, political) poles, which are upon occasion terribly necessary and always irreplaceably singular" (1988b, 148), then a deconstructive analysis of a concrete political situation must account for its choice of determined contexts. In other words, if deconstruction is itself nothing: "Deconstruction, in the singular, is not 'inherently' anything at all that might be determinable on the basis of this code and of this criteria. It is 'inherently' nothing at all" (1988b, 141), then on those occasions when it moves beyond the neutral description of "relations of force" and adopts a specific position, how can it account for the particular set of historical, philosophical, or semantic determinations which its rhetoric presupposes? Since we live in a world in which political choice is not determined by a single code, then Derrida's selection of determined concepts must be accounted for by his prior selection of enabling contexts. Why, on some occasions, does he try to deconstruct referentiality and, on others, affirm its necessity? Who is choosing contexts? There are contexts in which appeals to racism are deemed ethical. Why did Derrida not inhabit one of these? Ultimately, a choice has to be made based on something more solid than whimsy or expediency, otherwise infinite regress begins to resemble infinite bad faith.

The fourth solution, the one which I endorse, is basically an extension of the third. Peter J. Wilson (1983) reports on studies that show that chimpanzees can learn symbolic language in a laboratory situation because, in that radically altered environment, there is an advantage to using their latent linguistic abilities. In other words, since in a laboratory the environment is, in large measure, human language, success in that milieu requires that a chimp tap whatever inchoate language capability it might have. I think that an analogous claim can be made for Derrida's apartheid essays. As long as Derrida is able to negotiate the environment generated by his own textual theories, he can continue deconstructing such concepts as *anthropos*, freedom, choice, value, and reference with impunity. However, when placed in a different environment, the environment of pressing political issues where deconstructing binary oppositions risks accommodating those for whom division and supplementarity offer welcome relief from such metaphysical totalizations as the claim that *all* human beings ought to be treated with dignity and respect, Derrida chooses to reject deconstructive hyperlucidity for a kind of plain talk. In this new environment, deconstructing metaphysical structures is clearly inadequate—here, it appears, one must surrender to certain metaphysical concepts, especially those clustered around the idea of humanism.

As long as what is meant by *environment* remains undefined, there is nothing in this analysis with which Derrida would disagree.

However, I think that, in order to prevent the kind of buck-passing that renders deconstruction ethically suspect (if only for its neutrality), it is crucial to follow the lead of anthropologists such as Wilson, and a host of others, and attempt to specify an environment that is not simply that of a determined sociopolitical regime, or even of a minority context within such a regime.

The larger environment to which human beings belong is their evolutionary heritage. Within this context, I believe that it is possible to affirm a version of humanism, not one that simply substitutes man for god, making man, the generic as well as the gender, the measure of all things, but one that situates human beings within a vast evolutionary hierarchy. Such a product must step outside of the deconstructive worldview and appeal to a number of the more radical theories in contemporary science. I believe that Derrida's attempt to create common cause among deconstruction and such fields as genetics and cybernetics simply ignores the astounding, and astoundingly classical, implications of much postpositivistic science. When he claims that contemporary science has dispensed with such notions as soul, life, value, choice, and memory and works exclusively in the deconstructed medium of writing, Derrida is, in fact, either ignoring or distorting a host of recent developments in neurobiology, artificial intelligence, genetics, chaos studies, and cosmology.

Perhaps the most remarkable discovery of certain strains of twentieth-century science, one that should rattle the bones of the champions of deconstructive destabilization, is that order, identity, truth, humanity, ethics, and aesthetics are legitimate concepts whose reality is an emergent feature of cosmic evolution. Furthermore, it is becoming increasingly feasible to account for the specificity of literature, and of art in general, in a way that does not merely emphasize their ability to serve as cultural fractures, but rather as vital technologies in our biocultural evolution. In other words, we may be in position to conceptualize literature as something other than a superstructural manifestation of some infrastructure, be it libido, modes of production, or arche-writing. Paradoxically, it is science that may be setting the stage for this new understanding of literature. If literature is an agent of loss, absence, and death, as it certainly is, then it is also the site for the production of truth and beauty. And if such concepts strike the contemporary ear as hopelessly naive, it is because the remarkable complexity of the interpenetration between nature and culture that generates them has been obscured by the reigning consensus that science is still essentially nineteenth-century positivism.

Inasmuch as Derrida gets his science wrong, which I believe he does, he is unable to stabilize his view of meaning on anything more solid than the fault lines of *différance*. And yet, he knows there are contexts in which even truth, identity, and possibly even beauty must be affirmed. Whereas Derrida leaves the determination of these contexts up to vague generalities such as "relations of force," thereby making moral agency highly problematic, I propose to argue that the interpretative community which selects for such humanistic concepts is, indeed, history—not the minuscule slice of it, say the last four or five thousand years that typically constitutes the normal meaning of the term—but the ten- or twenty-billion-year history of our evolution into human beings from out of the inconceivably simple constituents of the early universe. The humanism that Derrida must simultaneously disown and invoke need no longer be viewed as a chimera of Enlightenment optimism, or of bourgeois hypocrisy, but as a concept defensible within, although not restricted to, the field of science. The world of modern science, either systematically ignored by contemporary cultural theorists or misinterpreted by facile philosophical translations of quantum mechanics and relativity, is only now, with recent developments in cosmology, sociobiology, and dissipative systems and chaos theory, able to account for an evolutionary community that makes Derrida's choice of emphasis in his essays on apartheid defensible in a nonrelativistic way.

2

An Evolutionary Ontology and Epistemology

Whereas most contemporary schools of critical theory, including deconstruction, are fundamentally dualistic in maintaining that the world of human beings is determined primarily, or exclusively, by culture, an evolutionary framework situates human culture within a natural hierarchy. Part 2 explores the implications of an evolutionary paradigm for such basic ontological and epistemological problems as the nature of knowledge, truth, time, and identity. In addition, the relationship of literature to the natural and cultural worlds is addressed from an evolutionary perspective.

Chapter 7

Stepping Outside the Deconstructive Language Game

Although it claims to be unsystematic and resistant to formalization, it is clear that, like any other philosophical style, deconstruction consists of a number of recognizably consistent strategies, gestures, approaches, and narratives. In other words, deconstruction slices up the world in a recognizable way—no first-year literature graduate student would confuse an essay by Derrida with one by, say, Frank Lentricchia. Another way of thinking about this is to employ Wittgenstein's notion of a language game. A game in general, and a language game in particular, must include two fundamental components: a set of pieces and a series of permissible moves. Of course, a game may include rules for the creation of new rules or new pieces, but it must also always exclude some kinds of pieces and some kinds of rules, lest it be so general and universal as to be meaningless. Deconstruction, therefore, can be viewed as a language game. Its tokens are the terms and concepts it disposes of, and its moves the arguments, claims, and style it generates.

In order to propose an alternative to deconstruction, one that can be viewed as more valuable than deconstruction, it will be necessary to change the rules of the deconstructive game somewhat. However, since progress implies the possibility of comparing a present state with a previous one, rules cannot be changed so precipitously as to render comparison impossible. Neither can we make merely cosmetic changes in the rules of the deconstructive game, for then we would, in fact, be engaging in an essentially Derridian drama. What is needed is a series of rule changes that create enough difference so that progress (or regress) is measurable but not so much that it is unlocatable.

The rule change I propose is that we be allowed to ask the questions "Why?" and "How?" regarding Derrida's fundamental presuppositions about the nature of the world. Derrida, in agreement with Heidegger, sees such questions, inasmuch as they are part of a series of concepts including causation, origin, priority, explanability, and reason, to be essentially metaphysical. Consequently, Derrida never asks "Why?" except in the limited deconstructive sense, the sense that assumes that, in fact, such questions can have no answers that lie outside of the system they are interrogating, or "How?" except in order to determine historical and institutional contexts for the emergence of metaphysical concepts.

Let us assume that the world is as Derrida describes it, namely a fabric of mobile and infinitely divisible traces constantly congealing into more or less determinate structures. The rule change I propose is to be able to ask the following questions: (1) Why is the world as it appears to be? (2) How did it get to be that way?

There are a number of different ways to approach questions of this kind. Let me sketch a few of the most interesting.

The creationist answer. The world is the way it is because it corresponds to some divine plan that accounts for both the "why" and the "how." If the universe is deconstructible, that is, if totalizing views of it are doomed because of their inadequacy to what is out there (the deconstructive version of mimesis), it is because the creator willed it to be so.

The illegitimacy approach. This is Derrida's style. Questions concerning the origins and the natural history of the world are axiomatically defined as metaphysical, so they are never asked. Derrida does make frequent claims about the nature of language, consciousness, time, etc., but he never accounts for these in any way that would adequately satisfy one who is not playing according to the rules of deconstruction. For example, does arche-writing apply only to human consciousness? If not, how far down the evolutionary ladder can we go and continue to use concepts such as dissemination? Is a paramecium's world a tissue of traces? A virus's? A rock's? A molecule's? A proton's? A quark's? In other words, is the ontology of deconstruction essentially a human epistemology, an anthropocentric phenomenology, or does it have roots in the prehuman universe? The illegitimacy approach eschews such questions by assuming their ontotheological nature and thereby resolving that the only appropriate and interesting posture toward them is to deconstruct them.

The phenomenological approach. This is a version of the illegitimacy approach. Despite his frequent critiques of Husserl and Heidegger, Derrida has never stopped being a phenomenologist. Basically, phenomenology is a philosophical attitude that presupposes (at some level) the centrality of Husserl's *epoché:* the provisional bracketing of ontological speculation. Ultimately, phenomenologists are primarily concerned with the world as it appears to human intentionality. Although Husserl himself recanted this position somewhat toward the end of his career, and despite Heidegger's claims to have developed a phenomenological ontology, the idea that philosophy should concern itself with the way the world presents itself to an intentional consciousness is common ground for such otherwise disparate philosophers as Husserl, Heidegger, Merleau-Ponty, Bachelard, Foucault, Barthes, Derrida, and Rorty. I think this attitude goes back, ultimately, to the Cartesian division between an unextended thinking substance and extended matter (it is no accident that one of Husserl's most powerful books is entitled *Cartesian Meditations*). Basically, phenomenologists believe that human consciousness, with its residence in language, memory, imagination, and intersubjective culture, forms such a thick filtration medium between the world and its perception that, for all intents and purposes, Being is only knowable as it presents itself to consciousness. Such a position can result in a kind of Berkelian idealism or in the constructivist conviction that nature is a social construct; for our purposes, the specific form that a phenomenological attitude takes is not as important as the basic decision to restrict epistemology to intentional analyses.

Given such a definition, Derrida is certainly a phenomenologist. The difference between the phenomenological position outlined here and the illegitimacy approach is that, for such phenomenologists as Husserl and Heidegger, the reduction of the natural attitude does not entail the necessary consequence that thereby all relation to truth has been equally suspended, whereby for Derrida the absence of an *hors-texte* implies that truth must heretofore be conceived of *sous-rature*. Furthermore, the concepts of *hylé* for Husserl and Being for Heidegger, while not strictly "natural," are nevertheless extracultural, while for Derrida any recourse to such concepts as nature or the extracultural is immediately suspected as a gesture of domination and exclusion.

Interestingly, a modern Cartesian and strange bedfellow of the phenomenologists is Noam Chomsky. On the surface, there appears to be no point of convergence between Derrida and Chomsky. Whereas Derrida has no pretensions to scientific rigor, Chomsky's work is classically empirical. Furthermore, unlike Derrida, for whom any notion of universality is de jure suspect, Chomsky's goal has always been to uncover the elements and rules of a universal grammar. However, despite such clear differences, Chomsky and Derrida share the phenomenological conviction that human language and culture are sui generis and not adequately explained by an evolutionary perspective. To my knowledge, Derrida never makes this claim explicitly, but it is clear he believes something like it from the total absence of any sustained treatment of biological evolution in his work. Chomsky, as is typical of a U.S. empirical scientist, addresses the subject directly.

> But human language, it appears, is based on entirely different principles [than animal communication]. This, I think, is an important point, often overlooked by those who approach human language as a natural, biological phenomenon: in particular, it seems rather pointless, for these reasons, to speculate about the evolution of human language from simpler systems—perhaps as absurd as it would be to speculate about the "evolution" of atoms from clouds of elementary particles.
>
> As far as we know, possession of human language is associated with a specific type of mental organization, not simply a higher degree of intelligence. There seems to be no substance to the view that human language is simply a more complex instance of something to be found elsewhere in the animal world. (1972, 70)

Let me repeat, between Chomsky and Derrida there are unbreachable gulfs. For one thing, Chomsky certainly believes that there is a neurophysiological structure underlying our linguistic ability. Derrida probably does too, however he would undoubtedly want to claim that its significance is in no way knowable in itself, but exists exclusively as a historically and culturally constructed phenomenon. However, there are traces of Derrida's "Il n'y a pas de hors texte" in the preceding quote, specifically in its anthropocentrism, just as there is a Cartesian flavor to Derrida's repeated uneasiness with empiricism or its phenomenological counterpart, the natural attitude.

In *Positions*, Derrida parries repeated efforts by Houdebine and Scarpetta to make him accept the absolute alterity of matter by explicating his frequently repeated position on empiricism.

> If I have not very often used the word *matter*, it is not, as you know, because of some idealist or spiritualist kind of reservation. It is that in the logic of the phase of overturning this concept has been too often reinvested with "logocentric" values, values associated with those of thing, reality, presence in general, sensible presence, for example, substantial plenitude, content, referent, etc. Realism or sensualism—"empiricism"—are modifications of logocentrism. (1981b, 64–65)

Derrida goes on to explain that his concept of writing or of text is neither sensible nor visible, but the point is plain to see. Nature, for Derrida, is part of a series of concepts forming the infrastructure of metaphysics or logocentrism. This position is not that different from Husserl's *epoché* or Heidegger's idea that the Being of beings is not a material substratum but the poetic challenge of Appropriation (*Ereignis*).

The evolutionary attitude. Neurophysiologist Pierre Changeux argues that "A given behavioral act may indeed engage, *simultaneously* and *necessarily*, groups of neurons which appeared at different periods in the evolution of vertebrates" (Lieberman, 1984, 21). Philip Lieberman uses this quote to riposte Chomsky's position that natural language constitutes an abrupt evolutionary adaptation that is unique to Homo sapiens. Lieberman hypothesizes that human language evolved from neural and motor structures that we share with lower animals.

> In my view, the abstract, logical aspects of human language that are formalized by linguists in the rules of a grammar and the metatheory of "universal" grammar share a common neural base with the cognitive behavior of other animals. In this model the language and cognition of human beings may be more com-

plex than that of other animals, but it is based on similar neural mechanisms and has similar formal properties. (1984, 35)

Lieberman's position, although certainly at variance with Chomsky's, is diametrically opposed to the fundamental axioms of deconstruction. A certain evolutionary model places human language and culture at the top of a hierarchy of selective adaptations, but it does not suggest that the world that humans experience is a cultural prison-house.[1] On the contrary, this view maintains that everything that we do as a species, from our rituals to our sciences and arts, is part of a continuum with profound connections to the world out of which we evolved. In short, whereas for Derrida interdisciplinarity would mean the demonstration that all the disciplines are actually the products of arche-writing, an evolutionary approach makes room for a meaningful, unnarcissistic dialogue among the arts, the humanities, the social sciences, and the natural sciences.

Let us now return to the questions "Why?" and "How?" To repeat, I am asking of Derrida's implicit worldview two allied ontological questions: "Why the deconstructionist's world and not another?," and "How did this world come about?" I am assuming that deconstruction is not an idealism, and that it consequently intends its claims to be references to the universe in which we live. If the universe has, in fact, evolved by establishing, at the human level, a sort of Manichean struggle between metaphysical reification and deconstructive sensitivity to the underlayer of *différance*, an evolutionary model would need to account for mechanisms whereby this state of affairs was selected or be condemned to posit it as an inexplicable given. It would not take it for granted that this is the necessary deep nature of reality, but would ask two sorts of questions. First, given all the available evidence—empirical, analytical, aesthetic, historical, etc.—is the deconstructive view a good fit to reality? Second, how could one account for the survival of such a universe if, as evolution assumes, nothing is etched in granite. Would we, for example, need to resort to a kind of Laplacian determinism, arguing that, given a set of initial conditions, it is inevitable for the deconstructive universe to have evolved. This view, an interesting twist on the anthropic principle, could be called the "textual principle." Has the universe always been a frail edifice built on the ghostly traces of *différance*? If so, evolution is merely an embellishment, a vain and futile flourish to mask an eternal underlying bed of textuality. This view, in its similarity to the views of David Bohm, might be called the "seamed web" principle. Is Derridian ontology an inexplicably contingent development? Or is it the price paid for other sorts of evolutionary successes? There are undoubtedly other kinds of evolutionary accounts of deconstruction. However, all I wish to emphasize at this point is that, in a theoretical perspective which accepts evolution as the best available model for the universe, any cosmology, even a negative one like deconstruction, must be accounted for in some way, either as a development with positive survival value, an inevitable product of some unspecified initial conditions, as a component of some larger structure, or as a contingent state of affairs with no survival value that has somehow managed to survive as the deep structure of the universe.

I think that it would be impossible for Derrida to play the evolutionary game because most of its rules clash with the rules for deconstruction. At the heart of the matter is the irreconcilable difference between evolution and deconstruction on the issue of representation. While deconstruction sees any gesture of empirical science as essentially limited by its adherence to metaphysical limits: "but it [*Of Grammatology*] is also a question about the limits of this science [the science of writing]. And those limitations, on which I have insisted no less, are also those of the classical notion of science, whose projects, concepts, and norms are fundamentally and systematically tied to metaphysics" (Derrida 1981b, 13), the evolutionary game presupposes a basically realist view of the physical, chemical, and biological worlds. If, for deconstruction, classical science is systematically tied to metaphysics, then so is evolution. Consequently, deconstruction cannot ask "Why?" or "How?" in an evolutionary sense. It can only ask why of this why, and how of this how, and once one gets the knack of such deconstructive recursion, it can get a bit tedious.

Like all relativisms, deconstruction must see the notion of progress limited to some historical, philosophical, scientific, or institutional paradigm. Perhaps the best illustration of this point of view is Foucault's vision of history as a discontinuous succession of regimes of truth/power.

"Truth" is to be understood as a system of ordered procedures for the production, regulation, distribution, circulation, and operation of statements.

"Truth" is linked in a circular relation with systems of power which produce and sustain it, and to effects of power which it induces and which extends it. A "regime" of truth. (Rabinow 1984, 74)

Or, to put it more succinctly, "Nothing is fundamental" (247). Paisley Livingston (1988) calls this kind of paradigm relativism "framework relativism" and casts some of the blame for its legitimation on such influential philosophers of science as Kuhn and Feyerabend. According to Livingston, framework relativism "contends that there exist radically divergent frameworks, so that beliefs that are true in one are false in another" (1988, 23). Despite their celebrated and frequently acerbic public debate, Foucault and Derrida are both prisoners of the paradigm paradigm. Their difference is that whereas for Foucault a rigorous historical inquiry can describe various constellations of power/truth, Derrida, for example in "Signature Event Context," contends that, insofar as it is never in principle possible to saturate or isolate a context, paradigms are essentially impossible to delimit. For both, however, Truth must be vitiated (Foucault puts it between quotation marks, Derrida *sous-rature*) by the belief that it is purely contingent and contextual. Consequently, it is difficult to see how Derrida (or Foucault) could make room in their thought for either a notion of progress or a philosophical worldview that takes the theory of evolution as its central tenet.

I have often imagined a naive or skeptical neophyte in the rules of academic inquiry asking a deconstructionist why he or she should believe that deconstruction is more valuable than any other methodology, even one which, like Christian exegesis, is, by all accounts, alien to the deconstructive horizon. What evidence would the deconstructionist offer, since deconstruction is, among other things, the deconstruction of the notion of evidence? In short, deconstruction cannot, as I see it, account for its own value. Of course, some philosophers, such as Rorty, affirm the inability to account for one's beliefs as a sort of liberation from metaphysics, but I have known too many used car salesmen who were also liberated from metaphysical requirements for evidence to have much faith in such affirmations.

As opposed to deconstruction, in my version of the evolutionary game not only are progress and reference good moves, but it is also permissible to argue for the greater truthfulness and value of the game itself. Whereas deconstruction must constantly deconstruct it-self, the evolutionary game can claim that it is more valuable than other games, that it is the game of games. Evolution, therefore, can risk totalization.

There is an economy here that I would like to emphasize. Totali-zation is considered a baneful term in almost all contemporary critical discourses. Part of the reason for this is its etymological relation to the political notion of totalitarianism. In fact, I suspect that the cli-mate that has proven so favorable for deconstruction and its penum-bra of relativisms stems from the understandable horror that the various totalizing fascisms of World War II have produced in the intellectual world. Sadly, the facile identification of totalization and totalitarianism has suggested that the only way to keep totalitarian-ism at bay is to eschew all totalizing and to assume that freedom can only be safeguarded by appeals to fragmentation and relativism. In effect, much contemporary criticism is arguing that relativism is a liberation philosophy, and, despite Derrida's uneasiness with the identification of deconstruction with a kind of "ideology of liberation, the liberation of desires, the liberation of man, the philosophy of freedom" (Derrida 1986c, 34), there is nonetheless a clear line of thought in Derrida's recent work that equates deconstruction with resistance to totalitarianism. "To put it in a word, deconstructions [Derrida now frequently uses the plural, to underline his refusal to allow deconstruction to become a master concept] have always repre-sented, as I see it, the at least necessary condition for identifying and combating the totalitarian risk in all the forms already mentioned" (1988a, 647).

The price deconstruction must pay for its refusal of totalization is paralysis. What I have been calling a model is of necessity a totali-zation. However, contrary to much opinion, not all totalizations are the same. Some totalizations are indeed monstrous. There is no need to offer a catalog here of even the most recent examples of horrific totalizations. Yet, it must not be forgotten, there have been scores of beneficent totalizations. For example, where would the feminist movement be today if feminists had considered it fascistic to claim that all women are people deserving equal protection under the law and equal access to employment and education? Could an effective campaign against racism be mounted without some appeal to the principle of universal human rights? And is not the Constitution of the United States an example of a magnificent, flexible, and self-modifying totalization?

It is not at all a given that all totalizations are equivalent to totalitarianism and that, as a consequence, it is politically suspect to espouse them. Totalization of some kind is a requisite of progress, so any philosophy that eschews it can only analyze interminably, it can never suggest alternate scenarios.

I think that all paradigms are economic systems whose value is always a balance sheet of profit and cost. Deconstruction pays for exemption from empirical verification by its inability to imagine a future that is superior to the present. The evolutionary paradigm must also pay a price. It pays for the power and effectiveness of totalizing theories with the possibility of error. To make this point, I need to introduce a concept that is central to Karl Popper's thought: falsifiability. A claim is falsifiable when some kind of evidence is, in principle if not in fact, adduceable to prove it erroneous. Although on many accounts deconstruction is probably false, it is not falsifiable. That is, there is no way that any of its assertions can be refuted from within its own axiomatic premises. Its radical brand of skepticism, often turned willingly against itself, generates no claim about the world or itself that might be disproved. Floyd Merrell (1985) discusses the dogmatic nature of deconstruction in relation to what he labels the *deconstructive principle,* the absolute faith of deconstruction that all texts are deconstructible.

> There is obviously no procedure for ascertaining whether a given text is non-deconstructible; that is, whether it is through and through decidable, for all texts are, according to the *deconstructive principle* absolutely undecidable, and therefore no text is non-deconstructible. The decision has obviously been made a priori, and from outside the domain of writing. Hence there is, and there can be, no real decision procedure, only *dogma.* (75)

In other words, Derrida cannot, in principle, respond to the skeptical reader introduced above who asks why he or she should believe the deconstructive worldview rather than a Christian one. Just as deconstruction must have faith that all theological texts can be deconstructed, a Christian perspective requires faith that all deconstructions are but tokens of human folly. And, as religious wars have always shown, competing faiths, even ones that share many presuppositions, do not tend to promote reasonable discussion and self-correction.

The evolutionary frame can make claims about greater or lesser truth, value, and beauty precisely because its claims are always falsifiable. It is important to read the preceding sentence in an affirmative rather than a skeptical way. The typical deconstructive interpretation of any such admission, namely that the possibility of truthful and valuable statements and events depends on the coequal possibility that these statements and events be not true or valuable, is that, inasmuch as the condition of truth is untruth, the concept of truth must be conceptualized as a metaphysical *effect* of an underlying level of undecidability. This argument is erroneous. Its error lies in a common confusion, that between falsifiability and falsity. An example might make this error clearer. Suppose Wallinsky claims that all grupes are blue. To say that this statement is falsifiable is simply to be able to imagine conditions that would render it false. For example, Wallinsky would have made a false claim if someone were to produce a red grupe. The falsifiability of Wallinsky's claim lies in the conceptual, not the actual, possibility of a nonblue grupe. Consequently, and this is the crucial point, that Wallinsky's belief is falsifiable in no way implies that it is necessarily tainted with falsehood. It may, in fact, be true that all grupes are blue. If that is the case, then Wallinsky has made an absolutely true, though falsifiable, claim. Of course, since Wallinsky is a finite being, she will never know if, in some far corner of this universe or under her feet in another universe, there doesn't lurk a red grupe, or that the rules governing the synthesis of grupes might not change in the future, allowing for the possibility of a red grupe, so she is content to call her claim true in an essentially provisional and open-ended way. My point is that a falsifiable claim is true until disproved, and even though for all we know it may be absolutely true, its value is by no way determined by such transcendental considerations. Deconstruction wrongly conflates falsifiability with an inherent and atemporal internal falsity; to describe the position in its most abstract form, deconstruction equates the possibility of error with the necessity that truthful statements be impossible in principle. The evolutionary paradigm, on the contrary, rejects dogmatism, and accepts the possibility that all its claims may be false as the price it must pay to be able to affirm, for example, that Barbara

Johnson is simply wrong when she claims that the Copernican idea that the earth goes around the sun is not an improvement over the idea that the sun goes round the earth, and that, on the contrary, the Copernican cosmology is indeed more accurate, faithful to nature, and *valuable* than the Ptolemaic scheme.

Chapter 8

An Evolutionary Ontology

The Big Bang

What I have been calling the evolutionary paradigm is informed by the theory that our universe is an evolving system. This theory, which has been adumbrated in preceding chapters, will be presented systematically here.

Whatever his topic, whatever the regional goal of a particular textual exercise, Derrida is always attempting to question what he believes to be an essential occidental presupposition, the determination of Being as presence. If deconstruction is anything, it is the demonstration that presence and the present are not primordial attributes of Being. Like Derrida, I also find the concept of presence to be inadequate to an accurate description of the natural and cultural worlds. The concept of presence implies, among other things, a static and deterministic view of Being. Basically, presence is a Platonic concept inasmuch as it privileges Being over becoming and timelessness over time. However, unlike Derrida, I do not intend to deconstruct presence, but to situate it, and the cluster of concepts that it controls, within an evolutionary cosmology. If we are careful about defining the field of their applicability, there is as little wrong with using the concepts of presence and the present as there is in defining planetary motion according to Newton's equations. Presence and Newtonian mechanics are special limiting cases of larger, more inclusive theories; however, they are not, for that, simply flawed.

Although there are many dynamic worldviews, the one that I feel has the greatest explanatory power and the most empirical verification is the theory of cosmic evolution. Evolution is commonly equated with Darwinian or biological evolution. A fundamental presupposition of this book is that biological evolution is simply a refinement of a much larger system, a universe that has developed from utter simplicity to at least the complexity of the human mind. Following the lead of such scientists as Stephen W. Hawking (1988) and Ilya Prigogine (1984), and especially of the philosopher of science J.T. Fraser (1978), I will use the term *evolution*, when associated with such terms as *cosmos* or *universe*, to refer to the increasing complexification of the entire universe.

The best available model for the universe is that it began in some sort of primordial explosion, popularly known as the big bang, ten to twenty billion years ago, that it has evolved to its present state, and that it is undoubtedly still evolving. In a recent essay, Jean Audouze (1987), head of research at C.N.R.S., describes the history of the universe as falling into six basic periods that I will briefly summarize.

The first phase, lasting approximately one second, includes the big bang, a cosmological model suggested by a series of discoveries in the early part of the twentieth century. In the 1920s, U.S. astronomer Edwin Hubble discovered that the spectra of other galaxies (whose existence he had discovered in 1924) are shifted toward the red, indicating that they are receding. Furthermore, the velocity of a galaxy's retreat is proportional to its distance from us, implying that the universe is not static, as had been thought previously, but a dynamical, expanding system. In 1965, Arno Penzias and Robert Wilson, working at the Bell Telephone Laboratory in New Jersey, detected a microwave background radiation with a temperature of approximately 3°K which, since it was later discovered to have the same values in all directions, is assumed to be the distant trace of some primordial fireball. These and other discoveries led to theory that the universe began in a pinpoint approximately twenty billion years ago, whereupon it commenced to cool and expand.

Because of limitations imposed by Heisenberg's uncertainty principle, it is meaningless to consider time intervals of less than 10^{-43} seconds. Between 10^{-43} seconds and 10^{-35} seconds after the big bang the symmetry among the four fundamental forces (the strong nuclear force—an extremely powerful but short-range force that keeps atomic nuclei together, the weak nuclear force—a short-range force involved in beta decay as well as the decay of other nuclei and particles, gravity—the force [or, in general relativity, the warping of space-time] that binds massive bodies, and electromagnetism—the force governing attraction and repulsion among charged particles) was broken first with the separation of gravity and then when the strong nuclear force branched off. At 10^{-10} seconds after the big bang, the weak nuclear force split from electromagnetism, and the universe had the four forces that characterize it today. The universe's first second saw the appearance of quarks (the fundamental components of hadrons, which are particles responding to the strong nuclear force) and leptons (particles affected by the electromagnetic and weak forces, but not by the strong force) and the subsequent "confinement" of quarks into pi mesons (the lightest meson, a combination of a quark and an antiquark), protons (a positively charged particle composed of three quarks), and neutrons (a neutral particle, consisting of three quarks). By the end of the first second, according to the work of Andrei Sakharov, quarks and antiquarks had practically annihilated each other, except for one quark for every billion antiquarks. The result was a tremendous amount of radiation (there are 10^9 photons for every baryon in the universe today) and a slight imbalance of matter over antimatter that constitutes the material of the universe.

The next phase described by Audouze extends to three minutes after the big bang. During these first three minutes, continued cooling and expansion allowed for the formation of lighter elements such as deuterium, helium 3, helium 4, and lithium 7.

During the third phase, lasting one million years, hydrogen was formed, the universe became transparent to radiation, an event that allowed for the photons generated by the synthesis of hydrogen to radiate outward constituting the 3°K background radiation, and density fluctuations, which would be the seeds of galaxies, appeared.

Audouze's fourth phase encompasses the time from one million years to one billion years after the big bang. The central event of the fourth phase is the creation of the universe's large-scale structures, its galaxies and clusters of galaxies, from the density fluctuations of phase three.

The present, Audouze's fifth phase, is characterized by the life cycles of stars, at least one of which, our sun, born some 4.555 billion years ago, has enabled the creation and evolution of life on earth.

Finally, Audouze speculates that, if the universe contains enough matter, it will cease expanding and contract into another big crunch in about fifty billion years. If, however, the density of the universe is less than a critical number, it will continue expand and cool, perhaps reducing itself to a series of black holes that will gradually disappear.

Of course, much has been left out of this thumbnail sketch of the evolution of the universe. Such exciting recent theories as inflation, supersymmetry, superstrings, and Stephen Hawking's (1988) speculations (that a theory of quantum gravity should generate a model of the universe as finite yet unbounded space-time that does not require a singularity at its beginning because it does not begin in the sense assumed by the standard big bang model) have been omitted because, although they are of vital importance to cosmological speculation, their resolution would in no way alter the basic thrust of the arguments presented in this book. The point I wish to emphasize is that all contemporary cosmologies that take into account the mathematical and empirical evidence currently available to the natuzral sciences agree that the universe is a dynamical, evolving system. Furthermore, certain preliminary observations can be made concerning this system that will prove valuable in our attempt to present an alternative to deconstruction.

First, at its beginning, the universe was unimaginably simple. Before the four fundamental forces began dividing, 10^{-43} seconds after the big bang and at the searing temperature of 10^{32}°K, the universe was perfectly simple, consisting of a single "superforce." Cooling and expansion caused the universe to break its primordial symmetry, generating a branching and looping structure of increasing complexity.

Second, our universe is lawful. Although there is much controversy concerning the inevitability of the laws of physics, it is indisputable that the universe displays enough regularities for scientists to ask questions of it and expect meaningful answers. As will be explained in a subsequent section, the concept of lawfulness is not simply synonymous with the notion of determinism, but covers a much broader field, including systems that are, for all intents and purposes, chaotic. However, be that as it may, it can be safely argued that it is the lawfulness of nature that allows for its explanation in scientific terms.

Third, the laws of nature are not atemporal. For example, when, near the very beginning, the universe consisted of X and Y bosons, laws governing the confinement of quarks into baryons (nuclear particles composed of three quarks) had simply not evolved. Conversely, the laws appropriate to the description and study of living systems are in no way predictable or explainable from the laws of quantum mechanics. A reductionist view of the universe, which presupposes that an understanding of the universe's simplest components is synonymous with an understanding of the universe, is therefore untenable.

Fourth, some form of the anthropic principle is doubtless correct. That is, the universe in which we live is the kind of universe whose laws allow, at least in certain of its neighborhoods, for the emergence of creatures like us.

And fifth, if the universe evolved to the point that one of its products feels compelled to ask questions about the regularities that enabled its own creation, then human beings are part of the universe's self-referential feedback system. The universe can be seen as a reflexive loop that has the remarkable property of generating novelty by regression, recapitulation, and recursion. If that is the case, the phenomenological duality described earlier, in which a kind of bracketing forecloses investigation of the prehuman cosmos on its own terms, choosing instead to focus on the world as it appears to a human consciousness, is a dangerous abdication of our chief responsibility to the universe, to be an instrument of its introspection and evolution.

Emergent Evolution

I wish to continue this discussion by focusing on two important features of cosmic evolution: hierarchy and novelty.[1] Although hierarchy and novelty are usually, if often implicitly, classed as antonyms in current critical discourse—hierarchy implying a kind of rigidity inimical to creativity—attention to the logic of evolution suggests that the opposite is the case: invention actually is enabled by certain kinds of hierarchies.

In *The Postmodern Condition*, Lyotard claims that, in our postmodern era, the nineteenth-century, Hegelian, speculative hierarchy of knowledge has been invalidated, leaving a flat network of disciplines.

The "crisis" of scientific knowledge, signs of which have been accumulating since the end of the nineteenth century, is not born of a chance proliferation of sciences, itself an effect of progress in technology and the expansion of capitalism. It represents, rather, an internal erosion of the legitimacy principle of knowledge. There is erosion at work inside the speculative game, and by loosening the weave of the encyclopedic net in which each science was to find its place, it eventually sets them free.

The classical dividing lines between the various fields of science are thus called into question—disciplines disappear, overlappings occur at the borders between sciences, and from these new territories are born. The speculative hierarchy of learning gives way to an immanent and, as it were, "flat" network of areas of inquiry, the respective frontiers of which are in constant flux. (1984, 39)

There is much in Lyotard's account of the present state of science and knowledge that rings true. The kinds of erosion, slippage, and interpenetration of fields of knowledge he describes are, indeed, occurring at an increasing pace. I do take issue with Lyotard, however, on his central thesis. Although our era is in the midst of great flux, I do not think that we are witnessing the crushing of hierarchies into flat networks of reference, but rather the complication of older, more primitive hierarchies into even more intricate hierarchical structures. In other words, postmodern culture is using the flexibility, energy, and efficiency of hierarchies to generate novel kinds of hierarchies. If there is such a thing as postmodernism, it is not, as Lyotard, Derrida, Virilio, Baudrillard, Feyerabend et al. imagine it, the deconstruction of classical hierarchical systems into textual relays, but the generation of new hierarchies of such complexity and beauty that, when viewed from certain myopic theoretical perspectives, they can appear to lack dimension. In short, whereas postmodern and deconstructive theory agree that hierarchy is a necessarily anachronistic and ultimately arthritic concept that must be replaced by postindustrial horizontal reference, I believe that if our era is indeed in the process of reinventing itself in astoundingly imaginative, and potentially hideously monstrous, ways, it is because we are rediscovering the tremendous fecundity and power of hierarchical organization.

The universe may not be nearly as deterministic as Hegel, but Hegel's dialectical eschatology is much closer to the preferred strategies of nature than Derridian dissemination.

Needless to say, the idea that the universe or parts of it are arranged hierarchically is an old one. Already clearly present in Aristotle's thought, a hierarchical view of nature or society reappeared in the work of John of Salisbury, St. Thomas Aquinas, Nicolas of Cusa, Jean Bodin, King James I of England, and Thomas Hobbes among others. The Renaissance world view was, according to Carolyn Merchant,

> an earth-centered hierarchical cosmos extending upward from the four inanimate elements, which were mixed together to form the minerals, vegetables, and animals found in the sublunar region of change, to the unchanging ether-filled spheres of the seven planets, with their associated hierarchies of angels, above the moon. Beyond the planets was the sphere of the *primum mobile*, source of the daily rotation of the heavens, then the sphere of the fixed stars and zodiacal constellations, and finally the Empyrean heaven of God. Together they comprised a living chain of being, each member a step in a stable, ordered, spherically-enclosed world, each member sharing some particular feature with the steps below and above, yet excelling in some unique characteristic. (1980, 100)

Other hierarchical cosmologies, such as Renaissance neo-Platonism and natural magic, shared the basic Renaissance belief that the cosmos was a great chain linking all its elements in an immense organic system. I suspect that when hierarchy is deprecated in deconstructive discourse, it is something like a great chain of Being which is at issue. Although such a worldview is certainly superior to postmodern textuality, I agree with its critics that it is an inadequate model of the universe because it tends to be rigid and deterministic. Once the idea of a universal order preestablished by a supreme entity is shaken, as it was repeatedly in the scientific era, it becomes difficult to imagine the cosmos as a perfect and essentially unchanging harmony. In fact, rather than fixity, it is becoming increasingly clear that the most appropriate category with which to describe the universe of which we are a part is innovation. In the wake of a number of seminal theoretical advances, such as Darwin's theory of evolution, Hubble's discovery of a cosmic red-shift, quantum mechanics, relativity, systems and chaos theory, it is now possible to resurrect the basic architecture of Renaissance hierarchical cosmology by infusing it with creativity. The new hierarchy of Being is not a chain, but a dynamical system that cannot help, it seems, but beget novelty.[2]

Philosopher of science Karl Popper, a champion of creative evolution, divides the universe into three "worlds" (Popper and Eccles 1977, 16).

World 3 (the products of the human mind)	(6) Works of Art and of Science (including Technology)
	(5) Human Language. Theories of Self and of Death
World 2 (the world of subjective experiences)	(4) Consciousness of Self and of Death
	(3) Sentience (Animal Consciousness)
World 1 (the world of physical objects)	(2) Living Organisms
	(1) The Heavier Elements; Liquids and Crystals
	(0) Hydrogen and Helium

Although it is clearly an oversimplification of a much more complex system, Popper's arrangement of cosmic evolution into six stages and three overarching categories is extremely valuable for two reasons. First, it emphasizes a point that is widely ignored in humanistic research, namely that the best available model for the universe is an evolutionary one. Second, despite much misdirected wishful thinking, practically nothing in the universe is distributed laterally, but tends to arrange itself hierarchically. In fact, these two notions are really one—the universe *is* its hierarchical evolution.

The specific form of the evolutionary hierarchy proposed by Popper is one in which simpler, lower levels become the microstructure of higher, more complex levels. Whatever the fundamental stuff of the universe might be (quarks, X or Y bosons, superstrings, or infinite regress), it constitutes the building block, not the meaning, of everything else. In other words, as opposed to the Platonism of reductive thinking, which assumes that the fundamental stuff of our universe is somehow more "real" than its more complex products, Popper's hierarchy refuses to equate primitiveness with reality. Popper's hierarchical levels are all equally real, although not equally complex.

If we begin with less esoteric objects, such as Popper's (0)— Hydrogen and Helium—that is, protons, neutrons, and electrons, then it is clear that the reductionist's agenda is in a sense unimpeachable. As long as we respect Einstein's equations for the translation of matter into energy, then it is certainly the case that everything in the universe is made of (0). However, just as this imaginative regress to the universe's elements confirms the reductionist position, it simultaneously renders it trivial. If we agree with Popper that "in a universe in which there once existed (according to our present theories) no elements other than, say, hydrogen and helium, no theorist who knew the physical laws then operative and exemplified in this universe could have predicted all the properties of the heavier elements not yet emerged, or that they would emerge; or all the properties of even the simplest compound molecules, such as water" (1977, 16), then the value of reductionism is analogous to the value of using yesterday's racing results to bet on today's races. Popper's claims concerning compound molecules are applicable, a fortiori, to levels (2) through (6). In other words, Laplace's demon, given complete information about the state of the universe at (1), could not have predicted its future evolution. Reductionism, which proposes that subsequent evolutionary levels can be understood exhaustively by studying their antecedent levels, implies a static or deterministic universe. The theory of emergent evolution, on the contrary, hypothesizes that the universe has been, and is still, capable of genuine innovation.

However, both reductionism and emergent evolution presuppose that the overall organization of the universe is roughly hierarchical. As we shall see, not all hierarchies are identical (in fact, they are probably arranged hierarchically, or more properly, they have probably evolved into a hierarchical structure), and they are frequently capable of tangling themselves to a point of nearly impenetrable complexity. Causation, for example, can proceed laterally, top-down, bottom-up, or in what Douglas Hofstadter (1980) calls strange loops. Be that as it may, the essential point is that Derrida's belief that hierarchies are metaphysical hypostatizations of an underlying unhierarchical bed of arche-writing is simply wrong. Recently, evidence has been accumulating from a large number of disciplines, ranging from particle physics to fractal geometry, that nature prefers to organize itself in hierarchical structures. Popper's diagram is, in fact, clearly hierarchical in that the series of levels on the right (1 through 6) roughly recapitulate the temporal evolution of the universe as it is explained in most viable cosmological models.

I suppose that this idea is relatively uncontroversial, and that, except for creationists and certain mystics, most people would accept the hypothesis of an evolving universe. However, I presume that while most poststructuralist or postmodern theorists would agree that the universe has probably developed in an evolutionary manner, they would contend its structure is not hierarchical. Perhaps, as suggested above, this position stems from too simplistic a concept of hierarchy, one that equates hierarchy with rigid, linear systems. Or perhaps the Marxist liberationist tendencies in much postwar critical theory automatically assume that hierarchies are human inventions serving the interests of the powerful in their attempts to oppress the disenfranchised.[3] Whatever the case, it is indisputably true that, in almost all contemporary critical theory, the notion of hierarchy is accorded explicit or implicit negative value. One of the purposes of this book is to invert this valuation. I would like to argue that hierarchies are "natural," that is, they are to be found throughout the prehuman world, and that they are indispensable to an understanding of the place of human beings in their natural and social environments. As opposed to Derrida, who frequently invokes Nietzsche's imperative to cultivate *active forgetfulness*—"The latter [Nietzsche's *Ubermensch*]—who is not the last man—awakens and leaves, without turning back to what he leaves behind him. He burns his text and erases the traces of his steps. His laughter then will burst out, directed toward a return which no longer will have the form of the metaphysical repetition of humanism, nor doubtless, 'beyond' metaphysics, the form of a memorial or a guarding of the meaning of Being, the form of the house and of the truth of Being. He will dance, outside the house, the *active Vergesslichkeit*, the 'active forgetting' and the cruel (*grausam*) feast of which the *Genealogy of Morals* speaks" (Derrida 1982, 136)—the concept of hierarchy that is at issue here has at its core *active remembering*. The hypothesis that the universe is an immense hierarchical system implies that more primitive levels in the hierarchy are *rememberd* by the more complex overlays to which they serve as both microstructure and history. An evolutionary hierarchical system is therefore historical because it claims that lower levels are not just the components of more complicated higher levels, but their past. The universe can be seen as a vast palimpsest retaining remnants of its entire history.

The theory of hierarchical evolution implies that the universe builds upon its previous inventions, incorporating the essential features of a given level into its subsequent emergent stage. In other words, the macrostructure of a given level becomes the microstructure of the next. Thus, living organisms are composed of heavier elements that themselves are composed of simple elements. Even such nonmaterial phenomena as human consciousness, scientific theories, and works of art need to be embodied in a material substratum that is itself ultimately composed of some kind of elementary particle.

Any theory of creative evolution, such as Popper's cosmology, raises questions about the degree of freedom that emergence implies. The notion of freedom can range from the minor liberties allowed in a deterministic system (the prisoner is free to choose between death by firing squad or death by hanging) to a kind of freedom that lays waste to everything that preceded it (can God choose to be limited?). Clearly the theory of emergent evolution rejects the pseudoinnovations of essentially deterministic systems. The question still remains, however: How free is emergence? Can the laws or regularities of a lower evolutionary stage be violated by a higher one?

One clear consequence of the theory is that upper levels are constrained by lower levels. That is, whatever emergent features a complex level of organization might possess, it cannot violate the regularities of its constituent microstructures. For example, biological entities cannot transgress the laws of physics, although they can transcend them. There is also a slightly less recognized form of constraint—top-down constraint. In a complex hierarchical system, global organization constrains or channels its constituent lower levels. Paul Davies quotes theoretical biologist Robert Rosen who claims that biology, in fact, constrains physics: "far from contemporary physics swallowing biology as the reductionists believe, biology forces physics to transform itself, perhaps ultimately out of all recognition" (Davies 1988, 158).

More interesting than the issue of constraint, however, is the question concerning the degree of lawfulness of nature's various levels. For example, although it is difficult to imagine how we could get around the rules that determine the range and strength of the strong nuclear force, it is somewhat easier to imagine the manipulation of biological laws. In fact, compared to the laws of physics, biological rules appear to be rather malleable. Despite the crudeness of our current speculations concerning alternate forms of life, it is certainly *imaginable* that such technologies as genetic engineering and neural-computer interfaces could radically influence not just the application of biological regularities but their very nature. And of course, the cultural realm, Popper's world 3, is so capable of routinely modifying its own rules that many philosophers (relativists, constructivists, and deconstructionists) are tempted to believe that, in fact, it has none.[4]

While it does indeed appear that some of nature's laws are always respected and others routinely transgressed, a nonhierarchical model would find it difficult to account for lawfulness except in an ad hoc manner. In other words, a nonhierarchical or deconstructive model of nature would be reduced to a kind of taxonomy of lawfulness: an essentially empirical catalog of the varying rigidity of certain laws. For the deconstructionist living in a flat world, any attempt to systematize degrees of lawfulness would be dismissed as a totalizing gesture.

The hierarchical model proposed here removes the awkwardness of such Borgesian lists. If the universe is a palimpsest of its evolution, with each level incorporating the lawfulness of its predecessors while adding new degrees of complexity and creativity, then it follows that we may expect that the farther down the evolutionary tree one descends, the more recalcitrant are its specific laws to retroactive modification. We can hypothesize that the older a form of natural regularity is, the simpler, more determined, and less ductile it tends to be. In other words, the rigidity of a level's lawfulness is a factor of its complexity and its age. I suspect that, as one proceeds backward from the present, the resistance of natural laws to alteration increases exponentially; however, the essential point is that, as with our habits, recent acquisitions tend to be more plastic than older ones. World 3, human culture, being a remarkably callow invention by cosmic standards, yet one of enormous complexity, is therefore governed by somewhat loosely defined and constantly reinvented laws. Popper's world 2, the levels of cosmic evolution that generate subjectivity, is older and less complex than culture, so is far less manipulable—yet, we can speculate that with growing sophistication in the fields of artificial thought the very nature of consciousness and self-consciousness might be changed. Farther down the scale, in Popper's world 1, change becomes more challenging. As I suggested previously, it is conceivable that research in genetic engineering might be able to change the meaning of life, yet such fundamental change would clearly be far more difficult to effect than the equivalent at the cultural level. Finally, although we might certainly invent new chemicals and discover new elementary particles, it is not so clear how top-down intervention could alter the basic principles of the universe's oldest and, by relative standards, simplest levels, those of chemistry and physics.

There are two possible objections to this theory. The first would suggest that, since scientific paradigms appear to change as quickly as aesthetic ones, the distinction I am making is questionable. This objection relies on Kuhn's definition of scientific paradigms (1970), one that this book contests. My basic argument is that transformations in scientific perspective, as in the change from the Newtonian to the Einsteinian paradigms, or from a linear deterministic view of nature to one focusing on nonlinear, chaotic processes, do not signal actual changes in the nature of lower level regularities, merely in our knowledge of them. In other words, scientific revolutions tend to be primarily, although not, as outlined above, exclusively, epistemological, not ontological. Aesthetic revolutions, on the other hand, routinely modify the very Being of art, not merely what humans know about it. Again, I am not arguing that there is a clear binary opposition between art and the sciences. My argument is simply that as one descends the evolutionary scale, change tends to be more epistemological and less ontological, whereas if the direction is reversed, and one ascends, epistemology tends to become increasingly more difficult to distinguish from ontology. No level of evolutionary development, no matter how old, is purely exempt from fundamental change; nor, for that matter, is any evolutionary level, no matter how recent, free from fundamental constraints, especially since it will always need to respect its constituent lower level constraints. My argument is simply that as one descends the evolutionary tree, the *probability* of effecting fundamental change decreases.

The second kind of objection to this theory would adduce as counterevidence one of the consequences of quantum theory, retroactive causality. Such bizarre causality is, in fact, an empirically observable and verifiable phenomenon. This is an important point, so I would like to dwell on it for a moment. Let us compare two different kinds of reverse causality: the quantum effect and the way in which a literary event can alter its own history. Shimony reports on the work of Alley, Jakubowicz, and Wickes of the University of Maryland and, independently, the work of Hellmuth, Walther, and Zajonc of the University of Munich.

> Both groups found that a photon behaves like a particle when particlelike properties are measured and that it behaves like a wave when wavelike properties are measured. The remarkable novelty of the results is that the experiment was arranged so that the decision to measure particle-like or wave-like properties was made after each photon had interacted with the beam splitter. Consequently the photon could not have been "informed" at the crucial moment of interaction with the beam splitter whether to behave like a particle and take a definite route or to behave like a wave and propagate along two routes. (Shimony 1988, 51)

An extension of this idea is John Wheeler's hypotheses that the logic of the quantum level suggests that observer participation in the present may retroactively determine the distant past of the universe.

> The elementary quantum phenomenon in the sense of Bohr, the elementary act of observer-participancy, develops definiteness out of indeterminism, secures a communicable reply in response to a well-defined question. The rate of carrying out such yes-no determinations, and their accumulated number, are both minuscule today when compared to the rate and number to be anticipated in the billions of years yet to come. The coming explosion of life opens the door, however, to an all-encompassing role for observer-participancy: to build, in time to come, no minor part of what we call *its* past—*our* past, present, and future—but this whole vast world. (Wheeler 1988, 4)

Wheeler's basic idea is that the universe is an enormous feedback–feedforward system using quantum retroactive causation to bootstrap itself into new configurations. Although Wheeler's cosmology is by no means accepted by a majority of researchers in the field, it is certainly not inconceivable that the universe's own past may be subject to revision through present intervention.

Now, let us compare this interlevel causation with an intracultural example. Perhaps influenced by Freud's concept of *Nachträglichkeit*, many contemporary literary critics have described the tendency of literature to modify its own history. There are several simple modes of reverse causation in the literary field that I will not discuss here. Instead, I will focus on what I think is the most interesting version of such intervention: the ability of literature not simply to alter a culture's predisposition to include certain authors and texts in the canon, but actually to redefine the rules that define literariness in general. In other words, the set of laws which a culture implicitly uses to identify a certain kind of discourse as literary is itself subject to modification by a work of literature. This sort of hermeneutic strange loop, in which a member of a set can influence the definition of the very set granting it definition, is common in the literary world. Consider, for example, how modernist poetry has redefined what conditions language has to fulfill to be considered poetic. Of course, it is far from clear how much freedom literature has to reform itself. Is there, one might legitimately ask, a core of literariness, a set of natural classical literature principles, that is resistant to modification? This question, although seemingly Platonic in form, is, I believe, now approachable from the perspective of chaos theory. However, for the time being I will hold it in abeyance, and emphasize simply that it is indisputable that, at the very least, literature is capable of modifying some of its constitutive rules.

The two types of retroactive influence outlined above, one of the quantum level by human observers, the other of cultural definitions of literariness by the intervention upon the culture of a literary work (or works), appear to contradict the hypothesis that the more deeply embedded levels of cosmic evolution are more resistant to modification than more recent stages. This is, however, not the case. In fact, retroactive causality in quantum mechanics in no way affects the fundamental principles of the quantum level. On the contrary, the laws of physics, at least of the best current explanation the subatomic world, define the nature of particle physics as a probabilistic realm engaged in a feedback relationship with an observer. To use the vocabulary of Heidegger, quantum causality can affect the ontic level of the world, the specific, contingent configuration of beings, but not the ontological status of microphysics. To do that would require a fundamental change, such as one that results in quantum phenomena behaving like macrophysical, deterministic objects. It is unclear how such a transformation of quantum regularities could be brought about, although it is conceivable that the enormous recalcitrance of the more primitive layers of the cosmos to basic changes in the nature of their lawfulness could be compensated for, in the future, by the exponential growth of human creativity (perhaps what Wheeler calls "observer-participancy").

As opposed to this picture of world 1, things are quite different in the world 3 literary model. Here, not only are particular ontic manifestations of literariness constantly coming in and out of Being, but the very ontological definition of literature, its very Being, is routinely modified. It is, in fact, ridiculously easy, by cosmic standards, to transform the basic principles underlying literary language. The emergence of the novel in the seventeenth and eighteenth centuries as a major literary genre, with its reliance on mechanization (the printing press) and its tendency to remove the experience of literature from the public to the private arena, constituted a transformation of basic principles of literariness. The same could be said of film, concrete poetry, and Robert Wilson's theater. Literature is capable of affecting the standards through which it is perceived and judged because, like the rest of world 3, it is intrinsically more pliable than lower evolutionary levels.

Unfortunately, things are not as simple as I have outlined them. Although I think that the inverse rule of resistance to change is a reasonable hypothesis in the main, it does obscure a feature of hierarchies that will be discussed at length in an upcoming chapter. For the moment, let me just add to the preceding discussion that what I have been calling the laws or regularities that constitute the specificity of an evolutionary level are not, themselves, a flat amalgamation of laterally related elements. In fact, an interesting thing about hierarchical arrangements is that once one is attuned to their presence, they appear everywhere. Not only are the basic stages of cosmic evolution arranged hierarchically, but the laws that constitute them as separable and definable levels are themselves arranged in a hierarchy. Thus, biology is a set of regularities that includes but transcends the regularities specific to the chemical world. This set, furthermore, includes a subset that is specific to biology itself, and this subset is itself a hierarchical system that mirrors the larger picture of evolution in containing subsystems that are more resistant to change than others. For example, that life should establish a self-regulating internal environment, which nevertheless maintains commerce with the larger environment, is a far more difficult principle to alter within the biological realm than, say, the rules governing the structure and dynamics of the nervous system in mammals. I speculate that the universe is a hierarchical continuum of hardwired to softwired systems (Popper's cosmic levels) that are themselves internally arranged in a manner roughly isomorphic with the entire universe. In addition, as cosmic evolution proceeds, its hierarchical levels tend to get more tangled, with an enormous range of feedback and feedforward loops, such as those Wheeler describes as possibly connecting human observers with quantum fields. Although it may appear that I am teetering on the brink of a favorite deconstructive metaphor, the hall of mirrors or infinite regress, since I am describing sets of hierarchies embedded within other hierarchies and embedding within themselves still more hierarchical structures, I believe that such a nest of hierarchies is quite different from Derridian dissemination. The universe resists deconstructive reduction because its overall hierarchical architecture functions as a kind of backbone that both guarantees stability and allows for all manner of internal level violation.

I suspect that it is precisely because hierarchy appears to be a kind of natural default option that nature is able to balance Being and becoming, conservation and innovation, and absolutes and contingencies with such delicacy. Although the universe is no great chain of Being, nor a Hegelian eschatology, neither is it the lateral sprawl envisioned by Derrida.

Chapter 9

The Evolution of Time

As Derrida correctly argues, truth and representation are essentially temporal concepts. However, whereas for Derrida time means either the punctuality of the present or the infinite deferral of the arche-trace, J. T. Fraser, perhaps the foremost philosopher of time, claims that time is an evolutionary hierarchy of different temporalities.

Because an evolutionary view of time is, to my knowledge, alien to contemporary critical theory, it might be useful (for diacritical reasons) to introduce a discussion of this theory with a summary of Derrida's concept of temporality. As I have already argued, a major component of Derrida's deconstruction of presence is his insistence on the trace-network structuring the present. For Derrida, the present, or the now, is constantly supplementing itself because it has no Being in the philosophical sense. As opposed to a long tradition that sees time as a series of discrete and indivisible now-points, Derrida argues that the present is merely a web of temporal anticipations and retentions. As usual, Derrida's position is accurate enough to make it convincing. Yet I believe that it is thoroughly misleading because of the error that, for programmatic reasons, a deconstructionist cannot avoid making—the collapsing of hierarchical levels into a flat, though highly articulated, network. Specifically, much of what Derrida says about time is accurate when applied to certain stages of cosmic evolution, but when presented in an undifferentiated and therefore confused thesis that ignores the basic fact that the universe is hierarchical, it generates all manner of incoherence and inconsistency.

Most philosophical treatments of time, from Aristotle's to Derrida's (which, in many of its positions, is clearly indebted to Husserl and Heidegger), are incomplete insofar as they assume that time is a single, ahistorical phenomenon. Whether one is trying to discover the essence of time or seeking to deconstruct a presumed metaphysical consensus that the essence of time is wed to the integrity of the Now, time has been typically assumed to be simply "out there," a fundamental component of reality. Even the most unsettling revolutions in the way we think about time, the theories of special and general relativity, share this basic assumption. Whereas in special relativity time in an inertial frame is assumed to be relative to the observer, and in general relativity, the fundamental fabric of reality is postulated to be a four-dimensional time-space, there is no suggestion in either theory that, over and above its plasticity and relativity, time has evolved along with everything else in the universe. Space-time provides essentially the same sort of temporality for a meteorite as for a lemur, and, to the extent that this is an oversimplification, it suggests a fundamental problem not only with Einstein's work, but also with any cosmology that eschews the cumulative and hierarchical nature of time. What has just been suggested in regard to Einstein is applicable, a fortiori, to Derrida. Within his phenomenological perspective, Derrida is quite correct in deconstructing a reductively linear conception of time. However, deconstruction tends to suggest that the Aristotelian notion of time that it undermines is, in fact, a metaphysical hypostatization of an underlying *différance*, time as deferring/deferred trace structure, whereas an evolutionary theory of time would refuse the suppressed/suppressor model in favor of a hierarchical one: metaphysical time is neither *the* truth nor a defensive attempt to constitute one, but simply a historical remnant of what was, at one time, the most advanced and unpredictable kind of temporality available in the universe

My exposition of an evolutionary model of time derives almost totally from the work of J. T. Fraser. Although it would be impossible to reproduce here even a small proportion of the riches his books hold, in the interest of developing a theory of time that corrects the misleading simplifications of deconstruction, I will nonetheless attempt to outline the rudiments of Fraser's remarkably subtle and original insights into the nature of time. Fraser's basic thesis is that time is inadequately conceptualized as the unchanging abstract fabric of reality. Instead, he suggests that the correct model for time is that of an evolutionary hierarchy of increasingly complex temporalities. Part of the beauty and persuasiveness of Fraser's theory is that it recasts the fundamental stages of cosmic evolution, such as those suggested by Popper, in temporal terms. Fraser's theory supplements the classificatory system usually employed to describe the evolution of the universe with a temporal description of each stage in the history of the universe. Time, therefore, is no longer understood as a background for reality, but as an evolving fabric of laws constitutive of reality.

In order to describe the temporalities Fraser posits as the stuff of cosmic evolution, it would be helpful, first, to consider his concept of extended *umwelts*. German biologist Jakob von Uexküll (1957) defines an *umwelt* as the sum of the possible stimuli able to affect an organism's receptors and the possible actions produced by its effectors. The world of a biological organism is contained within the horizon of its possible perceptions and its possible actions. Any event occurring outside this horizon simply does not exist in the world of that organism. Thus, a poem does not exist for a raccoon, except as a series of auditory or visual stimuli that are not perceived as poetry but as environmental noise. It is as if the raccoon existed in Abbott's (1952) two-dimensional flatland and was confronted by three-dimensional poetry. The two-dimensional raccoon would see all of the poem it could, its two-dimensional components, but, since poetry is simply not part of its *umwelt*, it would not be able to distinguish "Among School Children" from a humanlike voice uttering nonsense. The important point here is that reality is not a fixed objective concept for the entirety of biological evolution, but is defined by a level-specific ability to process information. Information that is unavailable to an organism simply does not exist for that organism.

If we expand Uexküll's theory to include nonbiological entities, then we could argue that the world available to anything in the universe is simply the sum of the information it is able to exchange with its environment. And, since one way to define evolution is as the gradual complication of information processing capacities, then evolution could be conceived of as the expansion of the world. The more sophisticated an entity's capacities to receive, store, manipulate, and transmit information, the more world it has at its disposal.

Fraser extends the *umwelt* principle in two directions. First, he proposes that exosomatic sensory prostheses, such as telescopes, have their own specific *umwelt*. A radio telescope, for example, has an *umwelt* that is restricted to electromagnetic radiation. A poem would be as alien to it as it is to a raccoon. Although Fraser does not make the point explicitly, it is clear that one of the evolutionary advantages of Homo sapiens is that we are able to extend our biological *umwelt* through the invention of such prosthetic devices. In fact, the growth of modern science is clearly dependent on our ability to register data that would normally be outside our ken. Much of modern technology can be conceived of as prosthetic sensory organs through which the slice of reality available to us has been expanded to an unprecedented extent in organic evolution.

In addition, Fraser claims that each major stage, or, in his vocabulary, integrative level, of nature is defined by a specific *umwelt*. This view has two consequences that will prove central to my subsequent arguments. First, the notion of language is expanded to a range of applicability that far outstrips the normal anthropocentric limits implicitly imposed by most contemporary critical theory. Second, the hierarchical evolutionary model developed by Fraser, insofar as it is constructed of superimposed layers rather than of revolutions that either annihilate preceding stages or render them inaccessible, allows for an inhabitant of a later integrative level to "speak for" an earlier one. Since they are so important, these two ideas will be developed separately and at some length.

Deconstruction, and most contemporary critical theory, assumes that the notion of language is tantamount to human language. Even when Derrida seems to extend the concept of language to include all codes, such as genetic and cybernetic codes, he does so in a superficial manner. Refusing to engage in any detailed analysis of nonhuman codes, his mention of them is, to my knowledge, just a kind of name-dropping. Of course, in his attempt to generalize the concept of arche-writing to include the entirety of reality (*différance* is "the becoming-time of space and the becoming-space of time, the 'originary constitution' of time and space" [1982, 8]), he must extend the deconstructive idea of the trace to the nonhuman world. However, Derrida's extension is essentially top-down, an assimilation of prehuman codes to the anthropic realm that is Derrida's domain. For example, an essential component of deconstructive temporality is the idea that the present is internally articulated by retentive and protentive traces. Without this becoming-space of time and becoming-time of space, deconstruction would be unthinkable. Consequently, it is difficult to imagine what Derrida could possibly mean when he implicitly attributes a present, past, and future to the genetic code if, as Fraser argues, temporalities more primitive that those associated with biological organisms simply do not have a present. Although, as I suggest in chapter 20, there is reason to suspect that Fraser's analysis of temporal asymmetry may be incomplete, it is nevertheless not given that genes are in any nonanthropomorphic way describable by the notion of a present. If, as Fraser suggests, it is necessary to avoid the anthropocentric assumption that human temporality is shared by nonhuman or nonbiological entities, then Derrida's deconstruction of the living present would be meaningless when applied to much of the universe. To assimilate primitive temporalities to the phenomenological horizon that informs Derrida's deconstruction of phenomenology would, therefore, be critical imperialism.

As opposed to Derrida's anthropo-chauvinism, Fraser claims that what are commonly called the laws appropriate to the universe's emergent levels can be fruitfully conceived of as languages.

> There are good reasons to believe that each of the major integrative levels of nature must be described in different, level-specific languages. By language is meant a class of signals and symbols in which the laws and regularities of nature must be expressed so as to satisfy the critical and practical intelligence of man, the formulator and tester of these laws. When the regularities and laws of the integrative levels are appropriately expressed, they too are found to be level-specific and hierarchical. To wit, each level-specific language and body of laws subsumes the languages and laws beneath it. (1978, 26)

Therefore, a phrase such as "the laws of chemistry" must be understood to have two, isomorphic meanings. It means both the formulations human beings devise to describe the organizational regularities constitutive of the chemical *umwelt*, as well as the organizational regularities of chemistry itself. The only way to avoid the unfortunate idealism of many cultural constructivist positions is to respect the otherness of nature by attempting to speak its languages. The language of chemistry, as spoken by chemists, is part of what Ilya Prigogine calls "a dialogue with nature" (Prigogine and Stengers 1984) precisely because it respects the language of the interactive regularities specific to the chemical *umwelt* enough to acknowledge it as nonhuman while simultaneously seeking to translate it into a language accessible to human beings. Were such translation impossible, it would have been inconceivable that human beings could have so successfully summoned the prehuman world to respond to our interventions. Without the correct equations, it is impossible to combine elements to form water. With them, it is routine. Nature snubs monologues, but responds, occasionally begrudgingly, to attempts at dialogue.

If, as many theorists contend, human culture is incarcerated within a "prison house of language," then, in the light of Fraser's extended *umwelt* principle, we must reinterpret this postindustrial jail to include everything (making it a rather whimsical prison—one from which there is no escape because it includes the entire universe). The integrative levels of which Fraser speaks are nothing but the laws and regularities that define a certain level of cosmic evolution. When Newton discovered the inverse square law of gravitational attraction, he entered into a real dialogue with the large structures of the universe because he had learned to listen to their language. This kind of listening, at once humbling and exhilarating, is precisely what we sacrifice when, in our hubris, we assume that nature is nothing but a skewed reflection of our own structures of understanding.

In a subtly insidious way, mainstream postmodern theory is a remarkable ruse to eradicate the otherness of the prehuman world. "Our perceptual categories," says Robert Merrill (1988, viii), "give the only shape to whatever is called 'real' that it can ever have, and thus response to the real is no different in nature than from our response to art." In a trivial way, Merrill is, of course, correct. The real is indeed a construction. However, the crucial error in Merrill's formulation is the chauvinistic assumption that our perceptual categories are ours alone. Being a palimpsest of our evolution, we share perceptual structures with our entire past. Furthermore, we are not the only participants in the construction of the real. As Frederick Turner once said in conversation, other entities in the universe have a say in what constitutes reality, and although we conceivably have more votes in the constitution of the real, it is only at our peril that we convince ourselves that ours is the sole and sovereign voice in the cosmos. The funny thing is that if by "our perceptual categories" someone meant the point of view of white, middle-class males, Merrill would be justifiably outraged, but, when the "our" uncritically does violence to a host of Others in the cosmic community, a critic as sensitive to the dangers of projection as Merrill can call this line of thought "life-enhancing."

In fact, by refusing to imagine the possibility that an entity that has poked its head into world 3 can still engage in a meaningful dialogue with worlds 2 and 1, all the various cultural relativisms that so characterize contemporary critical discourse are thinly veiled idealisms. I realize that to call deconstruction an idealism is likely to be met with disbelief from those of its proponents who assume that the deconstruction of presence has long since laid to rest the ghost of idealism; however, it is precisely idealism, perhaps the essence of idealism, to presume that the temporality of human semiotics is the temporality of all semiotics.[1] If "there is nothing outside the text" means that everything is a text, then we would do well to wonder if there is, indeed, something like *the* text, and, if not, if the text of organic chemistry is written in the same language as the text of literature.

Of course, in attempting to avoid the pernicious idealism of Merrill's "our," we should not move too far in the other direction, toward a postmodern worldview in which nature is conceived of as a kind of Wittgensteinian Tower of Babel. If each integrative level of cosmic evolution speaks its own level-specific language, then it is legitimate to ask how communication is possible at all. Isn't the situation somehow akin to a nightmarish version of Wittgenstein's language games—players of chess trying to apply the rules of their game at a checkers tournament? It is precisely to avoid such a dilemma that the notion of hierarchy is indispensable. I think that the crucial feature of flexible hierarchies is that they are able to use available resources more efficiently than nonhierarchical systems. Rather than excluding lower levels from the functioning of the whole, complex hierarchies are characterized by a capacity to engage in intricate backloops, reaching down to lower levels in order to tap information that may not be available in higher levels. In a temporal hierarchy in which simpler levels are also older or more primitive kinds of time, this nonexclusion principle amounts to a kind of systemic memory. The languages of the basic integrative stages of cosmic evolution are un-Wittgensteinian because they are embedded in a hierarchical tree within which communication occurs freely as long as level distinctions are maintained to some degree. In other words, the biologist does not hesitate to use the languages of chemistry (as in molecular biology) precisely because he or she understands that chemistry does not stand alongside biology as a competing language game but serves as its microstructure. If communication is the ability to listen to an Other rather than oneself, then hierarchies are perhaps the only way to enter into a genuine dialogue with genuine alterity.

Fraser's extended *umwelt* principle claims that interlanguage communication is possible because higher level languages already speak, that is, already are, lower level languages: "Each integrative level of nature has its level-specific language and man, as a hierarchical system, is open to his environment on all these levels" (1978, 126). Thus, by using physics, human beings can speak for fundamental particles (although not necessarily successfully: this dialogue, like all dialogue, is always subject to misunderstandings and misinterpretations—the noise of communication) because human beings are, in part, the language of particle physics. If we were not, if the physical world were an alien realm that we could at best *represent*, then deconstructive claims about the absence of a metatext would be accurate. However, the extended *umwelt* principle suggests that there is, indeed, a metatext, and this metatext is nothing other than the hierarchical structure of emergent evolution.

The extended *umwelt* principle forms the basis of Fraser's cosmology. The meat of his argument, however, is his strikingly original view of time. Basically, Fraser argues that the evolution of the universe can be thought of as the evolution of time. According to Fraser, time, which has traditionally been conceptualized as a rigid background for events, must be rethought as a hierarchical evolutionary system. Therefore, the levels of emergent evolution as outlined by Popper and many others can be seen as increasingly complex temporalities.

The most primitive temporality posited by Fraser is the atemporal: "There are processes which determine Umwelts that must be regarded as *atemporal*. By this is meant that there are no means, even in principle, whereby time can be recognized if such processes are examined entirely from within. In these worlds nothing can correspond to the idea of event, to conditions of before/after, to future/past/present, to causal connections, or to beginnings and endings" (1978, 23). This should come as a shock to many contemporary theorists. The very project of deconstruction, with its dependence on a phenomenological notion of time to deconstruct, is perfectly meaningless in realms of nature that know no time whatsoever. It is equally a shock to those who view Parmenides's idea of a plenum as primitive idealism. In fact, in a universe dominated by photons, gravitons, and neutrinos, that is, in the very early universe, the theory of special relativity suggests that any distinction between before and after is impossible.[2] For a particle traveling at the speed of light, or one traversing a distance that is in the order of the Planck length, all events are simultaneous. It is only from the perspective of higher temporalities that the path of a photon, for example, can be divided into temporal units; the photon itself experiences no delimitable events. It exists in an atemporal plenum, in which everything occurs simultaneously.

> It follows that in a universe of purely relativistic energy, containing only photons, gravitons, and neutrinos, as judged from the point of view of any of the traveling particles, is one single happening. Of course, photons have no opinions but we may have some on their behalf, through the extended umwelt principle. (Fraser 1978, 30)

It is indeed curious that eternity may not be a mythological utopia but the simplest language spoken by everything in the universe. Perhaps the universality of some concept of eternity in the theological and philosophical speculation of human beings stems from our ability, through the extended *umwelt* principle, to experience timelessness. This is nonanthropocentrism with a vengeance.

When the universe cooled enough for its energy to be trapped into stable elementary particles (perhaps around $10^{4°}$K), a new kind of temporality emerged. Quantum mechanics teaches us that the world of fundamental particles is characterized by a kind of ghostly smear of probabilities. It should be noted that this view of quantum mechanics, the Copenhagen interpretation, is not universally accepted, the list of skeptics being lead by none other than Einstein. The most common antiquantum view, the so-called hidden variables theory, claims that the indefiniteness characteristic of quantum systems is not an objective fact, but merely indicative of the observer's ignorance of some as yet undiscovered variables that render the system objectively definite. In other words, an objective description of a quantum phenomenon would, indeed, yield definite data if human scientists were aware of the hidden variables characteristic of an individual system. Unfortunately for those who cling to a view of reality that demands that it be definite and delimitable at all of its integrative levels, the hidden variables theory has not been confirmed by experimental evidence. Describing the failure of number of recent experiments aimed at establishing the validity of the hidden variables hypothesis, Shimony says: "A more natural interpretation is that the objective state of the photon in the interferometer leaves many properties indefinite. If the quantum state gives a complete account of the photon, then that conclusion is not surprising, since in every quantum state there are properties that are indefinite" (1988, 52). Therefore, the best available theory for quantum systems is, according to Shimony, that:

> If the quantum state of a system is a complete description of the system, then a quantity that has an indefinite value in the quantum state is objectively indefinite; its value is not merely unknown by the scientist who seeks to describe the system. Furthermore, since the outcome of a measurement of an objectively indefinite quantity is not determined by the quantum state, and yet the quantum state is the complete bearer of information about the system, the outcome is strictly a matter of objective chance—not just a matter of chance in the sense of unpredictability by the scientist. (47)

The objective indefiniteness of a quantum system, along with other well known properties such as its ability to behave like a particle if particlelike properties are measured and like a wave if wavelike properties are measured, and the correlation between two quantum entities when they are separated by a distance across which no communication is possible (assuming the limit of communication is a distance that can be traversed by something traveling at the speed of light), render the quantum-mechanical realm frighteningly bizarre by the standards of classical physics. Indeed, as I suggested earlier, quantum mechanics makes Derrida's deconstruction of Husserlian phenomenology somewhat trivial, since Husserl's principle of principles is clearly violated, and viciously, by the quantum world.

Quantum temporality is characterized by Fraser as prototemporality. Prototemporality is actually also protospatiality, since thing and event are barely distinguishable at this primitive level. The prototemporal *umwelt*, in accordance with quantum theory, is composed of particles and events whose essential, objective, existence is a distribution of probabilities. Specifically, cause is only weakly distinguishable from effect because momenta and positions can only be described probabilistically. Events exist in the prototemporal *umwelt*, so that we can legitimately claim that it possesses time, but causation, sequence, before/after, etc., have no linear clarity and can be described only by using the language of probability. Prototemporal entities are not distinguishable (all electrons are identical, for example), consequently, even though they can be counted, it is impossible to arrange them in any kind of order.

Clearly, prototemporality is alien to any traditional concept of presence. It is, therefore, difficult to see the applicability of deconstructive principles to an essentially aleatory temporality. In fact, it is becoming increasingly clear that, contrary to a fundamental deconstructive axiom, metaphysics, whatever it is, is hardly that to which there is no *simple* outside. Derrida's project, to demonstrate that, in the absence of such a simple exterior to metaphysics, the only option is to demonstrate its internal fissures, is largely invalidated by the observation that *most* of the universe is simply exterior to metaphysics.

The large structures of the universe, the realm analyzed by Newton, constitute the main example of Fraser's next integrative *umwelt*, the eotemporal. In the eotemporal world, space and time are cleanly distinguishable. Although there is clear temporal succession on this level, with identifiable and delimitable events, it is, according to Fraser, a kind of succession without a vector. This kind of temporality is common in physics, where equations preserve time symmetry, that is, where equations are invariant with regard to a change in the sign of time. "The laws of science," according to Stephen W. Hawking, "do not distinguish between past and future" (1988, 144). What this means is that, in the eotemporal *umwelt*, time is pure succession without a preferred direction. Fraser explains this with a graphic analogy.

This kind of time may be compared to a series of blazes on trees, indicating a trail, but not to an arrow, indicating a preferred direction. Endings and beginnings of processes can be identified but they cannot be distinguished from one another; they both ought to be described by the same word—which we do not have, since our conscious experience of time is not eotemporal. Causation here is deterministic; the dynamics of this world is that of action and causation. (1978, 23–24)

Fraser disputes the commonly held view that the second law of thermodynamics generates an arrow of time. In fact, he argues that no physical process can possess a temporality higher than that of pure succession that is characteristic of the eotemporal. The basic reason for this, according to Fraser, is that it is impossible to conceive of a temporal vector without a *now* against which the current of time can be gauged. Consequently, since the eotemporal *umwelt* has no present, neither can it determine a preferred temporal direction. In other words, physical systems, like the series of blazes in the forest, determine a kind of temporality in which it is impossible to assign a now to a given instant of time. In the absence of a present, temporal succession is completely reversible and cannot define an arrow of time.

With the emergence of life, we cross from Popper's world 1 to his world 2. The biotemporal *umwelt* is the time peculiar to living organisms. According to Fraser, its distinguishing feature is the appearance and development of the present. Here, as opposed to the rigidly linear temporality of the eotemporal, an increasingly better defined present opens time up to a number of important asymmetries. As biological organisms become more complex, the past is increasingly distinguished from the future, beginnings and endings grow increasingly asymmetrical, and goals, purposes, and teleologies gain greater definition.

A minimum condition for living systems is that they be capable of maintaining their difference from their environment. The homeostasis of an organism is tied largely to its ability to coordinate various periodicities and rhythms. An organism's biological clocks, ranging from the response to electromagnetic rays striking its skin, to circadian periods, population clocks, lunar periods, circannual rhythms, and genetic cycles, need to be coordinated, otherwise its interior environment would become hopelessly muddled. It is precisely the selective pressures to tune an organism's clocks that, according to Fraser, selected for the emergence of a now.

> Thus, I would imagine evolving a continuously richer inner landscape of rhythms. It would comprise a map of external periodicities, a store of periodicities which have no external correspondences, and a system of control to keep the clocks in the shop from becoming mutually destructive. (1978, 76)

As is often the case in evolution, complexity and simplicity appear as a pair joined in dialectical dependence. There is clearly an advantage in complexity, since a complex entity can choose among a wider range of options when faced with challenges from the environment. In fact, cosmic evolution as outlined by Popper, Audouze, Fraser, and countless others is little else then the history of successively more complex structures and processes. However, uncontrolled complexity can be disabling. Consider, for example, the librarians in Borges's "The Library of Babel" (1964) trying to decide on the appropriate wine to have with dinner. Although complexity is inherently valuable, its desirability depends on the accompanying development of a means by which possibility is collapsed into actuality. Complexity is only advantageous if, as it generates options, it can isolate and make concrete choices. These choices, in turn, create greater complexity, as when the election of a chief of state can lead a nation to undergo a renaissance of technological, scientific, and aesthetic research. If a major survival advantage of a living system is that its spectrum of endogenous periodicities can better map and affect environmental cycles, then the evolution of life must have included the machinery necessary to synchronize its multiple clocks. The minimum condition for the maintenance of a system composed of a large number of rhythmic subsystems is a now against which their harmonies can be compared. The biotemporal *umwelt*, synonymous with the life of living organisms, is the insertion of "meaningful present in the pure succession of the eotemporal world" (Fraser 1978, 80).

It is interesting, and somewhat ironic, that what for Derrida constitutes the locus of logocentric repression of the joyousness of dissemination, the present of presence, is, according to Fraser, the invention of a mode of temporality that liberated matter from the rigid linearity of the eotemporal *umwelt*. The astounding freedom of life, its ability to adapt rapidly to its environment as it simultaneously influences its surroundings (until, with the advent of man, the environment becomes largely a human invention), to look increasingly forward into the future and back into the past, to develop neural systems able to entertain multiple causalities and, eventually, counterfactual causality, in short, the evolution of evolution itself that is characteristic of world 2, is the product of a biological present. The now is not the repression of a complex and delicately branched temporality, it is its ground.

Although I take issue with Fraser's radically emergent view of temporal asymmetry, preferring to see the present as an evolving temporality (the full exposition of this theory will be deferred until chaos theory has been discussed), Fraser is doubtless correct in asserting that biotemporality is synonymous with a strongly delineated present and its attendant protentions and retentions. So when Derrida associates *différance* with death: "And thereby let us anticipate the delineation of a site, the familial residence and tomb of the proper in which is produced, by *différance*, the *economy of death*" (1982, 4), I might be tempted to agree, were it not that death itself is unthinkable outside the biotemporal *umwelt*. In short, insofar as Derrida ignores the evolutionary and hierarchical nature of time, he tends to translate his suspicions concerning the hegemony of the present into a general condemnation of its significance. It is precisely because deconstruction is anthropocentric that, when confronted with temporalities that do not properly belong to the higher *umwelts*, it seeks to deconstruct them. Fraser's suggestion that the biotemporal *umwelt* includes the eotemporal, prototemporal, and atemporal *umwelts* as its microstructure permits a nuanced description of time that simultaneously refrains from metaphysical universalization and allows itself the room to affirm the present as the most complex temporality allowed nonhuman biological organisms.

With the evolution of man, a temporality much like that described by Husserl and Derrida emerges out of the biotemporal. Human time, called by Fraser the nootemporal *umwelt*, constitutes an amazingly complex and involuted temporality. Stretched between expectation and memory, the human present is a process of constant adjustment to the changing topology of the past and the future. Whereas the future and past tend to be weakly defined and increasingly fuzzy as they spread out from the present for prehuman biological creatures, nootemporality projects into a future that can be multiple, counterfactual, and extended beyond the death of an individual human. It also projects into a past that is constantly being reinterpreted and includes cultural information preceding the individual's birth. "Let us recall that long-term planning and memory, conscious experience, selfhood, and concern with abstract and symbolic causes populate the umwelt of the neocortex. In contrast, the mammalian and reptilian brains attend to those needs that demand immediate satisfaction" (Fraser 1987, 184).

Because humans exist in large measure in the symbolic world that their temporality supports, a world largely defined by language and other representational systems (visual and auditory for the most part), they typically project their curiosity concerning beginnings and endings beyond the scope of an individual, or of a given culture, to ponder first causes and eschatologies. Nootemporality coupled with what d'Aquili, Laughlin, and McManus call a "cognitive imperative" (d'Aquili, Laughlin, and McManus 1979), the need to create models to account for the data of experience, suggests that those theological, philosophical, and aesthetic grand narratives, far from being oppressive examples of fascist totalization as deconstructive and postmodern theory maintains, are an indispensable product of the mode of time in which humans live.

In the feedback manner typical of evolution, nootemporality is both the product and the cause of the huge human neocortex. Long-term memory, the symbolic manipulation of experience, intersubjective community, reflexivity, the creation of counterfactual models for reality, and the ability to travel into the indefinite future and past are actually part of an evolutionary continuum whose increasing development and complication was both the product of evolution and the main selective pressure for the emergence of the human brain. Therefore, if by metaphysics we mean the creation of theories, such as mythical systems, religious cosmologies, aesthetic narratives, and scientific hypotheses that seek to account as well as possible for the entirety of Being, then it would be a cruel and baneful trick to play on our culture to convince it that the temporality that constitutes our freedom from the relative determinism of the lower *umwelts* is actually a repressive machine.

Fraser speculates that a more complex temporality than the

nootemporal is constituted by human society. Sociotemporality is a collective temporality that transcends the inorganic, organic, and mental temporalities out of which it emerged. Specifically, sociotemporality is characterized by two temporal functions of society, the socialization of time and the collective evaluation of time. The socialization of time involves "the timing of collective actions through synchronization and scheduling" (1987, 188), while the collective evaluation of time is "the creation and maintenance of value systems that guide the conduct of the members of a society. Such systems derive their authority from the history and the plans of the group, as seen by its members" (188). Taken as a whole, sociotemporality can be seen as the tendency of human beings to form societies in which a social present (defined as the time needed to coordinate communication among members of a group—for example, the time it takes to send a letter and receive a reply) needs to be maintained and for which certain moral codes provide both coherence over time and the raw materials for social change.

Fraser urges caution concerning the exact nature of the sociotemporal *umwelt* since he speculates that it is a relatively new integrative level still in the process of forming itself. However, he does make a number of claims concerning the specific sociotemporal configuration of the contemporary world.

Although Fraser does not make this point explicitly, his various analyses suggest that there is a hierarchy of sociotemporal *umwelts*, stretching from perhaps the family unit to the currently popular idea of a global village. In between, we would expect to find such entities as movements, institutions, nation-states, and multination conglomerates such as Europe 1992. Fraser's emphasis, however, is clearly on the global implications of sociotemporality. For Fraser, once the world's population achieves a threshold limit of social complexity, specifically the complexity necessary to constitute and maintain a global sociotemporal now, sociotemporality will begin to replace nootemporality as the hallmark measure of time. "[I]f a significant portion of the earth's population reaches a certain level of social complexity, the global socialization and evaluation of time will subsume the office of the individual as the primary measure and measurer of time" (1987, 342).

Fraser argues that the world is currently in a metastable boundary between nootemporal and sociotemporal dominance. He sees the social present contracting to a state of near simultaneity, a condition he labels the "time-compact globe." In other words, communication technology has made possible a global coordination of time to the extent that it is now conceivable that a global present is emerging to challenge the individual nootemporal present for temporal hegemony.

Fraser's evaluation of the implications of a time-compact globe is fairly grim, echoing the views of mainstream postmodern thought in many ways. I will summarize as briefly as possible the main features of Fraser's understanding of the time-compact globe before proceeding to criticize it.

1. Communication technology is yielding an increasingly sharply defined global present. As a result, the responsibility for remembering the past and planning the future is shifting from the individual to the global community.
2. Our civilization is focusing more and more on the present and the immediate future with a subsequent diminution of interest in history.
3. The "greying of the calendar" involves the smoothing out of distinctions between day and night, days of the week, and among the seasons. As a consequence, ancient cyclical rhythms based on these differences are in the process of losing their influence on the means by which human beings constitute their world.
4. The control of birth, and possibly of death, are affecting the quality of our private time. Since, according to Fraser, the desire to finesse time through procreation and bargaining with death contributed greatly to the creation of nootemporality, societal control of birth and death due to ecological pressures could radically affect the "texture of time."
5. Social time is growing more and more homogenous. Two primary causes for the homogenization of time are the bomb and the computer. Nuclear weaponry requires that "the global present be kept as narrow as communication techniques permit, so as to help each nation better safeguard itself against an attack by another" (1987, 325). The result is industrial and economic concentration and "the regimentation and scheduling of private life."

Computers lead to a homogenization of thought and a reduction of the range of ideas flowing through the culture because they "demand a way of talking to them, which carries with it a way of thinking: this communicates itself to peoples' assessments of the nature of reality and to the scale of values" (1987, 327).

6. Sociotemporal art, as symbolized by the various Disneylands, becomes a simulacrum of life, a simulacrum whose main purpose is to promote the ideal of our culture: "the good life, good fellowship, no deep search for meaning, interesting gadgetry, light entertainment, and mass-reproduced art" (1987, 333).

My criticism of Fraser's notion of sociotemporality can be divided into two themes. First, I find his description of the time-compact globe unduly bleak. In many ways, Fraser's time-compact globe resembles Foucault's description of the modern period as characterized by the increasing channeling of human beings by the microphysical technologies of power and discipline. In upcoming chapters, I will take issue with such a view of the present, arguing that sociotemporal complexity is not the ominous shadow of the technological arm of Western metaphysics, but an evolutionary process whose potential for good could be squandered if only its potentially pernicious effects are highlighted.

Second, although I agree with Fraser that we are entering a period of global time compaction, I have severe reservations about the thesis that such developments signal the evolution of a new integrative level. For one thing, it is unlikely that if sociotemporality were a new evolutionary *umwelt* we, as nootemporal entities, would be in a position to know about it. Just as frogs have no knowledge of properly nootemporal events except insofar as they intersect their biotemporal *umwelt*, it is reasonable to assume that, if the globe were itself a new kind of evolutionary being, nootemporal creatures would only be able to have knowledge of that slice of it that appears in our *umwelt*. Simply, that Fraser can discuss a sociotemporal *umwelt* is a powerful argument against it. Of course, it might be argued that sociotemporality signals our evolution along cultural, rather than biological, lines. If that were the case, there would be no level violation in our ability to envision sociotemporality, because we would be, at least in part, sociotemporal ourselves. Although this argument is internally consistent, I find no reason to believe that such cultural evolution is not simply an extension of traditional human social/biological coevolution rather than the emergence of a new integrative level.

Another source of my skepticism concerns the clear evolutionary trend, at least in the biotemporal and nootemporal levels, toward consciousness and self-consciousness. For that trend not to be broken, sociotemporal entities would need to have a collective consciousness and self-consciousness that qualitatively exceeds that available to human beings. Of course they might, and we are blind to it. It is difficult to imagine how such an argument could be refuted, so it does not strike me as terribly interesting. Another sort of claim might be that sociotemporal units like nation-states display many of the hallmarks of consciousness: they act, they reflect upon their actions, they scrutinize and criticize themselves, and they alter their behavior based on environmental pressures. This argument is compelling until one considers the fact that, except in some Rousseauian fantasy, human beings have always been social animals and that, as a consequence, we have always been participants in sociotemporal units such as families, kinship groups, or tribes. In fact, Fraser argues that nootemporality and sociotemporality "have evolved together: nootemporality and sociotemporality have complemented throughout history" (1987, 310). Since it is difficult to see how nootemporality can be conceived without sociotemporal institutions, that is, if their complementarity is essential and not a historical contingency, then should they not be viewed as components of a single, complex temporality?

To be fair to Fraser, he readily admits that sociotemporality did not begin to approach the status of a separate *umwelt* until it surpassed (assuming that it already has) a given level of complexity.

> This relation [between nootemporality and sociotemporality] is likely to change, however, if a significant portion of the earth's population reaches a certain level of social complexity. Thereafter, the global socialization and evaluation of time will subsume the office of the individual as the measure and the measurer of time. . . . I believe the necessary level of complexity has been or will soon be reached around a time-compact globe. (310)

His claim, therefore, is that, although sociotemporal entities were once inextricably tied to nootemporal creatures, the increasing complexation of sociotemporality has yielded a new evolutionary level of complexity, the time-compact globe. In other words, sociotemporality is a component of nootemporality until it exceeds a threshold level of complexity, at which point it undergoes a discontinuous leap into a new *umwelt*. Although this argument has the advantage of respecting the dynamics of evolutionary change, I am still unconvinced, for reasons not unlike those offered above. Again, if the time-compact globe describes an *umwelt* more complex than that available to human beings, it should in principle be outside our knowledge horizon. That it is not suggests that Fraser is wrong. Furthermore, the idea of a time-compact globe seems to be only quantitatively, not qualitatively, different from other sociotemporal units, such as families and nation-states, so it is unconvincing to maintain that it represents a leap of evolution. Finally, the time-compact globe appears to have only as many of the attributes of consciousness and self-consciousness as its members do, making it unlikely that it represents a novel *umwelt*.

My own view is that sociotemporality, or the time of such communal entities as families, tribes, linguistic groups, institutions, nation-states, multinational confederacies (both political and economic), and, eventually, the time-compact globe, is a real kind of time demanding rigorous study. Its current complexation, due (in the main) to advances in communications technology, is causing novel new opportunities and conflicts for human beings, but I see no reason to define it as a new, evolutionary *umwelt*. Therefore, although I will discuss sociotemporal issues as they arise in the rest of this book, I will depart from Fraser by refusing to grant sociotemporality the status of a separate integrative level, preferring instead to consider the time-compact globe as an intra-nootemporal phenomenon. In a way, my decision will affect the argument of this book only slightly. I fully agree with Fraser that the nature of time is changing as the world becomes globally integrated. If Fraser is right, and he is about most things, and we are witnessing the emergence of a new *umwelt*, then there will be much time for him and other thinkers to correct my shortsightedness.

To conclude, a temporal theory of evolution suggests that evolution moves in the direction of temporal complexity. As opposed to the neo-Darwinian view that defines progress as greater reproductive ability, or, what amounts to the same thing, greater potential for biological survival, Fraser's theory of temporal evolution suggests that evolution should be viewed as the increasing complexation of time.

However, as entities become more complex, they must pay for their larger *umwelt* with an increase in both fragility and potential for conflict. It is quite true that, in the event of a nuclear holocaust, cockroaches would be much more likely to survive than human beings. In fact, dinosaurs were much more complex than cockroaches, and we all know what survived. But, if fragility, especially at the level of populations, is the issue, there is no need to stop at cockroaches. Surely protons are more likely to survive nuclear winters than either humans or cockroaches, and photons are, to our knowledge, indestructible. Clearly, survival is unable to account for any notion of progress by itself. It is, however, possible to recast neo-Darwinism in such a matter that the notion of progress is salvaged. Fraser's model suggests that entities inhabiting more complex *umwelts* literally have more time than their lower-*umwelt* counterparts. If this is so, then Being is not an abstract substratum that all entities have in equal amounts. Inhabiting a more complex *umwelt* is tantamount to having more world with which to interact. Thus, as we proceed up Fraser's hierarchy of temporalities, the amount of Being available to an entity increases. Or, to put the matter slightly differently, I am suggesting that the quantity of Being per unit of clock time expands as an entity's temporality becomes increasingly complex. At the level of biology, this means that more complex animals enjoy a more intense life than simpler animals. In terms of an absolute clock time, cockroaches may have outlived dinosaurs, but in terms of time measured as a function of the complexity of temporal experience, it might be argued that there is not enough clock time left in the universe for cockroaches to outlast dinosaurs.

Fraser's temporal model allows us to modify the neo-Darwinian view of evolution by conceding that evolutionary progress cannot be gauged according to increasing reproductive success or even increasing resistance to annihilation. In fact, the opposite appears to be the case—the more complex temporal *umwelts* are actually more vulnerable than the lower ones. In short time-scales, evolution may proceed, as Gould argues (1989), according to sheer contingency. But in the long term, if the evolution of subatomic particles into human beings is any indication, evolution seems to so favor complex temporalities that it is willing to pay for the time it buys with the growing fragility, vulnerability, and precariousness of existence.[3]

In addition to fragility, another cost of temporal complexity is the potential for greater conflict. As time evolves from the atemporal *umwelt*, it slowly gains definition and breadth until, with the advent of biological organisms, it becomes possible to consider the future and remember the past. Consider, for example, that the order of evolution of the senses is touch, taste, hearing, and sight. According to Fraser, the evolution of biological sensing mechanisms is the evolution of a larger and more clearly defined future.

> The type of signals an organism is able to receive determine the amount of future time it has to react to the presence of friend, foe, or food. Signals by touch make this future perspective very brief, hearing extends it. In general, then, as organic evolution created the multiplicity of living forms, the separation of future from past became better defined." (1978, 91)

As sense organs are increasingly able to prospect in the future, neural structures develop with the complexity to store more and more information in memory (a crucial development is the increasing importance of the hippocampus, which has been shown to be crucial to long-term memory). The resulting enlargement of an entity's temporal horizon is paralleled by its increasing freedom from deterministic behavior patterns. Greater temporal complexity offers greater freedom. However, freedom implies choice, and choice invariably causes conflict.

Fraser argues that each level in the evolution of time is both more complex than the preceding phase and the source of an increasing potential for conflict. The nootemporal and sociotemporal *umwelts* offer the greatest amount of freedom available in the known universe and probably the greatest amount of conflict and anxiety as well. Because we are able to entertain counterfactual realities, to imagine a past and future of infinite horizons, to consider the possibility that all our comforting teleologies and eschatologies may be nothing more than illusions, to picture our own death, and, perhaps most importantly, to engage in a new kind of evolution, cultural evolution, which sacrifices the mindless security of random genetic variation for the frightening responsibility of collectively generated choices, we are prey to far more anxiety than denizens of lower *umwelts*. It is easy to see, therefore, why some people, tired of conflict and responsibility, long for a return to a more primitive *umwelt*, such as that suggested by Derrida's eotemporal realm of arche-writing. In fact, I even wonder if Fraser's unremittingly dreary description of the sociotemporal time-compact globe may not be motivated by his own uneasiness with the immensely complex new conflicts surely in the process of being invented by the current moment in the evolution of time. Devolution has its comforts, and nootemporality coupled with the extended *umwelt* principle makes this kind of time travel quite possible for humans. Whether it is a desirable turn involves our understanding of time, evolution, and progress.

Chapter 10

The Integrity of Integrative Levels

In the previous chapter, I described Fraser's cosmology as consisting of successive layers of temporal complexity, ranging from the atemporal *umwelt* and culminating either in the nootemporal or the sociotemporal. Although this rough sketch is essentially correct, it glosses over a crucial complication. Let us consider nootemporality. The sharp temporal asymmetry characteristic of human time sits atop a hierarchy of lower temporalities to which we have both direct and indirect access via the extended *umwelt* principle. This much has already been discussed. However, such a formulation suggests an intralevel integrity that Fraser is far from supporting. In the Derridian spirit it might be legitimate to ask: What constitutes an integrative layer? Is the nootemporal *umwelt*, for example, uniformly identical to itself? Is it of whole cloth, nootemporal through and through? Does any non-nootemporal element infect the integrity of the nootemporal qua nootemporal?

In fact, Fraser is far from supporting such an apparently metaphysical position. According to Fraser, it is not the case that only the microstructure of nootemporality consists of a nested hierarchy of lower *umwelts*, nootemporality itself remaining an undifferentiated whole. On the contrary, even what is properly nootemporal is itself articulated in a manner reminiscent of the overall hierarchy of which it is a part. Fraser calls the intra-nootemporal version of the lower *umwelts* moods.

The atemporal mood is the suffering of the schizophrenic who feels the pull of chaos and panics for the loss of nootemporal reality. The prototemporal mood is the feeling engendered by a Jackson Pollock painting, with its incoherent islands of coherence, or by listening to the talk of an autistic child. The eotemporal mood is the oceanic feeling of Freud, a sense of directionless time. The biotemporal mood is the happiness or fright of an hour that has no distant futures or pasts. The nootemporal mood is the reasoned feeling for human reality at its fullest. (1987, 292)

The nootemporal *umwelt*, therefore, is itself a hierarchical structure recapitulating its own evolution. "Accordingly, the theory of time as conflict assumes that the human mind, beyond displaying its peculiar nootemporal features, also subsumes functions that are appropriate to the lower temporal Umwelts" (Fraser 1978, 25). Interestingly, Fraser rehabilitates an old notion, the idea that ontogeny recapitulates phylogeny, in the service of an evolutionary ontology.

There is enough evidence to suggest that the sense of time in man (conscious experience of time that determines the nootemporal Umwelt) is the outcome of phylogeny, that is, of the evolutionary history, which passed through steps that correspond to the hierarchy of temporal Umwelts; also, that these steps are recapitulated in their main features in the ontogenic development of the child. It is thus that the mind of man can be said to subsume all lower temporalities and possess the capacity for cognitive exploration of these Umwelts. (1978, 26)

Fraser is arguing for two kinds of subsumption within an overall hierarchical system. One is the literal fact that human minds are simply the result of a complex organization of elements that themselves belong to pre-nootemporal *umwelts*. We may liken this situation to the way in which a work of architecture, say a church, includes the spatial and temporal characteristics of its elements (wood, mortar, stone, nails, metals, molecules, atoms, protons, etc.). The other is the sense that even the nootemporal *umwelt* itself is arranged hierarchically, with certain of its levels reproducing the overall evolutionary history that yielded something like human minds. In our church analogy, this idea suggests that the properly nootemporal experience of walking through a church consists of temporalities that reproduce the temporal logic of lower level *umwelts*. For example, the sense of the divine frequently engendered by churches is intra-nootemporal atemporality, the experience of its masonry eotemporal, and so on. Fraser explains:

> Along the hierarchical ladder each higher "language" (used here in its extended meaning) subsumes the morphologies of those beneath. For this reason even abstract statements of formal communication tend to retain traces of their origins. As bio-semioticists would quickly point out, to support such ideas we must understand them; to support weights, we must stand under them. (1978, 126)

A properly nootemporal event, such as the perception of sound by human beings, is itself a palimpsest of different temporalities. Human subjects cannot distinguish sound bursts separated by less than 2 msec, so such an experience is essentially atemporal. If sounds are separated by more than 2 msec but less than 20 msec, two sounds are heard, but it is impossible to say which came first. Such a temporality, in which causal sequence is smeared out, is prototemporal. Slightly longer periods between two sounds, on the order of 20–50 msec, allow a human subject to identify sound bursts, then count and arrange them according to sequence, thus identifying an eotemporal *umwelt*. The biotemporal *umwelt* is represented in nootemporal experience by what Fraser calls the physiological present, the minimum processing time needed to perceive not merely signal sequence but signal length. This minimum time, Fraser speculates, is sufficient to allow a biological organism to engage in reflexive responses, but not long enough to permit conscious decision. The nootemporal perception of sound is a series of sound bursts separated by enough time to allow the subject to choose consciously among various kinds of response. Finally, the sociotemporal present would be constituted by the minimum amount of time it takes for a social group to process information about the sound.

It would be possible to adduce a tremendous number of examples of similar relationships. For example, it is remarkable how the ontogenesis of human thought as described by Piaget, namely the sensorimotor period, the preoperational period, the stage of concrete operational thought, and the stage of formal operational thought, mirrors (in part) Fraser's sequence of temporal *umwelts* and the process of evolution in general. John McManus (d'Aquili, Laughlin, and

McManus 1979) describes Piaget's stages of mental development in terms that make their isomorphism with evolution quite clear.

> More clearly, these criteria [for the succession of mental stages] are as follows: (1) each stage of functioning is a necessary result of the previous one and prepares the following one; (2) each stage must be defined by a unity of organization that characterizes conduct at the stage; (3) the organization of the functional structures at each stage integrates the preceding structures; and (4) the succession of stages must be universal in order if not in rate of development. (187)

The point of these examples is that they suggest a kind of self-embedding in which a component of a hierarchical structure can internally replicate the overall pattern of which it is a part. It is possible, although extremely speculative, to suggest that this structure is an example of a phenomenon that chaos theory, which is the subject of part 2 of this book, labels self-similarity—the tendency of certain hierarchical systems to form similar patterns across different scales. Furthermore, self-similarity may be a crucial component of a set of natural processes that are responsible for the most dimly understood capacity of evolution: the generation of novelty. For the purposes of this chapter, however, I would simply like to conclude with the observation that the levels of Fraser's cosmology are in no way metaphysical concepts if, by metaphysics, we understand the conviction that a concept be simply delimitable around the impermeable borders of its self-identity. Yet, for their lack of metaphysical closure, neither are Fraser's *umwelts* contingent trace structures. Clearly, there is a third choice.

Chapter 11

Identity

Deconstruction makes common cause with much contemporary philosophical and critical thought in seeking to undermine both the identity of objects and the identity of the self. Deploying such weapons as Freudian psychoanalysis, semiotics, phenomenology, Heideggerian destruction, and, of course, his own idiosyncratic analytical style, Derrida has tirelessly sought to demonstrate that identity, whether of an intentional object or of a supposed phenomenological self, is a kind of metaphysical chimera.

As opposed to this typical deconstructive view, I believe that there are ample grounds, both ontological and ethical, for affirming the concept of identity. The basis for my claim is the hypothesis that the evolution of the universe as summarized in Fraser's temporalities can also be considered as the evolution of greater and greater identity. In general, as Fraser's temporalities become increasingly complex, the identity of events within them grows proportionately stronger. And, as events acquire greater identity, entities to which events are occurring become increasingly easier to identify. If identity is defined as the possibility of distinguishing one entity from another, then it is possible to trace the following short history of the evolution of identity.

In the atemporal *umwelt* there is no identity. Since events are not distinguishable, the notion of identity is meaningless.

Prototemporal entities are weakly distinguishable and have only a statistical identity. It is impossible in principle, for example, to distinguish two electrons except insofar as quantum mechanical effects are taken into account. The problem of electrons, as Kaku and Trainer argue, is that they all look alike: "Every student of chemistry learns that all electrons are the same. There are no fat electrons, or green electrons, or long electrons" (1987, 182). The only way to differentiate one electron from another is through probabilistic quantum effects. Physicist Paul Davies explains: "From the quantum angle, an electron is not simply an electron. Shifting energy patterns shimmer around it, financing the unpredictable appearance of photons, protons, mesons, even other electrons. In short, all the paraphernalia of the subatomic world latches on to an electron like an intangible, evanescent cloak, a shroud of ghostly bees swarming around the central hive" (1983, 162–63). Of course the role of the observer in quantum mechanics stabilizes this pullulating tribe of real and virtual particles, but the point is that, at its own prototemporal level, a given electron is distinguishable from another one only in a fuzzy, probabilistic way.

Eotemporal identity is better defined than stochastic, prototemporal identity. As atoms combine to form molecules, and molecules form larger structures, the possibility of distinguishing one eotemporal object or event from another increases. For example, distinguishing between two rocks is remarkably easier than distinguishing between two electrons. Of course, we are here discussing the possibility of top-down identification, but it should be clear that the possibility of such top-down differentiation is a factor of bottom-up identity. The reason prototemporal objects and events are so difficult for scientists to distinguish is that they are inherently weakly differentiated. Analogously, eotemporal objects and events are relatively easy to identify because they themselves are able to distinguish among each other. Of course, this level-specific differentiation must not be understood anthropomorphically. It is properly eotemporal and takes into account only that knowledge available at the eotemporal level, knowledge consisting of such information as gravitational and inertial mass, velocity, charge, and so on. In the knowledge horizon of the eotemporal world, to the extent that a given object can exert greater gravitational attraction on an asteroid than on a chunk of limestone, it is able to distinguish between them.

Although primitive biotemporal creatures, such as single-cell animals, are only minimally distinguishable, and as such possess a more or less eotemporal identity, the direction of Darwinian evolution is toward greater and greater individuation of members of a taxon. Interestingly, the higher mammals, such as the elephants, Cetacea, Canidae, Felines, and nonhuman primates, display increasingly complex social structures. There is a long tradition that suggests that the needs of a society and the desires of the individual are in an eternal zero-sum struggle. Although it is certainly true that there is an essential conflict between self and society, between the needs of the one and the needs of the many, what is often overlooked is that a well-coordinated social group is a precondition for sharply defined individuals. In other words, such inventions as kinship, ritual, corporate action, symbolic communication, and shared histories simultaneously create a self and its conflict from the group. Paradoxically, that which a self rebels against, its shared Being with others, is precisely the evolutionary condition for the creation of a self in the first place. Just as linguistic creativity depends on an immense hierarchy of embedded rules and conditions, biological individuation is the product of an organism's definition within a community. Although frequently thought of as promoting uniformity, ritual activity, such as that displayed by chimpanzees, may actually promote the simultaneous seepage of self into communal space and the chiseling of a far stronger self than would have been possible in its absence. As Laughlin and McManus argue,

> The increase in reliance on social action as an adaptive strategy in mammals is related to an increased range of intragroup personality differentiation, including wider differentiation in temperament, greater role differentiation, a longer period of time for development of adult patterns of ontogeny, and more variation in autonomic system tuning. (d'Aquili, Laughlin, and McManus, 82)

Social creatures tend to have personalities (or, in the case of primitive social creatures such as ants or the members of a jellyfish colony, group role identities) and are therefore able to distinguish among themselves. As social groups became more complex, the pressures for stronger intragroup differentiation probably grew in intensity. These epigenetic pressures, coupled with such preadaptations as neural mechanisms developed for mapping the difference between organism and environment, for accounting both for the influence of the environment (including other organisms—predators, prey, group members, etc.) on the organism and of the organism on its environment, and for distinguishing between future and past, undoubtedly selected for the hallmark of nootemporal identity, the development of a self symbol. "In due course," Fraser argues, "the set of symbolic actors on the inner stage had to be enlarged so as to include a new symbol, one which could be held responsible for the responses of external objects. In its most sophisticated form, in the nootemporal world of Homo sapiens, this new object is the self of man" (1978, 104).

There is much in Fraser's description of the time-compact globe to support the thesis that sociotemporality generates a weaker sense of identity than nootemporality. For example, Fraser's emphasis on the homogenization of values, thoughts, ideals, and tastes in the contemporary world suggests that, for him, the sociotemporal time-compact globe is less sharply individuated than nootemporal creatures. Of course, one problem with such a line of thought, as Fraser himself is quick to acknowledge, is that if the world is indeed becoming a single entity, then it is unclear to what it can be compared in order to assess the strength of its identity. Nevertheless, if, as Fraser claims, it is possible to address (with great caution) the question of the nature of sociotemporality, then it is also possible to hazard some guesses concerning the state of its individuation.

Although, as I stated in chapter 10, I do not believe that the sociotemporal time-compact globe represents a higher *umwelt* than nootemporality, I will consider the notion of identity from a sociotemporal perspective as if Fraser's analysis were correct.

If sociotemporality is, indeed, a more complex *umwelt* in the process of evolving, there is every reason to suspect that it will be more sharply individuated than nootemporality. The major support for my supposition is faith in large-scale evolutionary trends. One of the narratives embedded in Fraser's evolutionary schema is that of irresolvable conflicts at a given integral level spurring discontinuous leaps of complexity. As I have tried to demonstrate here, the tendency in the evolution of time seems to be squarely in the direction of greater complexity and individuation. It would indeed be very odd if such a long-standing trend were to be broken with the advent of sociotemporality. My own view is that the trend will not be broken, and that if, as Fraser assumes, sociotemporality represents a post-nootemporal *umwelt*, then the time-compact globe will resolve conflicts deemed unresolvable at the nootemporal level, create problems unimaginable at the nootemporal level, and generate an *umwelt* that is more individuated than those belonging to lower levels of temporal complexity.

If sociotemporality is really peeling itself off from nootemporality, then my guess is that it will find ingenious means of coordinating its component temporalities, and that one of these means will be an inconceivably well-articulated identity. If, on the contrary, the time-compact globe is simply a further complexation of the nootemporal *umwelt*, then I would conjecture that it is in the process of further refining nootemporal identity. I say this in the face of what appears to be global homogenization. While it is certainly true that shopping malls, fast-food strips, television, computer technology, and multinational corporations have resulted in a certain flattening of local differences, I believe that this compression is more than compensated for by two related phenomena, one clearly already at work, the other a conjecture on my part. First, the time-compact globe is necessitating that groups previously viewed as undifferentiated lumps, such as women, ethnic minorities, homosexuals, or peasants be considered as consisting of distinct individuals. Second, I speculate that after our culture is over its adolescent infatuation with the power of contemporary information technology, it will respond to the challenge of an information-rich environment by cultivating the valuable resources of idiosyncracy and originality. One way that this could be accomplished may be in the form of a radically increasing life span made possible by nanotechnology.[1] If we were to live much longer than the life span dictated by our biotemporal reproductive cycles, if our playful childhood years were extended significantly, if our habitation in a sociotemporal world were to increase the complexity of social relations, if most of our biotemporal material needs were met routinely, and if our brain capacity could be enlarged through computer-neural interfaces, then it is possible to conceive of an unprecedented increase in both our sociability (Fraser's time-compact globe) *and* our individuation, perhaps enough of an increase to signal a new, evolutionary *umwelt*.

A fuller development of these ideas must await the introduction of chaos theory in part 3, but, in general, my position rests on the assumption that complex systems function most efficiently when they balance the need for order, predictability, and coherence with the need for originality. If the time-compact globe is to continue to increase in complexity, it must learn to compensate for the new kinds of uniformity it will create with the cultivation of sharply articulated individuals.

Having outlined the hypothesized relationship between Fraser's temporal *umwelts* and the concept of identity, I would like to return to the issue broached at the beginning of this chapter, namely the relation between the theory of evolving temporalities and the contemporary uneasiness with the notion of identity. I propose to consider a concept that is at the heart of deconstructive, Lacanian, and postmodern attacks on identity—the self.[2]

Douglas Hofstadter (1980) speculates that the brain stores information about objects in the world in multineuron networks (more precisely, in a combination of the spatial distribution of neuron groups and the timing of neuronal firing). He calls these networks "symbols." Symbols may be simple, such as those standing for a physical object, or they may be complex, such as those representing abstract concepts. The point, in either case, is that a large constellation of lower level neuronal communication can be "chunked" into a higher level entity, a symbol. In turn, these networks of symbols get chunked into "subsystems." In other words, subsystems are to symbols what symbols are to neurons. The most important of these complex symbols is the "self."

Hofstadter's view of the self is much like that of Popper, who argues that the self is the active component of the brain. "The active, psycho-physical self is the active programmer to the brain (which is the computer), it is the executant whose instrument is the brain" (Popper and Eccles 1977, 120). Similarly, Hofstadter claims that the self-subsystem monitors and keeps track of lower level brain activity.

> A very important side effect of the *self*-subsystem is that it can play the role of the "soul," in the following sense: in communicating constantly with the rest of the subsystems and symbols in the brain, it keeps track of what symbols are active, and in what way. This means that it has to have symbols for mental activity—in other words, symbols for symbols, and symbols for the actions of symbols. (1980, 385)

According to Hofstadter, the brain's self-regulation through the self-subsystem is probably what we call consciousness. In Fraser's terms, however, the self can be seen as the most individuated component of the nootemporal *umwelt,* an emergent evolutionary feature necessitated by the immense amount of information that the human brain must routinely process.

A recurrent focus of Derridian deconstruction is on the supposed metaphysical collusion between self and voice. Much of Derrida's early work, especially *Speech and Phenomena,* is an attempt to expose and deconstruct the metaphysical identity of voice, presence, and self-presence. For Derrida, the supposed ideality of the voice, the proximity it promises between thought and expression, is a token of a larger, logocentric presupposition: that truth depends on the possibility of erasing the signifier. The voice, therefore, has always been privileged over writing because, among other reasons, it is presumed to efface itself in the presence of living thought and its intentional signifieds.

Needless to say, Derrida seeks to deconstruct the privilege of the voice as well as the integrity of the self. Although I have no desire to argue for an integral self, instead preferring to see the self as an evolutionary development that shares with all of evolution the characteristic of provisionality, it is interesting to speculate that the relation between self and voice may not be an example of metaphysical repression of arche-writing but an accurate record of the emergence of a self-subsystem.

Fraser suggests that selfhood emerged when the neural and peripheral organs governing audition had developed sufficiently to make them an important conduit for information. Specifically, since hearing depends on a more highly developed ability to organize the world temporally than sight, it might be that "physiological correlates would have to have included the need for enlarged neural complement in the brain, and an increased use of temporal coding to assist the spatial coding of sight" (1978, 106). Furthermore, it may be precisely the absence of the kind of relation between hearing and time that Derrida seeks to deconstruct that prevented other, higher hominids from developing language and its correlate, a strong sense of self. "The intimate connection between language and selfhood, between naming and identity is well known; the absence of language might thus be the most important reason why even hominids did not evolve identities comparable in importance to that of the identity of man" (Fraser 1978, 106). Derrida's attempted deconstruction of language, voice, and self may be an attempt to deconstruct Homo sapiens. To the extent that Derrida repeatedly argues that the Anthropos is a dangerous concept that ought to be dismembered, and that Hegelian dialectic is the essence of phallo-logocentrism, it is not inconceivable that evolution is precisely what Derrida means by metaphysics.

The sad irony surrounding deconstruction is that the examples we have of animals which are like us in many respects but with a much fuzzier sense of self, the nonhuman primates, suggest that deconstructed humans may actually be far more linearly deterministic in their behavior than the most metaphysical of people. What Derrida fails to realize is that the arrow of evolution, toward stronger and better defined identity, is the arrow of increasing freedom. A strong self, rooted in the present, is better able to spread itself temporally between the future and the past than a weak self. A strong self is also able to empathize with others and to engage in that productive commerce with one's conspecifics and culture that probably constitutes the greatest hope of happiness available to human beings. Inversely, deconstructed selves with feeble attachments to the present are likely to display the pathetic narcissism and self-interest that are characteristics of our most brutal and sanguinary of tyrants and sociopaths. Greek literature punished individuals with hyperbolic senses of self; world history has repeatedly witnessed the bloody excess of people with weak selves. Although neither extreme is desirable, I cannot help but think that, given a choice between Alexander and Hitler, I would choose the student of Aristotle over the book burner.

Evolution seems to favor complexity, organization, multiple temporalities, symbolic variation, culture, and strong individuation. Of course, what I am describing should not be viewed as a free lunch. There is a price to be paid for evolutionary success. Just as freedom accompanies increasing complexity, conflict and anxiety accompany freedom. Each integrative phase is characterized by a level-specific kind of conflict. According to Fraser, these conflicts are unresolvable at a given level.

> By unresolvable is meant that, by means indigenous to an integrative level, its conflicts may only be maintained (and thereby the continued integrity of the level secured) or else eliminated (and thereby the level collapsed into the one beneath it). If the

conflicts vanish, so does the integrative level. However, the unresolvable conflicts of each level can and do provide the motive force for the emergence of a new level. But a new umwelt, from its very inception, may once again be identified with certain unresolvable conflicts of its own. (1978, 27)

A conflict at a given level, therefore, can only be resolved at the cost of an even greater conflict at a higher level. Evolution is another name for this economy. Even the term *resolutions* is a kind of misnomer, since the freedom it buys is paid for by a kind of conflict that was not possible at the previous level. Human beings are both happier and more anxious than chimpanzees; we create poetry and beautiful gardens, but we also need to balance our checkbooks. Consciousness of death, tragedy, loss, neurosis, divorce, disease induced by our own environmental excesses, sociopathic behavior, self-destructiveness, large-scale war, genocide, the sword of nuclear annihilation hanging over our planet, and all the other horrors to which human history is a testimony may be the price paid for Popper's world 3. It is, I suppose, understandable to decide the price is too steep, but such an attitude strikes me as sadly adolescent. If the price we pay for life is death, then our children are a symbol of an unresolvable nootemporal conflict. Would a deconstructionist deconstruct the long and painful process of giving children a history, a sense of self, and, most importantly, a set of values? Guppies, which carry their history in their genes, have a terribly faint identity and rigidly hardwired values. To some this may be an attractive model for human life, but I reserve the right to accuse people who champion it of moral laxity and abdication of responsibility. It is, I believe, an evolutionary imperative that human beings assume the burden of the unresolvable conflicts of nootemporality if they are to engage in the tragic process of creating beautiful and terrible solutions to problems that do not exist among creatures with dim identities. And, if I am wrong and Fraser is correct and we are in the process of ceding our dominion over time to a new *umwelt*, then I propose that we do it graciously, with that wonderful combination of joy and sadness good parents have when they see their children leaving them for a larger world.

Chapter 12

An Evolutionary Epistemology

The World as Hierarchical System

An important consequence of Fraser's theory of temporal evolution is that as time evolves so does the knowable world. The major support for this claim comes from the extended *umwelt* principle. Uexküll's notion of a biological *umwelt* can be expanded to inform a general epistemology. The knowledge available to an entity is thereby defined as the sum of the possible information it can register (be in-formed by), manipulate, and transmit. Of course it is impossible that any given entity actually registers and transmits all the information it is, in principle, able to handle, so actual knowledge will always be less than that which defines an *umwelt*. An *umwelt* is always the horizon of potential knowledge accessible at a given evolutionary stage.

Consequently, there is no such thing as *the* world. Like everything else in an evolutionary cosmology, world is an evolving object whose definition becomes confused if level distinctions are not respected. Since the world is a function of the *umwelt* of entities experiencing it, there is literally more world available to entities occupying upper *umwelts* than for denizens of lower levels.

A second consequence of Fraser's theory is that it does not simply substitute biocentrism for anthropocentrism. An extended *umwelt* concept of knowledge extends to the entire universe. Every entity in the universe, from the most primitive to the most complex, exchanges information with its environment. A rock obeys the laws of Newtonian physics as well as the regularities of its molecular and particle levels. The idea of obeying laws, anthropomorphic though it may sound, is, I think, a perfectly appropriate way to describe the way in which entities can respond appropriately to ambient information. Thus, a rock falls in response to gravity (whether we understand gravity in relativistic terms, as a warp in space-time, or, in quantum terms, as the exchange of gravitons) because it has "knowledge" of its environment. Of course, this knowledge is not conscious, since consciousness does not belong to the eotemporal realm, but it is knowledge nonetheless. Since the extended *umwelt* principle suggests that knowledge is the exchange of information, and since everything in the universe exchanges some kinds of information with everything else, then we can postulate that knowledge is a hierarchically arranged continuum of increasingly powerful information-processing capabilities.

Representation and Truth

It goes without saying that at the heart of postmodern attacks on traditional epistemologies, as well as at the center of Derrida's critique of logocentrism, is a deep mistrust of the notion of representation. Any semiotics claiming that signifiers stand in some simple, univocal, delimitable, and punctual relation to signifieds or referents is judged to be an index of the metaphysical repression of textuality. It is in the nature of signs, according to Derrida, to be the traces of other signs, which are themselves nothing but traces. Furthermore, the present of a sign in consciousness is spread out between protention and retention, so, in addition to its ontological status as the trace-network of other signs, the sign is a temporal web of future and past traces. Simply, that of which the sign is a sign, the signified or the referent, is itself a sign. In the absences of a transcendental signified (or signifier), that is, of an element outside the play of the signifier that can function as absolute reference or standard, representation can only be thought of on the basis of Derrida's model of dissemination. Reference is never to something outside the game of reference, hence representation is essentially a kind of unmasterable game.

To the extent that truth has traditionally been defined as the correspondence between a statement and slice of reality (which could be the statement itself), that is, between a representation and a represented, it too falls under the sway of dissemination and the trace. If, as Derrida contends, the distinction between representation and represented is one of *différance*, one being the difference from and the deferral of the other, no principled theory of truth can be maintained. Truth becomes an effect of arche-writing, not its basis. A consequence of this notion is a widespread belief that truth and representation are repressive metaphysical impositions whose deconstruction promises some kind of liberation. I am repeatedly astounded at the number of well-meaning people, critics, philosophers, historians, and artists, who simply take it for granted that truth is precisely what they are supposed to undermine. This imperative depends on a vaguely defined and loosely conceptualized identity among truth, patriarchy, hierarchy, and oppression. For example, the issue of *Art Papers* (1986) to which I have already made several references, and which is subtitled "The Crisis in Knowledge: Poststructuralism Postmodernism Postmodernity," includes a "Lexicon: Guide for the Perplexed, II." In it *phallogocentrism* is defined as "the union or identity of logocentrism and phallocentrism, . . . a recasting in psychoanalytic terms of logocentrism's predisposition towards own-ness, the proper, linearity and hierarchy, and its assumption that meaning is transparent to investigation (and thus to mastery and manipulation)" (7). Representation (the "transparency of meaning") is conflated with linearity, hierarchy, mastery, and manipulation. To that we might add science, closure, totalization, and a probably endless series of other terms that add up to the concept of truth.

Although I agree with many of the ends espoused by certain deconstructionists, such as feminism, artistic experimentation, and social transformation, I believe that the skeptical position toward truth that they adopt as an expression of their liberationist ethic is at best ineffectual and at worse pernicious. In opposition to the widespread hostility toward the concept of truth, I would like to argue that truth, and its coconcept, representation, are crucial components of cosmic evolution whose repudiation by human beings would be morally questionable. The problem with deconstructive views of truth is that they tend to define the concept in a sweepingly homogenous way, invoking such suspect generalizations as "Western metaphysics" and "onto-logocentrism" which, even if they are assumed to be *sous-rature*, nevertheless do betray deconstruction's vaguely paranoid stance. If instead of understanding truth and representation in a grossly restrictive way, as the dream of the absolute reduction or obliteration of the signifier, we picture these concepts arranged in an evolutionary hierarchy, we could simultaneously dispense with the implicit Cartesian dualism of deconstruction as well as its self-serving assumption that truth and representation are filaments in some metaphysical spider's web.

By giving the natural world its due, that is, by acknowledging that no concept can be properly understood without taking into account its prehuman and human history, we might be able to arrest our culture's mad dash to deconstruct or otherwise disassemble anything that smacks of truth. By comparing the truth available to a chemical, to a lower animal, and to a human being, it might be possible to locate a hierarchy of truth and representation whose most complex component is Popper's world 3 or Fraser's sociotemporal *umwelt*. Such an interpretation of the concepts of truth and representation would define them as anything but oppressive. In fact, an evolutionary perspective could resurrect these notions from the casket built and supposedly nailed shut by recent critical theory.

The return on the sacrifice of an absolute frame of reference need not be infinite caution, but the possibility that we could once again entertain the notion of progress without guilt. In other words, giving up *the* truth for an evolutionary palimpsest of different truths might allow us to claim that it is precisely because absolute truth is an asymptotic limit that the amount of truth available to an entity is directly proportional to the complexity of its representations. Evolution is an economy, it makes up for the loss of metaphysical security by reinstating the sense of progress that many postmodern theorists think is an anachronism.

When Derrida interrogates the concepts of truth and representation insofar as they participate in the logocentric tradition's tendency to order the play of signification around the presence of immediately and unambiguously available signifieds he is, of course, correct. Any theory of human language, such as Wittgenstein's in *Tractatus Logico-Philosophicus* (1955), that privileges the near mathematical equality between a set of signifiers and a set of signifieds or referents is inherently weak. However, the question remains—is not the previous sentence correct because it is a better fit to a certain state of affairs than statements of a metaphysical turn? If not, then why should anyone believe it? If so, then what is at issue is not representation and truth per se, but certain inadequate representations of representation and certain incomplete theories of truth. Representation and truth are, as Derrida willingly concedes, indispensable. But whereas Derrida concedes their necessity grudgingly, seeing it as the resilient edifice of metaphysics that deconstruction must ceaselessly seek to undermine, I would like to suggest that only an anthropocentric view of truth and representation needs the corrective, or perhaps prophylactic, measures afforded by deconstruction.

An epistemology that is not confined to the world as it appears to human beings must base its notion of representation on a more general concept than phenomenological intentionality. To that end, I would like to propose an epistemology founded on the idea that representation is a process of information exchange. Being, as Frederick Turner once told me in conversation, is simply an information loop. Anything in the universe that is in-formed by its environment and in turn in-forms its surroundings can be considered as possessing Being. In short, Being is the exchange of information among beings. It follows that non-Being is defined by the absence of information exchange: an "entity" that neither informs or is informed simply is not.

If by representation is meant the ability to produce an inner map of external conditions, then it is clear that only higher animals are able to represent the world. However, if we consider representation as an evolving concept, then it appears that such biotemporal and nootemporal representation, clearly requiring a complex central nervous system, is simply an upper level description of a hierarchy constitutive of Being in general. Defined as the possibility of information exchange, or as the imprint of an outside upon some interior registering mechanism, Being is always representation. Although an entity existing in the prototemporal *umwelt*, such as an electron, represents its world in an essentially stochastic manner, to the extent that it exists at all it registers a certain amount of the information available in its statistical world. Similarly, a rock's sensitivity to the environment available to it is a kind of representation appropriate to the eotemporal *umwelt*, a range of information exchanges that is wider and more complex than that available to an electron, but primitive and narrow compared to the world of the crudest biological entity.

The concept of representation, therefore, must be seen as an evolving process of information transactions. I appreciate that many theorists might be uncomfortable about applying the notion of representation to entities unable to create an internal model of their environment, fearing that such an extension of a human concept may be nothing more than anthropomorphism. This problem, analogous to the one encountered earlier in discussing Fraser's evolutionary definition of language, is inevitable and unavoidable whenever a member of one *umwelt* uses an upper level language to describe a lower level one. In a way, there is no rebutting a skeptical critic who argues that it is, in principle, impossible to know if rocks represent anything. My only response to such a charge is that the skeptic's argument can be used in a Cartesian way to doubt anything, from the existence of other minds to the existence of a world in general, and that such idealism can no more be refuted than can the existence of colonies of invisible rabbits living in our homes. We must simply trust the dialectic between our senses and our minds to sketch a relatively accurate image of our environment, and, insofar as that environment seems to be best described by evolution, we must assume that even skeptical idealism has been made possible by its habitation in lower *umwelts*. We can, therefore, use Fraser's extended *umwelt* principle to argue that even though representation is a concept whose genesis as concept occurred in the nootemporal *umwelt*, because the nootemporal *umwelt* is itself a palimpsest of its evolution, the microstructure of nootemporal representation is a hierarchy of lower, less complex, kinds of representation.

If we define truth traditionally, as the correspondence between representation and represented, then an evolutionary theory of representation ought to yield an evolutionary theory of truth. A hierarchical epistemology suggests that, as we proceed up the levels of complexity constitutive of Fraser's *umwelts*, two things happen: representations become increasingly detached from stereotypical exchanges between entities and their environment, and, as a consequence, truth becomes increasingly problematic. Simply, the more time available to an entity, the more likely a mismatch between representation and represented.

In the atemporal *umwelt* there is no time for error, so neither is there time for truth. The atemporal *umwelt* describes a world in which decisions cannot be made, so that even the metaphor of Laplace's demon offers a view of determinism too weak to describe adequately this integrative level in which the distinction between truth and falsehood is meaningless.

The prototemporal *umwelt*, subsisting in a smeared-out time, defines a kind of truth that is essentially stochastic. Of all the *umwelts*, the prototemporal perhaps best approximates a world sketched out according to the protocols of deconstruction. In this disseminated *umwelt*, truth follows the logic of arche-writing: a relatively uncontrolled, vaguely delimited result of the corporate action of traces and traces of traces. All the stochastic textual effects that Derrida postulates as the repressed of logocentrism are, in fact, the truth available to an integrative level in which time is weakly separated from space (the becoming-time of space and the becoming-space of time). Prototemporal representation is hardly the adequacy between signifier and signified, or between symbol and reality, but the fuzzy commerce among fuzzy trace-networks. When the universe consisted exclusively of quantum mechanical entities, truth was a self-bootstrapping collocation of different likelihoods.

Logocentrism elegantly describes eotemporal epistemology. In fact, the eotemporal *umwelt* can be mapped quite successfully onto Derrida's concept of metaphysics. In this deterministic, Laplacian level, truth is rigidly causal. Whereas the atemporal *umwelt* is *before* truth and error, and the prototemporal *umwelt* describes a relation between truth and error that is weakly differentiated and fundamentally stochastic, the eotemporal world defines a kind of truth characterized by determinable fidelity to, and deviation from, symmetrical causal sequences. For example, the regularities in the eotemporal *umwelt* demand that two hydrogen atoms and one oxygen atom can combine to form water, and that water can be reduced to the same constituents. H_2O, then, is an eotemporal description of truth, and H_3O an eotemporal description of error. That this might seem counterintuitive, or, as suggested above, anthropocentric, is, to repeat, the result of forgetting that truth is a nootemporal concept being used, under the authority of the extended *umwelt* principle, to generate a lower level description. If we accept the level specificity of eotemporal representation and truth, then we are in a position to qualify them as the tendency for eotemporal entities to assume fixed configurations as defined by the laws of physics and chemistry. In other words, to a certain, level-specific extent, eotemporal entities "know" the lawfulness of their *umwelt* and obey it for the most part. This is why science works. And yet, since the universe is not, as most of the nineteenth century thought, a perfect machine designed by God to work smoothly forever, but an evolving system open to chance and capable of generating waste and novelty, eotemporal regularities are not followed slavishly. If they were, the universe would not have evolved after the emergence of eotemporality. Events like the attempted creation of H_3O happen routinely, and even though many of these deviations pass away as natural monstrosities, certain of them increase the available complexity in the universe so as to create selective pressures for their survival. Of these, certainly the most significant was biogenesis.

With the emergence of plant and animal life, a kind of truth that begins to approximate classic philosophical epistemologies comes into being. Darwinian evolution yields a central nervous system and, with it, internal maps of the external world. Insofar as they allow for a time lag between stimulus and response, these time lags give biotemporal entities more time to consider alternatives. It is precisely the delay of biotemporality, the ability to determine present action using archival information and glimpses of possible futures, that both creates a larger world and a more precarious one. In other words, biotemporal entities have at once more truth and more error available to them. Because a dog possesses some deliberative capability, it can find nutrition in forms it would not normally encounter, thereby increasing its chances of nutrition were its usual prey to disappear. However, the price it must pay for this increased nutritive flexibility is that it can be fooled into trusting a human being with a net behind his or her back.

As with evolution in general, an increase in freedom, that is, an expansion of the world, simultaneously expands the range of choices available and the range of possible errors. As Fraser argues, greater freedom implies greater conflict. Therefore, the concept of truth might be defined as a hierarchy of increasing freedom to choose and increasing sources of poor choice. The biotemporal *umwelt*, with its developing ability to extract salient features from the world and to manipulate them internally through abstraction and recombination, develops a kind of truth that has evolved beyond metaphysics but that has not yet developed the neural capacity to conceptualize metaphysics as something in need of deconstruction.

Saul Kripke's version of Wittgenstein neatly summarizes the conflict inherent in the nootemporal *umwelt*. Simply, Kripke repeats Borges's parenthetical challenge to the reader toward the end of "The Library of Babel."

(An *n* number of possible languages use the same vocabulary; in some of them, the symbol *library* allows the correct definition *a ubiquitous and lasting system of hexagonal galleries*, but *library* is *bread* or *pyramid* or anything else, and these seven words which define it have another value. You who read me, are You sure of understanding my language?) (Borges 1964, 58)

Borges's narrator calls into question the reader's presupposition that he or she knows the rules for reading that are operative at the moment of reading. Similarly, Kripke interprets Wittgenstein's famous principle of language games, as developed in *Philosophical Investigations*, to mean that one can never be certain which language rules are being observed during a linguistic event. In the absence of a set of transcendental metarules to serve as a stabilizing template, it is never possible to know apodictically in which language game one is engaged. In Derridian terms, since discourse has no metaphysical ballast to secure its signs, it is possibly already another text at the moment of its transmission and reception.

As an idealization of an exclusively nootemporal epistemology, the principle of language game slippage is an accurate, though limited, account of how the mind processes language. However, because both Wittgenstein and Derrida fail to consider the evolutionary history of language, they tend to overemphasize language's potential for slippage at the expense of its capacity to enable the collapse of possibility into actuality.

The nootemporal *umwelt* continues the biotemporal world's tendency toward an increasing habitation in the hypothetical. Long-term memory, symbolic thought, and, especially, language give the nootemporal *umwelt* a sharp temporal asymmetry between an infinite past (first cause) and an infinite future (eschatology). Within the space carved out by these temporal poles, the nootemporal world has time enough to create labyrinths as complex as those devised by Borges, Derrida, or Wittgenstein. It is a token of the flexibility of the huge human neocortex that it can inhabit deconstructed worlds. However, I think that there are two reasons why a deconstructive theory of representation and truth is inadequate.

Although the nootemporal *umwelt* is certainly capable of generating deconstructive skepticism, since nootemporality is also its own embedded hierarchical microstructure, there is no such thing as simple nootemporal truth. The human neocortex is rooted in the evolutionary successes of its lower *umwelts* for which Derridian or Wittgensteinian skepticism has no meaning. In other words, since human beings are not simply their upper level neocortical world, the truth of a representation is dependent upon the entire evolutionary hierarchy of which the nootemporal is a partial record. In fact, it is only through a radical Cartesian dualism that language can be conceptualized in a Derridian way. If, on the contrary, we concede that the truth of language is a vast hierarchy of different, level-specific truths and languages, then deconstruction begins to appear as a continuation of the least nuanced of nineteenth-century philosophical idealisms. The Other is not simply the human other, but the otherness of the natural world whose emergent feature we are. This Other also has a say in what constitutes truth, and to ignore it is to commit the most grievous of chauvinistic imperialisms.

The features of nootemporality described by Derrida are the price paid for the genuine evolutionary advantage of our residence in a complex integrative level: the flexibility to make choices, most of which are simply unavailable in lower *umwelts*. There is a widespread, but to my mind, erroneous, view that complexity and choice, like society and the individual, are opponents in a zero-sum game. In fact, although greater complexity does require more sophisticated methods of information management, the evolutionary advantage of complexity is that it allows for flexible responses to an environment, which includes, as perhaps its major component, language. Complexity is selected for by evolution because it enlarges the numbers and kinds of decisions an organism can make. Ultimately, survival depends on making choices, not on deconstructing them. Of course, nootemporality does require an extraordinarily complex hierarchical, heterarchical, and recursive neural mechanism to both generate its world and to respond to it flexibly, and such neural complexity inevitably gives rise to conflicts and aporias unthinkable at lower levels. It is precisely this cost of neural complexity that Derrida and Wittgenstein falsely posit as the essence of the human habitation in language, ignoring that what is bought with deconstruction is the ability to sacrifice the ghosts surrounding a possibility in the cruel, but beautiful work of decision.

Regardless of whether sociotemporality does or does not constitute a new *umwelt*, it is likely that the explosion of information technologies is altering the nature of truth and representation. In other words, if Fraser is right, the time-compact globe is becoming an entity in its own right with its own means of representation and truth assessment. If I am right, then sociotemporality is, as it always has, making nootemporal truth and representation more complex. In either case, it is possible to speculate on the epistemological implications of a world increasingly penetrated by relays of information.

In a context largely defined by Fraser's notion of a time-compact globe, Lyotard claims that truth is becoming increasingly uninteresting in a postmodern world.

> The question (overt or implied) now asked by the professionalist student, the State, or institutions of higher education is no longer 'Is it true?' but 'What use is it?' . . . Seen in this light, what we are approaching is not the end of knowledge—quite the contrary. Data banks are the Encyclopedia of tomorrow. They transcend the capacity of each of their users. They are "nature" for postmodern man. (1984, 51)

At the end of his study, Lyotard suggests that the future of knowledge is either in a totalitarian hoarding of information or in the democratic availability of information to the public. The first possibility is a kind of hybrid composed of Foucault's vision of the disciplinary society, Baudrillard's era of the simulacrum, Derrida's worldwide computer, and Orwell's *Nineteen Eight-Four*. The second possibility, in which the terrorist attempt to make different language games isomorphic is renounced, is, for Lyotard, a model of a postmodern world that obeys the human desire for freedom and justice.

In general, postmodern analyses of truth tend to divide themselves into optimistic camps, such as that described by Lyotard, and pessimistic ones, such as that described by Fraser and Derrida. Usually, the debate concerns the exact nature of knowledge in a world largely dominated by computerized information technologies. Simply, is the sociotemporal *umwelt* leading to a global control of knowledge, manipulating people by smearing out representational differences and substituting simulacra for representeds, or is it pointing in the direction of such informational mayhem that there will be room left in the interstices of knowledge for individual freedom? On one side is the global computer, on the other deconstructive interventions.

With the proviso that sociotemporality is difficult to describe at best, I would like to suggest a third possibility. I agree with Lyotard that sociotemporal truth and representation will increasingly inhabit computerized information relays. In fact, I suspect that sociotemporality will witness the increasing identification of ontology and epistemology; what *is* will be increasingly governed by what is *known*. Already experiments in virtual reality are beginning to render the boundary between Being and representation somewhat hazy. Just as nootemporality increases the spectrum of choices available to an entity to include counterfactual ones, sociotemporality will make choosing futures much less dependent on the regularities of lower *umwelts*. However, I do not believe that the implications of such a view need fall into one of the two camps outlined above, and this for two reasons. First, although less tied to lower *umwelts* than nootemporality, sociotemporality will nevertheless be constrained by its evolutionary past. Second, although potentially far more ominous than nootemporality, sociotemporality is also potentially far more auspicious. If the imperative to choose responsibly is not abdicated by our sociotemporal future, then it is possible to imagine a world of unprecedented fecundity and productivity. That this world will also be tragic, fragile, anxious, and rife with conflict to an equally unprecedented degree seems to be obvious, but, as I argued earlier, such is the price of freedom. In sum, then, as opposed to the typical deconstructive and postmodern visions of sociotemporality, I hypothesize that, as truth becomes increasingly performative, as representations gradually replace representeds as the definers of Being, and as the range and quality of information available to control, manipulate, and communicate increases exponentially, it is possible, although by no means inevitable, to imagine a world in which human beings, through their participation in sociotemporal communities, take part in the increasing democratization of information technologies, availability of information resources, and control over the nature of their Being. Of course, everything could go to hell in a handbasket. There are no guarantees in an evolutionary epistemology.

Having sketched the nature of truth and representation at the various integrative levels described by Fraser, I would like to make a number of general observations on the philosophical implications of an evolutionary epistemology. An evolutionary view of representation and truth considers these concepts as embedded hierarchies of often tangled levels. Derrida is correct insofar as he suggests that there is no such thing as *the* truth or *the* concept of representation. However, his view is limited because it is either anthropocentric or prone to level confusion. Specifically, by positing that the essence of logocentric notions of representation is a nostalgia for what never existed, pure unmediated presence, and, furthermore, that truth has always been structured by the presupposition that Being must be defined by something like Husserl's principle of principles, Derrida erects a man who is part boogey but mainly straw. I would suggest that the metaphysics that Derrida derides is little else than the desire to finesse the conflicts inherent in the nootemporal and sociotemporal *umwelts* by a retreat to the relative simplicity and predictability of the eotemporal. I am not arguing that such nostalgia for presence has been incorrectly diagnosed by Derrida, nor that his sense of its inevitable recrudescence is misguided. On the contrary, and to borrow from Sartre's existentialism, logocentric rigidity represents the temptation to flee from the hard work of freedom. In other words, logocentrism is time regression, the attempt to recapture what did, in fact, once exist but which has been both surpassed and enveloped by subsequent evolutionary phases.

If deconstruction were simply a vigilant watch on the perhaps universal tendency to abdicate freedom for the limited pleasures of determinacy, it would be a useful, though limited, cautionary philosophical and ideological gesture. However, deconstruction does not just warn against logocentric calcification, it suggests that metaphysics is actually the repression of an "underlying" structure of reference traces that Derrida labels dissemination, textuality, and arche-writing. At the level of arche-writing, representation runs rampant; in the absence of any transcendental anchor, truth becomes a mirage. In opposition to Derrida, I am claiming that the proper antidote to logocentrism is not dissemination, but a systemic view of the human mind and human culture as a palimpsest of their evolution. Such a position would have the beneficent effect of providing both a needed conservative ballast on rampant reference and the tools necessary for innovation. Evolution is the history of previous successful solutions to the problem of existence. In a fundamentally Hegelian way, evolution does not abandon inherited inventions, but incorporates them into subsequent levels as their skeleton. If, as is becoming increasingly clear, evolution's overall vector is away from determinism and toward self-correcting and self-organizing systems, then the human brain, when viewed as a component of its social interconnectedness, may, in fact, be the most complex entity in the universe and the most free.

On the issue of freedom, I am in agreement with Derrida. Like him, I advocate freedom from metaphysical calcification. However, I suggest that freedom does not stem from a Cartesian gesture of decapitation or from the phenomenological epoché, but from an acknowledgment of the deep evolutionary history of minds and societies. In other words, freedom can only stem from a base of stability, and our evolutionary past offers precisely such a support for the élans of human creativity. Of course, stability and innovation are relative things. There was a time when some sort of fish was the most inventive and unpredictable entity in the universe. Its freedom was paid for by billions of years of prior evolution, just as ours has been paid for by an inheritance that includes what now appears to be the fish's sluggishly deterministic world. But, just as the fish evolved because it did not forget the wisdom of the primitive beasts out of which it emerged, human beings can be free only if they pay for their freedom with memory. Just as we build memorials to our war dead, lest subsequent generations forget the blood upon which they stand, human beings must be vigilant to remember, with both humility and arrogance, the glories and holocausts of evolution. Anything less then that, any constructivist forgetting of the fish's sacrifices, confuses the short-lived and hollow illusion of freedom offered by deconstructive analysis with the genuine freedom bought by attention to the past we carry within us.

Having sketched the outlines of an evolutionary theory of representation and truth, I will now consider two specific kinds of knowledge available to human beings. The first, knowledge as shared representation, opens the possibility of direct communication between human beings and the natural world. The second, knowledge as representations of the world, suggests a way to avoid the idealizing tendencies of contructivist theories of scientific knowledge.

It should be noted that the remainder of part 2, but especially the next two sections, will be concerned primarily with knowledge from a nootemporal perspective, that is, with questions concerning human epistemology. Although some attempt will be made to speculate on the nature of sociotemporal knowledge, such efforts will be centered on the impact of sociotemporality on nootemporal knowledge. Even if a semiautonomous sociotemporal *umwelt* has knowledge of the world from its perspective, I suspect that it is structurally impossible for a nootemporal creature like myself to have any but the fuzziest sense of what the experience of such knowledge might be.

Knowledge as Shared Representational Modes

In my initial exposition of the extended *umwelt* principle, I mentioned Fraser's hypothesis that residents of an upper *umwelt* can experience the more restricted worlds of lower *umwelts* by engaging in a kind of time travel. It is still not clear, however, in what sense such continuity is to be understood. In this section and the one that follows, I hypothesize that the extended *umwelt* principle may have one of two modes. The first, possible only for nootemporal and biotemporal beings, is to represent something as object. The second, a mode of knowledge available to the entire world, is to represent the way something represents the world. The former, experience as indirect representation or knowledge as knowledge of something, is the subject of the next section. In this section, I would like to address the possibility that knowledge may be understood as shared knowledge—that is, as the direct experience of the representational modes of lower *umwelts*.

The kind of shared experience I have in mind is not that afforded by the human imagination. Human beings, and possibly other mammals, are able to represent information that is not accessible to their sense organs. In fact, our ability to exist in counterfactual worlds, in bizarre scientific hypotheses such as Hawking's imaginary time, Everett's many worlds view of quantum mechanics, or even the standard Copenhagen interpretation of the quantum world, and in the teleologies and eschatologies of traditional mythological and theological speculation, is clearly a cornerstone of the incredible plasticity and inventiveness of the nootemporal *umwelt*. We could, therefore, suppose that the extended *umwelt* principle relies exclusively on our imaginative faculty. Although the imagination is an important aspect of the enormous span of the nootemporal world, to suggest that communication with lower *umwelts* occurs solely through the imaginative faculty leaves the extended *umwelt* principle open to charges of idealism or anthropic imperialism. In other words, if all we know of the nonhuman world is filtered through nootemporal representations, such as scientific theories and imaginative recreations, then there is no possibility for empathy with prehuman creatures and things.

All nonhierarchical epistemologies must reduce human communication with non-nootemporal entities to heavy distortion at best and narcissism at worst. The only way to entertain the possibility of a kind of direct commerce with the world is if we conceive of the universe as a hierarchical system in which the uppers levels contain, as their microstructure, lower levels. Human communication with lower *umwelts* becomes possible, then, because we *are*, in part, these levels, or, to put the matter slightly differently, because these levels are actually earlier versions of ourselves upon which evolution based its subsequent development but which it never abandoned.

Such an evolutionary, hierarchical view of shared knowledge resolves the old dilemma of interlevel otherness. Clearly communication with something that is totally alien would be impossible, yet communication with an other conceived of as a version of oneself is the essence of solipsism. If, however, other entities in our world are evolutionary stages of which we are still composed, then communication is neither impossible nor superfluous. The notion of hierarchy gives the other its dignity while relieving it of the burden of pure and unbreachable alterity.

Therefore, the idealist dangers of the top-down kind of communication implied by the imagination model are mitigated if to it we add a level-specific model. This model suggests that, since the world of a given evolutionary level includes the worlds of lower integrative levels, the general modes of knowledge opened up by a specific *umwelt*, although not its specific representations, are available to the higher *umwelts*. In other words, it is possible to imagine a resident of an upper level *umwelt* directly experiencing lower level worlds because the hierarchical structure of the higher *umwelt* includes, as its fine structure, the information-processing technologies of the lower integrative levels. Needless to say, by direct experience I do not mean something like what Derrida understands to be the dream of metaphysics—the erasure of the signifier. All experience is representation, that much goes without saying. My point is that a hierarchically arranged entity can experience its constituent levels in two ways:

with top-down representations of a given *umwelt* and with level-specific representations of the world as experienced by that *umwelt*.

A simple example might help. Let us compare the *umwelts* of a rock (eotemporal), a rat (biotemporal), and a human (nootemporal). I am claiming that the human can participate directly in the worlds of the rock and rat in two ways.

First, imagination allows the human to attempt to see the world as if he or she were a rat or a rock. Although this approach has undeniable advantages, it is perhaps a better description of how a human being acquires human knowledge than how he or she communicates with lower *umwelts*. Actors pretending they are rats or rocks are de jure doomed to failure because, among other things, rats and rocks cannot pretend.

Second, insofar as the nootemporal *umwelt* includes the biotemporal and the eotemporal, the human can experience the worlds of a rat or a rock. For example, when I walk, I have biotemporal knowledge through my muscles and my autonomic nervous system. When I fall, when I am subjected to acceleration, and when I demonstrate the physical law that two objects cannot occupy the same space, my experience is eotemporal.

Perhaps the most important consequence of this hypothesis is that it claims that human knowledge need not be actually or potentially conscious. Even Freud, who did more than anyone else to popularize the idea of an unconscious, could never conceptualize the unconscious as anything but a relatively sophisticated brain process. Freud's id may be primitive, but it is certainly no more primitive than the biotemporal *umwelt*. I am suggesting that level-specific knowledge of the world of a rat or a rock is, for the most part, so primitive that it is, in principle, unavailable to conscious reflection except as a top-down theory or fiction. The reason for this is quite simple: most of the universe's lower *umwelts* do not include something like consciousness, so the knowledge available to them cannot include nootemporal (or advanced biotemporal) consciousness. It is becoming increasingly clear in such fields as neurophysiology and neural net artificial intelligence that the conscious part of the brain sits atop an immense and tangled hierarchy of subconscious processes. Perhaps the best demonstration of this claim is through introspection on introspection. A little introspection reveals how remarkably inefficient introspection is. No amount of introspection can reveal anything but upper level mind events. When it comes to the majority of the brain's work, introspection is useless. Try to figure out how words come to you as you speak the most banal of sentences to get my point. Therefore, if even the great bulk of upper level brain events are unconscious, then a fortiori events occurring in lower mental or physical *umwelts* are essentially unconscious. When I stand up and walk, I am using a part of my nervous system that I share with a rat, and because a rat's brain is not large enough to allow self-reflection, I am (in principle) not in a position to raise my direct knowledge of walking to consciousness. A rock's *umwelt* is orders of magnitude smaller than a rat's, since it does not include the world opened up by a nervous system. Yet, when a human falls, his or her body has knowledge of gravity that is identical to the knowledge that a rock can possess. In short, the theory of direct, shared knowledge claims that a hierarchically arranged system can experience directly the *kinds* of knowledge typically associated with its embedded layers, but, because such knowledge must be level-specific, it occurs mainly below the level of conscious awareness.

I would like to add a note of caution to this theory of interlevel communication. If it needed to monitor the functioning of every neuron, a human brain would crumble under the weight of its own officiousness. In fact, as Douglas Hofstadter (1980) argues, hierarchical systems tend to seal off lower level information from direct higher level awareness except in the form of "chunked" summaries. Thus, an architect need not know how to manufacture nails in order to design a house. Instead, he or she relies on chunked knowledge of nail making, namely that it is possible to have a contractor order them from a manufacturer. I appear, therefore, to be contradicting myself. On the one hand I am claiming that Fraser's extended *umwelt* principle enables interlevel communication, on the other I am acknowledging that, for the most part, higher levels abjure the clumsiness of lower level detail for the usefulness of chunked summaries. However, I think that the contradiction can be resolved if we are careful to distinguish between two kinds of information available to a hierarchical system.

The first, Hofstadter's, is a kind of translation of lower level information into a form that is useful at an upper level. Chunking is a summary of lower level processes encoded in upper level language.

For example, when I press "save" on my computer, I am chunking a series of commands and paths written in machine language that I do not need to understand; when I turn on my radio, I am chunking its circuitry and the laws of electromagnetism; and when I move my arm, I am chunking the laws of biology, chemistry, and physics. Hofstadter's concept of chunking, therefore, sacrifices precision for flexibility and direct knowledge of lower level events for the pragmatic advantages of delegation.

As opposed to chunking, Fraser's extended *umwelt* principle suggests that besides summaries of lower level information written, as it were, in upper level languages, levels in a hierarchical system have direct access to their own microstructure. Thus, whereas my brain works best when the various societies of neurons of which it is composed send each other, and especially the complex supersocieties that probably constitute consciousness, chunked summaries of their work, I, as a holistic organism, nevertheless have knowledge of the kind of knowledge to which my individual neurons are open. Of course, neurons are rather primitive biotemporal entities, well below the threshold of consciousness, so my level-specific knowledge of my neurons cannot be conscious. Furthermore, the biological usefulness of neurons is not in "how" they know, but in "what" they know, and to that I only have access in a highly chunked way. Nevertheless, since neurons are part of me, and since their *umwelt* describes a horizon of possible knowledge, I too have direct knowledge of the kinds of information exchanges they are open to.

Because the concept of selfhood has all too frequently been restricted to that part of a human being that is self-conscious, such lower level knowledge tends to be neglected or denied. It is only when we reject the phenomenological reduction of the self to consciousness that the economy between chunking and the extended *umwelt* principle as direct representation can be articulated. Whereas much contemporary theory considers hierarchies as oppressive and ethically suspect, I am arguing that a kind of genuine connectedness with nature is possible precisely *because* human beings are part of an immense natural hierarchy. Of course such level-specific communion with lower *umwelts* should not obscure what is properly and remarkably human, the stunning freedom of the nootemporal bought, in part, through the sacrifices implicit in chunking. However, if, as many feminist and ecologist theorists maintain, a crucial concern of our postmodern society should be the establishment of a genuinely respectful relation to nature, I believe it is important for our souls that we remember such commerce is possible due in large measure to nature's passion for hierarchy.

Indirect Representation

The kind of level-specific knowledge described in the previous section constitutes the basic, precritical connectedness of upper levels in Fraser's hierarchy with the levels beneath them. Although its importance cannot be stressed enough, insofar as it serves as a kind of glue uniting disparate elements in a hierarchy, it is nevertheless knowledge that is for the most part unavailable in useable conscious form for nootemporal creatures. In other words, although direct knowledge connects human beings with the rest of the universe, it does so largely at an subconscious level, so it is not available for the proper work of nootemporality—the creation of theories, hypotheses, or works of art except at a presomatic and somatic level.

This section will deal with the common notion of representation, knowledge as the extraction of information from an object. I would like to add, at the outset, that the difference between knowledge as direct representation and knowledge as indirect representation is not always clear. It would, in fact, be exceedingly difficult to isolate their contributions to our knowledge of the world. In actuality, I assume that they are always inextricably intertwined, each doubtlessly influencing the other's modes of information processing. Nevertheless, I think that it is useful to treat them separately both for reasons of clarity and because relation does not mean identity; that two kinds of knowledge might always be in a position to influence each other does not mean that they are indistinguishable.

The dominant contemporary epistemology is constructivism. A weak form of constructivism states the truism that all nootemporal representations are human constructions. The more common radical constructivist position argues that all human knowledge, including scientific knowledge, is purely the product of historical, economic, and institutional pressures. In what follows, I will criticize radical constructivism for committing a level confusion by conflating nootemporal constraints on scientific knowledge with the capacity of science to model lower *umwelts*. Then, I will attempt to surpass constructivist limitations by presenting a general theory of nootemporal epistemology that addresses the relation between knowledge and that of which it is knowledge from a hierarchical evolutionary perspective.

Scientific truth is part of larger epistemological category, the ability of residents in the nootemporal *umwelt* to make upper level description of both upper level and lower level phenomena. I accept as a guiding premise Derrida's view that any theory of representation that postulates the possibility of a general and universal one-to-one relation between mind events and world events, that is, a logocentric concept of representation, clearly needs modification. The mind is an emergent feature of the biological world, specifically it is the systemic, parallel, and partially distributed organization of the brain's biochemistry. As an emergent feature of the biotemporal *umwelt*, the nootemporal brain would be redundant were it simply the mirror of nature. However, I do not abjure mimetic theories of representation, as long as mirroring is clearly distinguished from imitation. The mind is not a mirror of nature, it imitates nature. To mirror is to create a lifeless copy of something assumed to be "out there." To imitate, on the contrary, is not to reproduce an object, but a process. The mind imitates nature in the sense that nature is not, as nearly the entire philosophical tradition would have it, a stable object of phenomenological intentionality or a Cartesian automaton, but an active, spontaneous, generative, hierarchical, and creative evolutionary process. The mind simply does the work of nature at a higher pitch, that is, it is more active, spontaneous, generative, hierarchical, and creative than the lower evolutionary levels of which it is composed.

As one ascends the evolutionary ladder, an entity's environment increasingly becomes a factor of the entity's own activity. In other words, evolution is increasingly performative. At the level of human beings, there is an intricate feedback relation between the world as perceived by individual minds and the world that is performed into being by various interpretative communities. Material products of human minds, such as clocks, are clearly real. But, as Popper has argued, nonmaterial, world 3 products, such as theories, interpretations, works of art, nations, marriages, and institutions, are equally, and perhaps in their impact on the lives of people, more real. The mind, therefore, especially in its essential commerce with sociotemporality, is an active participant in deciding the nature of the universe of which it is the product.

Assuming a traditional correspondence theory of truth, there is clearly no such thing as *the* truth at the nootemporal level. A seemingly innocent statement about the eotemporal world, such as "Water is composed of hydrogen and oxygen," can be surprisingly problematic. The nootemporal world is so complex that, even when it is engaged in describing an *umwelt* that time has collapsed into relative stability, it can muddy things up with infusions of higher level information. Thus, Wittgenstein's demon can always claim that "Water is composed of hydrogen and oxygen," or some chemical-mathematical representation of the same fact, was meant as a poetic evocation of mood rather than as a denotative statement. It is undeniable that such confusion is always possible. And, although we are able to use history, institutions, gestures, and linguistic markers more or less successfully to engage in context control, thereby specifying which level-specific language is currently operative, the kinds of context slippage signaled by Wittgenstein and Derrida are an unavoidable component of nootemporal representations.

However, I think that the sort of constructivism that maintains that interpretative contexts have no basis beyond the contingent stability lent by nootemporal institutional, political, and historical determinations mistakes the price paid for nootemporal truth with the truth itself. For example, although science is undoubtedly a nootemporal cultural phenomenon and, as such, clearly a human construction subject to political, economic, historical, and gender pressures, its existence in world 3 by no means exhausts the range of its reference. Thus, while it is undoubtedly true that even an innocent-sounding claim such as "The dominant hemisphere of the brain is involved in the production and reception of language" is rife with complexity, from its level-specific claims to pre-nootemporal *umwelts* to the metaphorical and cultural nature of such terms as *dominant, production,* and *reception,* it is by no means clear that the historical forces or epistemes that make such semiotic resonances possible fully determine the claim's epistemological value.

A radical constructivist view of science is anthropocentric insofar as it ignores the hierarchical nature of the universe. By way of contrast, a modest realist position would maintain that a function of science, though by no means its only function, is to allow human beings to employ a particular nootemporal formalism, mathematics, in order to communicate with the natural world. In other words, science attempts to translate the languages of our evolutionary past into nootemporal terms. It chooses mathematics because, as Fraser suggests, mathematics is an upper level translation of the fundamental mathematical reality of the lower *umwelts*. To put the matter simply, science works, it has cross-cultural instrumental efficacy, because nature is mathematical enough to respond to the scientist's equations. The inverse square law of gravitation is not a sociopolitical construct except on a trivial level—on the contrary, it is the translation into nootemporal terms of certain mathematical principles underlying the eotemporal *umwelt*. Thus, physics, chemistry, and biology are what Ilya Prigogine calls "a dialogue with nature," that is, a dialogue with the extant remains of past evolutionary inventions. In other words, science is a conscious peek into our past. To claim otherwise smacks suspiciously of the worst kind of Renaissance humanist creationism: the belief that "man," which in its contemporary incarnation becomes "institutions," is the measure of all things. Humans may have the largest ruler, but theirs is not the only one.

An evolutionary epistemology would eschew metaphysical certainty and constructivist smugness in favor of conceptualizing knowledge as a range of probabilities. In general, I hypothesize that, from the perspective of Popper's world 3 (the human world of culture and language), the probability of correctly mapping a given cosmic level increases with its decreasing complexity and malleability. The more primitive layers of the universe have a high probability of being represented adequately because they are simple and determinate enough to be mapped by the mathematical formalisms employed by the natural sciences. That is why experiments on lower *umwelt* regularities are repeatable and conform to the scientific method in general. Therefore, we should expect that the probability for objective knowledge increases as the object of inquiry decreases in complexity.

I should hasten to add that all of Fraser's *umwelts* are infinitely complex; however, since (as modern mathematics has shown us) not all infinities are equally large, it is possible to claim that lower *umwelts* are, in fact, both infinitely complex yet much simpler than upper *umwelts*. I would also add that these lower levels can be mapped using other representational means, such as literal and metaphoric natural language. Such representations tend to have a higher probability of correctly mapping the referent than nootemporal representations of nootemporal objects, but, since they are inherently more complex than quantitative formalisms, they can never approach the high probability of correspondence to lower *umwelts* enjoyed by mathematics. Of course, they frequently do not aspire to such rigor, thereby making its probability a moot point. In general, using natural language rather than mathematics to represent the natural world sacrifices determinism for flexibility and semantic richness. My basic point, however, is that scientific epistemology is so well represented by a correspondence theory of truth because atemporal, prototemporal, and eotemporal objects and processes are relatively simple and determined systems conducive to rigorous mapping by mathematical formalisms.

The intermediate levels of cosmic evolution, the social sciences, are too complex and too ductile for adequate quantitative mapping, yet not so complex and ductile that such mapping is completely useless. Therefore, the social sciences are best represented by a combination of mathematics and natural language. This kind of hybrid representational system is able to map a much greater and more complex range of information than can the natural sciences, in part because it must include, as its microstructure, Popper's world 1, but it must pay for its power with a lower probability of accurate correspondence between map and object.

The nootemporal representations of nootemporal objects, the humanities and the arts, deal with a fabulously complex evolutionary level that is still in the process of creating itself, so the rigor of traditional mathematics (an exception, perhaps, is chaos theory, about which much will be said in part 3) is nearly useless in representing it. At the nootemporal, the correspondence theory of truth is vitiated by the complexity of the object of representation, the complexity of the medium of representation (natural language and the arts), by the fact that, since representation and represented are partially on the same evolutionary level, representation is frequently self-reflexive and prone to continual self-modification, by the necessity to respect the constraints imposed by the lower *umwelts*, and by the fact that the level itself is largely inchoate. Therefore, the modes of representation typically applied to nootemporal fields like the arts and the humanities are rich enough to summarize an enormous amount of information, but their robustness must be bought at the price of a relatively low probability of a strict correspondence with their representeds. As such, they are better figured as paintings than as maps. In general, nootemporal representations tend to become more map-like as the object *umwelt* becomes simpler, and more painting-like as the object *umwelt* becomes more complex.

In fact, it is here that Derridian deconstruction, Wittgensteinian skepticism, and Foucauldian historicism appear to be fruitful epistemologies. There are several reasons for this. First, there are certainly constructivist pressures on all nootemporal truth determinations. Second, a Gödelian kind of dynamic suggests that self-reference always leaves a margin of undecidability or incompleteness. Third, nootemporality, especially in its interface with Popper's world 3 and Fraser's sociotemporality, has not been totally invented yet, so its callowness seems to preclude classic truth representation. Fourth, to the extent that nootemporality is primarily futural, it is unclear how a statement about what has yet to come into being could possibly be held accountable to standards for truth. In fact, at the nootemporal level, epistemology and ontology, or knowledge and that of which it is knowledge, are frequently indistinguishable. And, if Fraser's speculations concerning the emergence of a new evolutionary level, the time-compact globe, are accurate, this merging of epistemology and ontology will continue. More and more of reality may become virtual, although, as I have said on several occasions, I do not believe that we are witnessing the ascendancy of the similacrum as described by Baudrillard.

Although the potential for grafting and misappropriation increases greatly when nootemporality represents itself, since nootemporal truth claims are, by the very nature of nootemporal freedom, inherently unstable, I do not think that it is necessary to follow deconstruction into the relativist abyss. Even purely nootemporal truth claims, such as those pertaining to aesthetic objects, can, I think, be weighed against standards. That is, as long as we do not commit level confusions and expect nootemporal truth claims to approach the objectivity possible when referring to the lower *umwelts*, it is possible to rescue nootemporal epistemology from the debilitating antifoundationalist positions of current deconstructive and postmodern theory. Specifically, in the next chapter, I will argue that it is possible to use an evolutionary epistemology to suggest a theory of literature and literary criticism that respects both the ambiguities of the human world and its anchorage in the lower *umwelts*.

In sum, an evolutionary epistemology is able to account for the qualitative difference between truth claims in the arts and humanities, the social sciences, and the natural sciences by arguing that the very notion of truth must be applied in a level-specific manner. The kind of constructivist epistemology to which Derrida subscribes is inadequate because it neglects the hierarchical nature of truth. That is, although Derrida correctly assesses the provisional nature of representations of nootemporal objects, he incorrectly extends their ductility to all representations. Furthermore, by ignoring the fact that even nootemporal representations are constrained by their microstructure—by the higher probability of a correspondence between representation and represented at the level of the nested lower *umwelt* components of nootemporal representations—Derrida's deconstruction of truth and representation condemns itself to being a limited and regional enterprise.

Chapter 13

Collapsing the Literary Function

The gist of the preceding chapter is that nootemporal truth involves the construction of models whose accuracy can only be partially gauged by comparison with the physical and cultural environment. The reason for this is that, while some of these models involve the prehuman *umwelts* (that is, emergent events that have already, so to speak, solidified) or the nootemporal past (previous cultural developments, ideas, works of art, or political institutions), the major vector of nootemporality is toward the future.

Of course, even when dealing with already stabilized cultural contents, truth cannot be conceived of as a one-to-one relation between representation and represented. There are two basic reasons for this. First, the nootemporal represented, being a recent and marvelously complex evolutionary development, is still highly malleable. Since it is still in the process of inventing itself, especially as it is expanded by its sociotemporal components, it is unlikely that nootemporality can be represented in a totally rigorous way. Second, since in the nootemporal *umwelt* representation and represented are partially at the same level of description, an inevitable element of Gödelian incompleteness and paradox creeps in. Perhaps the simplest way of describing this Gödelian limit on adequateness is to observe that nootemporal representations are themselves part of the world they describe. In other words, participancy or performativity in nootemporal representation complicate the applicability of truth criteria that are relatively straightforward when dealing with more primitive integrative levels.

These problems are compounded when nootemporal representation is involved with modeling the future. In that case, it is clearly difficult to imagine how a correspondence theory of truth could be meaningful. How can the adequacy between representation and represented be judged when the represented does not yet exist? And yet, I suspect that future modeling may be the most important work that humans do. Furthermore, I believe that, as opposed to science, which models the past, it is art that best performs the crucial function of modeling the future. The question, then, becomes one of value. It is rather simple to assess the value of a scientific claim—the scientific method provides an elegant and nonauthoritarian way to determine the truth value of a scientific theory. It is, however, much more difficult to gauge the truth value of artistic models. We have, in fact, arrived at a crucial question, the question of standards in aesthetic judgment.

Although I hope that the conclusions reached in this chapter might prove applicable to the other arts, I would like to broach the issue of truth or standards in aesthetic work by limiting my focus to literature and criticism. As has been the general practice in this book, I will begin the analysis of literary truth by presenting the difficulties inherent in a deconstructive view of the issue. Then I will attempt to enlist an evolutionary framework to suggest a resolution to these problems. Using the epistemology described in chapter 12 as a foundation, I will present a theory of literature and criticism that is essentially compatible with the recent work in genetic and cultural evolution known as sociobiology.[1]

Despite the widespread belief that deconstruction is devoted to the transgression of limits, I believe that the theoretical and practical consequence of deconstructive principles is a kind of textual idealism. I have already outlined the key axioms of deconstruction, such as indeterminacy of meaning, lack of closure, and rampant textual displacement. Insofar as deconstruction has been seen as a methodology to be applied to the criticism of literature, its fundamental premise is that all literary texts are essentially resistant to totalizing interpretation.

It is clear, however, that deconstruction is not concerned primarily with literature. Properly speaking, Derrida's work is an attack on traditional ontologies and epistemologies. Derrida claims that the relation between consciousness and its intentional objects is itself propped on the abyss of difference, writing, or text. In other words, Derrida's most radical argument is that the world itself is a kind of text, as are human minds, and that the relation between them (and, of course, the relations among humans) are, roughly speaking, iso-morphic with the relation between a critic and a book. Textuality is not something reserved for literary texts—it is, according to Derrida, a fundamental ontological state. Consequently, to the extent that experience is reading, Derridian indeterminacy, or arche-writing, is the deepest attribute of Being. Just as Thales said that all is water, Derrida says that all is text.

A deconstructive view of the relations among world, literary text, and critical text would see them as a nexus of textual connec-tions. Since all "real" things are the products of arche-writing, all texts are incessantly bleeding into one another. The deconstructionist argues that there is nothing outside the text because there is nothing but text. Literature, criticism, all forms of writing, thought, experi-ence, the material world: all are simply different hypostatizations of an underlying arche-writing. Consequently, it is impossible to assign fixed identities to anything. If any identity is merely a temporary crystallization in a hyperfluid, multidimensional set of circuits, then, insofar as they are provisional reifications of an underlying protean dance, literature, criticism, and reality are eminently deconstructible metaphysical concepts.

If the natural world, the social world, literature, and criticism are all text, and if the deconstructive critic obsessively demonstrates that any attempt to adopt a standpoint in any one of these in order to evaluate the others is necessarily doomed, it follows that a decon-structive analysis must deemphasize what it perceives as metaphysi-cal identities and relations in order to focus on their organizing princi-ple: *différance* or textuality. At this level, distinctions between self and world, self and other, self and literature, literature and criticism, and culture and nature, insomuch as they are themselves derived from arche-writing, are understood as repressive, ontotheological dichoto-mies. A philosophy of difference, deconstruction must ultimately es-chew the differences that every human culture has employed to erect its cosmology for a kind of rarefied Ur-difference, dissemination, where, paradoxically, everything ends up looking strangely like everything else.

As opposed to Derrida, for whom literature is ultimately the *différance* of other textual manifestations, I would like to argue that literature and criticism are the scene of nootemporal truth formation and, as such, have specific evolutionary value. Whereas for the deconstructionist the relations between literature and criticism are characterized by such fluidity that even the identity of these realms is rendered suspect, I will claim that these relations are best described by a decrease in "textuality" and a resultant increase in the possibility of identity.

I believe that deconstruction misconstrues the purpose of literary criticism because its theory of literary language is flawed. In its essentially Cartesian fashion, deconstruction treats literature as if it were a transcendental phenomenological category. That is, like all idealisms, deconstruction gives an exclusively upper level description of structures that are, in fact, a dialectic between their purely nootemporal characteristics and that portion of their evolutionary history that serves as bottom-up support. By way of contrast, I suggest that an adequate theory of literature and criticism must entail what sociobiologists Lumsden and Wilson (1983) call gene-culture coevolution.

I hypothesize that literature is an emergent evolutionary development of Homo sapiens, a development whose chief survival value involves the creation of a privileged arena, Popper's world 3, in which the culture represents, evaluates, criticizes, and, when necessary, reformulates, its most fundamental hypotheses about the world. According to this theory, literature constitutes what Turner (1986) calls a "liminal space," a kind of marketplace in which the decisions a human society must make concerning its very nature are given or denied value.

Whereas deconstruction is unable to speculate about the evolutionary origin of literature, preferring to see it an "always already" existing snakes' nest of unstable traces, a sociobiological theory of literature postulates that the value of literature stems from its ability to aid a culture in the difficult work of choosing its future. Specifically, literature is seen as simultaneously generating cultural possibilities and ordering them in a hierarchy that enables decision. "Great literature," according to Frederick Turner, "is the achievement of an unmistakable clarity and intelligibility in the teeth of the proclivity of every word, every sentence, to collapse entropically into divine indeterminacy" (1985, 34–35). In other words, the identity of great literature does not, as deconstruction would have us believe, melt into the interstices of its multiple textual layers. On the contrary, the best literary works orchestrate their component structures so that out of their harmonic interaction can emerge an experience of heightened unity and identity.

Probably stemming from the rituals of early human hominids, literature offers human society the opportunity to consider those crucial decisions that affect the nature of its Being, decisions concerning its gods (theology), its place in the universe (cosmology), its morals (ethics), its social organization (kinship or politics), its techniques for assigning value to objects (economics), its preferred ways of defining knowledge and of assigning the requirements for making truthful statements (epistemology), its definitions of Being (ontology), and its understanding of art (aesthetics). Literature enhances the survival potential of humans through its ability to perform the following three functions: (1) to enable innovation by generating variations of previous cultural choices, thereby offering positive or negative models of the essential issues I have outlined; (2) to highlight certain variations in such a way as to situate them in a hierarchy of value; and (3) to present these delimited choices to the culture for debate and criticism. In sum, I am suggesting that literature is most fruitfully understood as an activity through which human beings create models of the possible effects of concrete choices. These models allow the culture to evaluate itself and either to make certain adaptations or to reinforce and transmit those elements that it perceives as healthy and productive.

Art in general, and literature in particular, are not, as in the Kantian tradition to which deconstruction belongs, disinterested activities cut off from the natural world. On the contrary, they have an evolutionary purpose. Lumsden and Wilson hypothesize that culture works in conjunction with genetics to alter the very nature of evolution.

> As a result [of gene-culture coevolution], evolution is accelerated. The genes continue to hold culture on a leash; in each generation the prevailing epigenetic rules of mental development affect which cultural innovations will be invented and which will be adopted. Yet culture is not just a passive entity. It is a force so powerful in its own right that it drags the genes along. Working as a rapid mutator, it throws new variations into the teeth of natural selection and changes the epigenetic rules across generations. (1983, 154)

Inasmuch as literature is an integral component of culture, it can be seen as a powerful evolutionary adaptation that renders somewhat obsolete the sloppily stochastic pattern of random mutation characteristic of purely genetic natural selection. By presenting a society with alternatives in an incomparably more efficient manner than mere genetic variation and by introducing an element of control in the form of the possibility of intersubjective debate and criticism, culture in general, and, within culture, literature in particular, participate in the evolution of evolution itself, from ponderous genetic mutation and selection to nimble cultural change. In other words, literature participates in the establishment of gene-culture coevolution, a positive feedback system in which genes generate epigenetic rules for cultural practice and cultural practice creates selective pressures for the survival of certain genes. In fact, not only does literature participate in gene-culture coevolution, it probably helped bring it about. Activities as demanding as the creation and reception of literature must have exerted selective pressures on the brain of early humans favoring the increasingly complex neural organization necessary to contain the tremendous amount of information constitutive of culture. Through a feedback loop, literature helped to create the genetics able to support it. In other words, in a quite literal way, literature invented human beings.

If, as I am proposing, literature is a model through which factual and counterfactual possibilities may be staged so that human societies can make choices in a safer and faster manner than if they had to depend exclusively on empirical information, then what is at stake in the liminal space of literature—indeed what the notion of choice is all about—is the capacity to identify and rank possibilities. The ability to identify such important concepts as self, other, society, and environment has positive survival value. As I argued in chapter 5, one of the major directions of evolution is toward the generation of entities better able to make distinctions. Whereas deconstruction wages war on the concept of identity, I am claiming that literature is one of the technologies Homo sapiens have developed to render themselves more social by becoming more individuated.

Let me hasten to add that my view rests on the premise that there is no such thing as identity if unreasonable demands are made on the term. Since the concept of identity is central to a sociobiological theory of literature and literary criticism, I will briefly recapitulate the central arguments of chapter 5. Basically, I maintain that the major direction of biological evolution has been toward greater individual identity. For example, let us consider the separate organisms constituting a jellyfish colony. For all intents and purposes, jellyfish are a perfectly deconstructed species, since they are simply a structure (text) consisting of primitive animals that, because they are all essentially identical, have no identity. Indeed, most lower forms of life are based on the principle of repetition, either literally, as when single-cell animals divide, or metaphorically, as in the case of colonial jellyfish, where each organism within the colony is much like all the others. As we proceed up the evolutionary scale, however, individual animals become increasingly differentiated from others of their species, thereby enabling the formation of articulated social groups that, in such complex taxa as hominids, involve intergroup role distinctions, divisions of labor, and intricate social hierarchies.

The ability to make finer and more nuanced distinctions can be thought of as a kind of exchange. The more individuated an organism becomes, the more its sense of "oneness" with its environment and its conspecifics is sacrificed for the alienation and conflict that accompany differentiation. For example, among the costs of being human is a high degree of alienation not only from other humans but also from one's self, due largely to the fact that our huge brains are able to generate conflicting desires, self-consciousness, internalized others, and awareness of death. Individuation, however, yields a remarkable profit. For one thing, the social environment of higher animals is richer than that of lower animals, so that group and self divisions are compensated for by the increasing opportunities for play, nurture, love, and altruism. But there is an even greater profit: as animals possess more finely delineated identities, the more information they are able to exchange with a world partially of their own making. Consequently, as I have argued, the better able an organism is to individuate itself and its environment, the more world it has at its disposal. And the larger its world, the greater its potential freedom. By the time we reach the human stage, individual identity is sharply defined, group identification has become so crucial that our genetically inherited neural structure cannot reach anything approaching its potential without extensive socialization, and our world has increased to include objects and concepts that have no objective correlative.

Deconstruction, in concert with much contemporary critical theory, views identity as a major tool of the ontotheological repression of textuality. I find this pervasive view both erroneous and profoundly dangerous. Not only is identity not the strongman of some metaphysical Gestapo, but its formation is a seminal activity of human beings. Our brains routinely organize a jumble of sensory information into objects, and a tangle of memories, hopes, desires, thoughts, and anticipations into a sense of self. We do this effortlessly, without any conscious executive control, because our brains have evolved in such a manner so as to construct relatively stable identities out of seas of ghostly data. The explanation for our identity making is quite simple, yet it has been routinely ignored in recent critical theory: were we unable to organize ourselves and our world in such a way as to erect unity out of diversity, actuality out of potentiality, and reality out of traces, we would soon succumb to those elements in our environment that threaten us and, sooner or later, we would either cease to exist, give way to a species better able to map its surroundings, or evolve into such a species.

Let me repeat that I am not using the word *identity* in any absolutist or idealist way. Our identity making is, as Derrida correctly claims, highly fluid. If, instead of the metaphor of presence that Derrida so vigorously contests, we use the metaphor of a probability curve, then it will be clear that identity making need not be unconditional to be a real and concrete biological activity. Identity can thus be defined as the probability that a concept will settle into a recognizable pattern that is distinguishable from other patterns. The higher that probability, the stronger the identity, the lower, the more it resembles Derrida's dissemination.

Whereas Derrida uses his notion of arche-trace to argue the essential continuity between surface identities, I am claiming that differentiation, as the origin of identity, is, in fact, all there is to identity. We can dispense with the deconstruction of identity once we no longer harbor a nostalgia for absolute purity. We are left with a lesser or greater probability of differentiation and are content to call that identity. Furthermore, as opposed to Derrida, for whom identity, in its filiation with what he calls Western metaphysics, is ultimately something to be deconstructed, a sociobiological perspective postulates that identity, as a token of advanced evolution, is a positive concept that ought to be affirmed. Identity enables choice. It is the abdication of the plenum of indeterminacy for the dangerous, but essential, vulnerability of the determinate. Werner Heisenberg, one of the sources of modernist uncertainty, was all too aware of the perhaps tragic necessity of decision.

> In the practical decisions of life it will scarcely ever be possible to go through all the arguments in favor of or against one possible decision, and one will therefore always have to act on insufficient evidence. The decision finally takes place by pushing away all the arguments—both those that have been understood and others that might come up through further deliberation—and by cutting off all further pondering. . . . Even the most important decisions in life must always contain this inevitable element of irrationality. The decision itself is necessary, since there must be something to rely upon, some principle to guide our actions. Without such a firm stand our own actions would lose all force. (1958, 205)

Only a creature with an identity can die, only a decision can be wrong. Conversely, of course, only something that can die can be said to live, and only that which can be wrong can make correct or valuable choices. That Derrida would doubtless insist that these binary oppositions be deconstructed would be proof enough of the devolutionary nature of his enterprise. Biological evolution (and, I suspect, cosmic evolution) proceeds via decision, and decision is only possible if a manageable number of choices have been identified and ranked according to relative value.

Before proceeding to discuss the role of criticism in this evolutionary model of literature, let me anticipate an objection to this theory. The power and beauty of literature have long been associated with its evocative ambiguity. Most readers, both naive ones and literary critics, are quickly bored by literature that is overly simplistic. It would seem that literature is most enthralling when, as the deconstructionists would argue in essential agreement with the New Critics, it resists calcification. This objection is well founded in the main. Its error is not in the position it defends, but in the implications it draws from that position. These implications are best illustrated if we consider the converse of the ambiguity claim. If anything is more vapid than excessive simplicity, it is excessive complication. A purely ambiguous work would be unreadable for any reader except one for whom ambiguity were a theoretically desirable quality, and then, as I will shortly argue, such a theory would appreciably reduce the work's ambiguity.

Controlled ambiguity, however, is certainly conducive to aesthetic pleasure. We are a complex animal, and we demand of our art a certain depth. This innate attraction to the multidimensional does not, however, invalidate the theory I am developing, for two reasons. First, literature is an inherently complex cultural phenomenon because it is tuned to a vast hierarchy of phylogenetic levels. We experience literature on all these levels, from its ability to stimulate our phylogenetically and ontogenetically earlier and more primitive brain components up to its ability to engage our higher cortical functions. Second, the theory does not demand univocal decisions. All that the theory requires is that literature identify concrete cultural possibilities. To identify, as I have noted, does not mean to reduce to unity. Identity is simply the probability that something can be distinguished from something else. A choice is impossible if it is not perceivable, and perception, as phenomenology has taught us, must be of an intentional object. In other words, this theory restores to literature its claim of innovation, as long as by innovation we understand the imaginative embodiment of a set of cultural choices that had, up to that point, existed only as pure indeterminate possibility. Reduction, in turn, is valuable in that it encourages decision. A culture that refuses to consider alternatives, either because it feels that it possesses the truth, or, as postmodern theory would have us believe, because it is convinced that no real choice is possible, is unable to adapt to changing physical or historical conditions, and is therefore vulnerable to absorption by other cultures, to internal decay, or, more probably, to both. Cultural acedia is as dangerous as cultural hubris. A vigorous literary tradition is both a defense against cultural gelation and, in its absence, a warning that such stiffening may already be far advanced and, what is even more dangerous, may be parading as revolutionary literary theory.

Let us now turn to criticism. The concept of criticism has two general meanings in contemporary literary studies. There is what Geoffrey Hartman (1981) calls criticism of the reporting or reviewing kind, the kind of criticism that generously aids a reader puzzled by a difficult or recalcitrant work. The other kind of criticism, what is currently called critical theory, is actually philosophy, or that branch of philosophy that has traditionally dealt with art, aesthetics. Despite their differences, however, both of these kinds of criticism perform what amounts to the same function. Inasmuch as practical criticism always has theoretical underpinnings and inasmuch as theory is only meaningful in the light of its possible realization, there is perhaps not much actual difference between the two. But even if their distinction were to be presumed, both can, in fact, be understood as limiting the range of possible meanings ascribable to a work of literature. Practical criticism does this openly and straightforwardly, telling the reader what a text means. Literary theory is a bit more subtle, but no less effective in its constricting function. Any coherent theory will tend to generate readings consistent with its fundamental principles. While this is surely obvious with critical theories such as Marxism or feminism, it might be objected that deconstruction produces the opposite effect. Deconstruction seeks to explode meaning, to open a text so that it can never be contained within any delimitable catalog of interpretations. Yet even here, I would argue, theory is performing its traditional function, the generation of a coherent hypothesis about how an object or a system functions. Perhaps the most powerful proponent of this view of theory is Popper, who argues that, in fact, there are no such things as pure sense data, that even the work of our sense organs is guided by the brain's active interpretation of inputs.

> [T]he neurophysiology of the eye and that of the brain suggest that the process involved in physical vision is not a passive one, but consists in an active interpretation of coded inputs. It is in many ways like problem solving by way of hypothesis. (Even the inputs are already partially interpreted by the receiving sense organ, and our sense organs themselves may be likened to hypotheses or theories—theories about the structure of our environment, and about the kind of information most needed and most useful to us.) (Popper and Eccles 1977, 45)

According to Popper, theory is defined as an active sorting, cataloging, comparing, and organizing of sensory information that occurs throughout the hierarchical structure of the nervous system, from the peripheral sense organs to the higher cognitive functions of the neocortex. Popper's position, that theory or hypothesis formation is a primary task of the central nervous system, can be extended to the domain of literary theory. Every theory of literature is an abstract network of relations, expectations, norms, and hierarchies that filters and arranges incoming data. As such, all literary theory is a hypothesis employed to make sense of literary texts.

Even deconstruction, then, is a relatively coherent theory that selects those elements of literary texts that fit into the nexus of decisions it has made concerning their relative value. Despite the pretensions of deconstructive critics to the generation of an untethered textual mobility, the fact is that deconstructive kinds of readings are no different in their schooling function than other sorts of analyses. Deconstructive criticism has a signature style, and the essays it generates tend to show a family resemblance. All those lexical, stylistic, and thematic markers that serve to identify any school of criticism are powerfully at work in both the work of Jacques Derrida and that of his acolytes. Deconstruction may claim to open up a Pandora's box of disseminated meanings; what it actually does is to repeat tirelessly the same kinds of readings, to search unflaggingly for and find the same sorts of textual aporias, to unearth obsessively the same kind of trace (*différance*, writing, hymen, *pharmakon*, etc.). To paraphrase Jerry Aline Flieger and myself, no deconstructive reading would ever fool a PMLA blind panel (Flieger and Argyros 1987).

Until recently, criticism has been viewed as playing a supporting role to the literary text. Lately, however, due primarily to the work of such Derridian critics as Hartman and J. Hillis Miller, there has been an attempt to elevate the status of criticism by postulating it as having always been a quasi-literary text. My view is that, if status is understood in terms of cultural influence, literature and criticism form a heterarchy; that is, either can, at the proper time, occupy the dominant position to which the other is subservient. I do think, however, that there is an important difference between criticism and literature. Whereas Hartman prefers to focus on the textual overlapping between literature and criticism, pointing out the narrative, metaphoric, and fictional elements they share, I would argue that criticism has a delimitable cultural function. Despite many fuzzy edges and overlappings with other discourses, criticism can be viewed as a set of theories about literature that are, for the most part, conscious and therefore available for social debate, rejection, or acceptance. As Robert Scholes argues: "And that is the whole function of criticism. It is a way of discovering how to choose, how to take some measure of responsibility for ourselves and for our world" (1985, 72).

Criticism, or the kind of analytic or philosophical discourse of which it is a subset, almost exclusively engages the neocortical regions of the brain, its primary sphere of influence being the dominant hemisphere of the cerebrum. Literature, on the other hand, can trigger a much wider range of neural and hormonal events. Especially in its performance, great literature tunes in to all the levels of the remarkable evolutionary palimpsest of our species' nervous system. As most theoreticians of literature from Aristotle on have known well, literature is as effective in speeding up breathing (a brain stem function) and in producing emotional response (probably a limbic system function) as in provoking temporal and spatial conceptualization (a function of the two hemispheres of the neocortex, and, probably, of their interaction across the corpus callosum). In other words, although literature's choices are partly accessible to the conscious, self-reflective level of the human brain, they also affect an enormous range of brain states, most of which are not directly available to conscious examination. Criticism, therefore, especially in Popper's sense of conscious theory formation, serves to further delineate those choices already made by literary works. Criticism reduces the complex psychic arsenal of a literary text (itself already a reduction of pure cultural possibility) to those categories of analytic or synthetic thought within the purview of the higher cortical functions, to the world 3 realm of conscious evaluation and selection.

Whether of the practical or of the theoretical variety, criticism performs what its etymology suggests, it separates and chooses. It separates what has already been separated, and chooses among previous choices. Whereas, for the deconstructive critic, criticism is a wedge thrust into the faults of a text in order further to crumble it, a sociobiological theory of literature views criticism as an instrument of hypothesis synthesis. Furthermore, such a theory postulates that the generation of synthetic theories of literary meaning participates in cultural value formation. Criticism, therefore, is a kind of intersubjective forum in which the various ethical, aesthetic, political, and philosophical variations identified and arranged by literature can be consciously evaluated. In other words, criticism chooses what it judges to be either a more valuable specific reading (because it has already chosen a more valuable theoretical position) or a more important philosophical view (because it has already developed that view in the act of encountering specific texts). In either case, criticism completes the work of literature: to sacrifice the adamantine sweep of undecidability to the necessity of choice.

Literature is a human activity through which the immensely complex structure of culture is provisionally collapsed into a number of concrete possibilities. (I am, of course, using the verb *to collapse* to suggest a filiation between the function of literature in culture and the role of the observer in quantum mechanics. In both cases, it is a question of a certain kind of choice.) These possibilities are either deemed to be desirable, and given value, or judged to be undesirable, and thereby devalued. In either case, literature offers human societies choices, and choice is crucial for a culture's survival. Criticism is a further restriction of the range of acceptable options. Criticism is a bet. Its success, therefore, depends less on the accuracy with which it analyzes the state of the present, than on its ability to predict, and perhaps influence, the future. In other words, just as a stock market analyst helps his or her client by recommending investment vehicles that he or she thinks will be more valuable in the future, the critic should aid a community of readers to choose appropriate interpretations of literary works with the understanding that, inasmuch as he or she is participating in literature's evolutionary role, his or her interpretations, like those of certain market analysts, may on occasion be performative.

The position maintained here, therefore, is the antipode of deconstructive literary theory. Whereas deconstruction argues that the concept of literature is an artificial hypostatization of a limitless and mobile text to which there is no outside, a sociobiological model of literature and criticism maintains that literature is an evolutionary adaptation of human culture that aids it in the precarious work of deciding its very nature. Of course, this nature can never be single or rigidly determined. Should that ever be the case, our species would be extremely vulnerable to unpredictable changes in our external or internal environment. In fact, it is a hallmark of human beings that we transcend the fixity of genetic determinism through gene-culture interaction. Literature can never offer the final mode of Being —or to use deconstructive terms, literature can never be an ontotheological essence—because that would make us as vulnerable to changing conditions as dinosaurs. I am arguing that, by reducing the synchronic diversity of cultural options to a manageable number, literature makes diachrony possible. Literature and literary criticism are part of an open-ended evolutionary pattern: the incessant sampling and subsequent adoption or rejection of possibilities that has enabled the breakneck speed of cultural development since the emergence of Homo sapiens from Homo erectus some 500,000 years ago.

In conclusion, literature can be thought of as an adaptation of Homo sapiens to facilitate the handing of the main baton of evolution from the biological or genetic realm to the cultural realm. It is important to add that I am not arguing a dualistic, or blank-text cultural position (similar to Foucault's for example). We are biological organisms, and as such much of our behavior, our ideas, and the forms of our relations are governed by our genetic makeup. However, as Lumsden and Wilson argue, the remarkable feature of human beings is that we have developed a partially autonomous kind of organization, culture, which, through its back-looping relation to the genetic level, has speeded up our evolution to an extent unprecedented in the animal world. Literature, then, is one of the ways in which our species both facilitates its choices and rewards itself for the pang that always accompanies the road not taken.

In its turn, criticism, whether practical or speculative, is a reduction of the variations generated by literature to the higher cortical level of concepts, hypotheses, and theories. Whereas good literature engages the entire brain, from the reptilian stem to the huge human neocortex, criticism tends to function primarily at the level of ideas.[2] As such, it serves the purpose of further defining the nature of the distinctions wrought by literature and of providing an intersubjective forum for the consideration and "criticism" of these choices.

Finally, the culture-literature-criticism network is an enormously complex feedforward and feedback system functioning on many levels simultaneously. Literature is both a part of culture and an instrument of cultural change; criticism is both parasitic on literature and an integral part of literary development; and, finally, literature/criticism interacts with the other components of culture, to both perform a cruel selection and to enable the healthy proliferation of new possibilities.

Chapter 14

Betting with Cultural Universals

How then, does such an evolutionary or sociobiological theory of literature help us to make aesthetic judgments? If, as I suggest, literature and criticism can be viewed as kinds of wagers, are we to assume that all bets are equally likely to be winning ones, or can they, to some degree, be evaluated in advance?

As I argue in chapter 6, although classical correspondence notions of truth are increasingly viable as a represented's *umwelt* becomes older and simpler, when dealing with noo/sociotemporal events such as literature and criticism, we must be content with a kind of probabilistic performative relation between a literary or critical representation and its possible effects on the culture.[1] In other words, truth is conceptualized as weakly predictable and marginally reproducible at this level. Consequently, the question of standards does not involve a metaphysically binding set of literary norms, but the possibility of evaluating noo/sociotemporal aesthetic events along a scale of greater or lesser likelihood to engender productive effects.

In general, the only way the future can be predicted is on the basis of past patterns. Such patterns range from the sphere of mathematical linearity (the next integer after n will be $n + 1$), to the somewhat lower certainty of quantum events (at the quantum level, specific events are totally unpredictable, but their corporate probabilities, the wave function, are known with a high degree of accuracy), to the increasingly more unpredictable, but still quite deterministic, events characteristic of the eotemporal and biotemporal *umwelts* (predicting solar eclipses, planetary orbits, estrus cycles, reflex responses, etc.), to weakly predictable events (population distributions, size of offspring, timing of earthquakes, etc.) to very weakly predictable events (weather patterns, the stock market, horse races, most noo/sociotemporal phenomena, etc.) to genuinely random events (a throw of dice, chance meetings, the New York City subway schedule, etc.). It will be noted that predictability tends to decrease with increasing systemic complexity, that is, as one goes up the evolutionary scale, but that this is not the case exhaustively, especially insofar as purely random events can be found at every integrative level. Furthermore, prediction techniques appropriate to one level frequently "jump" a level and prove useful at a much higher, or much lower, level. For example, the essentially statistical predictability at the quantum *umwelt* is the only way to make decent weather predictions or to predict genetic inheritance at the level of populations. Despite this messiness, however, it does appear that evolution yields a world which is increasingly less predictable and, as a consequence, increasingly free.

Whatever the probability of success or the nature of the forecast, all prediction assumes the existence of patterns in nature. Were nature not lawful in some way, that is, were it to offer no regularities at all, not only science, but also scientists would be impossible. Therefore, although the level specificity of the term should be respected, pattern-based predictability is the only concept that can lend itself to the development of a theory of aesthetic truth.

The next part treats what I believe to be the most exciting recent development in the study of apparently random processes, the still inchoate chaos theory. Therefore, as an introduction to that analysis, I would like to conclude this part with a few observations on the applicability of patterns to the study of aesthetic events. Although ever diligent not to find lawfulness where there is only accident, an evolutionary aesthetics realizes that choices, both creative and critical, must be made and that the best ones are usually made on the basis of the success or failure of previous choices. Specifically, this chapter suggests that the existence of cultural universals, or cross-cultural tendencies to organize the world in similar ways, could serve as a kind of foundation for aesthetic decision making that is neither parochial nor rigidly normative.

Since noo/sociotemporality has issued from lower *umwelts* and includes them as its microstructure, many of the patterns that the natural and social sciences have discovered could be of value in predicting the future. These patterns might be either formal or thematic. In general, they range from our genetic inheritance (epigenetic rules that predispose us to conceptualize our environment in certain ways, to prefer certain themes or formal devices, and to deem as valuable certain behaviors, objects, and structures), to the consequences of our embodiment (the tendency, for example, to see the world in terms of the basic binary oppositions highlighted by Lakoff and Johnson [1980]: In/Out, Up/Down, Container/Contained, Self/Other, etc.), to our existence in a universe in which Newtonian mechanics, Einsteinian relativity, and Heisenberg's equations both enable and limit what we can do and what we can know. In other words, the hierarchy of temporalities outlined by Fraser forms a kind of fundamental background against which our projects could be compared.

If the result of lower *umwelt* constraints on noo/sociotemporal events is indeed a series of patterns or cultural universals, then such knowledge could serve as a heuristic guide for both the production and the evaluation of literature, and art in general. Of course, it is not evident to a majority of contemporary theorists that the concept of lawfulness is applicable to human culture except in a purely local manner. Perhaps the major thrust of currently hegemonic "framework relativisms" such as deconstruction is that cultural uniformities are contingent historical phenomena having no predictive value. For example, although Foucault's regimes of truth/power are hypothesized to generate a tremendous number of regularities through a combination of disciplinary or channeling technologies, the point of Foucault's epistemes is that regimes of truth/power are radically relative and discontinuous—no information culled from one of them will necessarily be of value in analyzing another. Two other powerful contemporary proponents of this position are Richard Rorty (1989) and Barbara Hernstein Smith (1988), both of whom maintain that all values are radically contingent on social, institutional, economic, and ideological contexts.

I would suggest that such contextualist theories are the result of what Freud called the narcissism of small differences. Just as certain Greeks cannot see how alike Greeks and Turks are, preferring to create unbreachable gulfs out of small differences (specifically, religion), I think that framework relativists are simply too close to their field of study to see anything but the real, but overemphasized, differences separating cultures. I imagine that a Martian could not help but notice that an African bushman and a Dallas yuppie share much more than mainstream constructivists would care to admit.

Consider the following thought experiment: The yuppie is dropped into the middle of the bushman village. Furthermore, neither she nor the bushmen speak each other's language. It seems to me that the amount of information that could be exchanged from the very beginning is tremendous, and that in very little time very sophisticated and complex nonlinguistic communication would occur. Gradually, as the yuppie and the bushmen grow to understand each others' language, rituals, beliefs, etc., communication would approach, though perhaps never reach, the semantic richness possible between members of the same culture.

Why is this the case? One explanation is that human beings are so generalized that they adapt quickly to different cultural environments. This theory would maintain that the yuppie enters the bushman village as a Lockean blank slate and learns everything from scratch. However, given the enormous complexity of cultural knowledge, it stretches the thought experimenter's credulity to postulate that starting from absolutely no shared knowledge people from radically different cultures could quickly engage in complex communication.

A slight modification of the blank slate explanation would maintain that the yuppie and the bushmen initially share some cultural presuppositions and that these commonalities could serve as a basis for future exchanges. Although somewhat attractive, this theory contradicts itself since it assumes the existence of those shared cultural codes whose necessity it was intended to refute.

A much more satisfying explanation for cross-cultural communication is suggested by Hofstadter's ASU metaphor (1980). Hofstadter proposes the following thought experiment: Consider a map of the United States with all the geological features in their proper place but with no linguistic markers. Next, imagine that you are told to transform this bare-bones map into a road map for a projected trip. The point is to add names at all levels of detail, from states, mountain ranges, rivers, and major cities down to small byways, villages, parks, and streets. Hofstadter calls the result of this personalized map of the USA an ASU—an "Alternative Structure of the Union."

How much like a standard map of the USA will various peoples' ASUs be? Needless to say, there will be many variations. For example, close to home, an individual's ASU will tend to reproduce the

USA map quite well, while far from home we would expect that the match at the level of local detail would be rather poor. In other words, my ASU will be a very good match of the USA map around Manhattan (where I was brought up) but only remotely like it around Atlanta (where I have never been). Yet, all in all, almost all ASUs will be rather good approximations of the USA. Ask nearly anyone to create an itinerary that would get him or her from New York to Los Angeles and the odds are that he or she will make reasonably good choices. Of course, there are people who do not know where New York is (some of them living in New York), but the point here is not to argue for pure objective correlations, just for a statistically interesting commonality.

Why should most people's ASUs resemble each other globally while diverging locally? Hofstadter's answer is that most people have two general kinds of agreement on the nature of the map: they agree on the location of major cultural centers (cities like New York, San Francisco, or Los Angeles) and they are working with maps upon which a number of external geological reference points, such as lakes, mountains, or rivers, have been already inscribed. Although no two ASUs will be identical, two people comparing an itinerary will be able to communicate because their ASUs share enough information to assume some sort of common ground.

Of course, listening to two potential travelers argue over the best itinerary from Ithaca, New York, to Mountain Home, Arkansas, one might assume that their ASUs have nothing in common. One might then conclude that ASUs must be determined purely by their creator's specific geographic context. However, a sober look at even their ASUs will quickly convince the relativist skeptic that such local disagreement is only possible because of the huge amount of global information that is shared. In other words, they can argue about byroads because they are working with the same large-scale map.

The point of Hofstadter's metaphor is that it illustrates a way in which it is possible to conceive of isomorphism among different brains. The analogy works like this: The given geographic features of the map represent lower-level phenomena common to the environment of all human beings. Large cities represent core "symbols" that are based on these environmental givens. These chunked, upper-level neural societies represent concepts, classes, ideas, or images shared by a large majority of human beings, though not by any par-

ticular individual. Small towns and local features represent the idiosyncratic particulars that make human beings so delightfully distinctive. Roads are "triggering paths," the various neural pathways that
can be used to excite a given symbol. And a trip corresponds to a
thought, a complex interaction of symbols and triggering paths.
Hofstadter explains the significance of the analogy:

> The fact that all ASU's have some things in common, such as
> the East Coast, the West Coast, the Mississippi River, the Great
> Lakes, the Rockies, and many major cities and roads is analo-
> gous to the fact that we are all forced, by external realities, to
> construct certain class symbols and triggering paths in the same
> way. These core symbols are like the large cities, to which
> everyone can make reference without ambiguity. (1980, 375–76)

Let me, in a rather tentative way, suggest kinds of knowledge
that are equivalent to the geographic data on an ASU. Roughly speaking, the shape of the map itself, that it is a map and not a random
piece of paper, such things as its ink, paper, and chemistry correspond to what we share with the rest of the universe—the atemporal,
prototemporal, and eotemporal *umwelts*.

Geographical features such as the Rocky Mountains are our biotemporal heritage, especially our common heritage with the higher
primates. Here we find Kant's a prioris, thinking in terms of cause
and effect, the existential primitives such as in/out, us/them, and
up/down discussed by Lakoff and Johnson, as well as symbolic
thought, kinship, value hierarchies, division of labor, nurturing the
young, ritual, war, and possible aesthetics. In short, the Rocky
Mountains are our genetic ties with our mammalian past.

Major cities like New York would correspond to Chomsky's
hypothesized universal or deep semantics, such noo/sociotemporal
universals as long-term memory, natural language, belief in a deity,
the predisposition to organize the world in narrative, eschatological
cosmology, the fundaments of the imagination as analyzed by
Bachelard—fire, earth, wind, and water, respect for the dead, poetry,
music, dance, theater, architecture, agriculture, gardening, social eti-
quette, animal husbandry, face-to-face sexual intercourse; the assignment of positive value to love, generosity, altruism, sharing, commu-

nity, revenge, payment of debt, and righteous hatred; and the assignment of negative value to cheating, lying, stealing, adultery, murder, smallness of spirit, and snakes. That is, certain features, structures and dynamics of our world are so important to all human beings that we would be as likely to agree on their nature and meaning as any two U.S. citizens on the location of New York City.

Smaller cities such as St. Louis would be represented culturally by what the framework relativists always adduce as proof of the radical contingency of all meaning and value: the important regional cultural coloring lent to all the preceding. St. Louis represents regional style, taste, or predilection. Here is the difference between the Judeo-Christian creation story and that of the Hopi Indians, alternate forms of social organization, different embodiments of patriarchy, food preferences, subtle variations in kinship structure, and differences in the determination and administration of justice. It should be noted that although these cultural differences are real, their absoluteness must not be overemphasized. I may disagree with Muslims on the wisdom of eating pork, but our disagreement is made possible in the first place by all the cultural and biological rules upon which we agree, such as the nature of taboo, transgression, and reverence.

Finally, Mountain Home, Arkansas, is the tantalizing and utterly inexplicable phenomenon of local taste. However, since the private or the eccentric can constitute a crucial dose of variation or perturbation in cultural evolution, they are phenomena to be prized and cultivated. Here I would include historical contingencies, artistic genius, the French love of snails, and, in general, the irreducibly and deliciously unique point of view each individual or each minority brings into the social arena.

Sharing a largely common neural architecture and living in a world that, especially at the atemporal, prototemporal, eotemporal, and biotemporal levels, is fundamentally the same across cultures, it is not at all strange that most people map their environment (including symbols for other people and for themselves) in ways that are, for the most part, isomorphic. Therefore, Hofstadter believes that there is, in fact, much more transcultural commonality, especially at the more global level, than is commonly thought.

> The fact is that a large proportion of every human's network of
> symbols is *universal*. We simply take what is common to all of

us so much for granted that it is hard to see how much we have in common with other people. (1980, 376)

By focusing solely on cultural differences, theorists such as Derrida, Foucault, Smith, Feyerabend, and Rorty underestimate the amount of our evolutionary inheritance that is shared. Although I believe that cultural differences are an important component of our species' survival advantage, so I am in no way advocating the imposition of a set of cultural universals that imperialistically subsume all cultures into a rigid paradigm, I think that radical antifoundationalists have systematically ignored the basic fact that cultural differences have not descended from heaven but have been enabled by the huge arsenal of similarities all humans share. In other words, it is because there are cultural universals that local divergences are healthy injections of novelty into cultural evolution. By analogy, it is only because two players of chess agree on a basic set of rules that they can create unforeseen moves; in the absence of such a common ground, they could not even play chess, so innovation would vanish into a vacuous catalog of pure possibilities.

It is precisely this issue that prompts an instructive thought experiment by Lumsden and Wilson. Imagine, they say, that there are three different modes of intergenerational information transmission. One they label *eidylon*. The eidylons are a group in which all knowledge is encoded genetically. Because they must learn to be eidylons, they have the illusion of choice and development, but in fact what they learn is rigidly encoded in their genes. Even the illusion of choice is a genetically encoded mandate. The eidylons are a stunted culture, frozen onto a genetic track. Much like lower mammals, they confront their environment with stereotypical strategies of survival. As long as their environment remains stable, they survive quite well. A rock, after all, is better at some things than a human being. But in the face of novel situations, the eidylons' locked-in responses offer them no flexibility, so they are as vulnerable as a rock in the path of a steamroller.

A second limit-case culture is whimsically called *xenidrin* by Lumsden and Wilson. Xenidrins, although equally improbable and grotesque as eidylons, are actually what most contemporary cultural relativists and social constructivists maintain Homo sapiens indeed are. Xenidrins are blank-slate creatures. These radical Lockeans come into the world with no genetic predispositions. Whereas eidylons think they have free will, though in fact they do not since, in every concrete instance, the choices they think they make have already been made by their genes, the xenidrins live in a world in which all possibilities have an equal probability of realization. In contrast to the reductionist eidylons, the xenidrins are highly chunked creatures whose lower *umwelts* are effectively overwhelmed by cultural freedom. Without any genetic knowledge to channel their behavior, xenidrins are totally generalized. Their world is a Foucauldian succession of regimes of power/truth—a discontinuous series of culturally invented and constructed worldviews governing the nature of knowledge and of Being.

Lumsden and Wilson sum up the eidylon/xenidrin distinction as follows.

> The xenidrin mind is entirely the product of the accidents of history, the place they live in, the foods they encounter, and the stray inventions of words and gestures. If we watch eidylons and xenidrins for short periods of time, their outward behavior might appear similar or even identical. But a close inspection of the growth of their children would reveal radical differences in the way their minds work: exquisite automata versus brilliant driftwood, iron will versus protean fidelity. (1983, 56)

I believe that many well-meaning cultural critics distrust those who, like Lumsden and Wilson, attempt to present a genuinely interdisciplinary and holistic view of human culture informed by a biogenetic evolutionary perspective because they believe that any mention of evolution and genetics is tantamount to a reduction of human freedom to its eidylon caricature. As an antidote to this correct, but misplaced, fear, deconstructionists and social constructivists replace one caricature, the eidylon view of culture, with another, the xenidrin one. And yet, xenidrins are, in the end, no more free than the dronelike eidylons. The problem with xenidrin culture is that its members must continually reinvent the wheel. For example, it took evolution billions of years to come up with something like Chomsky's (1972) deep grammar, the universal predisposition toward certain constellations of syntactic and semantic rules. Rather than impeding the freedom and inventiveness of human language, deep grammar serves as the ground upon which the world's languages stand and through which they can communicate in non-trivial ways. In other words, deep grammar guarantees both difference from and respect for the Other. If no such deep grammar existed, humans would have to invent language with each generation. Let us imagine that a species evolved with precisely such a blank-slate mind. Would it not be highly likely that, in the struggle to survive, they would be supplanted eventually by a rival group that had evolved a brain able to transmit genetically the basic architecture of language so that their children could spend their crucial developmental years most efficiently learning, and learning to manipulate, the subtle complexities of one of a number of permitted languages? In general, xenidrinlike cultural transmission of information vital to a culture's survival is simply too cumbersome and inefficient and would, surprisingly quickly, be overwhelmed by an alternate means of inheritance.

> Even if a species could be created to resemble the xenidrins, with pure cultural transmission, evolution would eventually carry it from the blank slate and into a culture based on gene-culture transmission. We went on to calculate the average number of generations needed to take a xenidrin-like species away from its extreme condition. We found that the time is reduced to just a few generations if there are many choices available. (Lumsden and Wilson 1983, 60)

The third possible kind of information inheritance, adumbrated in the preceding quotation, is gene-culture transmission. Chomsky's deep grammar/surface grammar distinction is a perfect example of gene-culture inheritance. Basing his theories, in part, on the ability of children to create grammatically correct sentences when exposed only to either minimal or defective examples, Chomsky concludes that human beings are equipped with a kind of innate knowledge, a basic deep grammar that predisposes them toward certain syntactic, phonologic, and semantic structures. Chomsky's point is that language is not transmitted in an eidylon manner (otherwise we would all speak one language) or in xenidrin fashion (otherwise we could not explain the ease and efficiency of language acquisition), but a combination labeled by Lumsden and Wilson as gene-culture coevolution.

Evolution has bequeathed to us an incredible array of rules and regularities that serve as predispositions subject to cultural and environmental influences. In other words, culture is, indeed, the most powerful force in the lives of human beings, but its potency is not based on some supposed xenidrinlike autonomy. On the contrary, it is because culture has access to so much genetic deep-structure that it can allow human beings the freedom to be unpredictable. To repeat, gene-culture transmission does not minimize the role of culture in the development and transmission of information. In fact, as Aoki and Siekevitz (1988) argue, it appears that the very physical structure of the brain is sensitive to environmental forces and is routinely altered during early childhood. We are certainly not eidylons. Even lower animals are not, although they are more eidylonlike than Homo sapiens. On the contrary, we are the remarkable dialectic between old inventions that have become encoded in our genes and an openness to unforseen possibilities. So many of us can pretend that we are xenidrins precisely because we are not, because the freedom to ignore our evolutionary past is enabled by all the rules, principles, and predispositions we are spared from learning.

The idea of gene-culture coevolution is, I believe, an extraordinary resolution to the cultural universal—human freedom dilemma. If cultural universals were rigid we would be eidylons, easy prey to the environment or to a more protean culture. If we were totally free, with no cultural universals, we would be xenidrins, drunk with the romance of anarchy, and just as cruel, narcissistic, inefficient, and impotent as anarchists tend to be. Instead, gene-culture coevolution provides us with genetically encoded predispositions toward certain solutions to the problems presented by existence, solutions that free us up to make other, more pressing and more complex choices. In short, we are freer for having ASUs preinscribed with geographical and cultural features than if we had to start with a blank piece of paper every time we wished to take a trip.

Epigenetic rules—a combination of genetic and cultural transmission—predispose humans across various cultures to make certain sorts of decisions. Among these epigenetic rules Lumsden and Wilson list the following: incest avoidance, organization of colors into similar wavelength clusters centering around the four basic colors (blue, green, yellow, and red) perceived by the brain's visual apparatus, the preference of infants for particular shapes as well as the predictable changes in such preferences with increasing age, the common facial expressions to communicate "fear, loathing, anger, surprise, and happiness" (1983, 68), the tendency of newborns to prefer "sugars over plain water and in this descending order of preference: sucrose, fructose, and glucose" (69), typical anxiety responses of young children when facing strangers, and phobias.

> Phobias typically emerge full-blown after only a single unpleasant experience, and they are exceptionally difficult to eradicate, even when the victim is carefully reassured and coached by a psychiatrist. It is remarkable that the phobias are most easily evoked by many of the greatest dangers of mankind's ancient environment, including closed spaces, heights, thunderstorms, running water, snakes, and spiders. Of equal significance, phobias are rarely evoked by the greatest dangers of modern technological society, including guns, knives, automobiles, explosives, and electric sockets. Nothing could better illustrate the peculiar and occasionally obsolete rules by which the human mind is assembled, or the slowness of man to adapt to the dangers created by his own technological triumphs. (70)

That most cultural relativists are probably as afraid of snakes and spiders as most Amazon tribesmen should be food for thought. The point, of course, is not that epigenetic rules are rigidly binding prescriptions that determine the shape and direction of culture. Such biological determinism, along with its opposite, a blank slate kind of cultural determinism, are precisely what Lumsden and Wilson are criticizing. Their purpose is to rehabilitate the notion of free will in a way that is neither metaphysical nor reductionist. Our long evolutionary history has deposited layer upon layer of successful decision in our genes, and it is only by standing on the shoulders of the regularities that constitute our past that genuine free will is possible. In other words, epigenetic rules are simply the voice of our intersubjective and interspecies legacy; they are the influence of a demanding but loving teacher who knows that he or she can only pass on the gift of creativity to his or her students if he or she first carefully transmits the salient ideas and texts of their culture.

If we take the notion of cultural universality to indicate a statistically significant proclivity among all cultures to engage in certain similar practices and to cognize the world in similar ways, then the number of activities, structures, and conceptual frames common to all known cultures is staggering. Frederick Turner quotes anthropologist George Peter Murdock's list

> of items . . . which occur, so far as the author's knowledge goes, in every culture known to history or ethnography . . . age grading, athletic sports, bodily adornment, calendar, cleanliness training, community organization, cooking, cooperative labor, cosmology, courtship, dancing, decorative art, divination, division of labor, dream interpretation, education, eschatology, ethics, enthnobotany, etiquette, faith healing, family, feasting, firemaking, folklore, food taboos, funeral rites, housing, hygiene, incest taboos, inheritance rules, joking, kin-groups, kinship nomenclature, language, law, luck superstitions, magic, marriage, mealtimes, medicine, modesty concerning natural functions, mourning, music, mythology, natal care, pregnancy usages, property rights, propitiation of supernatural beings, puberty customs, religious ritual, residence rules, sexual restrictions, soul concepts, status differentiation, surgery, tool making, trade, visiting, weaning, and weather control. (Murdock 1968, 231)

To this list, Turner adds "combat, gifts, mime, friendship, lying, love, storytelling, murder taboos, and poetic meter"; certainly there are others. Without a doubt, not one of them will appear in identical form in two or more cultures. Yet, they are so recognizable cross-culturally that, like cities of various sizes on Hofstadter's ASU, they can be used to initiate sophisticated and complex communication between members of wildly different cultures.

Epigenetic rules can be thought of as the interstices between biology and culture, much like the relation between geological features and the cultural structures organized around them on an ASU. Cultural universals should not be imagined to be the imperialistic imposition of a hegemonic civilization on cultures unable to defend themselves with indigenous anthropologists, but as a token of the common evolutionary roots of all human beings. As I have argued, the direction of evolution is toward greater individuality and sociability. The individual, necessary to infuse unpredictable seeds of novelty into a culture, is, in fact, enabled and supported by those common bonds, norms, practices, rules, and codes that constitute a human culture. It is precisely because human culture is so complex that, in the absence of islands of stability such as the cultural universals outlined above, it would quickly succumb to the frenzy of its own freedom. Far from being the sticks of cultural oppression, cultural universals are a kind of secure and steady pole on which cultures can lean in order to be able to imagine the future.

If, as I am arguing, aesthetic production in general, and literature in particular, can only be judged adequately in relation to its as yet unrealized performances, and if such judgments must nevertheless be made if a culture is not to fall into the acedia of deeming everything or nothing valuable, then the only available option is to base decisions on those natural and cultural regularities, trends, and patterns whose own structure is a hierarchy of previous choices.

The kinds of cultural universals that prove useful to artists and critics can be divided into two categories: formal and thematic regularities. Even though, as much contemporary criticism has effectively shown, form and content are never simply exterior to each other, neither are they so implicated in each other that a classical division between them would be simply invalid. Therefore, while recognizing the somewhat artificial distinction I am maintaining, I would like to conclude this chapter by suggesting a few ways in which thematic and stylistic regularities could help create a useful map of literary judgment.

Turner speculates that one index of a literary work's value might be the number of cultural universals it embodies: "it would be tempting to propose that a work of literary art can be fairly accurately gauged for greatness of quality by the number of these items it contains, embodies, and thematizes" (1985, 26). If cultural universals are the cities with which a culture reinvents its own ASU, then it would indeed appear that the more of them it has at its disposal, the more likely that its map will be able to integrate predictable structure with the insanity of creation. It is to be hoped that a culture confident of its past will tend to treat it neither as a burden nor as a destiny, but as a gift.

In general, cross-cultural anthropological studies could yield a weighted list of the incidence and importance of various themes in human literary work. Although such a list would in no way constitute an absolute standard against which literary innovation would be gauged, it would, I suspect, be a stunningly accurate tool with which to make heuristic guesses of a work's potential importance. Specifically, I believe that such a list of cultural universals would include those themes that we have come to identify with the great works of Western literature: war, peace, illumination (coming to knowledge or its opposite, renouncing the quest for knowledge), transcendence, eschatology, teleology, socialization, freedom, fate, politics, morality, love, sacrifice, loyalty, hatred, revenge, tragedy, and whimsy, among others. Inclusion of such themes in a work of literature certainly does not guarantee success, but I think that their exclusion does invite failure.

Of course, it could be argued that hegemonic groups determine the value of certain themes, and that a sampling that included women, blacks, or whatever other disenfranchised group one chose to consult would yield a differently structured hierarchy (or, even though I doubt it, no hierarchy at all). I agree that groups at the margins ought to be able to vote in what constitutes our collective history and what might be the shape of our future, so I applaud such an expansion of anthropological inquiry, even though I suspect that most framework relativists might be sorely disappointed by results that, I think, would prove that although local interpretative communities might certainly differ in the relative weight they assign to cultural universals, their thematic ASU would not differ to the point of unrecognizability from the ASU of most other human cultures.

Form, of course, must be considered from a genre-specific perspective. It is needlessly procrustean to try to make general rules to which the lyric poem as well as the novel must conform. With that proviso, however, a number of hypotheses can be proposed concerning the formal properties of literary texts. Turner suspects that a biological auditory present yields a cross-cultural propensity for a three-second poetic line. Furthermore, the near universality of meter suggests that even the most radical attempt at free verse will, even despite itself, either incorporate some form of measure or, if not, be meaningful only when measured against the brain's formal expectations.

An even more speculative hypothesis, which will be defended in part 3, is that literary genres have a deep grammar that both unites them and creates the space for their obvious differences. This grammar, under siege in the contemporary critical environment, is narrative. Narrative is a remarkable invention of human beings, a technology with which literature can be simultaneously random and definite. Furthermore, even manifestly nonnarrative literature, such as the lyric poem, is, in fact, best conceptualized as kinds of holographic fragments of larger, ghost narratives that they presuppose and develop.

In addition to the three-second line, meter, and narrative, an evolutionary aesthetics might explore formal universals such as the relation between actors and audience in theater, the importance of the voice in poetry, chapter breaks in prose narrative, length of works, and the use of characters, descriptions, conventions signaling realism, fantasy, adventure, or comedy, implied narrators, metaphors, symbols, and allegories in all the genres.

The evolutionary aesthetics presented here suggests that human future projection cannot be purely free (although it can delude itself into thinking that it is), but must, if it is to be as free as possible, use the entirety of its past as a springboard. It is precisely because noo/sociotemporal truth is not metaphysical that we have a responsibility to base our creative sallies on the only kind of criteria that do not necessarily degenerate into an imperative for slavish and sterile imitation of the past: a sense of the trends and patterns that nature has manifested in the evolution and self-organization of matter and energy into those fragile and inventive natural entities that we are.

3

Chaos

Part 3 augments the evolutionary ontology and epistemology outlined in part 2 with ideas drawn from chaos theory. The capacity of chaotic systems to coordinate simultaneously the requirements of order and innovation is suggested as an alternative to both metaphysical and deconstructive views of the world. Evolution and chaos are conjoined to generate a hypothesis that most robust events and objects in nature and culture are the result of hierarchical, dynamical, feedback-dependent, and nonlinear processes. This chaotic-evolutionary worldview is then applied to such themes as the nature of time, mind, beauty, and ritual. Part 3 concludes with three speculative chapters investigating the future of narrative, the possible resuscitation of the notion of progress, and the relation between art and the sacred.

Chapter 15

A New Paradigm

The heliotrope can always be *relevé*. And it can always become a dried flower in a book. There is always, absent from every garden, a dried flower in a book. . . .

— Jacques Derrida

All the great cultural florescences began when the purpose of gardening changed from food for the body to food for the spirit. Poetry begins with "anthologies"—flower collections. . . . Poetry is gardening or cultivation of the language. A garden is the marriage of culture and nature—and their common source.

— Frederick Turner

A Word of Caution

In general, attempts to make common cause between the sciences and the humanities have been either banal or guilty of unwarranted inference. Claims that the nature of artistic creativity is much like the creativity necessary for scientific work, that scientists and humanists are merely dealing with the same world using different languages, or that science is a quantitative way of expressing what the arts embody metaphorically, can tend toward such generality that they end up saying practically nothing. Other kinds of arguments, such as those conflating quantum indeterminacy or Einsteinian relativity with appeals to the undecidability of cultural phenomena are frequently guilty of either getting their science wrong or of committing grievous level confusions. For example, it is by no means obvious that a state of affairs typical of the prototemporal *umwelt* should have any necessary bearing on noo/sociotemporal events. It may, but to

227

avoid the errors attendant upon reductionism, it will be necessary to employ an argument other than the typical one that suggests that recent discoveries in quantum mechanics prove that the universe is fundamentally indeterminate. In other words, it is horribly reductionist to suppose that quantum mechanics is the "deep" truth of Being that spreads its effects throughout the rest of the universe. If, as I have claimed earlier, the universe is the history of its complication, then it remains to be demonstrated how its most primitive and simple components should determine the characteristics of upper level structures. Quantum indeterminacy is an appropriate description of the behavior of particle/events on the order of subatomic particles, but it is nothing less than a bad faith explanation of why I muff my backhand in tennis.[1]

And yet, the thrust of this book is that there is, indeed, a means to repair the damage wrought by the Cartesian division of the universe into mindlike culture and bodylike nature. Virtually all the criticisms I have leveled against deconstructive and postmodern thought involve their tendency to deny the pressure of lower level *umwelts* on the nootemporal or its concomitant, the sociotemporal *umwelt*.

I think that there are two kinds of solutions to this problem, both of which have already been discussed at length.

First, the question of Being, whether in its Heideggerian or Derridian form, must be abandoned if by Being is meant an essence or a horizontal network of references. Phrases such as "the truth of Being" or "the Being of beings," and their deconstruction, are, if unqualified, meaningless. Being is a palimpsest of its history, a complex and multilayered onion whose layers are its past. Only such a hierarchical model of Being can account adequately for a universe that has, according to the best theory currently available, evolved from a state of unimaginable simplicity to its current level of equally unimaginable complexity.

Second, Fraser's extended *umwelt* principle hypothesizes that a creature is able to speak the languages of its constituent lower *umwelts* in three ways. First, inhabitants of the noo/sociotemporal *umwelt* have developed the ability to translate lower level regularities into a code, science, that is meaningful to humans. Second, the powerful human neocortex has the ability to inhabit imaginary worlds. Although the evolutionary value of the imagination stems, I think, from its capacity to model alternate futures, it is nevertheless able to generate empathetic links with both human and nonhuman beings. Third, to the extent that an entity's microstructure is the history of its evolution, it has direct access to its past. However, this access is via level-specific languages, so that it is largely unconscious (since most of the universe is unconscious).

Having summarized the basic principles of the evolutionary cosmology presented thus far, it will perhaps be useful to mention some of their possible shortcomings.

First, it is not clear from the preceding discussion why there should be evolution at all. Or, to put the matter in Heideggerian terms, why there should be something rather than nothing. Furthermore, even if existence is taken as a primitive and axiomatic dimension of the universe, why is the universe not a static or disintegrating system? After all, the second law of thermodynamics seems to suggest that disorder should be the principle vector of any complex system. From where, therefore, does complexity come?

Second, assuming that evolution is the generation of increasingly complex layers of matter and energy, and assuming further that the hierarchical theory that forms the basis for most viable cosmologies is valid, it is unclear why levels of complexity that are widely divergent should communicate in any but the most trivial ways. After all, my rocklike self is hardly available to those higher cortical functions that are, in the end, what I consider to be the real and genuine me. In my own personal value hierarchy, the Newtonian or eotemporal parts of me, the material clockwork that certainly underlies much of what I do and am, are clearly not as important to me as my ideas, thoughts, hopes, aspirations, or judgments. In other words, my intentional, mental layers are so nearly identifiable with my sense of self that a long tradition has maintained that they are my exclusive genuine Being. Although this book is clearly aimed at criticizing what I maintain is a kind of residual dualism in deconstruction and postmodernism, I do not wish thereby to neglect or minimize the clear temptation our species feels to reject its constitutive lower levels as inessential. Fraser observes that there is a general tendency of upper integrative *umwelts* to resist acknowledgment of their lower level origins. "Once the integrative level of human self was born and the nootemporal umwelt emerged, its features came to be protected against collapse into the integrative level of life no less strongly than life protects itself against collapse into the inorganic" (1978, 125). This inverse of Freud's death instinct is described in more general terms by Hofstadter, who calls "chunking" the capacity of upper levels in hierarchical systems to require only general descriptions of lower level functions. For example, knowledge of the nature, or even of the existence, of quarks is totally superfluous to one learning to fly cast, although it is undeniable that his or her quarry—the trout—his or her tackle, as well as his or her own body are ultimately composed of quarklike things.

> The point is clear. Each level is, in some sense, "sealed off" from the levels below it. . . . Although there is always some "leakage" between the hierarchical levels of science, so that a chemist cannot afford to ignore lower-level physics totally, or a biologist to ignore chemistry totally, there is almost no leakage from one level to a distant level. That is why people can have intuitive understandings of other people without necessarily understanding the quark model, the structure of nuclei, the nature of electron orbits, the chemical bond, the structure of proteins, the organelles in a cell, the methods of intercellular communication, the physiology of the various organs of the human body, or the complex interactions among organs. All that a person needs is a chunked model of how the highest level acts; and as we all know, such models are very realistic and successful. (Hofstadter 1980, 306–7)

It is clear how Hofstadter's concept of "chunking" could be used as a convincing argument for dualism. The upper levels of the human organism, it might be argued, are sealed off from its lower levels, so that even if it were conceded that to understand properly the human cultural world we must take its evolution from lower levels into account, the significance of this knowledge could be minimized as being essentially theoretical and of nearly no practical value. Just as the laws of high-energy physics do not offer any intrinsic guidance to the moral questions that arise along with the development of nuclear weapons, so it might be argued that, in general, any attempt to wed the humanities to the sciences ignores the effects of chunking whereby distant levels in a hierarchy are sealed off from one another.

Third, although I think that the dangers of reductionism have been dealt with adequately, it is nevertheless appropriate to remain cautious concerning the temptation to explain systemic behavior through recourse to the regularities of its component parts or subsystems. The explanatory ability of natural science might inflate human pride to the point that our hubris knows no bounds. Although I think that the natural classical position argued here leads in the opposite direction, we should nevertheless be wary of any glib importation of lower level languages into the arena of upper level decision making.

Fourth, it is possible that the universe has not evolved. It may have been created by God, or it may, in fact, be a human construction. We must not forget that the price paid for a rejection of explanation by authority is an ineradicable margin of uncertainty. Although I think it is, ultimately, a good thing that I have no convincing argument against the existence of invisible (i.e., unperceivable) rabbits, it is nevertheless possible that the world teems with them.

Finally, I may be guilty of some kind of chauvinism. It is possible that, despite my cautions, my basic presuppositions have been informed and distorted by some combination of the following views: white, male, academic, middle class, capitalist, etc. I am all of these, so, in a sense, I simply plead guilty. The extent to which the theories presented in this book have been channeled by my necessarily limited being-in-the-world is for others to determine, bootstrapping being a notoriously inefficient way of getting anywhere.

I do not propose a definitive solution to these problems in this book. Indeed, I suspect that an essential attribute of the noo/sociotemporal *umwelt* is inherent openness and ambiguity. Of course, I differ from Derrida in that whereas for him it is morally desirable to demonstrate and generate aporia wherever possible, I believe that a healthy culture is one that balances its production of new possibility with the perhaps tragic realization that without choice pure potential is at best insipid and at worst fascistic. Nevertheless, there is no reason to believe that noo/sociotemporal questions can be answered with the kind of quantitative sharpness to which eotemporal problems readily lend themselves.

In fact, it is the economy between clarity and aporia, or between order and chaos, that I believe is the best answer available to the kinds of questions adduced above. In part 1, chapter 3, I discussed Derrida's views on the notion of randomness. Perhaps the most interesting conclusion to be drawn from this analysis is that, despite his insistence on the nonbinary nature of deconstructive concepts, Derrida's view of Being is essentially Manichean. On the one side lies metaphysics, the totalizing machine eager to synthesize all exteriority into a master teleological dialectic. On the other side, the rest—a battery of traces that will not return to the father. The commerce between these two camps can be one of two kinds for Derrida. The metaphysician relentlessly tries to finesse *différance* by seeking to incorporate it into the system as a potentially recuperable detour. The deconstructionist, for his or her part, accepts the metaphysical urge (without, however, seeking to account for its tenacity or its usefulness) and, with a certain amount of self-righteousness, defines his or her work as a Sisyphian struggle against an enemy that can never be defeated.

Randomness belongs to the series of deconstructive concepts that serves as an Ariadne's thread through Derrida's work. Like its fellow nonconcepts, randomness figures in Derrida's work as the stubborn but inevitable remainder that haunts deterministic systematization. And although Derrida clearly understands that neither randomness nor determinism can stand in isolation, his allegiance and his agenda are clear. Deconstruction would be nothing were it not the systematic demonstration and affirmation of that which exceeds the economy of the Paternal logos. All of Derrida's attacks against meaning, idea, totality, and stability can be understood as the effort to insinuate an unablatable margin of randomness in deterministic structures.

Although Derrida has repeatedly taken great pains to maintain that he does not believe that metaphysics is an enemy to be defeated in the name of freedom, he nevertheless consistently adopts an oppressor/oppressed model in his analyses of logocentrism and the trace or of determinism and randomness. In the remainder of this book I will enlist the still callow science of chaos in the effort to suggest that the image of determinism as the oppressor and randomness as the unablatable oppressed is a fundamentally inaccurate and dangerously misleading metaphor for the physical, biological, and cultural worlds. It is becoming increasingly conceivable that both determinism and randomness are relatively rare limiting cases of a class of chaotic dynamical processes that combine the stability of determinism with the unpredictability of randomness. Chaos theory offers a view of the dynamics of the natural and social worlds that might make the notion of metaphysics as well as that of its deconstruction, both oppressor and liberator, seem strangely anachronistic.

The Local and the Global Models

Commenting on the intuitions that fueled the recent discovery of chaotic dynamical systems, Gleick says: "The tradition of looking at systems locally—isolating the mechanisms and then adding them together—was beginning to break down" (1987, 44). Gleick suspects that the long tradition of scientific reductionism, the idea that to know something it is necessary and sufficient to analyze it down to its simplest components, is currently being challenged by a new paradigm that emphasizes global structures. "Chaos breaks across the lines that separate scientific disciplines. Because it is a science of the global nature of systems, it has brought together thinkers from fields that had been widely separated. . . . It makes strong claims about the universal behavior of complexity" (5).

In the current climate of literary and cultural criticism, Gleick's vocabulary would be characterized as reactionary. Derrida's hostility toward teleological or dialectical syntheses, Foucault's insistence on the radical discontinuities structuring regimes of truth and power, Rorty's neopragmatist interpretation of Wittgensteinian forms of life or language games, the scientific anarchism of Feyerabend, and the radical axiological relativism of Smith are examples of a general disposition to doubt and vilify any tendency toward generalization, essentialization, unification, and universalization. Perhaps no one expresses this contemporary allergy toward the whole better than Lyotard, who defines the urge towards globalization as terrorism.

> A recognition of the heteromorphous nature of language games is a first step in that direction. This obviously implies a renunciation of terror, which assumes that they are isomorphic and tries to make them so. The second step is the principle that any consensus on the rules defining a game and the "moves" playable within it *must* be local. . . . (1984, 66)

Interestingly, among the many kinds of evidence that Lyotard adduces to convince his readers of the ineluctability of his conclusions are those drawn from the sciences. Lyotard's postmodernism is not to be understood as ideological or theoretical fiat, but, we are led to believe, if only by implication, as the consequence of new developments in the natural and mathematical sciences. Therefore, Lyotard enlists such allies as Gödel, Thom, and Mandelbrot in his campaign to reduce ethics to paralogy.

Although I think that Lyotard's appropriation of mathematics and science is biased and tendentious in general, one of his themes merits special attention—the question of whether the meaningfulness and pragmatic usefulness of language games, by which Lyotard means semiotic exchanges in general, are best described as local or global phenomena.

Lyotard correctly diagnoses the failing prestige of linear, or continuously differentiable, functions. "The conclusion we can draw from this research (and much more not mentioned here) is that the continuous differentiable function is losing its preeminence as a paradigm of knowledge and prediction" (1984, 60). The conclusion Lyotard draws from the decline of the linear paradigm is that we are on the eve of a new, postmodern science, a science which will concern itself with: "undecidables, the limits of precise control, conflicts characterized by incomplete information, 'fracta,' catastrophes, and pragmatic paradoxes" (60). In short, borrowing from Thom, Lyotard surmises that at best determinism will be a limited, local phenomenon and that the norm will be discontinuity, unpredictability, and contradiction. "All that exist are 'islands of determinism.' Catastrophic antagonism is literally the rule" (59).

Although Lyotard can hardly be criticized for not being aware of chaos theory in 1979, the date of the original publication of *La Condition Postmoderne: Rapport sur le Savoir*, what is remarkable here is how his vocabulary and emphasis, typical of much deconstructive and postmodern theorizing, differs wildly from that of Gleick. Lyotard talks about local determinism, Gleick of local unpredictability. Lyotard sees the death of global order, Gleick announces the birth of a new kind of global structure. Lyotard persists in deploying the traditional binary opposition between order and randomness, while Gleick suggests that chaos is a third term, a kind of dynamic disorder able to balance determinism with freedom.

Perhaps an even more poignant contrast is between Lyotard's emphasis on agonistics: "Catastrophic antagonism is literally the rule:

there are rules for the general agonistics of series" (59) and Prigogine's sense that nonlinear chemical reactions are able to inaugurate order and cooperation at macroscopic scales: "Moreover, in the case of a non-linear type of chemical reaction . . . long-range correlations appear. Particles separated by macroscopic distances become linked" (Prigogine and Stengers 1984, 180). Prigogine explains the implications of this view.

> We believe that this type of behavior is quite interesting, since it gives a molecular basis to the problem of communication mentioned in our discussion of the chemical clock. Even before the macroscopic bifurcation, the system is organized through these long-range correlations. We come back to one of the main ideas of this book: nonequilibrium as a source of order. Here the situation is especially clear. At equilibrium molecules behave as essentially independent entities; they ignore one another. We would like to call them "hypnons," "sleepwalkers." Though each of them may be as complex as we like, they ignore one another. However, nonequilibrium wakes them up and introduces a coherence quite foreign to equilibrium. (180–81)

In the place of Lyotard's general agonistics and paralogies, Prigogine suggests that, when nature is pushed into a far-from-equilibrium state, cooperation and communication is the rule. Minor local fluctuations in such systems, far from functioning as sui generis regimes of truth in a state of Hobbesian brush war with other "islands of determinism," are able to spread their effects throughout the system in such a way as to generate order out of chaos. The kind of isomorphism that is tantamount to fascist terror for Lyotard is precisely what Prigogine sees as the possibility of a renewal of man's relation to nature. Prigogine's version of postmodern science is not the cultivation of discontinuity and paradox, but a new dialogue with the natural world that respects both its otherness and our fundamental continuity with it.

However, as with all progress, such a postmodern science offers great hope as well as great danger: "This leads both to hope and a threat: hope, since even small fluctuations may grow and change the overall structure. As a result, individual activity is not doomed to insignificance. On the other hand, this is also a threat, since in our universe the security of stable, permanent rules seems gone forever" (Prigogine and Stengers 1984, 313). It is tempting to see Derrida's deconstruction and Lyotard's postmodernism as flights from the dangers of uncertainty. Derrida's "always already" precludes genuine innovation, and Lyotard's general agonistics would guarantee that local perturbations remain locked in place by the pressure of other, warring language games. In both cases, although local change is certainly possible, an essentially rigid cosmology prevents such local fluctuations from generating genuine global innovation. Whether the whole is "arche-writing" or "paralogy," the upshot is essentially the same: in the absence of a mechanism allowing for global communication and transformation, the system spends itself in the creation of local pockets of energy differentials. In one key respect, a system that is excessively continuous is identical to a system that is excessively discontinuous: they are both basically infertile, unable to change, adapt, or invent. As Prigogine argues, change, especially global change, in its embracing of uncertainty, is dangerous because it is potentially evil. However, the possibility of evil is, I believe, the price paid for our habitation of a dynamic, evolving universe. Derrida and Lyotard would attempt to prevent fascism by declaring it impossible. I suspect that Hitler, Pol Pot, Stalin, Botha, and their ilk might find such declarations amusing, but hardly inconvenient. The only ethical response to the spread of evil is not denial, but the systematic attempt to globally postulate and disseminate good. And if one's theoretical system has no room for such anachronisms, then that theoretical system is in de facto collaboration with terror.

Nonlinearity and Deconstruction

Until recently, scientific work has focused on linear systems. According to Davies, a linear system is "one in which cause and effect are related in a proportionate fashion" (1988, 23). In addition, linear systems are characterized by a simple relation between the whole and its parts, one in which translation between whole and component is possible with no distortion. In other words, in a linear system, the whole is equal to the sum of its parts. Examples of linear systems abound in nature, among them most waves, "electric and magnetic fields, weak gravitational fields, stresses and strains in many materials, heat flow, diffusion of gases and liquids" (24). Mathematical linearity, therefore, can be fruitfully compared to its philosophical counterpart. Linearity tends to be deterministic in a Laplacian way. Even if a linear system evolves, its evolution is discrete and sequential. Therefore, the time of linear systems is eotemporal, succession without a preferred direction. Consequently, since linear systems evolve predictably, they are subject to descriptive shortcuts. In other words, at a given time, t_1, it is possible to predict what the system will look like in the future, time t_2, without having to run the system in real time until t_2.

In deconstructive or postmodern discourse, linearity is ontotheological insofar as it suggests continuity, analyzability, and, ultimately, the immediacy of presence. The initial focus of Derrida's work, the deconstruction of the Saussurian sign, was, in large measure, an attempt to demonstrate that the supposed linear relation between signifier and signified, or between sign and referent, is, in fact, complicated by unpredictable and unmasterable perturbations. In many ways, Derrida's insistence on discontinuity appears to parallel the mathematics of nonlinear equations. In general, nonlinearity describes systems that change abruptly or discontinuously: the snapping of a rubber band, weather, or breaking a camel's back. According to Briggs and Peat: "In a nonlinear equation a small change in one variable can have a disproportional, even catastrophic impact on other variables. . . . Unlike the smooth curves made by students plotting linear equations in high school math classes, plots of nonlinear equations show breaks, loops, recursions—all kinds of turbulence" (1989, 24). Nonlinearity, especially inasmuch as it requires feedback—that is, equations in which output serves as input—is a crucial component of chaos, therefore it appears as if chaos theory might be remarkably similar to Derrida's deconstructive project. According to Hayles, "both discourses invert traditional priorities: chaos is deemed more fecund than order, uncertainty is privileged above predictability, and fragmentation is seen as the reality that arbitrary definitions of closure would deny" (1989, 314). Just as Derrida contends that metaphysical stability is, at best, a temporary hypostatization of underlying textual energy, chaos theory claims that deterministic linear systems, far from being the norm in the physical world, are merely special cases of nonlinear systems.

Consequently, chaos theory seems to be perfectly congruent with deconstruction. And although, with the exception of parts of

Hayles (1989 and 1990), I have not seen much evidence of it as yet, I suspect that this apparent compatibility may be implying to literary theorists that chaos is a validation of deconstruction. My own view is that such a claim is, for the most part, wrong. Basically, I agree with Hayles when she describes many of the differences between deconstruction and chaos.

> There are, of course, also significant differences between them. . . . One measure of these differences is disagreement among deconstructionists and scientists on how extensive chaos is. For Derrida, textual chaos is always already in Rousseau and in every other text. By contrast, scientists acknowledge that ordered, predictable systems do exist, although they are not nearly as widespread as classical science had supposed. . . . Where deconstructionists see an apocalyptic break with logo-centrism, scientists are likely to think of their work as a continuation of what went before. To a deconstructionist, to say someone is a recuperator is a damning comment; for most scientists recuperation is not an issue, because they see their work as enhancing rather than discrediting scientific paradigms. These differences are symptomatic of the different values the two disciplines place on chaos. For deconstructionists, chaos repudiates order; for scientists, chaos makes order possible. (1989, 316–17)

The gist of Hayles's article, and of her *Chaos Bound*, is that such differences are not as important as the significant parallels between chaos and deconstruction. While it is certainly true that deconstruction and chaos are both interested in highlighting the importance of nonlinearity, to claim that they are fellow travelers is, I believe, to make an unwarranted assumption. Some radical feminists and some fundamentalist Baptists may agree on the importance of highlighting the evils of pornography, but this overlap should not obscure the deep incompatibility of their basic presuppositions and political agendas. Similarly, I think that Hayles's last observation concerning the meaning and implications of chaos suggests that although deconstruction and chaos may be focusing on similar phenomena, their interpretations of these phenomena are incompatible because they are informed by fundamentally different worldviews. On the one hand, deconstruction seeks to affirm the destabilizing effects of unde-cidability; on the other hand, chaos theorists are intrigued by the appearance of order in apparently random systems. Deconstruction sees itself as a sentry watching for the recrudescence of order, whereas chaos scientists tend to be fascinated by the strange paths chosen by nature to order, universality, and beauty. And if such concepts seem alien to the language games that dominate contempo-rary critical theory, if they arouse suspicions of theoretical or ideo-logical disrepute, it is perhaps an index of how profound a paradigm shift we may be witnessing.

Chapter 16

Chaotic Systems

Studies in Boom and Bust

Chaos is, in large measure, a mathematical formalism, so that a discursive account of its basic tenets is bound to be partial and rudimentary. However, with this caution in mind, I believe it is possible to highlight those characteristics of chaos theory that have important philosophical implications.

At its simplest, chaos involves the study of systems whose random behavior is not the result of human error or ignorance, but is an ineradicable feature of even the perfectly smooth functioning of the system. Interestingly, nonlinear chaotic systems can be generated by civilized and deterministic algorithms. In fact, as opposed to the contortionist mathematics of traditional physics, including quantum mechanics and relativity, the mathematical formalism underlying chaos can be childishly simple. All that is required are algorithms incorporating the key features of nonlinearity and feedback. For example, a simple version of the logistic equation used by Robert May to model boom and bust cycles in animal population is $x_{next} = rx(1 - x)$, where x is the population, x_{next} is the population the next year, and r is a parameter describing the birth rate of the population. Such an equation, in which a future state of a system is a function of a past state, is feedback dependent and highly nonlinear—although for some values of the parameter feeding the equation back into itself produces a stable final figure for the population, for other, higher values of the parameter the system never locks into a single value. Figure 1 depicts population growth as modeled by the logistic equation. The horizontal axis represents the birthrate parameter, and the vertical axis the population's equilibrium points.

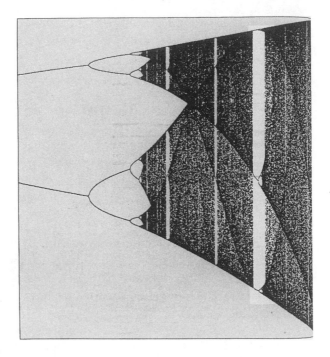

Fig. 1. Population growth as modeled by the logistic equations.

The important feature of this figure is the equilibrium points in the population plotted along the x-axis. With a small parameter, when the equation is fed back into itself a large number of times, it settles down to a fixed point. However, as the parameter increases, interesting things happen. First, there is the characteristic period doubling of chaos. Instead of finding a single basin of attraction, the logistic equation vacillates between two different levels. As the parameter is increased even more, bifurcations increase in frequency, finally losing all semblance of simple order as they lapse into chaos. In the chaotic region, the population never seems to find a stable point, jumping around the system in an unpredictable way. And yet, even in this sea of randomness, islands of stability reappear. This algorithm, and many others like it, suggest that the path from order to randomness in nonlinear systems is not smooth and sequential.

However, the bizarre thing about the logistic equation is not so much the appearance of randomness, but the ability of the system to find order in the midst of chaos. Gleick explains this strange phenomenon: "If you were following an animal population governed by this simplest of nonlinear equations, you would think the changes from year to year were absolutely random, as though blown about by environmental noise. Yet in the middle of this complexity, stable cycles suddenly return" (1987, 73).

As long as chaos is seen as the ability of deterministic systems to generate random behavior, it can be interpreted philosophically as suggesting that the condition of possibility of order is a fundamental structural randomness. Of course, such a claim is not unusual, given that quantum fuzziness is probably the microstructure of everything. However, such reductionism is precisely one of the traps chaos theory is, according to some of its key theorists, able to circumvent. As opposed to typical scientific analysis, chaos does not attempt to explain large-scale behavior on the basis of its constituent parts. In fact, Hofstadter's notion of chunking renders rather fatuous the argument that quantum indeterminacy has any direct effect on higher *umwelts*. As Crutchfield et al. explain:

> The source of unpredictability on a large scale must be sought elsewhere [than the Heisenberg uncertainty principle], however. Some large-scale phenomena are predictable and others not. The distinction has nothing to do with quantum mechanics. (1986, 48)

Instead of seeking solace in the kind of reductionism that deconstruction is prone to, that is, the kind of reductionism that seeks to explain order by recourse to its trace-structure, chaos proposes that it is precisely in global structure that meaningful clues concerning the relation between order and randomness must be found. Of course, a key feature of chaos, self-similarity or fractal scaling, suggests that nature might choose solutions to similar problems by generating structures that maintain recognizable family resemblances across scales, but that is not to say that the logic of a lower temporality can be imported, full-blown, into a higher one.

Thus, we are led to wonder about the meaning of something like the logistic equation. Perhaps a fittingly modest approach would be to see what mathematicians, physicists, and other experts have said. Robert M. May seems to think that the true importance of the logistic equation is that it demonstrates how even simple deterministic algorithms can generate remarkable complexity.

> I would urge that people be introduced to the equation $y = 4 \lambda x(1 - x)$ early in their mathematical education. This equation can be studied phenomenologically by iterating it on a calculator, or even by hand. Its study does not involve as much conceptual sophistication as does elementary calculus. Such study would greatly enrich the student's intuition about nonlinear systems.
>
> Not only in research but also in the everyday world of politics and economics, we would all be better off if more people realized that simple nonlinear systems do not necessarily possess simple dynamical properties. (Hofstadter 1985, 387)

At best, May's interpretation may lead to an evolutionary view of complexity, one that sees the evolution of the universe through increasingly complex *umwelts* as the natural result of certain recursive processes. At worst, it might suggest a kind of conceptual entropy, the tendency of certain simple mathematical formalisms and the physical processes they model to get out of hand quickly and inexorably.

Physicist Paul Davies concentrates on the bifurcations produced by the logistic equation. These bifurcations, or period doublings, appear not only to follow a pattern, but this pattern may be a universal feature of systems on the way to chaos. Davies interprets the work of Mitchell Feigenbaum as an indication of the way in which chaotic systems appear to be genuinely interdisciplinary, inasmuch as some of their features appear in widely divergent systems.

> It has been discovered that chaos arises in a wide range of dynamical systems, varying from heart beats to dripping taps to pulsating stars. But what has made chaos of great theoretical interest is a remarkable discovery by an American physicist, Mitchell Feigenbaum. Many systems approach chaotic behaviour through period doubling. In these cases the transition to chaos displays certain universal features, independent of the precise details of the system under consideration. (Davies 1988, 42)

Specifically, successive bifurcation points are separated by a distance in which each gap is 1/4.669 201 . . . of the previous one. Davies adds that "this implies a 'self-similar' form, with a rate of convergence that is independent of scale" (43). In addition, the rate by which the vertical distance separating the fingers of the bifurcations shrinks it by a precise ratio, 1/2.502 9 . . . . Davies' conclusion, that the "significance of these numbers lies not in their values but in the fact that they crop up again and again in completely different contexts" and that they appear to "represent a fundamental property of certain chaotic systems" (44) implies that randomness may not be simply unpredictable instability, but that it may have an underlying pattern and order. In other words, it appears that the simple opposition between order and randomness, which characterizes Derrida's speculations on the subject, may be inadequate. Chaos may be a totally new way of looking at evolving systems, one in which a kind of dynamic stability is able to transcend the distinction between dissemination and metaphysics.

It is interesting, and possibly disturbing to those theorists who are tempted to make allies of the new science of chaos and deconstructionist-type calls to indeterminacy, that what appears to excite many scientists and historians of science about chaos is not its randomness but the discovery of unexpected stability subtending apparently stochastic systems. For example, E. C. Zeeman introduces the proceedings of a Royal Society discussion meeting as follows. "The understanding of chaos and strange attractors is one of the most exciting areas of mathematics today. It is the question of how the asymptotic behaviour of deterministic systems can exhibit unpredictability and apparent chaos, due to sensitive dependence upon initial conditions, and yet at the same time preserve a coherent global structure" (Berry et al. 1987, 3). Certainly this is not the coherence of classical Laplacian linear and deterministic systems; yet neither is it the uncontrollable pullulation of the Derridian trace. In the same vein, Gleick refers to the conclusions drawn by James Yorke, whose mathematical analysis of May's population studies led him to the conclusion that chaos is strangely and unexpectedly orderly: "But Yorke had offered more than a mathematical result. He had sent a message to physicists: Chaos is ubiquitous; it is stable; it is structured" (1987, 76). Gleick's own analysis of logistical equations focusses on a basic philosophical problem. Many ecologists, like many philosophers, tend to identify themselves with one of two camps.

> Some read the message of the world to be orderly: populations are regulated and steady—with exceptions. Others read the opposite message: populations fluctuate erratically—with exceptions. By no coincidence, these opposing camps also divided over the application of hard mathematics to messy biological questions. Those who believed that populations were steady argued that they must be regulated by some deterministic mechanisms. Those who believed that populations were erratic argued that they must be bounced around by unpredictable environmental factors, wiping out whatever deterministic signal might exist. Either deterministic mathematics produced steady behavior, or random external noise produced random behavior. That was the choice. (78–79)

Despite his often repeated reservations concerning the metaphysical ramifications of binary opposition, Derrida does offer a rather traditional separation of chance and order in "My Chances." Although I have already quoted the following passage, I think that it bears repetition.

> Language, however, is only one among those systems of *marks* that claim this curious tendency as their property: they *simultaneously* incline towards increasing the reserves of random indetermination *as well as* the capacity for coding and overcoding or, in other words, for control and self-regulation. Such competition between randomness and code disrupts the very systematicity of the system while it also, however, regulates the restless, unstable interplay of the system. Whatever its singularity in this respect, the linguistic system of these traces or marks would merely be, it seems to me, just a particular example of the law of destabilization. (Smith and Kerrigan 1984, 2–3)

In many ways, Derrida is correct, of course. A certain play between chance and order is, in fact, crucial in most nonlinear systems. However, despite his incisive intuitions, Derrida makes two crucial mistakes. First, he assumes that randomness and code are in competition, and that this competition is a disruptive element within the systematicity of the system. Second, he assumes that the general law being observed in the struggle between order and randomness is the law of destabilization or, perhaps more succinctly, deconstruction. Derrida is wrong on these two counts because his initial assumption that the accidental and the orderly are engaged in some sort of rivalry that tends to disrupt the smooth functioning of a given system is unwarranted, given contemporary research in systems theory and chaos. Of course Derrida's formulations here are exceedingly sloppy. It is unclear, for example, what a system of *marks* is, or is not. However, despite Derrida's tendency to ignore the specificity of different kinds of systems, his point is quite clear. Systematicity is inimical to the internal conflict between the stochastic and the orderly. While this may be true for the kinds of limiting case, deterministic systems that chaos theory is finding to be the exception rather than the rule, such a view is quite meaningless in the context of nonlinear feedback systems. Rather than undermining the systematicity of systems, the coordinated interplay between the erratic and the deterministic *constitutes* the systematicity of chaotic systems. Chaotic systems are not a field upon which the claims of order and indeterminacy are disputed. In fact, it is precisely such a binary opposition, here between order and randomness, elsewhere between metaphysics and dissemination, that constitutes the most glaring dualistic rigidity in Derrida's thought.

Instead of requiring a choice between the imperative to deconstruct linear systems in order to unearth their arche-chaos, and the imperative to define chaos as supererogatory and thereby repress it, chaos theory suggests that determinism and randomness are not the only options available when describing the behavior of systems. Chaos offers a third possibility, and, curiously in light of how long it has taken to appreciate it, this possibility appears to be the one nature tends to choose in all its integrative levels when survival depends on flexibility and innovation.

Following his description of the debate between determinism and indeterminism in population studies, Gleick concludes that, to borrow one of Derrida's favorite formulations, chaos is neither one nor the other. "In the context of that debate, chaos brought an astonishing message: simple deterministic models could produce what looked like random behavior. The behavior actually had an exquisite fine structure, yet any piece of it seemed indistinguishable from noise. The discovery cut through the heart of the controversy" (1987, 79). There is some poetry in the idea that it is precisely the ability of chaotic structures to participate in Derrida's "neither/nor" that allows them to synthesize and transcend the opposition between order and randomness in a way that owes more to Hegel than to Derrida.

Fractal Attractors

The study of dynamical systems typically has recourse to two key terms: *phase space* and *attractor*.

Phase space is a mathematical tool used to depict the evolution of a system. It is possible to create a map of a system's development by tracing a graph that uses the system's degrees of freedom, its constitutive kinds of behavior, as its dimensions. For example, the phase space of an ideal pendulum can be represented by the follow aing graph plotting velocity versus position (fig. 2). All the information necessary to describe the dynamics of the pendulum is contained in the x-axis, representing its position, and the y-axis, representing its velocity. With no friction to slow it down, the pendulum will continue swinging back and forth forever, thus describing identical closed orbits, specifically ellipses, on the graph. The pendulum can be said to be attracted to the resulting closed orbit, which therefore is the pendulum's attractor.

The phase space of a real-world pendulum, one plagued by friction, is significantly different (fig. 3). In the presence of gravity, both the pendulum's velocity and the distance it covers with each oscillation will gradually decrease to zero. A spiral describes the descent of a real-world pendulum to its fixed-point attractor.

The important point is that in the case of a pendulum, position and velocity represent all the significant information constitutive of the system. Although a complete phase space description of a system usually cannot be reduced to just two degrees of freedom, the operation of constructing the phase space of a more complex system is essentially the same as that applied to a pendulum, except that a certain amount of chunking is required in order to keep the graph manageable.

Phase space, then, is a kind of visual metaphor of the evolution of a dynamical system. Or, using the vocabulary of the previous

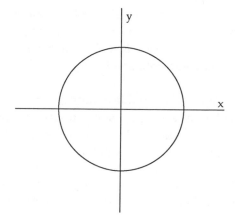

Fig. 2. A frictionless pendulum.

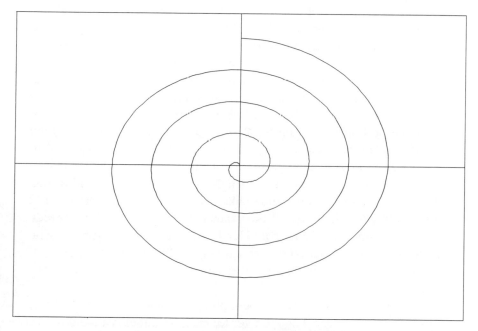

Fig. 3. A pendulum influenced by friction.

section, phase space is a model of a system, an abstract yet highly useful representation of the important information a system has to offer. And, since phase space is a dynamical model, it represents both the system's current state and its history.

> In phase space the complete state of knowledge about a dynamical system at a single instant in time collapses to a point. That point is the dynamical system—at that instant. At the next instant, though, the system will have changed, ever so slightly, and so the point moves. The history of the system can be charted by the moving point, tracing its orbit through the phase space with the passage of time. (Gleick 1987, 134)

The concept of an attractor follows directly from a phase space description of a system. An attractor is simply a region representing the equilibrium point of the behavior of a system. In other words, nature tends to be rather conservative when creating dynamical systems, apparently preferring those that find some kind of regular pattern. This pattern can be represented in phase space as a basin of attraction, a kind of magnet that draws the phase space to a recognizable shape. Another way of imagining an attractor is as an indentation on the surface of a system's phase space. If the evolution of the system is being traced by successive points in phase space, and if we imagine that these points can be represented by a marble, then clearly the marble will eventually find the indentation and tend to restrict its motion to the indentation itself or to its immediate neighborhood. If the indentation is a single point, the marble will funnel down to it sooner or later, much like water flowing out a drain, until it ultimately comes to rest. If the valley is more complex, it will guide the marble into describing some kind of recognizable trajectory. The point is that the indentation attracts the marble, or, in the terminology of dynamical systems, the attractor is a basin toward which the system is drawn.

Some systems, such as a pendulum influenced by gravity, tend toward a state of rest. The attractor for such a system is a fixed point. For a frictionless pendulum, the attractor is a closed loop. In general, simple systems such as oscillating pendulums have a comforting eotemporal regularity, and their attractors are rudimentary geometrical patterns. In fact, linear systems can perhaps be defined as systems generating tame attractors. Traditionally, such systems have been thought to be reducible to those generating three kinds of attractors—fixed point, limit cycle (closed loop), and torus. Although more complex than a fixed-point or a limit-cycle attractor, a torus attractor, describing a system composed of two independent oscillations (i.e., quasi-periodic motion) is still basically linear. In other words, fixed-point, limit-cycle, and torus attractors share a fundamental stability and predictability. Given pertinent information about their phase space, it is possible to predict the state of such systems at any given time in the future.

It is tempting to speculate that what Derrida understands as metaphysics might simply be a system generating a normal attractor. If by metaphysics is meant the desire to conceptualize the world as a system whose dynamics are reducible to a nontextual, fully present essence, then it would indeed appear that stable attractors function as some sort of transcendental signified. Any system whose behavior is guaranteed by an underlying determinable attractor would be ontotheological insofar as the attractor serves one of the traditional purposes of God—to control and channel the play of traces.

If a stable attractor is, indeed, a mathematical-visual metaphor for metaphysics, then we should expect that Derridian textuality would be described by the absence of an attractor. I suspect that the very concept of a basin of attraction would be condemned by Derrida as excessively onto-theo-logocentric. Furthermore, he would probably choose to characterize dissemination as a radically discontinuous play of traces whose phase space, if such a description of dissemination is even possible, would never settle into a recognizable pattern. The phase space of dissemination would be fundamentally anarchic, periodically congealing into metaphysical stability but then quickly undermining its temporary hypostatization with unpredictable and discontinuous leaps of textual free play.

Until Edward N. Lorenz discovered a new kind of attractor, it was thought that either a system would generate a fixed-point, limit-cycle, or torus attractor in phase space, or it was truly random and could be described by no attractor at all. In other words, dynamical systems were thought to one of two kinds—predictable or random. This belief was rattled when, studying fluid flows in the attempt to understand the seemingly unpredictable behavior of the weather, Lorenz revived Poincaré's three-body problem (that Newton's equa-

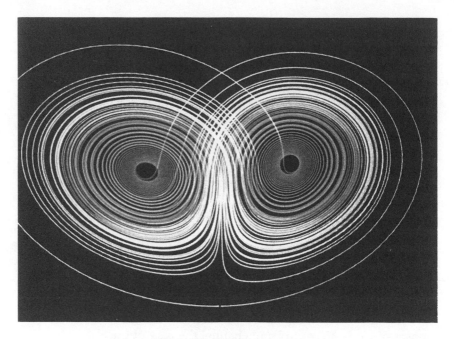

Fig. 4. The Lorenz attractor.

tions cannot be solved precisely when three bodies are involved) by devising a simple system consisting of just three degrees of freedom. Despite the unspectacular nature of Lorenz's system, it behaved rather bizarrely. The phase space of the Lorenz system is a kind of double spiral, a hauntingly beautiful set of butterfly wings or owl eyes. Although visually striking, the real interest of the Lorenz system is that it settles into an attractor that is neither stable nor random. The Lorenz attractor (fig. 4) is the first strange or chaotic attractor to be studied, and it inaugurated the serious study of chaotic systems.

The remarkable feature of strange attractors such as those discovered by Lorenz is that they are both confined within the finite space of a basin of attraction yet display a pattern of behavior that is nonperiodic. In other words, although a chaotic attractor never returns to a point it previously occupied in phase space, it is nevertheless still a recognizable attractor. A strange attractor is able to fulfill simultaneously two seemingly contradictory requirements—those of infinity and those of Procrustes—because in some manner it is able to squeeze an infinitely long line into a finite space.

In order to best explain the need to account for such a bounded infinity it might help to consider one of the most significant features of chaotic systems: their extreme sensitivity to initial conditions. In the torus attractor, two points on nearby orbits remain in close proximity with the passage of time. It is precisely the stable relation between two given points as a function of time that lends even the torus attractor its ultimate predictability. Things are quite different in the case of strange attractors. The seemingly random behavior of points on such attractors stems from the system's extraordinary responsiveness to even infinitesimal differences in original input. The reason for this extreme sensitivity to initial conditions is that chaotic systems are based on nonlinear equations in which feedback tends to magnify even the smallest differences in initial input into global divergences after only a relatively small number of cycles. The famous butterfly effect, in which the atmospheric disturbance occasioned by the flapping of a butterfly's wings is said to be able to alter the weather pattern halfway around the world, is a perhaps hyperbolic metaphor for the normal behavior of chaotic systems, their ability to explode minor fluctuations into global transformations. In the words of Crutchfield et al., in a chaotic system "microscopic perturbations are amplified to affect macroscopic behavior. Two orbits with nearby initial conditions diverge exponentially fast and so stay close together for only a short time" (1986, 51).

The problem, then, is to accommodate the dual demands of an exponential sensitivity to initial conditions and confinement to finite space. The solution—Lorenz's, Mandelbrot's, and Rössler's to be sure—but also, if we are to heed Prigogine's call to enter into a sincere and respectful dialogue with nature, one that nature has apparently selected (or one that selected for the kind of nature that could produce entities such as Lorenz), is the intricate beauty of fractal geometry.

French astronomer Michel Hénon, having heard a lecture on the Lorenz attractor, imagined that the best way to understand its astoundingly complex microstructure was by way of another metaphor. Henon believed that the apparently incompatible requirements of infinite detail and finite space could be met with an operation somewhat akin to the folding and stretching of dough. (Here I bow to the cultural relativists. Scientific knowledge makes a significant advance thanks to a culinary metaphor cooked up in France.) Pursuing the bread metaphor, Crutchfield et al. explain how chaos can produce fractal attractors.

> One can imagine what happens to nearby trajectories on a cha-
> otic attractor by placing a drop of blue food coloring in the
> dough. The kneading is a combination of two actions: rolling
> out the dough, in which the food coloring is spread out, and
> folding the dough over. At first the blob of food coloring simply
> gets longer, but eventually it is folded, and after considerable
> time the blob is stretched and refolded many times. On close
> inspection the dough consists of many layers of alternating blue
> and white. After only 20 steps the initial blob has been stretched
> to more than a million times its original length, and its thickness
> has shrunk to the molecular level. The blue dye is thoroughly
> mixed with the dough. Chaos works the same way, except that
> instead of mixing dough it mixes the state space. (1986, 51–52)

Chaotic attractors are fractal insomuch as they display layer upon layer of detail at greater and greater magnification. Furthermore, they are self-similar since their fractal depth tends to uncover microstructures that repeat the general shape of the system's macrostructure.[1]

Fractal scaling is able to accommodate the embedding of infinite complexity into finite phase space. Furthermore, fractal geometry is what allows chaotic systems to generate a dynamical structure that balances classical decorum and radical unpredictability. In fact, it is precisely this characteristic of chaos that is most vulnerable to misinterpretation, so it deserves a somewhat extended discussion. As I have indicated, chaos has occasioned much excitement in the scientific world not because it represents a mathematical vindication of those who, like Derrida, believe that the deep truth of our world is that it is underwritten by uncontrollable random effects, but because chaos offers a model of dynamical systems that is neither random nor deterministic. The importance of chaos for many scientists such as Crutchfield and Mandelbrot is that it is more than just a mathematical formalism. There is increasing evidence that the mathematics used to describe and generate dynamical systems may, in fact, subtend many vitally important natural processes. If chaos is to have implications for the humanities and the arts, it is because it allows us to model, and thereby understand, a strategy that nature has apparently chosen to deal with those of its problems most in need of creative solutions. Chaos may be the strategy selected by evolution to accommodate the dual demands of conservation and innovation, or, perhaps more accurately, evolution may be the strategy chosen by a chaotic universe to wrest complexity from the teeth of entropy.

A proper understanding of chaos, therefore, requires a novel definition of the term. Chaos does not mean simple randomness. Although it uses the power of randomness, chaos nevertheless channels it in productive ways. According to Gleick, Otto Rössler, the inventor/discoverer of a simple, ribbonlike attractor,

> felt that these shapes embodied a self-organizing principle in the world. He would imagine something like a wind sock on an airfield, "an open hose with a hole in the end, and the wind forces its way in," he said. "Then the wind is trapped. Against its will, energy is doing something productive, like the devil in medieval history. The principle is that nature does something against its own will and, by self-entanglement, produces beauty." (1987, 142)

Although the quote from Rössler, himself a relatively minor figure in the development of chaos theory, is of only passing significance in Gleick's narrative exposition of the history and meaning of chaos, I believe that it encapsulates, in a superbly concise fashion, several of the most astounding philosophical implications of this new science.

The usual interpretation of chaos is that it describes and studies systems whose behavior becomes discontinuous and unpredictable. The bifurcation diagrams studied by May, the aperiodic nature of chaotic attractors, the extreme sensitivity to initial conditions or perturbations displayed by all chaotic systems, the absence of a shortcut whereby the state of a chaotic system can be accurately described at a given time in the future, in short, the relative absence of causal connections between the present, past, and future in chaos, all suggest that chaos theory is the death knell of metaphysical totalizing systematization. In other words, chaos appears to validate Derrida's intuition that the world is not organizable according to principles that are essentially timeless (that is Laplacian—since in such deterministic systems time is illusory, the entire future of the system being in a sense already inscribed in any description of the system's present state).

The anti-Laplacian nature of chaos does not stem simply from the dynamics of chaotic systems. In fact, chaotic systems generated by mathematical algorithms are perfectly deterministic: although an observer might not know where the next dot on a chaotic attractor might land, the dot's location is, in a sense, included in the original algorithm. The same algorithm run an indefinite number of times will always yield the same pattern, so the system's freedom seems to be simply due to the observer's ignorance. However, this seeming determinism in chaotic systems neglects a crucial factor: sensitivity to initial conditions. Since nonlinear systems are extremely sensitive to initial conditions, and since initial conditions can never be specified to an infinite degree of precision (for reasons having less to do with observer ignorance than with quantum limits on the accuracy of any measurement), all chaotic systems are in a sense unpredictable, if by predictability we understand something like Laplacian determinism.

I support such a deconstructive description of chaos in a sense. In agreement with Derrida, I think that the metaphysics that he so assiduously contests is not the deep truth of Being, but merely a limiting case of chaos, something akin to Fraser's eotemporal *umwelt*. However, I differ from Derrida in two important ways.

First, I think that metaphysics is neither as pervasive nor as dangerous as Derrida claims. With the waning of traditional religious belief in the post-Enlightenment period, the rapid urbanization of the world, the general postmodern information crunch, and the seepage into the general culture of certain destabilizing implications of developments in natural science (such as relativity, quantum mechanics, and, now, chaos), metaphysical determinism has been gradually losing the prestige it enjoyed in medieval Europe. However, although certainly less hegemonic than in the past, metaphysics is still a significant component of the lives of most people. Some of its manifestations are unfortunate, and I join deconstructionists in the effort to eradicate them. I would include fascism, marxism, rigid social hierarchy, creationism, cults, sexism, racism, reductionism, idealism, and the postmodernism of Lyotard and Baudrillard among the undesirable expression of metaphysics. However, I am grateful to metaphysics every time my plane leaves on time, when my car starts, when all kinds of clocklike machines work, when medicines and vaccines are effective in preventing and curing infectious diseases, when bridges do not collapse, when the amount of money I have had deducted from my income for tax purposes matches the taxes I owe, when the sun rises every morning, and when my garden looks a little bit like what the seed catalogs predict.

Second, whereas Derrida chooses to emphasize the destabilizing potential of textuality, Rössler's interpretation of chaos underlines its productive capabilities. By focusing on self-organization and, perhaps more important, on the concept of beauty, Rössler is squarely at odds with the spirit, if not the letter, of deconstruction.

In my view, the most intriguing aspect of Rössler's quote is the idea that chaos is a way in which nature fools itself. If by "its own will" is understood the second law of thermodynamics, nature's own wicked deconstructor, then Rössler is suggesting that chaos and self-organization might offer a way to account for the otherwise unaccountable rise of order and organization in a universe that seems to be under the sway of Boltzmann's sentence of stochastic death.

The problem, then, is to account for organization, productivity, and beauty in a universe where the genuinely random influence of entropy seems to prefer the unremitting degeneration of things. The price paid for the deterministic, time-reversible Newtonian paradigm is a maniacally self-deconstructing universe. By way of contrast, chaos and Prigogine's model of dissipative far-from-equilibrium systems suggest the possibility of global increases in complexity and organization. Whereas the Newtonian-Laplacian view is ultimately pessimistic, the new perspective offers the hope of genuine progress. Furthermore, whereas the postmodern and Derridian interpretation of Newtonian mechanics claims that the only slice of Being that is meaningful is the local, self-organization and chaos suggest that nature's most remarkable transformations are global and holistic. Paul Davies describes the interface between chaos and self-organization in terms, and in a tone, that underscore their remove from the deconstructive paradigm.

> The emerging paradigm, by contrast, recognizes that the collective and holistic properties of physical systems can display new and unforseen modes of behaviour that are not captured by the Newtonian and thermodynamic approaches. There arises the

possibility of *self-organization,* in which systems suddenly and spontaneously leap into more elaborate forms. These forms are characterized by greater complexity, by cooperative behaviour and global coherence, by the appearance of spatial patterns and temporal rhythms, and by the general unpredictability of their final forms. (1988, 197–98)

Davies goes on to speculate on the possibility that the universe might have a "cosmic blueprint," a preferred direction of evolution: "Physical systems can display unidirectional change in the direction of *progress* rather than decay. The universe is revealed in a new, more inspiring light, unfolding from its primitive beginnings and progressing step by step to ever more elaborate and complex states" (198). Instead of the Newtonian clockwork paradigm, in which there is no genuine novelty since every possible future state in the universe is contained as a Laplacian homunculus in its present state, and instead of a view of the universe that characterizes it as the random succession of states with no direction whatsoever, Davies proposes that the universe's freedom may, in fact, be enabled by its fundamental predispositions. The universe is creative and unpredictable because, not in spite of, certain preferred patterns of development. "In this more *canalized* picture, matter and energy have innate self-organizing tendencies that bring into being new structures and systems with unusual efficiency" (200). Davies distinguishes between predeterminism and predestiny (or predisposition). Whereas predeterminism is classical Laplacian metaphysical closure, a view of the universe in which time and novelty are seen as mere illusions or products of human ignorance, predisposition is much like Chomsky's deep grammar, or Lumsden and Wilson's epigenetic rules—a kind of soft teleology that leaves much to serendipity.

Predestiny—or predisposition—must not be confused with predeterminism. It is entirely possible that the properties of matter are such that it does indeed have a propensity to self-organize as far as life, given the right conditions. This is not to say, however, that any particular life form is inevitable. In other words, predeterminism (of the old Newtonian sort) held that everything *in detail* was laid down from time immemorial. Predestiny merely says that nature has a predisposition to progress along the general lines it has. It therefore leaves open the essential unknowability of the future, the possibility for real creativity and endless novelty. In particular it leaves room for human free will. (1988, 201)

Simply, Davies believes that the cosmic blueprint is not a rigid master plan but a set of kindly encouragements to develop in certain ways. Playfully reformulating Einstein's famous maxim, Joseph Ford puts it this way: "God plays dice with the universe. But they're loaded dice" (Gleick 1987, 314). With a given throw, loaded dice are indistinguishable from ordinary dice. However, after a while, a pattern begins to emerge, and it becomes clear that the dice in question are not following the laws of chance. According to Davies, the universe works somehow analogously. It is free, especially in its choice of local detail, yet it seems to generate similar patterns time and time again. Like an immense chaotic attractor, the universe is both free and constrained, both random and determined. Rather than the false choice between untethered freedom and timeless determinism, the universe seems to have chosen loaded dice with which to play its games. "Of all the possible pathways of disorder," says Gleick, "nature favors just a few" (267).

If chaos is, as Davies believes, a kind of cosmic blueprint, that is, if chaotic patterns or dissipative structures underlie many flexible and creative natural and cultural processes, then the fundamental concepts of chaos—phase space, the attractor, sensitivity to initial conditions, fractal self-similarity, and self-organization—should prove useful in fleshing out the evolutionary ontology and epistemology outlined in part 2. Beginning with a reappraisal of Fraser's theory of temporal evolution, the remaining chapters of this book will seek to fulfill the promises made in the introduction by using a combination of evolutionary and chaos theory to suggest a number of alternatives to the deconstructive worldview.

Chapter 17

Temporal Asymmetry Reconsidered

My earlier discussion of Fraser's theory of temporal evolution suggested that Fraser's hypothesis concerning the origins of temporal asymmetry is the best one currently available. In fact, this issue is one that is hotly contested in contemporary philosophy of time. I deferred further analysis of this crucial question until the basic principles of chaos theory had been introduced because I think that, with the aid of chaos, it is possible to shed new light on this thorny problem.

Some theorists, many of them, like Einstein, physicists, believe that time is fundamentally reversible. According to this view, the physical universe is indifferent to the direction of time; consequently, something like an arrow of time is held to be a subjective, human imposition on an otherwise temporally isotropic world. Another position, held by Whitehead and contemporary process philosophers, maintains that temporal asymmetry is a primitive condition of the universe, and that, therefore, even the most basic physical processes, such as those occurring at the subatomic level, display a distinct temporal direction. Finally, Fraser claims that temporal asymmetry is an emergent feature of the universe, appearing for the first time with biogenesis. According to Fraser, with the emergence of life comes a present, or "now," a temporal dimension whose absence in more primitive levels of cosmic evolution prohibits the attribution of an arrow of time to any prebiotic entity.

I agree with process philosophers and Fraser that any theory of time that postulates that temporal asymmetry is merely a human illusion is untenable, and that, as a consequence, Whitehead's view, Fraser's view, or a synthesis of the two is likely to represent the nature of time most accurately. Using ideas stemming from the study of dissipative thermodynamic systems and chaos theory, I will attempt to present a view of time that respects Fraser's evolutionary temporal model while removing the awkwardness inherent in any attempt to date an arrow of time from the first appearance of biological entities. Specifically, I will claim that Fraser is correct in asserting that time has evolved along with everything else in the universe, but that he is incorrect in assuming that an arrow of time is the product of the emergence of life. Instead, it is much more reasonable to assume that an arrow of time is, itself, an evolving feature of our universe, developing from the faint temporal asymmetries associated with those initial inhomogeneities that kicked the early universe out of thermodynamic equilibrium and set its evolution in motion, to the sharply anisotropic temporality of the human cultural sphere.

Fraser's temporal cosmology is at odds with a long tradition in the natural sciences that maintains that time is not an objective component of the physical universe. Stephen Hawking states flatly that "the laws of science do not distinguish between the forward and backward directions of time" (1988, 152), and Einstein believed that time was a product of human subjectivity and was without a physical basis: "For us believing physicists, the distinction between past, present and future is only an illusion, even if a stubborn one" (Griffin 1986, x). Fraser's evolutionary view of time attempts to correct the widely held view that time is, at best, a subjective quality having no basis in objective reality. However, despite the beauty and explanatory power of Fraser's theory of temporal evolution, it does present a number of serious problems. For the sake of simplicity, let me reduce them to two seminal types.

First, if an arrow of time first appears with the emergence of biological entities, in what sense can the history of the universe before that "moment" be called evolution? It would appear that, by Fraser's own definition, the atemporal, prototemporal, and eotemporal *umwelts* could not be situated in a series with a preferred direction, since the very notion of temporal progression only becomes thinkable with the emergence of the biotemporal present. And yet Fraser clearly subscribes to an evolutionary view of time in which there is a logical vector leading from atemporality to biotemporality, implying that evolution itself has an arrow of time.

Gardner (1979), Prigogine (Prigogine and Stengers, 1984), and Hawking (1988) maintain that such a cosmological arrow guarantees a temporal asymmetry on the largest of scales. This asymmetry can be understood simply as the direction of cosmic expansion—"the cosmological arrow, the direction of time in which the universe expands rather than contracts" (Hawking 1988, 152)—or in an evolutionary sense—"If we assume that the universe started with a Big Bang, this obviously implies a temporal order on the cosmological level" (Prigogine and Stenger 1984, 259). Since Fraser's model requires that temporal direction be meaningless in the purely physical *umwelts*, his evolutionary model would have to maintain that the cosmological arrow is the result of retroactive observer participancy. Although this view, a version of Wheeler's (1988) theory of observer participancy in the self-synthesis of the world, is undoubtedly true at a certain level of description, it is still somewhat unconvincing to argue that had the universe ended before the appearance of biotemporal entities, it would not have evolved in any meaningful way.

A variant of the cosmological arrow view maintains that it is not simply entities and forces that evolve, but also the basic regularities or laws that constitute an integrative level. According to Griffin, the evolution of the fundamental laws of matter should itself display an arrow of time: "If this idea is accepted, then time, with its difference between past, present, and future, its 'moving now,' and its irreversibility in principle, will have to be recognized as applying to the fundamental laws of physics, for it will thereby be recognized that the so-called fundamental laws themselves have a history, that their importance in the actual world had a beginning and will have an end" (1986, 28). In sum, a cosmological arrow of time, whether it is measured against the scale of evolving laws, increasing complexity, or expanding space (all of which I believe to be descriptions of the same phenomenon) would define temporal asymmetry as the condition of possibility of evolution itself, thereby making Fraser's cosmology incoherent.

Second, Fraser's refutation of the widely held theory that the second law of thermodynamics guarantees a universal arrow of time is less than satisfactory. According to Davies there is a paradox inherent to the statistical nature of the second law. Statistically, it guarantees a macroscopic temporal asymmetry, yet microscopically, at the level of individual entities, time appears to be reversible: "All physicists recognize that there is a past future asymmetry in the universe produced by the operation of the second law of thermodynamics. But when the basis of that law is carefully examined, the asymmetry seems to evaporate" (Davies 1983, 125). Consider a bottle of perfume whose cap has been removed. Clearly, the perfume will evaporate and permeate the room. Equally as clear is the improbability that the vector of its diffusion would be reversed, with vaporized perfume gradually finding itself back in the bottle in liquid form. According to Davies, "the evaporation and diffusion of the scent provides a classic example of asymmetry between past and future" (126). Yet, Boltzmann's equations are essentially statistical in nature, guaranteeing that a large number of molecules will tend to find a state of maximum disorder (because there are far more such possible states than there are ordered states). "However," adds Davies, "any given individual molecular collision is perfectly reversible. Two molecules approach, bounce and retreat. Nothing time asymmetric in that. The reverse process would also be approach, bounce and retreat" (126). Davies's solution to the dilemma is to argue that it is, in fact, a level confusion, an attempt to compare temporalities that belong to two different orders of organization. "The mistake is to overlook the fact that time asymmetry, like life, is a holistic concept, and cannot be reduced to the properties of individual molecules. There is no inconsistency between symmetry at the molecular level, and asymmetry on a macroscopic scale. They are simply two different levels of description" (127). If Davies is correct, then time asymmetry could not be a purely emergent feature of our universe. For even if temporal asymmetry as guaranteed by the second law of thermodynamics is a holistic phenomenon, it certainly is applicable to a universe that has not as yet reached the biotemporal *umwelt*. Holism, as the system behavior of individual entities, is a possible state of objects in any *umwelt* with the possible exception of the atemporal, consequently Davies's synthesis of temporal asymmetry and symmetry would introduce an arrow of time to all of Fraser's integrative *umwelts*. If that is the case, then the possibility of temporal asymmetry is, indeed, dependent on entropy and not, as Fraser would have it, on the existence of a biological present.

Fraser's response to such an attempt to anchor temporal asymmetry in the fundamental nature of the universe is to argue that the second law of thermodynamics, by itself, cannot guarantee an arrow of time. Fraser maintains that eotemporal entropy only appears to have a preferred direction to an noo/sociotemporal observer. A human observer, rooted deeply in an anisotropic temporality, perceives entropy as displaying a preferred direction, but in fact he or she is only observing the world through a kind of temporal prism-house. The second law of thermodynamics is only temporally asymmetrical when viewed from a higher temporal *umwelt* than that associated with nonliving matter, so to assume that it is, itself, possessed of an arrow of time would be a kind of temporal imperialism.

Fraser's basic argument is that primitive *umwelts* cannot be temporally asymmetrical because they do not possess a present. Although he focuses on the statistical nature of the second law of thermodynamics, I think his main point is that whether one looks at prebiotemporal *umwelts* holistically or reductively, that is, either as aggregates or as mixtures of individual entities, they are, in principle, presentless and thus indifferent to the direction of time. It should be noted that in a later work, Fraser complicates this schema slightly, arguing that, in a sense, the two cosmic arrows—entropy and growth—offset each other in the prebiotemporal universe, thereby maintaining a directionless eotemporal temporality (Fraser 1987). I will defer a discussion of Fraser's later formulation until after I have had occasion to interpret temporal asymmetry from the perspective of Prigogine's theory of self-organizing systems. For the moment, I will simply say that it is not at all clear that only biological entities are able to define a present.

An opposing view of time is held by process philosophers such as Griffin who, following in the tradition of Alfred North Whitehead, maintain that temporal flux is a primitive feature of our universe: "For Whitehead, the reality of time, with its irreversibility, is based on the fact that *the actual world is composed exhaustively of momentary events that include, partially but really, preceding events*, which had in turn included previous events, and so on back" (1986, 10).

Griffin considers even the most elementary of particles as so many processes, with their own division into past, present, and future.

> Rather than thinking of enduring particles as the fundamental entities of the world, Whitehead sees each enduring object as composed of a rapidly occurring series of events, each of which includes aspects from its predecessors in that enduring object but also aspects from other prior events as well. Hence, Whitehead opposes the widespread view that an individual

atom is timeless; rather, it is a "temporally-ordered society" of actual occasions . . . . Since an individual atom (or even electron) has a temporal structure, time or temporality does not first arise as a statistical effect of the interactions among a multiplicity of atoms. (1986, 10–11)

While process philosophers would certainly take issue with Fraser concerning his interpretation of the second law of thermodynamics, the real point of contention is whether a present is a universal temporal feature or whether it indeed becomes thinkable only after the emergence of life. Holding, as does Fraser, that any definition of temporal asymmetry needs, as a minimal condition, a present, process philosophers argue that everything in the universe, from noo/ sociotemporal events to subatomic particles, is a process consisting of potential events passing into actuality through the present. Specifically, Griffin defines the future as the realm of as yet indeterminate possibility, the past as the set of events that are determinate, and the present as the instant of choice: "The *present* is the realm in which decisions are being made: some possibilities are being turned into actualities while other possibilities are being excluded from actualization" (2). Becoming, the continuous transformation of indeterminism into determinism, is a fundamental property of Being. Therefore, since the present divides the world into two asymmetrical regions, that of potentiality and that of actuality, an arrow of time is not restricted to biotemporal entities, but is a primordial feature of the universe.

Process philosophy views the second law of thermodynamics as merely one manifestation of a much deeper principle, that temporal anisotropy underlies all processes. As such, Whitehead's view of time is squarely at odds with Fraser's theory of evolving temporalities and, in a more limited way, with Davies's idea that time asymmetry is the property of collectives, not of individual physical particles.

I would like to propose a resolution to this apparent dilemma, a resolution that would simultaneously respect Fraser's basic temporal architecture and allow for a prebiotemporal arrow of time. I will begin by returning to Fraser. According to Fraser, evolution is fueled by irresolvable conflicts that develop within a given *umwelt*.

The theory of time as conflict identifies each of the major integrative levels with certain unresolvable conflicts. By conflict is meant the coexistence of two opposing trends, regularities, or groups of laws, in terms of which the processes and the structures of the integrative level may be explicable. By unresolvable is meant that, by means indigenous to an integrative level, its conflicts may only be maintained (and thereby the continued integrity of the level secured) or else eliminated (and thereby the level collapsed into the one beneath it). If the conflicts vanish, so does the integrative level. However, the unresolvable conflicts of each level can and do provide the motive force for the emergence of a new level. But a new Umwelt, from its very inception, may once again be identified with certain unresolvable conflicts of its own. (1978, 27)

For example, Fraser speculates that the competing demands of growth and decay constitute a biotemporal conflict resolvable only in the nootemporal *umwelt*. I would like to generalize Fraser's idea to include states of nonequilibrium at all integrative levels. While there must be a minimum amount of stability in an *umwelt* for it to be recognizable as a stable level of evolutionary complexity, it cannot be in perfect equilibrium if it is to be pushed to transcend itself. In other words, an integrative level must have enough stability to have a useable identity, but not so much that evolution becomes unnecessary or unthinkable.

Fraser's understanding of time as conflict accounts for the need for temporal instability within a given integrative level, however, in light of recent work in the science of self-organizing systems, it appears that in order to avoid the trap of stasis, Fraser must admit an element of temporal asymmetry into the most primitive *umwelts*. In order to see why this is the case, it would be well to recall that arguments such as Davies's maintain that the universe is divided into two temporal camps: microscopically, at the level of particles, the laws of physics are indifferent to the direction of time; macroscopically, when societies of particles are considered, the second law of thermodynamics guarantees a statistical arrow of time. And, even if we complicate this schema a little by adding a third category, the negentropic arrow of self-organization, it still suggests that there might be entire *umwelts* that know no time asymmetry.

Although primarily concerned with biological systems, Brooks and Wiley make essentially such a distinction concerning the whole of the natural world.

> The natural systems studied in physics, chemistry, and biology are made of up simple microscopic components. The laws describing the behavior of individual components are time invariant. Macroscopic systems made up of these components, however, always exhibit one of two forms of irreversible behavior. Those that follow the "arrow of time" . . . move in the direction of decreasing order and organization. . . . In contrast, other systems follow the "arrow of history" . . . , and move spontaneously toward states of higher order and organization. These systems are called "self-organizing." (1988, 51)

Brooks and Wiley recognize two forms of irreversibility—classic thermodynamic decay and self-organization. They contrast these global, stochastic processes with microscopic interactions that they define, as does Davies, as temporally symmetrical.

Two components of the Brooks and Wiley position need to be emphasized: (1) their microscopic/macroscopic opposition; and (2) their focus on the temporality of self-organizing systems. Both of these ideas receive extensive treatment in the work of Ilya Prigogine, although with a somewhat different emphasis. On one crucial point, however, Brooks and Wiley are in complete agreement with Prigogine—dissipative, far-from-equilibrium systems are inherently temporally asymmetrical.

> Some systems begin as collections of particles having no time asymmetry (no arrow of time). Fluctuations in the surroundings, the *boundary conditions*, may cause instabilities in the system (Jantsch termed this the "penetration of the environment into the system"). As a consequence, the system may "react" or "respond" in a physical sense. This would be accompanied by the production of entropy that would then be "exported" from the system into the surroundings. The system might then transform into a nonhomogeneous, or ordered, state. If this occurs, a time asymmetry will have been produced and the system may persist in an ordered state. This process is referred

to as "order out of chaos" or "order through fluctuations" (Prigogine and Stengers 1984). We will call it the "dissipative structures idealization," because it applies to systems whose macroscopic behavior can be explained totally by reference to products dissipated from the system irreversibly. (Brooks and Wiley 1988, 57–58)

The Brooks and Wiley interpretation of self-organizing systems theory is halfway between Fraser's position and that of Griffin. Whereas Fraser believes that an arrow of time only comes into being with the emergence of life, and whereas Griffin argues that temporal asymmetry is a primitive aspect of our universe, Brooks and Wiley maintain that although microscopic particles display eotemporal, directionless succession, nonequilibrium systems that are either decaying or self-organizing describe a temporal direction. If that is the case, as evidence from diverse fields is suggesting, then Fraser's model will have to be amended. Time's arrow appears to be tied less to biological systems than to certain instabilities or inhomogeneities liable to appear anywhere in the natural world.

Prigogine makes the points clearly: "All dissipative systems have a preferential direction of time" (Griffin 1986, 234). Whenever symmetry is broken in an entropy producing dynamical system, irreversibility and an arrow of time occur. Therefore, if, as many cosmologists have speculated, the entire universe is one unimaginably complex, far-from-equilibrium self-organizing system, then an arrow of time must be an inherent property of an evolving cosmos. Therefore, temporal asymmetry cannot simply be an epiphenomenon of macroscopic aggregates, but must, as process philosophy maintains, be a feature of the microscopic realm.

Prigogine's central thesis is that contemporary science is undergoing a paradigm shift from a concept of nature as fundamentally deterministic and reversible to a point of view that is sensitive to the tremendous number of processes that are probabilistic and irreversible.

We have repeatedly stated in this book that the reconceptualization of physics going on today leads from deterministic, reversible processes to stochastic and irreversible ones. We believe that quantum mechanics occupies a kind of intermediate position in this process. There probability appears, but not irreversibility. We expect . . . that the next step will be the introduction of fundamental irreversibility on the microscopic level. In contrast with the attempts to restore classical orthodoxy through hidden variables or other means, we shall argue that it is necessary to move even farther away from deterministic descriptions of nature and adopt a statistical, stochastic description. (Prigogine and Stengers 1984, 232)

Prigogine is committed to the view that, although nature displays many reversible processes, such as those that Fraser labels eotemporal, the processes that will prove of ultimate interest will be those displaying temporal polarization. Furthermore, he is convinced that macroscopic irreversibility is not simply a product of the laws of large numbers but is, in fact, the expression of an underlying microscopic arrow of time.

As we have emphasized repeatedly, there exist in nature systems that behave reversibly and that may be fully described by the laws of classical or quantum mechanics. But most systems of interest to us, including all chemical systems and therefore all biological systems, are time-oriented on the macroscopic level. Far from being an "illusion," this expresses a broken time-symmetry on the microscopic level. Irreversibility is either true on *all* levels or on none. It cannot emerge as if by a miracle, by going from one level to another. (Prigogine and Stengers 1984, 285)

Just as many cosmologists believe that the essentially featureless early universe must have begun its evolution because of a break in symmetry, Prigogine speculates that temporal asymmetry may be the seed out of which complexity arises at all levels of description. If that is the case, although some *umwelts* may be mainly atemporal, their very existence as well as the impetus pushing them toward self-organization into more complex *umwelts* must be due to an element of internal temporal polarization. In other words, deterministic systems are the fossilized record of generative irreversible processes.

In general, since they could run backwards as easily as they do forwards, deterministic systems display no temporal polarity. If a

Laplacian demon knew the initial conditions of such a system, he could predict its state at any moment in the future, so its future would be, in essence, no different from its past. Past, future, and present would coexist in a kind of atemporal plenum. We know, however, that many systems in nature are not linear or deterministic but are more properly described as chaotic. One of the central features of chaotic systems is that, even though they describe recognizable attractors, the exact trajectory of their development is so sensitive to initial conditions that it is impossible to map it in advance. The only way to know exactly what a chaotic attractor will look like is to run the recursive algorithm that generates it.

> The randomness of chaotic motion is therefore *fundamental*, not merely the result of our ignorance. Gathering more information about the system will not eliminate it. Whereas in an ordinary system like the solar system the calculations keep well ahead of the action, in a chaotic system more and more information must be processed to maintain the same level of accuracy, and the calculation can barely keep pace with the actual events. In other words, all power of prediction is lost. The conclusion is that the system itself is its own fastest computer. (Davies 1988, 54)

Prigogine has sought to "unify dynamics and thermodynamics, the physics of being and the physics of becoming" (Prigogine and Stengers 1984, 277). The result is that certain systems can be shown to be inherently unstable, probabilistic, entropic, and temporally polarized. "It also seems quite remarkable that irreversibility emerges, so to speak, from instability, which introduces irreducible statistical features into our descriptions. Indeed, what could an arrow of time mean in a deterministic world in which both future and past are contained in the present?" (277). In a sense, Prigogine's goal is to thwart the rapacious grasp of Laplace's demon. He would like to demonstrate that temporal irreversibility is not the product of human ignorance, but an objective property of certain natural processes. If that is the case, time's arrow is not simply a macroscopic statistical phenomenon that could, in principle, be reduced to timeless determinism by an omniscient observer, but an intrinsic feature of many systems. Simply, Prigogine would like to show that, in such systems, no amount of knowledge concerning their initial conditions would be enough to allow Laplace's demon to determine all its future states. If that is the case, that is, if systems exist in which it is *in principle* impossible to determine exhaustively their initial conditions, and if, in addition, such systems are extremely sensitive to these initial conditions, then their evolution will be objectively asymmetrical with respect to time. In other words, if *"for certain types of systems* an infinitely precise determination of initial conditions leads to a self-contradictory procedure" (262) because the initial conditions for such systems are inherently undeterminable, then an ineradicable element of instability, randomness, and irreversibility determines their evolution.

According to Prigogine, an "entropy barrier" acts as a selection principle, requiring an infinite information content for those kinds of initial distributions lending themselves to deterministic temporal reversibility. Such an entropy barrier prohibits the interchangeability of temporal vectors. "In other words, the second law becomes a selection principle of initial conditions. Only initial conditions that go to equilibrium in the *future* are retained" (Prigogine and Stengers, 276), thereby making temporal asymmetry a primitive axiom of our universe. Furthermore, according to Prigogine, a microscopic arrow of time is not the *product* of systemic instability and randomness. In fact, the relation of causality goes the other way, irreversibility constituting the condition of possibility of dynamical instability: "Intrinsic irreversibility is the strongest property: it implies randomness and instability" (276).

How, then, are we to reconcile Griffin and Prigogine's theory of inherent temporal polarity with Fraser's conviction that an arrow of time only emerges with the biotemporal *umwelt*? I think that Davies suggests a possible solution. Davies distinguishes between complete reductionism, the idea that "there *are* no emergent phenomena, that ultimately all physical processes can be reduced to the behaviour of elementary particles (or fields) in interaction" (1988, 139) and uncaused creativity, a view of emergence that assumes that "new levels of organization (e.g., living matter) are not . . . caused or determined in any way, either by the underlying levels or anything else. They represent true novelty" (140). Of course, neither Griffin nor Fraser would see themselves in the preceding descriptions. Yet, regarding time, I believe that Griffin and Prigogine's position is reductionist and Fraser's an example of uncaused creativity.

On the one hand, by postulating that temporal asymmetry is a primitive dimension of Being, process philosophy must define the human subjective sense of time as merely a version of an underlying arrow of time. On the other hand, although Fraser's cosmology of time is aggressively evolutionary, it nevertheless requires that an arrow of time emerge full-blown, like Athena from the head of Zeus, with the leap into biotemporality. Although time evolves for Fraser, temporal asymmetry does not; on the contrary, an arrow of time is a genuinely discontinuous event with no precedent.

I suspect that the irreconcilability of these two views, the reductionist always already and the radically emergent, is a level-specific conflict that can only be resolved at a higher level of analysis. I believe that the third possibility suggested by Davies—a view that conjoins reductionist principles with emergent self-organization, is precisely such an upper level solution. "If we accept that there exists a propensity in nature for matter and energy to undergo spontaneous transitions into new states of higher organizational complexity, and that the existence of these states is not fully explained or predicted by lower level laws and entities, nor do they 'just happen' to arise for no particular reason, then it is necessary to find some physical principles additional to the lower level laws to explain them" (Davies 1988, 142). Davies proposes that the tendency of far-from-equilibrium, open, nonlinear systems with feedback to undergo spontaneous global leaps of organization can accommodate the requirements of evolution with those of discontinuous emergence. In a similar vein, I would like to suggest that temporal asymmetry is a feature of all integrative levels, but that, like time itself, it has evolved in an essentially chaotic way consonant with the fundamental intuitions of Prigogine and Davies concerning self-organization.

Frederick Turner argues that the universe may be the result of a bottleneck.

The universe is the result of a scheduling problem. Everything that can happen, including nothing at all, happens as fast as it can. But logically certain things can only happen after other things. Hence periodicities occur, and events that depend upon the existence of periodicities. Room must be found in time to close-pack these events as efficiently as possible. The world is a branching flow-chart that regulates itself. The tree of life. (1985, 49)

Keeping to the spirit of Turner's idea, I propose to modify it minimally to suggest a fractal theory of time. Brooks and Wiley claim that evolution is characterized by an ever-increasing difference between maximum possible entropy, or the state of a system in which all of its possible microstates are equally probable, and actual entropy, or the state of a system in which its microstates are so constrained as not to be equally probable. Analogously, I hypothesize that the evolution of time is fueled by the difference between the amount of time necessary to exchange information and the amount of time available to accomplish this exchange. If an evolutionary *umwelt* is the totality of information available at a given level of complexity, then there will always be a misfit between the maximum speed with which information can flow and the actual time required for such processing. Normally, accommodations can be made, and a relative state of equilibrium can be maintained. Such states are equivalent to Fraser's *umwelts*. However, as Fraser himself points out, certain conflicts invariably arise that push an integrative level out of equilibrium. I believe that such conflicts are actually both the result and the product of nature's tendency to self-organize spontaneously. In other words, there is a feedback relationship between self-organization and disequilibrium: small asymmetries are able to expand asymptotically, kicking systems into a far-from-equilibrium state that itself can create further asymmetries. Evolution may be nothing more than nature expanding itself discontinuously so that it may have more time to process more information.

Fraser is quite correct in claiming that the evolution of time expands the amount of world. He is also correct in arguing that time evolves into increasingly more complex temporalities. I differ with Fraser, however, when he asserts that temporal asymmetry is an emergent feature of the biotemporal *umwelt*. Instead, I propose that an arrow of time has always existed, but that it has evolved from a state of near nullity in the atemporal *umwelt* to a sharply defined vector in the noo/sociotemporal *umwelt*.

The evolution of time, therefore, would be the evolution of temporal asymmetry. Fraser's chronons, objects with zero restmass and distances of the order of the Planck length, are genuinely atemporal.

However, their integrative level can be pushed into a far-from-equilibrium state introducing enough of a seed of temporal asymmetry into the atemporal *umwelt* to enable the emergence of prototemporal temporality. Although it is generally assumed that no arrow of time can be said to exist in the prototemporal *umwelt*—"Quantum theory denies all meaning to the concepts of 'before' and 'after' in the world of the very small" (Wheeler 1988, 13), there is reason to believe that, even in the prototemporal integrative level, a weak and admittedly fuzzy arrow of time exists. For example, Roger Penrose has speculated that "the initial smoothness of the universe ought to emerge from time-asymmetric fundamental laws.... Penrose points to the existence of certain exotic particle physics processes that display a weak violation of time reversal symmetry, indicating that at some deep level the laws of physics are not exactly reversible" (Davies 1988, 153).

I believe that an element of time irreversibility is precisely what prompted the initially featureless early universe to begin its evolution. An intriguing theory in this regard is the inflationary scenario, which posits a time reversible, initial smoothness reminiscent of Fraser's atemporal *umwelt* that subsequently undergoes a global and irreversible loss of symmetry.

> During the inflationary phase the universe was in a condition of perfect symmetry. It consisted of precisely homogenous and isotropic empty space. Moreover, because the expansion rate was precisely uniform, one moment of time was indistinguishable from another. In other words, the universe was symmetric under time reversal and time translation. It had "being" but no "becoming." The end of inflation was the first great symmetry break: featureless empty space suddenly became inhabited by myriads of particles, representing a colossal increase in entropy. It was a strongly irreversible step, that imprinted an arrow of time on the universe which survives to this day. (Davies 1988, 129)

The end of inflation may have been a monumental feat of self-organization, when the homogenous universe suddenly increased its total potential entropy, thereby creating a difference between maximum potential entropy and realized entropy. According to the Brooks and

Wiley hypothesis, an expanding phase space in which maximum potential entropy increases faster than actual entropy inevitably produces time asymmetry. Therefore, the expanding phase space of the atemporal *umwelt* might have been the seed for the weak temporal polarity of the prototemporal *umwelt*. Analogously, the expansion of the prototemporal *umwelt*'s phase space may have engendered the rather more pronounced thermodynamic arrow of time characteristic of the eotemporal *umwelt*.

If this scenario is accurate, Fraser's biotemporal present was, indeed, a massively discontinuous intensification of temporal asymmetry, but it was not its emergence ex nihilo. On the contrary, biotemporal temporal anisotropy would be simply one moment in the evolution of greater and greater temporal asymmetry. In terms of Fraser's later formulation, this theory would suggest that the two opposing arrows of time—"Growth and decay—decrease and increase of entropy—are simultaneously present in the universe. Let their coexistence be represented by the shaft of a headless arrow. We are entitled to think about this shaft as two arrows in one, pointing in opposite directions, thus offsetting the directional preference that a single arrow would represent" (1987, 279–80)—are never of equal length (or intensity) in any of the universe's integrative levels. Instead, I hypothesize as follows: (1) If growth is conceived of as the simultaneous increase in both maximum potential entropy and observed entropy with the condition that, as Brooks and Wiley maintain, actual entropy increases more slowly than maximum potential entropy; (2) and if decay is conceived of as the inverse—a simultaneous decrease in these two values, so long as the actual entropy decreases at a slower rate than maximum potential entropy; (3) and if any nonzero value of the difference between maximum potential entropy and observed entropy is equivalent to a measure of organization and of time asymmetry generating disequilibrium; (4) then the universe is temporally polarized through and through, though only statistically.

Furthermore, if Fraser's integrative levels represent discontinuous increases in both maximum potential entropy and observed entropy, as well as the maximum potential distance separating them, then we would expect that, as the universe gains in overall complexity, temporal asymmetry would undergo a concomitant sharpening of definition. I suspect that the universe has undergone successive stages of stability, growth, and decay, with the overall vector being long periods of relative equilibrium punctuated by discontinuous jumps (themselves occurring with increasing speed, measured by noo/sociotemporal clock time) where both maximum potential entropy and observed entropy, as well as the distance separating them, increase simultaneously. Thus, if the value of this difference increases with each jump in temporal complexity, then it is possible to argue that temporal asymmetry evolves along with the evolution of the universe.

To recapitulate, the universe's expanding phase space, the difference between the totality of information potentially available for processing at a given level of complexity and the amount of information that the level's constraints allow, creates the entropy differential that is a level-specific temporal anisotropy. Of course, this must be thought of as a statistical average, since not all systems within a given *umwelt* need to display its characteristic arrow of time. Even noo/sociotemporal human beings experience eotemporal, pure succession or prototemporal, probabilistic succession. However, I believe that each *umwelt* contains processes that display a measure of temporal anisotropy, from the faintest asymmetry inhabiting the atemporal to the pronounced temporal asymmetry of the noo/sociotemporal. Furthermore, just as an arrow of time becomes more pronounced and clearly delineated as time evolves, so does the relative importance of anisotropic temporal events, or the probability of encountering them. Until the biotemporal *umwelt*, the arrow of time is both weak and limited in scope, so it plays a relatively minor part in the functioning of systems. With biotemporality, and especially with noo/sociotemporality, temporal asymmetry becomes increasingly important and widespread, so much so that a sharp distinction between past and future is less an incidental characteristic of human beings than definitive of what it means to be human.

I believe that the far-from-equilibrium structures described by Brooks and Wiley suggest an explanation of the mechanism underlying the evolution of time into more complex temporalities with increasingly better defined arrows of time. If Turner's distinction between nature's desire to do things as fast as possible and the scheduling problem inherent in the necessity of following certain sequences is mapped onto the Brooks and Wiley model, then maximum speed would be analogous to maximum potential entropy and the need to adopt certain sequences would be analogous to actual or observed entropy. In other words, any system must experience the constraint of the nonidentity between the possibility of following all possible paths to an end and that of following only those allowed by the system.

There is an element of tragedy in evolution, a version of the quantum mechanical idea of collapsing the wave function. Systems are always slower than they might be if every possible temporal combination allowable in principle in a given *umwelt* were to be realized; yet, it is because of this tragic choice that something gets accomplished at all. A system in maximum temporal entropy would be rarified potential and little else. Like a thoroughly deconstructed world, it would spin so fast and in so many directions that the result would be a strange barrenness.

Since an integrative level must allow for the making of choices if it is to do anything, and since choice implies that the system must always run more slowly than it could if it were to devolve into pure possibility, then it follows that a given system or *umwelt* will always run a bit behind schedule. Derrida's notion of primordial delay (1982) is useful here, since I think it accurately describes the simple idea that the cost of preventing a system from disintegrating into maximum potential entropy is a discrepancy between what can be done and what needs to be done. Far-from-equilibrium systems are always a bit slow: their phase space is characterized by the difference between the need to work as rapidly as possible and the tragic necessity of choosing actual temporal configurations.

I hypothesize that when this situation becomes exacerbated, the conditions are right for a global leap of self-organization, increasing the temporal phase space of the system. Global and discontinuous expansion of a system's temporal phase space is intuitively represented as a kind of explosion. Indeed, the evolution of the universe is normally depicted as the physical expansion following an explosive big bang. As long as we realize that such expansion is, in fact, literally true regarding matter, but only metaphorically true when describing the increasing complexity of time, it is a useful visual representation of evolution. However, I would like to suggest that it is possible to view evolution inversely, as increasing contraction into more and more complex configurations. I suspect that a system creates more time for itself by imploding, that is by creating greater temporal depth. Needing to accomplish an infinite number of tasks infinitely fast, yet restricted to a finite temporality, time behaves like phase space when it is stretched and folded to accommodate exponential expansion in a finite space.

> The key to understanding chaotic behavior lies in understanding a simple stretching and folding operation, which takes place in the state space. Exponential divergence is a local feature: because attractors have finite size, two orbits on a chaotic attractor cannot diverge exponentially forever. Consequently the attractor must fold over onto itself. . . . The process of stretching and folding happens repeatedly, creating folds within folds ad infinitum. A chaotic attractor is, in other words, a fractal: an object that reveals more detail as it is increasingly magnified. (Crutchfield et al. 1986, 51)

I imagine the evolution of time to be a similar kind of stretching and folding. If that were the case, then Fraser's temporal *umwelts* would be increasingly complex because they would display greater fractal depth, that is, they would be a palimpsest of more and more complex, though self-similar insofar as they all display a similar pattern of temporal asymmetry, temporalities. The more complex a temporality, the better defined is its arrow of time, and the more means it has at its disposal to do things. For example, compare the primitive and deterministic temporality of a paramecium's nervous system to the incredibly complex way in which the human brain juggles a huge number of temporalities. However, just as Fraser suggests that the price paid for resolution of lower level conflicts at an upper level is the emergence of new conflicts that are themselves unresolvable at the upper level, the price for an increase in scheduling possibilities is an ever-increasing number of kinds of work that can be done. In other words, as Brooks and Wiley claim, the evolution of the phase space of a far-from-equilibrium system will always mean that maximum potential entropy increases faster than actual entropy. Although in the following quotation Brooks and Wiley are discussing matter, I think that an analogous argument can be made for time.

> For example, cosmological models suggest that the universe expands faster than the matter in the universe can distribute itself. The reason for the lag is gravitational effects that slow the ex-

pansion of matter. As a result, there is local clumpiness of expanding matter within expanding surroundings. The expanding phase space means that the entropy maximum (S_{max}) for the system is increasing through time. The expansion of matter and dissipation of energy from the clumped matter indicate that entropy (S) is increasing as a result of work being done. The ordering of the universe indicates that S_{max} is increasing more than S, so the accumulation of physical order is due not to local entropy decreases but to constraints slowing the increase in entropy. In other words, the system is constantly moving towards entropy maximum, but S_{max} is receding from the system faster than the system expands towards it. (Brooks and Wiley 1988, 58–59)

That is, as the universe creates more ingenious ways to do work, it simultaneously creates more work to be done. The tragedy of tragedy is that its resolution is simply the beginning of even greater tragedy, whose pathos is unimaginable at the level of the original tragedy.

A kind of primordial delay selects for the folding of time into itself, creating complexity, depth, and increasing asymmetry. This new state of complexity solves the scheduling problem at the original level, only to find itself in ingeniously novel bottlenecks. As time becomes more distinctly asymmetric, more space is created for remembered and projected work. Furthermore, entirely new temporal technologies emerge, such as parallel and distributed neural networks, ritual, narrative, art, and electronic, especially computerized, information processing. However, even as they allow for the exponential increase of information-processing technologies, they also create new dimensions of potential temporal speed against which any actual speed is deemed slow. Time's depth, the infolding of its phase space to create the intricate and beautiful filigree of nested temporalities described by Fraser is, itself, the most asymmetrical temporality imaginable. The ultimate arrow of time is time's fractal scales, the history of its tragic resistance against those limits that had, at a previous level, just set it free.

Chapter 18

Beauty and Ritual

Although, to my knowledge, Derrida has never engaged in an extended analysis of the concept of beauty (unless *The Truth in Painting* counts as one), the general contours of such an analysis are, I believe, not difficult to imagine. His deconstruction of beauty might include the demonstration of its filiation with the metaphysics of presence followed by the attempt to prove that beauty is dependent on some tracelike structure that is, itself, neither beautiful nor ugly. Or he might engage in a more Foucauldian kind of analysis, seeking to situate the historical, political, and institutional determinations of the concept. What Derrida would certainly refuse to do is to consider the possibility that beauty is not simply a product of cultural forces, but that it may have a universal natural basis. Not only would Derrida decline to speculate on the universality of beauty, he would doubtless avoid commerce with the concept of universality in general. In fact, as good a definition of deconstruction as any is the metaphysical conviction that nothing is universal.

In contrast to this sort of position, which I attribute to deconstruction but which has such currency today that, ironically, it has become naturalized, I propose to argue that, as long as the concept of universality is understood in the chaotic sense described in the previous chapters, it is possible to postulate a universal concept of beauty that is defensible both theoretically and ethically.

I believe that the historical basis for the hypothetical deconstructive position on beauty just presented is the combination of two notions, Kant's definition of art and the radical antifoundationalism that has come to dominate aesthetic thought in the postwar period. Specifically, two conjoined ideas—that the aesthetic is synonymous with disinterested contemplation and that abstract concepts such as beauty are social constructs—have made it nearly impossible to engage in a serious study of beauty in the current intellectual environment.

It is plausible that the curious elimination of the concept of beauty from much current aesthetic speculation stems, in large measure, from the hegemony of social constructivism as an explanatory theoretical matrix. Since social constructivism maintains that much, if not all, of the meaningfulness of the world is a construction of social, political, economic, ideological, institutional, and historical forces, no statement about the world can be assumed to have any extracultural reference. When Derrida says "There is nothing outside the text," he does not mean that the world outside of texts is not real, but that its fundamental Being is textual, founded on nothing more solid than discursive practices.

The basic claim of this book is that constructivist positions are correct as long as the concept of history they employ is not arbitrarily limited. In other words, if one wishes to maintain that there is nothing outside historical signifying practices, I see no justification in limiting the slice of history under consideration to a mere two or three thousand years. There is, indeed, nothing outside the text, but the text, meaning the totality of referential relations or languages constitutive of the world, must be understood to include the history of the entire universe. If we are the product of a combination of Darwinian evolution and Prigoginian self-organization, then a full understanding of the human world must include our total history, everything from the big bang to theories about the big bang, not just that small slice of it that myopic constructivists elevate to the whole.

I would like to argue, therefore, that although beauty is certainly a human concept, it is not simply an artifact of the cultural concept-smithy. On the contrary, I believe that the human concept of beauty has an extra—human language referent—that is, it refers to something real in the world. Furthermore, that to which it refers has a history, so more primitive versions of it can be seen in the prehuman world. To make my point, I would like to examine a rather ordinary example of prehuman ritual. The reason for my choice of ritual behavior is that I suspect that there is an intimate relation between ritual and beauty. It is perhaps no accident that most of our access to beauty is in contexts that are heavily ritualized, from religious ceremony, to theatrical performance, to the personal rituals we all employ to highlight the little corners of beauty we encounter

in ordinary life. If there is something noncontingent about the relation of beauty to ritual, then ritualized behavior may suggest both a
valuable access to the concept of beauty, and, in the case of prehuman ritual, a means of discussing beauty in a nonanthropocentric
fashion.

When chimpanzees consume a recent kill, they do so in a remarkably organized way. A series of ritualized patterns of interaction
while prey is eaten suggest that what is at stake in such "exchange
rituals" is less the acquisition of calories than the reinforcement of the
rather complex social world of chimpanzees. The following is a brief
description of the chimpanzee exchange ritual.

> A variety of vocal and gestural signals occurs in connection with
> the sharing of a carcass. The sounds, gestures, and facial ex-
> pressions seen during this stage are not specific to predation,
> though some may appear more frequently in this than in any
> other behavioral context. (Teleki 1973, 146)

What is perhaps most striking about this ritual is the nearly total
absence of aggression between meat requestors and meat controllers.
In fact, the exchange ritual seems to foster a high degree of cooperation and communication among the participating chimpanzees.
Using the classic ritual techniques of motor synchronization, or "tuning," and of intricately choreographed patterns of information exchange, the food consumption ritual of chimpanzees performs the
typical function of all ritual—to allow a member of a group, and of
the group itself, to represent a whole many of whose component
parts are individually inaccessible. In this case, the exchange ritual
appears to allow members of the chimpanzee group to form a concept
of community, that is, of the complex hierarchy of roles that constitutes chimpanzee society.

Charles D. Laughlin and John McManus speculate that the significance of such exchange rituals is that they involve the creation of
symbolic entities.

> All of these factors seem to indicate to us that chimpanzees
> recognize the entire period of predation—capture, carcass divi-
> sion and meat exchange—as conceptually distinct from other
> forms of interaction. To what degree the exchange ritual is also

a source of symbolization still remains unknown. It is not entirely unreasonable to hypothesize that the meat itself (with the
exception of brain tissue; see Teleki, 142) takes on the conceptual status of symbol for chimpanzee participants. (d'Aquili,
Laughlin, and McManus 1979, 107))

It begins to appear that the exchange ritual could be described as the
First Supper: a complex series of social interactions in which a community is organized around an object that, if we are cautious about
respecting level distinctions, might be characterized as sacred. I believe that the chimpanzee exchange ritual is a primitive, prehuman
version of religious ceremony. Like human religious ritual, it performs the functions of interpersonal coordination, role assignment,
and social communication. But more than that, the exchange ritual
follows all ritual in the construction of a new entity—the circumscribed space of the aesthetic.

Laughlin and McManus's hypothesis that the exchange ritual
creates a special social arena in which normal patterns of Being are
suspended is especially interesting in the light of Victor Turner's
theory of liminality (1986). Turner believes that ritual creates a state
of liminality, a kind of social margin in which the very foundations
of a culture are rehearsed, tested, tuned, enforced, and occasionally
altered. The liminal state is a kind of social laboratory where experiments concerning the symbolic objects most dear to a culture are
performed so that they may be affirmed, torn asunder, replaced, or
reconstructed. If rituals are the genes of a culture, then ritual liminality may be an ancient form of genetic engineering.

The chimpanzee exchange ritual clears an opening in which the
world normally available to individual members of the group suddenly expands to include nonphysical entities. A given chimp participating in the ritual has a sense of a complex object that it cannot
literally see: a social system whose very existence depends on such
rituals. Furthermore, it is likely that, in dividing up food and sharing
it according to rank and status, the chimpanzees create a primitive
sense of sacred symbolism. The meat, like Christian communion,
becomes less a source of energy than a symbolic entity representing
the genuine possibility of transcendence. Specifically, the meat as
sacred object both symbolizes the performative creation of a world
previously unavailable to lower mammals—the world of symbols and

ideas—and is a crucial instrument in the constitution of this higher evolutionary integrative level.

As I have mentioned, the creation and reception of beauty is almost always ritualized. On an intuitive level, it is perfectly clear why this should be so. Beauty has usually been associated with the gods, and, as such, it is simultaneously awe inspiring, terrible, and comforting. Our sense of beauty and our obsession with the sacred, both of which have displayed remarkable resilience even in our secular historical period, suggest that the nexus of beauty, ritual, and sacredness may be of far greater importance to us as a species than most contemporary philosophers suspect.

The necessity for this triumvirate begins to be apparent in the chimpanzee exchange ritual. I believe that the exchange ritual is a relic, a kind of phylogenetic artifact, of the kinds of conditions, activities, and behaviors that enabled our evolution into human beings. Whatever the specific environmental pressures that selected for the creation of the huge neocortex of our earliest prehuman and human ancestors, they doubtless selected for such things as symbolic thought, kinship, long-term memory, and, perhaps most important of all, what Peter J. Wilson calls the ability to make promises. To promise is to be able to envision a future that is unlike the present, to populate it with events that have not occurred, and to project one's own existence and responsibilities beyond the palpable here and now. Human beings tend to live in the subjunctive and conditional moods, carving out hypothetical regions of the world in which to situate the most treasured components of their Being. Somehow, millions of years ago, a chimpanzeelike creature evolved into a promising primate. I would like to suggest that the complex network of conditions, choices, pressures, and events that enabled this momentous leap could be economically characterized as beauty.

One of the problems with traditional Darwinian explanations of evolution is that they fail to account adequately for the discontinuities of evolving systems. The obvious example that comes to mind is perhaps the second most crucial event in the history of the universe, after its origin, namely the creation of life. But even a more sedate event, such as the enlargement of the neocortex in advanced prehominids, is not easily explained through recourse to a model of evolution based on the principles of continuity and linearity. Evolution is not a continuously integrable linear function. On the contrary, evolution is a heavily feedback-dependent, recursive, nonlinear system. Simply, evolution is chaotic.

The new science of chaos promises to shed much light on the way in which natural systems can generate order spontaneously, that is, without supernatural intervention. Prigogine's central thesis, that when natural systems are pushed into far-from-equilibrium conditions they have the ability to undergo discontinuous global organization, is of tremendous importance to the question at hand. It is almost certainly the case that our evolution into human beings was not a sober and gradual increase in cerebral mass, but a sudden, nonlinear leap in organizational complexity. This leap must have been chaotic, that is, it must have followed an irreversible trajectory consisting of the abrupt level jumps characteristic of feedback-generated, dissipative systems. Joseph Ford's aphorism, "Evolution is chaos with feedback," is also a definition of ritual. Ritual is evolution insofar as ritual is, in large measure, the sudden creation of precisely those symbolic entities such as community, kinship, taboo, gods—in short, culture—that constitute the invention of human beings.

At this point, the reader might wonder what all this has to do with beauty, especially with a nonanthropocentric definition of beauty. In fact, I would like to argue that the concepts under consideration—evolution, feedback, chaos, and ritual—combine to form a system which *is* the beautiful. Despite the awesome speed with which the universe has evolved, it is nevertheless an essentially conservative system. Once a solution works for a particular niche or integrative level, the solution tends to select for the maintenance of its own state of greatest equilibrium. But periodically, something occurs that kicks the system out of equilibrium. Disequilibrium can have an external origin, as in a significant change in the environment (which can itself be caused by the intervention of the system into its environment), an internal etiology, as when the system develops to the point where it is no longer in balance with its environment, or, most likely, by a dialectic between exogenous and endogenous causality. I suspect that, more often than not, such moments result in the destruction of the system. Occasionally, however, when conditions are right, such a far-from-equilibrium system can undergo a global leap of organization. At times, such events are truly creative— they bring into existence something that did not previously exist. An example, of course, is the creation of life, but in general I postulate that every evolutionary leap was occasioned by some kind of global leap of self-organization. And I think that this is precisely what constitutes the beautiful—the unpredictable and discontinuous emergence of higher levels of systemic complexity. When we read a work of literature that we are tempted to describe as beautiful, I suspect that, at the very least, the work is a self-similar system, displaying similar patterns at different levels of description, and that it functions as a nonlinear, dynamical system able to occasion global leaps of organization in the reader's mind.

If the chimpanzee exchange ritual is a remnant of the kind of event that pushed our hominid ancestors toward the creation of a human type of culture, then we must imagine that, in their own way, these chimps have an appreciation of the beauty of their performance. Their ritual is not simply mammalian reflex, their symbols are not merely bestial, and their kinship structures are not just mindless sexual behavior. In a real sense, these chimpanzees are Promethean. If the most intense selective pressure for the creation of human beings came from our ability to make promises, then the chimpanzee exchange ritual is part of an immense repertory of ritual behaviors through which we promised ourselves into being. By promising, we entertain counterfactual information in our brains and this, through a feedback mechanism, selects for more complex brains. So, if we interpret the chimpanzee exchange ritual as a precursor of the human habitation in the symbolic and hypothetical, then, in a way, apes such as these chimpanzees once promised themselves humanity.

There is something terrible about such transcendence, which is why, I suppose, we have tended to make beauty the province of gods who are as overpowering as they are comforting. But in the end, what is truly deserving of our awe and terror is the possibility that beauty may be a perfectly natural occurrence. We should abandon the traditional view of nature as a benign, stable, and unimaginative ground upon which humans impose their interventionist schemes. Instead, nature can now be seen as seething with beauty. What we gain by such an understanding of nature is a deeply satisfying sense of connectedness with the rest of the natural world. If beauty is indeed evolution, and if evolution is fueled by chaotic self-organization, then we are in a position to make beautiful things, that is, art, because we ourselves were invented in a beautiful disruption of ecological equilibrium.

Chapter 19

The Chaotic Mind

The Self

Despite the residual attraction of some form of mind-body dualism, I take it as fairly well settled that mind is simply a higher level description of brain, much as wet is a higher level description of certain molecular structures. Assuming then, that a great deal of our knowledge, from that associated with our lower *umwelts* to that which belongs properly to the noo/sociotemporal world, is stored in our bodies, it is reasonable to ask how it is stored and how it is routinely retrieved and manipulated. For the purposes of this chapter, I will focus on that part of noo/sociotemporal and sociotemporal knowledge that is stored and rearranged in the brain, excluding, for example, knowledge kept in books or computer banks.[1] How then, is this incredible feat of information technology accomplished?

Because it has been done so well elsewhere by people much more qualified than I, I will refrain from indulging in lower level, neurophysiological descriptions of brain activity. Instead I will make some tentative speculations from a highly chunked, upper level perspective. I wish to emphasize the hypothetical nature of these ideas. Their ultimate validation must await empirical research.

In the postscript to a chapter on mathematical chaos and strange attractors, Hofstadter introduces the concept of "locking-in," a description of how a system zeroes in on its most stable state: "The imagery I wish to convey is that of a system that seeks and gradually settles into its own most stable states, and the mechanism whereby it seeks and attains such loci of stability is *feedback*" (1985, 389). Locking-in is a process whereby a system uses iteration and feedback to find its most stable configuration. As such, it appears to be simply another way of describing the construction of a mathematical dynamical system that can be represented in phase space by an attractor. As is his wont, however, Hofstadter is not content to inhabit the disciplinary boundaries appropriate to a mathematician or a physicist. In his usual bold fashion, he proceeds to speculate that locking-in may be central to two crucial philosophical problems: the creation and maintenance of an identity, an I, and the retrieval of memory.

In order to situate a chaotic theory of mind, I will first translate some of the conclusions reached in chapter 5 into the language of chaos. In the wake of psychoanalysis, deconstruction, and social constructivism, the concept of the self has been thoroughly discredited in academic circles. Yet if we follow Wittgenstein's exhortation to philosophers to look rather than think, or Griffin's "hard-core commonsense . . . , the idea that the ultimate criteria for testing philosophical doctrines are those notions all people in fact presuppose in practice, even if they deny them verbally" (1986, 8), then it becomes clear that those who announce the demise of the self tend to cling to it with fierce tenacity. Indeed, my experience has been that it is precisely the gurus of the fragmented self who are most likely to wallow in self-indulgence and narcissism. Of course, I am not suggesting that the self can be equated with a Cartesian pinpoint. Marvin Minsky's idea of a society of mind (1986), in which the mind is pictured as a vast hierarchy and heterarchy of interconnected agencies, is undoubtedly a better metaphor for the mind's structure and activity than dualistic closure. However, as Hofstadter argues (1980), it would be bizarre if an organ as complex as the brain, rife as it is with symbols for nearly everything, including many things that are counterfactual, did not contain a symbol for itself. The self, Hofstadter suspects, is probably such a subsystem of the brain whose purpose is to monitor the complex nexus of symbols and representations constitutive of brain activity. In other words, the self is a symbol serving the executive function of mental self-reference—it is the mind including itself in its symbolic world. That the self-symbol is unlikely to be a single mental agency, that it is, itself, probably a fabulously complex network, goes without saying; the point, however, is that at a higher, chunked level the self's systemic articulations coalesce to give us that sense of identity across time and space that most humans share.

If our intuitive sense of a self is indeed an accurate representation of the brain's organization, then it follows that, given the essentially social nature of human consciousness, the self cannot be either a fixed essence or an isolated monad. It must be a dynamical system open to the world and especially to other selves. Borrowing from physics, Hofstadter calls this *mitsein* of the self "renormalization": "the way that elementary particles such as electrons and positrons and photons all take each other into account" (1985, 393). Bootstrapped into being, the human self is simultaneously the most strongly individuated self in the animal world, and the most communal. To my mind, the most fascinating contribution made by Hofstadter to the theory of self is that he believes that the self is constituted by and maintains itself through a dynamical process of level-crossing feedback and recursion. In other words, the self appears to have some of the hallmarks of a chaotic attractor.

> This close connection of locking-in to the deepest essence of personhood plays a central role also in Chapters 22 and 25, where "who" one is is portrayed as emerging from a "level-crossing feedback loop," in which a sophisticated perceiving system perceived limited aspects of its own nature, and by feeding them back into the system creates a type of locking-in. The locked-in loop is itself given a name, and that name, for every such system, is "I." (Hofstadter 1985, 394)

If instead of the choice between a Cartesian and a Deleuzian self, that is, between a transcendentally secure self and a disjointed schizo-self out for a walk, we were to picture the self as a chaotic attractor, then I believe that a model for selfhood might emerge that fulfills some of the correct requirements of classical conceptions of the self as well as the important contributions to the philosophy of self made by deconstruction and psychoanalysis. The self as a chaotic feedback loop locking-in on its attractor would be at once open to the world and to other selves, yet possessed of a deeply felt identity. A chaotic self would have a perdurable shape, the attractor, yet such a self would never repeat itself. Simultaneously Cartesian and Heraclitean, a chaotic self would be consonant with the intuition of much contemporary theory, that the self is not a fortress carried through time, but a dynamic, changing, multiple, and, at times, contradictory network, while not sacrificing the equally compelling idea that the self does indeed have coherence and integrity. Furthermore, if the self is a renormalized feedback system, then it is a radically intersubjective entity essentially open to the social world. And, since a chaotic self would be constantly crossing levels, creating tangled hierarchies and strange loops, then a large part of its being would consist of levels below the threshold of consciousness, thereby allowing room for Freud's subconscious and unconscious minds. In short, a chaotic, feedback-generated, level-crossing, renormalized self closely resembles the self most people have in mind when using the word *I:* a dynamical, open, temporally complex, multiple system with a profound sense of its own identity and stability.

Tangled Ideas

Having speculated on a chaotic self, Hofstadter proceeds to make an analogous argument concerning memory. Just as the self might be a form of chaotic locking-in, so memory might be a self-equilibrating, dynamical process: "In short, locking-in—that is, convergent and self-stabilizing behavior—will surely pervade the ultimate explanation of most mysteries of mind. One example is the question of memory retrieval" (1985, 94). Hofstadter is concerned with the mechanism whereby dimly remembered representations are conjured up through the use of vague associations. Using the ideas of cognitive psychologist Pentti Kanerva, he imagines that the haziest of associations function as a kind of seed that, when fed into the memory retrieval system, begins a complex feedback and locking-in process that often results in the production of the correct memory.

> The seed is fed into memory-retrieval mechanisms, which convert it into an output vector that is then fed back in again. This cyclic process continues until it either converges on a stable fixed point—the desired memory trace—or is seen to be wandering erratically without any likelihood of locking in, tracing out a chaotic sequence of "points" in mind space. (394–95)

Memory retrieval, therefore, might involve the introduction of a perturbation into a dynamical system that proceeds to use its output as input until it senses that it is tracing an attractor or that it is plotting points haphazardly. If it describes an attractor, it has accomplished its task; if it is disseminating wildly, it does the reasonable thing and throws in the towel.

I would like to suggest that Hofstadter's model of memory retrieval might be expanded to include the constitution, modification, and recovering of ideas in general. In order to pursue this possibility, let us return to the notion of cultural universals. As I hope is clear, I have used the term *cultural universals* somewhat rhetorically to underline the difference in perspective between an evolutionary epistemology and the various cultural relativisms I have had occasion to criticize. To repeat the main point of chapter 14, I hypothesize that knowledge is spread out along a scale ranging from the nearly universal to the highly idiosyncratic. The mind probably stores its ideas in some treelike fashion using hierarchical and heterarchical arrangements in order to facilitate the work of both mapping the world and actively rearranging its maps. Furthermore, it is unlikely that the mind uses only one strategy to store, manipulate, and create information; every indication that we currently have suggests that the brain is highly redundant, so I suspect that its ideas are stored as prototypes, abstractions, and lists, as well as structural, functional, and associative descriptions. And, contrary to what many language chauvinists might believe, it is quite clear that the mind avails itself of a congeries of information-processing techniques—linguistic, to be sure, but also visual, musical, olfactory, somatic, etc. Furthermore, I do not think that ideas are localized; using Minsky's society of mind metaphor, it is productive to imagine that an idea is a chunked symbol of a large number of subagencies working in a partially parallel, partially distributed, partially discrete fashion.

The metaphysical desire for certainty, which for Derrida is a primitive of our logocentric world, is a limit case of a much more modest typical mental strategy. Generally, the mind does not require absolute certainty to recognize an idea or a representation. For example, Minsky argues that if "chairness" were to consist of six functional, structural, and associative characteristics, something less than all six of these need be present in a nexus of representations for it to qualify as a chair. "In real life, no recognition-scheme will always work if it's based on absolutely perfect evidence. A more judicious scheme would not demand that every feature of a chair be seen; instead, it would only 'weigh the evidence' that a chair is present. For example, we could make a chair-agent that becomes active whenever five or more of our six chair features are in sight" (Minsky 1986, 201). Clearly there are thresholds under which there is confusion, and other thresholds under which there is negative certainty ("that is not a chair"). The exact nature of these thresholds need not concern us here, since they are probably highly protean in their sensitivity to environmental differences. The point is that noo/sociotemporal knowledge is probably arranged in a hierarchical structure of hypotheses about the world. These hypotheses, consisting of abstractions, theories, prototypes, narratives, associations, among other things, are matched against incoming data in a continuous synthesis requiring neither certainty (a complete match) nor even total agreement among the hypothetical criteria (a desk upon which one sits can count as a chair and as an example of epistemological flexibility). I think that ultimately there is little difference between the way so-called abstract concepts (freedom, love, etc.) and concrete concepts (table, this table, etc.) are processed. As Lakoff and Johnson argue (1980), it is probably the case that abstract concepts are conceptualized in terms of a number of core metaphors. Although metaphor is undoubtedly also at play in the way concrete concepts are conceptualized, I suspect that such concepts are processed more in terms of functional and structural descriptions. Nevertheless, both concrete and abstract concepts are probably confederacies of hypotheses containing elements of all of the mind's information strategies.

It is precisely this kind of confederacy that Hofstadter calls a symbol which serves as a default hypothesis about a given concept and its relation to some sort of referent. Needless to say, since conceptual confederacies are themselves forests of different hierarchically ordered agencies, they display a tremendous amount of systemic flexibility, rearranging themselves constantly in response to fluctuations in the exterior environment (the natural and social worlds) and to the interior environment (the mind).

Crutchfield et al. believe that chaos offers a way of conceptualizing free will in a world apparently dominated by deterministic laws: "Innate creativity may have an underlying chaotic process that selectively amplifies small fluctuations and molds them into macroscopic coherent mental states that are experienced as thoughts" (1986, 57). In addition, they also theorize that chaos might be the underlying principle of evolution: "Biological evolution demands genetic variability; chaos provides a means of structuring random changes, thereby providing the possibility of putting variability under evolutionary control" (57). If these ideas were combined, and if the product were infused into Minsky's notion of a society of mental agencies, it would be possible to imagine a model of mind that consists of a chaotic society of chaotic systems and subsystems.

I believe that what philosophy has called an *idea* can be fruitfully conceptualized as a symbol in Hofstadter's sense of a self-adjusting, feedback-dependent mental subsystem. As opposed to the logical positivists, who define an idea as a sovereign, simple, punctual, and irreducible piece of information; and as opposed to Derrida, for whom an idea is a temporary crystallization of an uncontrollably semiotic network of traces, Gleick suggests that an idea might be pictured as an attractor in mental space.

> Many other scientists began to apply the formalisms of chaos to research in artificial intelligence. The dynamics of systems wandering between basins of attraction, for example, appealed to those looking for a way to model symbols and memories. A physicist thinking of *ideas* as regions with fuzzy boundaries, separate yet overlapping, pulling like magnets and yet letting go, would naturally turn to the image of phase space with "basins of attraction." Such models seemed to have the right features: points of stability mixed with instability, and regions with changeable boundaries. Their fractal structure offered the kind of infinitely self-referential quality that seems so central to the mind's ability to bloom with ideas, decisions, emotions, and all the other artifacts of consciousness. With or without chaos, serious cognitive scientists can no longer model the mind as a static structure. They recognize a hierarchy of scales, from neuron upward, providing an opportunity for the interplay of microscale and macroscale so characteristic of fluid turbulence and other complex dynamical processes. (1987, 298)

One of the guiding motivations of deconstruction is the attempt to demonstrate that ideas are not Platonic essences. Derrida believes that the traditional conception of ideas posits them as fully present, securely circumscribed, and exhaustively specified signifieds. For Derrida, metaphysics is basically Platonism—the attempt to render the signifier transparent and, therefore, superfluous in the presence of the autonomous signified.

Chaos offers a nondualistic resolution to the Plato/anti-Plato opposition. If we were to conceptualize ideas as attractors instead of either essences or trace structures, then we would be in a position to meld the stability of determinism with the energy of serendipity. The crucial point is that we must stop thinking of ideas as things and begin to conceptualize them as dynamical systems. The mind, as Minsky asserts, is probably a society of agencies. Specifically, it is a supersystem composed of a highly complex and tangled hierarchy of subsystems. One of these, the self, has already been discussed. The staples of our epistemology, the various ways in which we have knowledge of the world—our judgments, desires, and concepts, for example—are also systems. These systems are themselves composed of subsystems and serve as subsystems of other subsystems. Some of these subsystems, certainly the most powerful ones, are linguistic, but some are not. Language is important, but it is no prison-house. However, since all of the mind's subsystems are interconnected in an intricate feedback and feedforward fashion, it is somewhat meaningless to speculate on the relative importance of language in constituting the cognitive world. Even such squarely nonlinguistic subsystems as music and visual art owe at least part of their being to information exchange with more linguistically oriented subsystems, so in the end what matters is that the mind is able to use its various component subsystems in the most efficient and appropriate manner given the demands of its environment.

If we think of ideas as dynamical confederacies, then we can describe the scale of cultural universals symbolized by Hofstadter's ASU in terms of chaos theory. For the sake of simplicity, I will restrict this discussion to the kinds of knowledge stored in our nervous system, that is, biotemporal and noo/sociotemporal knowledge, although it could clearly be extended to kinds of knowledge appropriate to the lower *umwelts*. The physical properties and the preinscribed geological features of Hofstadter's map are analogous to a range of biotemporal knowledge. Although dynamical, such knowledge probably traces simple, low-dimension attractors. Therefore, it tends to be nearly identical across cultures. For example, all human beings "know" to tremble when cold, to salivate when hungry, or to breathe fast during sex.

The bulk of human ideas, theories, beliefs, or desires can be represented by chaotic attractors of varying degrees of complexity.

Some ideas, such as Lakoff and Johnson's experiential concepts, "the central concepts in terms of which our bodies function—UP-DOWN, IN-OUT, FRONT-BACK, LIGHT-DARK, WARM-COLD, MALE-FEMALE . . . object, substance, container" (1980, 56–57), are primitive human concepts and are, therefore, as universal as the average U.S. citizen's knowledge of the location of New York City on a map. Not everyone can find New York on a map of the United States, but there is a fairly high probability that, given a large enough sample, a statistically significant number of people will. Similarly, although some people will claim that for them "Up is Bad," and that consequently the expression "Things are looking up" as meaning "Things are getting better" is an example of cultural imperialism, I expect that a cross-cultural sample would confirm the near universality of Lakoff and Johnson's basic concepts and their metaphorical conceptualization.

More complex ideas and beliefs trace even higher dimension attractors. In other words, although I am claiming that because all people have roughly the same brain and live in roughly the same world, their idea-attractors will be partially isomorphic, the more complex the attractor, the more room it leaves for local variation. Thus, the attractor *chair* is likely to be simpler than the attractor *god* or *beauty*. Nevertheless, if this hypothesis is correct, the truly amazing thing is that there should be a basin of epistemological attraction at all. Why should a New Guinea tribesman and a North Dallas professor be able to communicate on the nature of god or beauty? Of course, the cultural relativists say that they can't, that their discussion, if it were literally possible through a translator, would, in fact, be an instance of dueling ethnocentrisms. I say that such a view is philosophically unsound, but, more important, myopic and niggardly. *God* and *beauty* are cross-cultural attractors. Nearly every culture, I warrant, will have devoted a great deal of energy to developing, nurturing, and transmitting these concepts. Furthermore, their understanding will trace an attractor (or, perhaps more accurately, a society of attractors) in the mental phase space of its members that resembles the attractors in the mental phase space of the members of other cultures in enough ways that genuine intercultural communication is possible. Yet, because we are conceptualizing ideas as complex dynamical systems, a complete overlap will be impossible, thereby guaranteeing cultural autonomy and difference as well as the promise that communication is neither imperialistic projection nor mere tautology. Furthermore, since chaotic systems are susceptible to discontinuous global transformation, it is possible to account for the unpredictable generation and spread of new ideas, although it should be emphasized that the kinds of constraints outlined earlier limit the *probability* of such proliferation.

One of the unexpected bonuses of a chaotic epistemology is that it is able to rehabilitate the concept of depth. Beginning perhaps with Barthes's influence, depth has been a much-maligned notion of late. Given critical legitimacy by Barthes, aesthetic weight by Robbe-Grillet, and philosophical sanction by Derrida, the devaluation of depth has been highly successful. Derrida's repeated attacks on the supposed autonomy of the signified and his concomitant efforts to affirm the horizontal spread of the trace have tended to make deconstructive critics eager to condemn depth as another manifestation of the metaphysics of presence. And yet, as is usually the case with basic ideas, the notion of depth, especially in its positive, metaphoric sense, has displayed remarkable resilience.

If, following Minsky and Hofstadter, an idea is imagined as a dynamical society or confederacy of symbols, and, furthermore, if the internal organization of such confederacies is roughly hierarchical, then we would expect ideas to exist in mental phase space as intricately nested fractal structures. Thus, any concept is a chunked society of other societies, themselves chunked societies of yet other societies, and so on and so forth.[2] Interestingly, such hierarchies are frequently heterarchical, thereby generating what Hofstadter calls strange or tangled loops. For example, a given concept, say "city" may be a member of the confederacy of another concept, such as "country," while simultaneously "country" is in the confederacy of "city." Hofstadter speculates that such strange loops, when coupled with recursive dynamical processes, probably constitute the crux of intelligence. My point, however, is that even though conceptual confederacies participate in countless numbers of such tangled loops, the overall structure of which they are the chunked description is generally a hierarchy of nested subsystems. The more complex the concept, probably the more complex and deep its hierarchical tree. If such is indeed the case, then our intuitive sense that some concepts or thoughts are deeper than others may be an accurate description of how the mind works. A "deep" idea may simply be an idea with a more intricate systemic structure, with a more complex society of nested self-similar layers, with a higher dimension chaotic attractor, or, what is more likely, with a combination of all three.

A chaotic epistemology, therefore, yields the following hypothesis concerning that part of human knowledge that is stored or processed in the brain: noo/sociotemporal knowledge is processed neurally in the form of a mechanism that, in the presence of appropriate stimulation, is able to describe a network of chaotic attractors in mental "phase space." These attractors guarantee translatability from one culture to another, since they tend to be globally isomorphic. Yet, their random local configurations safeguard individual and cultural difference. Globally hard edged, they allow respect for the Other because he or she is seen as participating in the same world of thought, symbols, and concepts as me; locally fuzzy, they are a healthy caution that excessive chauvinistic assimilation is both impossible and, as an ideal, undesirable.

Since chaotic attractors are not fixed points but evolving systems, a chaotic epistemology would no longer picture concepts as Platonic islands; yet, since chaotic attractors enjoy a large measure of autonomy and identity, neither would they be conceptualized as Derridian texts. Instead, a concept or idea would be understood as the chunked or emergent product of a vast network of other concepts. Its constitution would be the result of renormalization and locking-in. In other words, concepts would be dynamical syntheses melding innate genetic proclivities with feedback from both the human (i.e., social) and prehuman environments. Once locked-in, that is, once a recognizable attractor has been formed or located, concepts would become semiautonomous, yet they would always maintain an intimate relation both to other confederacies and to their immediate, lower level societies.

To tap Hofstadter's ASU once again, the chaotic structure of an idea can be likened to the dynamics of a city. A city is both connected to other cities on the map and to its constitutive boroughs, neighborhoods, blocks, houses, rooms, and walls, not to mention its inhabitants and their cultural universe. A city's external connections (to other cities, countries, etc.) are more or less strong depending on a number of factors such as geography, traffic patterns, and communication and trade networks. Its internal connections are often tangled and generally fractal (boroughs are self-similar to cities, neighborhoods are self-similar to boroughs, etc.). Clearly, a city is a dynamical entity, interacting constantly with other cities or countries and with its own microstructure. In fact, a city is a system both constituted and supported by feedback from the outside and from the inside. A city is a vague, amorphous, and flexible system (where does New York City end?), yet it is undeniably real (as a New Yorker, I can attest to the overwhelming reality of New York). Although part of many vertical and horizontal networks and ever in dynamic flux, a city tends to have a real and unmistakable identity (few people confuse New York with Paris). And finally, some cities, such as the world's great cities, have greater depth, and a concomitant increase in identity, than lesser cities. This depth, stemming from their history and from the layers of human work, creativity, and imagination that combine to perform the city into being, is palpable and goes a long way toward explaining why some cities are more interesting, seductive, and beautiful than others. I think it is unnecessary to describe the analogy I have been suggesting in greater detail. Suffice it to say that, like cities, concepts or ideas are fractally self-similar, dynamical systems whose shape or amorphousness is the result of a dialectical feedback synthesis with both their environment and their history. Like cities, ideas maintain a fluid identity that is as inimical to Derridian dissemination as it is to metaphysical closure. Like cities, ideas are perdurable but probably never permanent. Like cities, ideas are nodes in communication links with other ideas, other people, and sociotemporal entities. And like cities, ideas can perhaps be best conceptualized as attractors, or eddies, in the turbulence of personal, social, historical, and evolutionary processes.

Some Social Implications

Having presented the rudiments of a chaotic epistemology, I will turn to the possible social and ideological implications of such a theory. One of the criticisms to which this model is vulnerable is the charge that it tends to be conservative and normative. If human concepts are, in part, the individual and intersubjective representations of real, and often oppressive, institutions, then is not the notion of a universal attractor, even if it is only weakly universal, in fact a call to a kind of resignation? I believe that the main motivation behind the blank slate, xenidrin kind of social constructivism that so dominates political and philosophical thought these days is a sincere attempt to prevent the validation and maintenance of unjust social institutions in the name of "nature" or "human nature." If there is no such thing as nature except as a social construct, then no institution or idea is any more fundamental or inevitable than any other. Since appeals to nature are thereby seen as merely self-serving attempts on the part of the ruling classes to maintain their power and prestige, a properly revolutionary epistemology would first need to demonstrate the artificiality and instrumentality of such calls to foundationalism. Of course, as I argued earlier, this typically Foucauldian strategy is ultimately impotent and dangerous because, having supposedly demonstrated that truth is the product of power, it can only legitimate its own concrete proposals through an appeal to its own ungrounded power. Since social constructivists are usually unwilling to participate in such an arena of raw power, they tend to define their political practice as the production of vigilance and criticism, not of substantive alternate political models. Unfortunately, having argued itself into the margin, social constructivism is likely to be given free reign there by those practitioners of political power, some of them brutal, who do not shy away from grounding their beliefs on any convenient foundation, be it God, nature, class struggle, or history.

However, the constructivist caution concerning the potentially evil uses of concepts such as universality is, in the main, a good one that deserves response. The theory I am presenting does, indeed, appear to sanction the status quo. For example, if such concepts as city, love, and beauty are universal attractors, then why should not genocide, racism, and patriarchy also be similar basins of attraction? And if the latter are universal, how can there be reasonable hope for change?

In a way, I plead guilty to these charges. A dispassionate view of the historical and contemporary world is a powerful argument for the universality of such concepts and of the social institutions they generate. And yet, one of the core hypotheses of this book is that human culture was selected for by evolution because of its flexibility and its proclivity for innovation. How, then, can universality and emergence be reconciled? How can a chaotic evolutionary theory balance its appeal for natural classical categories with the need to account for social transformation?

Clearly, change does occur. Evolution is proof enough of that.

The question at hand is whether cultural attractors inhibit change or enable it. In other words, is a view of human culture that sees it stabilized by natural classical categories conservative or progressive? Here, I will argue that chaos theory can be interpreted to suggest that, far from impeding social change, cultural universals are actually essential to the emergence of new cultural possibilities.

I will begin by reconsidering the sociobiological notion of epigenetic rules. The obvious advantage of encoding predispositions epigenetically is that it saves time and brain space. A somewhat more subtle advantage is that it offers a useful ballast against sudden and capricious change. As anyone who has ever attempted to invest in the stock market knows, the quickest way to insolvency is to buy and sell stocks every time the market changes direction. Such fickleness is almost always rewarded with much anxiety and little profit. Instead of impulsive trading, many successful investors seek to stabilize their investments by attempting to identify a meaningful trend before buying or selling securities. Epigenetic rules serve much the same function, preventing human beings from adjusting too swiftly to modifications in their environment. In fact, the conservatism of epigenetic rules is not an end in itself, but a means of promoting beneficial change. If it turns out, as I hypothesize, that the interface between epigenetic rules and their culturally dependent expression does, indeed, employ some sort of chaotic mechanism, then it is likely that chaos was selected as the basic blueprint of mental organization because it increases the odds that mental change will be slow enough to be appropriate to the environment, yet not so slow as to be maladaptive to external changes. Ultimately, too much novelty is indistinguishable from excessive conservatism. Both result in sterility. Healthy novelty is possible only when tradition is transmitted in the form of predispositions that are always open to modification.

Natural classical categories, or epigenetic rules, are a kind of systemic memory that serves as the background for productive change. Although it is true that certain sociobiological theories are dangerously close to biological reductionism, the kind of sociobiology associated with Lumsden and Wilson's theory of gene-culture coevolution (1983) is anything but reductionist.[3] In fact, by constructing a model of evolution in which pure Darwinian evolution has, in a sense, passed the baton of change over to cultural evolution, Lumsden and Wilson are able to claim explicitly that culture has effectively taken over from random genetic mutation the role of primary generator of variation. "Yet culture is not just a passive entity. It is a force so powerful in its own right that it drags the genes along. Working as a rapid mutator, it throws new variations into the teeth of natural selection and changes the epigenetic rules across generations" (Lumsden and Wilson 1983, 154). We are a promising primate. We live in the future, and we compulsively perform new realities into being. Culture is, among other things, a way in which to stage alternate forms of Being so that they may be considered, judged, evaluated, and then rejected, chosen, or modified. In other words, culture is the evolution of evolution from stochastic mutation to intersubjective decision. Of course, as anyone who has ever served on a committee understands all too well, intersubjective decision making can be infuriatingly slow, yet, Teenage Mutant Ninja Turtles notwithstanding, it is certainly more efficient than waiting for genes to mutate.

Epigenetic rules are a library of our past random and performative decisions. Being a compendium of past wisdom that the culture can consult, they offer a necessary and sanguine ballast for social change. Libraries are not a constraint on intellectual freedom; rather, they are remarkably enabling institutions, offering shoulders upon which the culture can stand. I do not think that it is an accident that one of the hallmarks of a free society is protection from censorship. That the more radical cultural relativists would deny the species-library that epigenetic rules constitute smacks of evolutionary censorship, and I suggest that we ought never censor knowledge in the name of freedom.

It is important to note that epigenetic rules do not constitute the entirety of our epistemological attractors. For one thing, an epigenetic rule, or chaotic symbol, is itself a confederacy of other symbols and probably belongs, as a member, to yet other confederacies. But more to the point, an epigenetic rule does not, in and of itself, constitute a human trait. Human children must be exposed to culture in order to become fully human, so epigenetic rules must be thought of as guides or head starts. Much of what we are is a product of culture. In fact, gene-culture coevolution can be translated into the terminology of chaos in such a way as to answer one of the crucial questions concerning the model of mind I am constructing—What is the mechanism whereby the mind's symbols turn chaotic? I think the answer to this seminal question can be found in the work of Ilya Prigogine. Basically, Prigogine argues that whenever certain systems are pushed into far-from-equilibrium conditions, they can begin to self-organize spontaneously. In other words, far-from-equilibrium systems can become negentropic and innovative. I believe that such systems do their generative work, in part, by tapping the creative energies of chaos. If that is the case, then it is tempting to see the mind's symbols in a constant state of disequilibrium occasioned by the conflict between their epigenetic proclivities and their inclination to test, alter, and vary them culturally. Gene-culture coevolution itself may be a far-from-equilibrium system in which culture is always out of phase with biology. If that is so, then we may consider epigenetic rules as kinds of attractors that are extremely sensitive to perturbations in the form of cultural input or feedback. These cultural fluctuations, which frequently take the form of promises—that is, ideas, narratives, scenarios, models, and hypotheses—are constantly being fed back into the epigenetic attractor, challenging it with new selective pressures and thereby keeping it out of equilibrium. Sometimes, the attractor proves superior to its fluctuations. They wallow around for a while, but fail to occasion substantive change. At other times, however, culturally induced perturbations are the kind of seed that chaos has taught us can induce global transformation.

We are a species for which the possible constitutes a major portion of our environment. Our brains, both individually and communally, are always renormalizing the present in terms of the alternate futures open to us. Yet our genes are stronger than our promises in the short term. Our libraries are immense, and often Borgesian. We are good authors, but we are also librarians.

Despite our astounding generalization and habitation in the hypothetical, our anchors are heavy. The price paid for protecting our species from capricious cultural change is that, even in the case of a trend that is likely to be long lived and robust, biology always lags behind culture, damping its sallies. We are currently in the process of promising ourselves any number of alternative futures. But promises are bets, and if bets are truly bets, they cannot be sure things. If cultural seeds are to push our traditional attractors into a new configuration, as I think they must if culture is to progress, then it will take work and time. Even though one of the central themes of this book is that the importance of conserving the past has been neglected too much in the academy in the latter half of the twentieth century, ultimately I applaud our contemporary lunatics, poets, and lovers—our artists, philosophers, and critical theorists—even when they infuriate me with their xenidrin fantasies, because they are the gardeners of a future that, although doubtless more anxiety producing than the present, promises pungent new fruit.

Chapter 20

Narrative and Chaos

Significant portions of our culture, ranging from performance artists
to academic critics, have grown increasingly chary of narrative. We
tend to express this discomfort in two ways. We either actively pursue the disruption of narrative through antinarrative experiments or
we concede the power of narrative but cynically assume that it invariably veils some ideological agenda whose demystification is the
proper work of analysis. In this section I argue that the first of these
positions inevitably undermines itself and that the second, although
useful in cultural criticism, is vulnerable to generalization into the
incoherence and impotence of radical social constructivism. In their
place, I will sketch the outlines of an affirmative theory of narrative.
Informed by an evolutionary and chaotic epistemology, this theory
will attempt to rehabilitate narrative by suggesting that it can be a
principle agent of cultural change.

It is, I think, unnecessary to give an extended account of the
attacks to which traditional narrative has been subjected in recent
critical theory. However, in the interests of framing the central concerns of this section, I will begin by outlining some seminal antinarrative positions.

1. Derridian deconstruction, with its emphasis on fragmentation, destabilization, bifurcated writing, multiplicity, and the
   nonlinear nature of the trace, tends to group narrative with
   logocentric, metaphysical discourse.
2. Radical feminist theory, especially that associated with the
   French (see Cixous 1976; Irigaray 1977; Kristéva 1974), suggests that traditional narrative is a prime example of patriarchal phallic hierarchical oppression. The French feminist

revolution is fueled by "writing through the body," a kind of writing that enacts a supposedly archaic female economy, a plural, scattered, polymorphic, autoerotic, contradictory, non-self-identical, and radically anarchic Being in the world.

3. From a neo-Marxist perspective, Jameson (1981) qualifies nineteenth-century narrative as linear and bourgeois, and condemns it for its participation in capitalist domination. In another typical, neo-Marxist gesture, Merrill (1988) asserts that narrative is a self-contained representational system whose function in postmodern culture is to bombard the population with simulations of the hegemonic capitalist value system. Defining contemporary U.S. ideology as the systematic passion for domination, Merrill argues that narrative is a paradigmatic tool of capitalism's oppression of marginal groups: "Narrative solves the problem of legitimation in the way the protagonist arises from the conflict or plot and in his counterposition to the antagonist. It, moreover, socializes an interpretive community to structures of human relations built on dominance which are then taken to refer to historical social structures" (Merrill 1988, 159). In other words, it is precisely the ability of narrative to create a systematic and hermetic symbolic world that renders it inimical to a kind of cultural critique that bases itself on historical and material conditions.

4. Cultural relativists, or radical antifoundationalists, tend to be skeptical concerning the value of any specific cultural practice. These "framework relativists," in Paisley Livingston's formulation (1988), frequently espouse antinarrative experiments hoping, thereby, to cast doubt on a natural basis for narrative. If nothing is natural, and if, as Barthes has argued, the attempt to pass off the contingent product of historical, ideological, institutional, and economic forces as a natural imperative is the essence of bourgeois conservatism, then the generation of texts that actively disrupt traditional narrative techniques describes a revolutionary praxis.

Another kind of cultural relativism, the social constructivist position that borrows much from Foucault's epistemes and genealogies, adopts a cynical attitude toward narrative. Narrative is seen as one way in which the social construction of reality is effected by the diffuse web of hegemonic power relations constitutive of a given regime of power and truth. Although constructivists tend to acknowledge the power of narrative, they see their ideological work as demystification, an attempt to unveil the oppressive codes functioning in all semiotic systems, including narrative.

5. Finally, with the exception of certain Marxist critics, practically no one in contemporary critical theory has any patience with totalizing or globalizing narrative. For example, although Lyotard does acknowledge the usefulness of small narratives (1984), especially as they function to exacerbate the generation of paralogies, he continues in the direction of William James by announcing the demise of grand narrative. In general, literary and cultural theorists tend to see grand narrative as the imperialistic imposition of a rigid teleological scheme on a world that either is or should be a web of differential textual energies.

That most proclamations of the death of narrative are delivered in classic narrative forms should give us reason to suspect that narrative is highly resistant to eradication. But I do not think that it is enough to grant narrative a certain cockroachlike refractoriness. On the contrary, I propose to claim that not only is narrative a stubbornly universal manifestation of human culture, but that it constitutes one of the most remarkable and desirable inventions of biological evolution. Thus, my goal is to sound a word of caution concerning a presupposition shared by many literary and cultural critics, namely that the proper place for narrative is on the semiotic dissection table. Although I have much sympathy for a properly modest constructivist position, I fear that, in our passion to demonstrate the tendentious textuality of everything, we have forgotten the private joy and political effectiveness afforded by a margin of innocence. Thus, mindful of the necessity of caution, in this chapter I nevertheless adopt a positive posture, arguing that it is precisely because narrative can encode oppressive epistemes that it can also function as a means of individual, cultural, and political empowerment.

In opposition to much contemporary critical theory, for which the constructivist worldview has become so naturalized that any recourse to information issuing from the natural and social sciences is understood exclusively in its ideological dimensions, I have attempted to argue that an interdisciplinary attitude toward knowledge, one that respects the alterity of scientific knowledge while remaining cognizant of the institutional forces that help forge it, might be able to rescue academic discourse from constructivist cynicism. Specifically, I believe that a chaotic sociobiological view of human culture suggests that narrative is both a product of, and a selective pressure for, our evolution into Homo sapiens. If narrative is, indeed, a seminal component of the dialectic human beings entertain with their cultural and natural environments, then it should be possible to affirm traditional narrative forms as crucial forces in the dynamics of cultural change.

The human brain is a remarkably fertile and resourceful processor of exogenous and endogenous information. It avails itself of a large number of strategies to record, manipulate, and create information about its environment. In fact, one of the chief selective pressures for the evolution of the human brain was the challenge to create a network of individual and intersubjective maps of the world. Narrative is among the most powerful of these maps because it allows for the constitution of a representational structure whose basic unit is the causal frame: actor—action—object. The essential feature of narrative is that it maps the world causally. Given the universality of narrative structures, both in everyday discourse and in the myths, cosmologies, and fictions generated by all human cultures, we must assume that the world is sufficiently causal to offer a species able to represent it in narrative forms a selective evolutionary advantage.

Needless to say, narrative is almost always considerably more complex than a simple, linear sequence, primarily because it allows for the nesting of causal frames within each other in a structure that Douglas Hofstadter (1980) describes as strange loops or tangled levels. What I am labeling traditional narrative in this section is precisely such a collection of nested causal frames. Thus, traditional narrative can be defined as a kind of information-processing strategy characterized by an overall causal frame, the general plot, which is itself composed of a frequently tangled hierarchy of nested plots and subplots.

The identifying feature of traditional narrative, what distinguishes it from antinarratives such as the French *Nouveau Roman*, is that it respects the necessity of an overarching causal frame supporting and stabilizing a hierarchical and heterarchical arrangement of subordinate causal networks. Grand narrative is a special case of narrative, distinguished from it by the pitch of the causal frame it describes. Whereas small narrative is energized by causal gradients on the order of a human life or of a number of human generations, grand narrative tends to flow between the inaugurating moment and the telos of a larger entity such as a nation, humanity, the spirit, or the universe. In general, there is no clear demarcation between small and grand narrative, so it is most useful to consider them as asymptotic poles on a scale.

As opposed to the widespread discomfort with globalizing narrative, I wish to argue that the potentially liberating capacities of traditional, small narratives apply a fortiori to those grand eschatological narratives with which all cultures have organized their cosmos. Oppression does not result from grand narratives, it results from evil grand narratives; in general, as the irony of Lyotard's grand narrative of the death of grand narrative suggests, the absence of grand narrative is not a choice available to us. In the contemporary intellectual arena, to be accused of globalization is tantamount to an ad hominem attack. However, I submit that no cogent position can refrain from globalizing. Consider the radical antifoundationalism that maintains that all values are the contingent and local products of a given performative community. Is it not reasonable to ask how one who argues this position knows that all values are contingent? Has he or she surveyed all real and possible worlds and reached the empirical conclusion that universality is inappropriate? If not, is it not a metaphysical and totalizing act of faith that authorizes such absolute relativism? In either case, a globalizing narrative is at work.

We tend to say "globalizing" when we mean that a theory is globalizing in a way that is not in accordance with our own, often unstated, globalizations. I suggest that to blame grand narrative for the evils of such worldviews as Nazi eschatology is as meaningful as savaging the printing press for its role in the production of *Mein Kampf*. We must abandon the reductive and vaguely paranoid belief that all grand narrative is equally linear, rigid, and imperialistic. There are grand narratives and there are grand narratives. Some are, indeed, like an automobile assembly line, but others are astoundingly complex, flexible, self-reflexive, and self-regulating. I would hope that having questioned the psychological and rhetorical economy of casting the first stone in the marketplace of narrative, the critical theory community might consider that the only real choice available to us is between rigidly linear narratives and the fertile and imaginative narratives that participate in most genuinely innovative human thought. Lyotard's paralogies will not lead to freedom. Political demagogues would like nothing better than a population mired in small-stakes contradiction, for, as psychological research has shown, individuals and groups that are overwhelmed by too much information or bored by too little will prove very receptive to the most rudimentary, and often barbaric, explanatory narratives.

In part, my argument rests on the findings of researchers in human evolution. Anthropologists such as Peter J. Wilson (1983) have argued convincingly that a central feature of Darwinian biological evolution is that it gradually yields a brain able to project itself into what Heidegger calls temporal ecstacies, a sharply defined future and past. Along with the development of long-term memory, symbolic thought, and, especially, language, the noo/sociotemporality of the human brain has, in the dialectical manner typical of evolutionary change, offered pressure for a neural structure whose key survival advantage is its ability to handle counterfactual speculation. And it is the mind's habitation in the world of the possible that is, as Douglas Hofstadter (1985), Jacques Monod (1971), and Richard Dawkins (1976) among many others point out, the real distinguishing feature of human beings.

The human brain evolved in such a way that it can surround itself with a cloud of alternate futures and, to a lesser extent, alternate pasts. The relative stability of the cognized past—stability lent by our biochemical inheritance, long-term memory, cultural knowledge, and language—is part of an apparatus that facilitates shrewder guesses about a future that is, in large measure, created by the very choices made by human beings. As Fraser defines it (1987), nootemporality is a highly asymmetrical continuum between hypothetical pasts (first causes) and endings (eschatologies): "It is characterized by a clear distinction among future, past, and present; by unlimited horizons of futurity and pastness" (367). Within the horizons of these nonempirical poles, the mind negotiates a vast array of temporalities, from the atemporal world described by sound bursts separated by about 2 msec or less, to subtly coordinated and recursive intersubjective temporality of ritual activity. The point, however, is that human time is essentially futural (why else do our brains take up so much space for memory, if not to help us in the difficult work of choosing a future), that it is a hierarchically arranged collective of different temporalities, and that it makes of Homo sapiens the most flexible and generalized biological organism.

Karl Popper has hypothesized that there are no such things as sense data (Popper and Eccles 1977). Information from the environment is a kind of challenge to the nervous system to engage in interpretation and hypothesis formation. According to Popper and Eccles, even the most rudimentary of information, such as the minutiae of vision, is interpreted by the nervous system over and over again before it becomes accessible to conscious reflection. Popper explains this idea as follows: "You will now see why I think that it is better not to speak of sense data as being primary. I think that we get a really beautiful picture of the organism and of the working of the mind if we see both as involving a hierarchy of levels at which these operations take place. These levels or layers are probably at the same time very largely evolutionary layers" (Popper and Eccles 1977, 432). Consciousness is a highly sophisticated generator of hypotheses that are in a constant feedback relation with their environment. In other words, the scientific method is a rather good description of how the mind works—a field of negotiations between theories about the environment and the natural and social constraints offered by the environment.

The loop formed by the mind's hypotheses and its world are, at various levels of description, its sensory data, its perception of objects, and the intricate theories it routinely constructs concerning that portion of the human world unavailable to the older mammalian sensory part of our nervous system—theories about what Popper calls world 3, the world of science, philosophy, theology, and art. In fact, I would venture to say that a workable definition of "mind" may simply be the predisposition of a complex biological organism to create explanatory theories or hypotheses about its ambient natural, social, and counterfactual worlds.

Should that be the case, then it is reasonable to ask what constitutes a worthwhile theory. There are many ways to evaluate a theory. Inasmuch as any theory about the world must somehow be a map of either an actual or hypothetical state of affairs, its success depends, in large measure, on the accuracy with which it depicts its object. Of course, maps can have many uses, from swatting flies to helping a motorist find a city, so it behooves us to respect the Wittgensteinian nature of theorizing. However, I suspect that the various possible applications of a map are typically arranged hierarchically in a given culture, just as they are for a given individual, with the emphasis being placed on those uses that exploit a map's ability to encode a richly articulated web of information. Therefore, it is likely that a theory will be successful insofar as it encodes the maximum amount of information about its object.

However, even with this proviso, certain problems still arise in such a cartography of theory. Not all theories are about objects of similar complexity. As I argue throughout this book, although both are equally impervious to saturation, being infinite sets, cultural knowledge is actually far more complex than either direct or indirect representations of lower *umwelts*. For example, it is relatively easy to program a computer to perform arithmetic tasks impossible for any human being, save the most infuriating idiot savant, to handle, yet it is wickedly difficult to create an artificial intelligence program that can participate in a simple social interaction with the flexibility and resourcefulness of most people. I believe that cultural knowledge is so difficult to translate into an artificial intelligence program because, beside the sheer amount of information it must handle, it is not a static representation of something "out there," but a set of mental maps whose very structure is constantly being altered by feedback from other real, remembered, or imagined minds. In other words, the human brain must map a world that is altered by the very process of being mapped, or, as I suggested earlier, maps become more paintinglike as the object *umwelt* become increasingly complex. This enormously complex feedback and feedforward relation between a given mind and its social and natural environment requires information processing capabilities of extraordinary sensitivity, storage capacity, flexibility, and vigor. In fact, I would suggest that if an individual's map of the social and natural landscape consists of a library of theories and hypotheses concerning his or her culture's basic beliefs, expectations, rituals, symbols, and sign systems, then this mental library will likely prove to be the most information-rich single entity in the universe.

If that is the case, then we would expect biological evolution to have equipped human beings with the cortical structures to manage such nexuses of information efficiently. To borrow from Geertz, it is the "thickness" of cultural knowledge that should make us suspect that primitive information storage and manipulation techniques, such as the flat, unhierarchized networks, webs, and trace structures championed by deconstructionists and postmodernists are simply too elephantine to have been selected by evolution. Although a web is certainly an improvement over even more elementary information technologies, such as a list, it soon falls prey to the rigidity of uncontrollable complexity. Complexity offers a clear evolutionary advantage only when it can be managed flexibly, and webs and trace networks are too cumbersome to be of much help to an organism more complex than an outdated artificial intelligence program.

It is here that narrative offers an elegant solution to the problem of human information management. We have, of course, developed scores of strategies, both in the form of neural structures and extrasomatic prosthetic aids—for example, our art works, libraries, and computer networks—to aid us in the difficult work of processing the complex cultural information that constitutes a major portion our world. Of these, undoubtedly the most powerful is language. And, of the strategies developed to store, manage, and create the remarkable semantic richness of natural language, I hypothesize that narrative is the most robust.

If, as I argue in chapter 19, our ideas are best understood as dynamical systems, then we would expect narrative to be a higher level dynamical system. In other words, narrative should be a system of systems. Furthermore, if narrative indeed proves to borrow its resources from those dynamical configurations that nature has chosen to enable the delicate dance between innovation and conservation, then it should be possible to claim that it is especially in the contemporary world, with its exponential growth of information, that the narrative techniques that humans have developed in the course of their evolution are most desperately needed. As opposed to Lyotard's apocalyptic proclamation: "We no longer have recourse to the grand narratives" (1984, 60), the sciences of chaos and of dissipative systems may offer the theoretical muscle to allow us to affirm the desirability, legitimacy, necessity, and morality of narrative in general and grand narrative in particular.

I believe that self-organizing systems and chaos theory can combine with anthropological research to suggest a plausible explanation for the ubiquity of narrative. Such an account would have three components that I will briefly summarize before proceeding to suggest a number of their possible consequences for the study of narrative.

1. The universality of narrative implies that it reflects an underlying neural substrate or a set of epigenetic rules predisposing human beings to organizing experience in a narrative manner. Therefore, we should expect antinarrative experiments to fail, either because they will display disguised narrative structures or, even in the absence of such unconscious narratives, the mind will automatically cast into a narrative mold even the most random and unconnected information. Of course, such default narratives tend to be linear and simplistic, but that is the price to be paid for the attempt to eradicate narrative.

2. We can assume that narrative is a good match to significant features of our environment, especially insofar as the natural and social landscapes are considered not in their static structure but as a set of dynamical, causal relations.

3. We can hypothesize that narrative is probably self-similar to those innovative processes in nature whose engine is chaos. In other words, the global dynamics of narrative serve as a cultural attractor, a self-adjusting algorithm through which all cultures of which we are aware seem to have spun their cosmos. Insofar as narrative is a remarkably efficient information-processing strategy whose function is to store, manipulate, and create the tremendous range of information constitutive of the world of human beings, it mirrors the basic process of evolution itself—a temporal, dynamical process that effectively mixes conservation and novelty in the open-ended and often tragic struggle to wrest choice from the teeth of textuality.

A narrative is a hypothesis about the nature of an existing slice of reality or about the potential consequences of certain variations on a model of the world. Inasmuch as narratives tend to be shared, they perform on an intersubjective, cultural level what our central nervous system does at the level of the individual. In both cases, models of reality are generated and compared with either other models or with incoming sensory data. As I suggested earlier, the basic feature of narrative is its temporal extension. Although narrative bashers frequently argue that the linearity of traditional narrative renders it a suspect agent of metaphysical or ideological repression (Jameson [1981, 285] refers to Bakhtin's "notion of the dialogic as a rupture of the one-dimensional text of bourgeois narrative"), I wager that it is actually impossible to offer an example of a truly linear narrative. To be sure, some kinds of narrative, such as pornography, do tend toward simplistic linearity. However, most interesting narratives, and certainly the plots of the great nineteenth-century (bourgeois) novels and the delicately articulated structures of our cosmologies and theologies, are anything but linear.

In fact, traditional narratives are among the most complex structures known to us. A common presupposition of contemporary thought is that complexity and teleology are engaged in a zero-sum game—a relation in which an increase in teleological dynamics must be paid for by a decrease in complexity. Implied in such a view is a conception of teleology as a deterministic frame inimical to the indeterminate richness of complexity. I believe that chaos offers a model of complexity that supplants this widespread notion by allowing for a relation between complexity and teleology that is best understood as a mutually enhancing feedback loop.

Complexity and flexibility are proportionately related to the teleological vector of what anthropologists Eugene d'Aquili and Charles Laughlin (d'Aquili, Laughlin, and McManus 1979) call a causal operator—the universal human imperative to explain phenomena by situating them in a causal frame. The causal operator generates narrative automatically, and, when applied to larger, cosmological questions, tends to favor temporal maps of reality that are stretched between a first and a final cause. I think that the contemporary allergy to grand narrative, especially when it is expressed as resistance to totalizing ideological systems, is remarkably wrongheaded. Our evolution into human beings undoubtedly entertained a feedback/feedforward relation to creation cosmologies and eschatologies. That is, the ability to imagine nonempirical first causes, infinite ends, and explanatory totalizing cosmologies—that is, grand narrative—requires an enormously intricate neocortex, whose gradual selection allows for even more complex cosmologies. Grand narrative and the human neocortex probably contributed to each other's selection, much like automobiles and highways. In fact, it may not be an exaggeration to suggest that grand narrative created us as much as we created it. Consequently, to renounce totalizing narrative now would be a terrible blow to our potential for progress. Of course, many postmodern theorists do not believe in progress, but then I would suggest that they can offer no reason to refuse the wisdom of our nonindustrialized conspecifics who go about creating the grandest of narratives without a trace of postmodern guilt.

Needless to say, not all narrative shares the sweep of such epics, but I believe that the essence of narrative resides in the creative energy of a temporal stretch between future and past that the narrative present enacts. The importance of narrative temporality is that, in its asymmetry, it provides those conditions of far-from-equilibrium systems that Prigogine claims are the means by which nature precipitates order out of randomness. In other words, the temporal instability instituted by the causal operator in traditional narrative is a kind of textual thermodynamic generator able to push the system into a chaotic state. Traditional narratives can be viewed as chaotic laminar systems, rivers characterized by an overall vector, the plot, itself composed of areas of local turbulence, eddies where time is reversed, rapids where it speeds ahead, and pools where it effectively stops. Extending William James's famous metaphor for consciousness: "Consciousness . . . is nothing jointed; it flows. A 'river' or a 'stream' are the metaphors by which it is most naturally described. In talking of it hereafter, let us call it the stream of thought, of consciousness" (1890, 239), I am suggesting that if narrative were conceptualized as a turbulent current, then it is possible to accommodate the modernist and postmodernist desire to respect multiple temporalities with the overall temporal anisotropy that appears to be the central feature of traditional narrative. Just as the energy powering a river is supplied by a topographical gradient, narrative tends to function like a dynamical system able to contain a congeries of different temporal relations, each with a specific ability to encode causal information, precisely because of the gradient generated by the temporal asymmetry constitutive of narrative causality. Traditional narratives employ modest temporal asymmetries, exploiting the human tendency to employ the causal operator on actual experience, while grand narrative or totalizing cosmologies tend to combine the temporal stretch of human time with our tendency to inhabit counterfactual or symbolic worlds, thereby creating a steep gradient between first causes and eschatologies. Ironically, it is precisely because traditional narrative forms have this overarching temporal vector that they are able to generate locally heterogeneous temporal relations. Without such a temporal gradient, narrative time tends to degenerate into smooth linearity or pure randomness, forms of information processing that are notoriously inefficient at either storing information or abetting its creation.

Using the insights offered by chaos theory, it is tempting to speculate that traditional narratives are, in fact, far-from-temporal-equilibrium dynamical systems capable of generating global order simultaneously with local randomness. The remarkable feature of chaotic systems is their tendency to settle into perdurable patterns, chaotic attractors, that are nevertheless highly sensitive to external fluctuations and initial conditions. In other words, dynamical systems satisfy the requirements of recognizable structure and flexibility. The fractal folds of narrative, its self-similar and frequently tangled layers of plot, subplot, monologue, and dialogue, allow a culture to store tremendous amounts of information in a stable form while simultaneously freeing that information to vary according to historical influences. In other words, narrative exists in the economy between Platonic fixity and Foucauldian relativity—describing a form that is at once cross-culturally universal and locally ductile.

Narrative's productive capability, its ability not only to model existing reality but to perform experiments on it, is enabled by the ability of chaotic systems to amplify minor local fluctuations into global structural transformations. It is precisely because narrative has a relatively stable overall structure that it is in a position to exploit the turbulence created by its constitutive temporal asymmetry. Without the stability offered by narrative, the emergence, storage, and transfer of new cultural information would be an essentially stochastic affair. Although random cultural inventions certainly occur, they tend to function like Derrida's version of Lacan's purloined letter—so cut off from any stable means for their encoding and delivery that they are extremely vulnerable to the noise of intergenerational transmission. Narrative offers culture both a remarkable data bank in which to store and transmit cultural knowledge and a flexible and turbulent laboratory in which to invent new knowledge.

I suspect that proclamations of the demise of narrative are understandable reactionary retrenchments in a historical period during which many long-held presuppositions concerning agency and responsibility are being radically questioned. Of course, nonnarrative islands are certainly possible, and, as I have already suggested, are actually a healthy local perturbation in narrative systems. However, the choice of totally dispensing with traditional narrative is simply not available to us. Nonnarrative prose or dramatic experiments inevitably challenge the mental causal operator to impose narrative structures where none appear to exist. Ironically, in an attempt to free the reader from linear narration, practitioners of the postmodern antinarrative induce him or her to impose the blandest of ad hoc narratives on the text. These compensatory narratives are inevitable. (How many readers can respect Robbe-Grillet's prescription for reading: "l'anecdote se met ainsi à foisonner: discontinue, plurielle, mobile, aléatoire, désignant elle-même sa propre fictivité, elle devient un 'jeu' au sens propre du terme" [Butler 1984, 75–76] and not make *Jealousy* into a narrative of an obsessive, jealous narrator?) Yet, without the challenge of a complex text, such compensatory narratives tend to be rudimentary and stereotypical. Since human beings experience their environment in a narrative way, they will invariably apply the causal operator on incoming data in order to make them into narrative. When processing a complex narrative, the disequilibrium between the mind's default assumptions and the text will, itself, generate fecund turbulence. However, when the mind is confronted by unmanageable complexity or unchallenging blandness, it tends to plug such information into relatively simple, linear, and deterministic default narratives. One way or another, any text will be made into narrative. If it is radically fragmentary, acausal, or antinarrative, it will be explained in terms of one of a number of simple causal frames. If, on the other hand, it is dynamically turbulent, it will challenge our backup causal frames and foster the emergence of new information. Thus, the real choice available to the literary community is not between metaphysics and dissemination, or between a male economy and a female economy, but between fecund traditional narratives and baggy default ones.

However, having accepted the inevitability of narrative, we should refrain from the other danger lurking in the current critical consensus. Although analysis is a desirable attitude, one that should be informed by a certain amount of skepticism and cynicism, it can easily turn into a smug metaphysics of paranoia. In many ways, the constructivist position is correct. Human cultures do construct much of their world through narrative. The chaotic complexity of narrative makes it a highly efficient way to encode a wide range of cultural presuppositions. And, if those presuppositions are deemed to be evil, it behooves the intellectual community to demystify them through the critical techniques bequeathed to us by poststructuralism. But in our analytic frenzy we should not forget that narrative itself is not the enemy. Instead of glibly condemning totalization, we should consider that to postulate analysis as an end is to adopt an essentially reductive and conservative attitude. Analysis is progressive only when its deconstructions are understood as prolegomena to thesis, creation, or poiesis. We live in a future that is largely waiting to be imagined, so it is an ethical imperative to resist the defeatism and acedia of radical constructionism. And, if we are indeed to refuse the facile identification of globalization with fascism, we must assume the frightening responsibility of offering ourselves a sampling of different futures with a certain amount of optimistic innocence. To do this, it is imperative to reject decisively the antinarrative prejudice, the monotony of demystification, and the allergy to globalization. A culture that is aware of its debt to the past will assume the risks of imagining a future, and I suggest that such habitation in emergence will inevitably exploit the sensitively self-modifying globalizations that narrative—small, but especially grand—is able to effect.

To summarize, I have argued that our evolution into human beings was, at least in part, the result of the selective pressures wrought on our brains by the powerful information processing and creating mental technology of narrative structures. As such, we are creatures whose experience is essentially narrative. Using some of the ideas offered by chaos theory, it is possible to view traditional narrative, and its most ambitious subset, grand narrative, as evolutionary adaptations able to tap the remarkable ability of chaotic systems to be simultaneously conservative and innovative in the difficult task of accumulating, storing, transmitting, and creating cultural information. Narrative is indeed mimetic. It imitates nature. However, in light of what we are currently learning about the behavior of dissipative systems, nature can no longer be conceptualized as a Laplacian clock, or Cartesian automaton, following strictly deterministic laws, but as a dynamical, evolving system whose defining characteristics are complexity, hierarchy, and emergence. Therefore, if narrative does hold a mirror up to nature, we must rethink the notions of nature and representation implicit in such a model. Narrative does not re-present an object, idea, signified, bit of information, or cognitive structure; on the contrary, narrative is isomorphic to the dynamics of nature—the cruelty and beauty of the deep dialectical interpenetration between conservation and creation.

Chapter 21

The Question of Progress

One of the prime motivations for this book is my belief in a nonconstructivist concept of progress. However, I am aware that there are many legitimate reasons why the notion of progress is viewed as highly problematic in today's intellectual climate. Let me begin by briefly listing several kinds of objection to the idea of progress.

For the most part progress has implied a rudimentary kind of teleology, the idea that a change can be labeled progressive when it moves in the direction of a fixed end. Such teleologies, whether they have been intellectual, political, economic, theological, or aesthetic, tend to be linear and Platonic in that they assume the existence of a goal serving as an eternal benchmark against which progress can be gauged. As our confidence in linearity and Platonism wanes, so does our faith in rigid teleological notions of progress.

It has frequently been argued that progress is an Enlightenment idea (although the chorus's famous "Ode to Man" in *Antigone* seems to suggest deeper roots), so that to apply it to an evolutionary model is anachronistic. In other words, since progress is a historically contingent notion, roughly contemporaneous with the rise of the bourgeoisie, it is meaningless to apply it to periods before the modern era.

Finally, theorists such as Foucault and Kuhn tend to argue that progress simply characterizes the presuppositions of the winner in paradigm wars. For such theorists, although it is possible to gauge progress within a given paradigm, indeed, for Kuhn, science may be defined as the field in which there is progress, it is far more difficult to argue for a global or transparadigm sense of progress. What is progressive for a liberal democrat may be regressive for a royalist.

In a way, my own view is rather close to one of Kuhn's formulations.

> The developmental process described in this essay has been a process of evolution *from* primitive beginnings—a process whose successive stages are characterized by an increasingly detailed and refined understanding of nature. But nothing that has or will be said makes it a process of evolution *toward* anything. . . . Does it really help to imagine that there is some one full, objective, true account of nature and that the proper measure of scientific achievement is the extent to which it brings us closer to that ultimate goal? If we can learn to substitute evolution-from-what-we-do-know for evolution-toward-what-we-wish-to-know, a number of vexing problems may vanish in the process. (1970, 170–71)

Although I differ from Kuhn for what I trust are obvious reasons, I do concur with him that as long as progress means movement toward closure—a fixed and timeless goal—then it is a concept that we would do well to modify. Which is not to say that in terms of its possible contribution to motivating societies to undergo transformations that even a rigid teleology is not to be preferred over the dreariness of no teleology at all, but that a view of progress such as that implied by Mr. Ramsay's march down the alphabet in *To the Lighthouse* is too rigidly linear to serve as a general model of progress.[1] In other words, progress may be enabled by a culture's aspirations toward Platonic goals, but progress itself cannot be properly described as the inexorable passage toward such ends.

In addition, I appreciate that different interpretative communities frequently disagree on what constitutes progress or on whether the notion itself is a meaningful description of time. Most traditional cultures, for example, have a cyclical view of time to which our modern understanding of progress is alien. However, the basic point of this book is that it is always possible to translate between interpretative communities in such a way as to make communication possible. Furthermore, I believe that such translation need not be of the *Nineteen Eighty-Four* or Nietzschean will-to-power kind espoused by Rorty, but that it can be based on the possibility that human beings share enough cultural universals, and have an active enough imagination, to consider alien worldviews without distorting them beyond recognition.

Fundamentally, the historical relativist sorts of positions presented above are correct during sufficiently small time scales. It is, for example, perfectly true that a certain notion of progress is intimately tied to the social, political, economic, religious, and technological transformations in Europe following the Renaissance. However, as I have argued previously, the relativist position depends on arbitrarily defining history in far too narrow a manner. If by history we mean something like the history of Homo sapiens, the evolutionary history of biological organisms, or the history of the entire cosmos, then certain long-standing trends are inescapable. One of these is the self-organization of the universe into increasingly complex entities. In this chapter, I will investigate the possible cultural ramifications of a definition of progress not as a culturally specific teleology, but as the general and nonteleological tendency in nature to increase its complexity.[2]

To summarize some earlier conclusions, I conjecture that the universe is a dynamical, evolving system describing a vector of increasingly complex and self-reflexive information-processing technologies set against the background of ballooning entropy. The complication of the universe is clearly a nonlinear, chaotic process, one that becomes increasingly tangled in level-crossing loops, and one that is accompanied by an increase in both maximum potential entropy and observed entropy.

Furthermore, I think it is possible to rehabilitate a kind of Renaissance humanism through recourse to a version of the cosmologists' anthropic principle by contending that the evolution of the universe has resulted in a hierarchy that, at least from the perspective of the earth, situates human beings as its most complex individual and corporate components. Indeed, unless one is a dualist or a creationist, it seems reasonable to speculate that human beings and their social institutions are the universe reflecting on itself, thereby creating information exponentially. What is commonly known as the postmodern era is, I think, precisely this seething process of information creation, management, and transmission.

Needless to say, many theorists do not see postmodernity as potentially progressive. Certain cultural critics, often informed by a style of analysis owing much to Foucault, consider our culture as one in which the technologies of control, discipline, channeling, marginalization, and oppression have grown so efficient that the concept of freedom has become simply one more site of power and truth.

Some Marxists, like Lentricchia (1988), believe that there is always a margin available for resistance, yet they share the mainstream Foucauldian view that the arrow of history does not describe a vector of freedom but one of increasing oppression. Derrida concurs with this view, seeing the hegemony of the West spreading throughout the world via the "global computer," but his response to the metaphysical web choking the postmodern world is unclear. Baudrillard (1983) is so convinced that postmodern information technology has created a world of rampant simulation that the only recourse he proposes is futile terrorism. Lyotard suggests that if we abandon the urge toward grand narrative, the postmodern world might find justice in the untotalizable buzz of its information circuits. And even Fraser postulates that we are witnessing the inauguration of a new *umwelt*, the sociotemporal, which is characterized by homogenization, uniformity, and a rejection of depth.

Many other cultural theorists, and in their wake, the majority of the academic critical world, concur in this assessment of postmodernity, tending to see it as the fantasy of Western technoscience gone berserk, a kind of cyber-Frankenstein about to debilitate the culture. For my part, I imagine that if rocks could talk, about four billion years ago they were probably saying something similar about their version of postmodernity—biogenesis. After all, life is messy, it is cruelly hegemonic, it radically transforms the environment, it creates such a babel of information that the material basis of Being appears to be threatened, it creates differences and disequilibria unknown in the eotemporal *umwelt*, and it brings death. I sometimes wonder if our oppression theorists are not just contemporary rocks, so terrified of progress that they desperately seek to define it out of existence.

Needless to say, progress, understood as complexation, *is* terrifying. I think that postmodernity describes a world on the cusp of great horror and great leaps of imaginative freedom or, more precisely, a world in which the potential for horror grows simultaneously with the potential for creativity. I fear that this symbiosis is unavoidable, and that attempts to evade it through either apocalyptic scenarios, Marxist nostalgia for the resolution of a class struggle that will soon no longer exist, if it ever did, ecologically oriented appeals to arrest technological development in the interests of respecting a natural world that has thereby been imperialistically characterized as stable and static whereas it has, in fact, always burgeoned with creativity, and countless other science, technology, and information phobias, are simply the understandable conservative fear of change in an era of radical ontological and epistemological transformations. In a bizarre and sadly amusing way, much contemporary theory is playing the role of the Catholic church in its struggles with Galileo— offering institutional prestige to the idea that progress is either an unthinkable or a politically undesirable concept.

In an earlier chapter, I criticized Fraser's characterization of our era as one that is metastable between nootemporality and sociotemporality. Although I agree with Fraser that once the world reaches a threshold of complexity it is likely that the nature of its temporality will be transformed, I think that it is possible to interpret this change differently. Specifically, I suspect that it is unlikely that we are in the process of arresting the long-standing evolutionary trend toward greater individuation, freedom, responsibility, and conflict. In general, I believe that we are in the midst of a phase change from a relatively deterministic, matter-centered universe to one in which matter will be seen as particular manifestation of an evolving hierarchy of information. Although we tend to have a matter bias, believing that the real is equivalent to the material, I agree with eccentric computer scientist and physicist Ed Fredkin (Wright 1988), who considers information to be the basic stuff of the universe. Matter is one form of information, but there are others, such as force, energy, and spirit. Spirit is highly chunked matter and its creation is clearly one dominant direction of cosmic evolution. And to the extent that the world is becoming increasingly dematerialized, as mainstream postmodernism has so compellingly demonstrated, human beings are the universe evolving out of its material phase into an era in which spirit will prove to be less a chimera of the primitive imagination than a significant, perhaps dominant, form of Being.

If Fraser is right, our world is evolving toward a global society characterized by a diminution of all the asymmetries that contributed to making us human: the disparity between our sense of historical time and eschatological time, individual and cultural distinctions, the differences between day and night and among the seasons, the disproportion between the hypothetical world of art and actual social life, and the distance between the profane and the sacred. If I am right, the social organization that has the highest probability of succeeding will increase all these asymmetries as it creates a more complex world, a world that, according to the axioms outlined earlier, could legitimately be called progressive. This world would witness the gradual merging of knowledge and reality with a concomitant sharpening of the distinctions among the kinds of knowledge available to human beings, the increasing individuation, sexualization, and information-processing capacity of its inhabitants through a radically lengthened life span due to nanotechnology and some form of computer-neural interface, the emergence of an immensely complex global state (perhaps to be compensated for by our return to some kind of tribal village system) in which the old nation-state allegiances are felt to be underpinned less by metaphysical necessity than by aesthetic choice (this is like the difference between killing someone biologically and doing it on stage), the increasing reverence for art that is at once classical and experimental, the rehabilitation of our old bio/noo/sociotemporal roles, such as sex roles and kinship roles, in a flexible and ultimately aesthetic manner, and the discovery of new forms of devotion to the sacred. An information-centered world could be, to resurrect an old Puritan idea, the setting for a new Eden. Of course, this Eden would have its contingent of snakes, and we would simply have to stop trying to legislate them out of existence. But with the snakes would come astonishing new possibilities for human freedom, imaginative transcendence, and creativity.

Where the future is concerned, there are, of course, no answers in the back of the book. However, assuming that my scenario is possible and desirable, then we might legitimately ask what form of contemporary social organization would be most likely to encourage our culture to make the new world as humane as possible.

I am repeatedly amazed at what is going on in the contemporary world. The communist grip on the imagination of oppressed people, of which there are still too many, is loosening, as is evidenced by the dramatic developments in Eastern Europe and the USSR. Even China, despite its recent reactionary reversion to high Maoism, has not been immune to the liberating power of the free flow of information. And Europe's rapid move toward a kind of confederacy in which the old nation-state boundaries will be more cultural than political and economic is a stunning historical event. There is still a Third World, there are still dictators of the right and of the left, the Near East is still a powder keg, in certain parts of the world, poverty, neglect, illiteracy, and cruelty are still a growth industry, and xenophobia, racism, and sexism remain as reminders of our roots in patriarchal tribalism. However, progress is not linear, and it is certainly not smooth. There will always be blacksmiths put out of work. In fact, much third world poverty is no longer predominantly the effect of lingering colonial politics, although there are certainly enough exploitative oligarchies around to concern me, but increasingly of economies whose main products are raw materials. In a world that is shifting its emphasis from matter to information, economies based on rubber or sugar will suffer. I have much sympathy for the people affected by these developments, but I do not think it is generous to suggest to someone whose horse cannot keep up with automobiles to get a faster horse.

And yet, despite its quickly fading prestige as a form of political and economic organization, especially among societies that have tried it, Marxism is still a dominant form of cultural analysis in the Western academy. Whether of the teleological or the demystifying type, academic Marxists tend to agree that capitalist/technological institutions are oppressive constraints on the freedom of human beings. I will conclude this chapter by suggesting the opposite, that it is precisely a form of multinational, free-market capitalism whose energy is channeled productively by a certain amount of socialist top-down control that is most likely to foster freedom, justice, community, and individual happiness in a world that is metastable between matter dominance and spirit dominance.

As with evolution at any level, the greater number of options available to a system the more likely it is that appropriate choices can be made. It is important to note, however, that sheer numbers of choices do not in themselves guarantee freedom. Too many nonhierarchic possibilities can swamp a system, causing it to generate no more options than a system with only a few possible states. However, in an efficiently organized, graded, and hierarchic system, the larger the pool of alternatives, the more likely the system is to make useful choices against the background of specific environmental selective pressures. Given a generally hierarchic and value-ordered social typography, it is likely that a society with greater resources will have a greater chance of survival than one with an equally complex organization but with fewer options. That is why I believe that, all things being equal, a free, democratic society that is aggressive in the creation and transmission of value is likely to do the work of evolution best. Furthermore, again all things being equal, a society able to use its human resources most efficiently is likely to have a survival advantage over one that squanders human potential. Although I am convinced that human society will always arrange itself hierarchically, I feel that a self-regulating meritocracy has the potential to be an infinitely more generative social hierarchy than rigid hierarchies based on inherited social and economic power. If value to a society is determined by one's intelligence, wisdom, or creativity, in other words, by one's competence in performing evolution, then questions of birth class, race, or gender will be seen less as a kind of biological destiny than as a source of aesthetic identity-making. The ethics implied here are not based on some abstract categorical imperative. On the contrary, I am invoking a cruel struggle for survival. My point is that a caring, nurturing, competitive, multiethnic, nonpatriarchal, flexible, democratic society able to cull talent from all of its human resources is likely to win the Darwinian struggle. This is social Darwinism without the grave error of equating survival with strength.

According to the theory expounded in this book, the universe values managed creativity above all else, and a society that is able to manufacture more innovation will be more likely to survive in the long run than a rigidly authoritarian one. I believe that a society whose most revered product is controlled novelty will tend to organize itself in a flexible and frequently tangled hierarchy because such social systems have a higher probability of success than those, such as traditional patriarchy or institutionalized racism, that simply exclude from the evolutionary arena vast amounts of potential human creativity. Of course there is no master plan guaranteeing this. Culture will always be a struggle in which agency is valued because it constitutes a bifurcation point where a system chooses its future. This future is open, though not indiscriminately so, so cultural agency is essential. However, I am suggesting that, given the universe in which we live, certain systemic configurations tend to survive better than others over time. Such systems, which prize flexibility, self-adjustment, and chaotic sensitivity to fluctuations, will be more likely to survive than systems whose rigidity may allow them short-term success but dooms them in the end. Agency is important because culture is a gamble. There are no guarantees at the races, but betting with the odds invariably produces better results over a period of time than betting randomly. Nazism and apartheid are not evil because of some suspect appeal to humanism, but because they are inefficient systems. The failure of right-wing authoritarian regimes, and of their left-wing counterparts, communist dictatorships, will, I hope, demonstrate that First World capitalist/socialist societies have a better than even chance of winning the political struggle for survival because flexible, self-regulating, chaotic hierarchies are the most powerful information-creating, -processing, and -transmitting systems available to us. In other words, I am speculating that the balance between the top-down, collective, constraints—especially in matters concerning large-scale medical care, legal protection, human rights, fostering of the arts, environmental issues, urban/suburban planning, and, in general, the exertion of moral and aesthetic guidelines—typical of socialist forms of organization and the bottom-up individualism, freedom, mobility, eccentricity, and energy of capitalism will produce forms of social organization that most closely resemble chaos: neither random, like the shopping strip cities polluting the American landscape, nor deterministic, like the bleak cities of Marxist-Leninist regimes, but chaotic, like the great cities of the world, those marvelous and enchanting places such as Venice, Paris, Barcelona, and San Francisco where the heart rejoices at the marriage of classicism and anarchy.

Ultimately, I believe that chaos offers a bracing vision of political normativity. If the universe is, indeed, a society of chaotic, self-similar layers, then it appears that everything in nature, from prebiotic dissipative systems, to the ecosystem of a river, to the organization of a primitive nervous system, to the dynamical flow of a human brain, to the shape of a kinship group, a city, a nation, or a world works best when it resembles a chaotic attractor; or, if you will, when it hangs in the tension generated by the disequilibrium between the imperative that information flow as quickly as possible and the imperative that it do so beautifully.

Chapter 22

Art and the Sacred

Ed Fredkin sees the entire universe as the solution to a computational problem (Wright 1988). He believes that physical and mental reality are products of a recursive algorithm that, through repeated feedback, has yielded this incredibly intricate universe. Exploiting a prevalent idea in chaos theory, namely that chaotic systems have no shortcuts, he speculates that the universe is merely the fastest possible way to answer some unspecified questions: "I can say I don't know how powerful God is; he cannot know the answer to the question any faster than doing it. Now, he can have various ways of doing it, but he has to do every Goddamn single step with every bit or he won't get the right answer. There's no shortcut" (43). Fredkin claims not to believe in God, at least not in a Judeo-Christian God, but rather in some sort of intelligent, but hardly omniscient, programmer. I mention Fredkin not because I agree with him—I don't entirely, especially concerning the possibility of a master programmer—but because he broaches the important issue of the relation between cosmology and theology.

The marginalization of art in contemporary society is a fairly well-accepted phenomenon. As all good students of the arts and humanities are wont to do, my students frequently rail against a society in which the value of art has greatly diminished. Anyone doubting this need only consult the patterns of government and private funding for the arts as opposed to the torrent of money flowing to scientific and technological research. I agree with my students, of course, when they argue that art should be at the core of a healthy society's cultural life. For that reason, I resent the modernist and postmodernist continuation of the Romantic tradition of situating the artist in opposition to mainstream society. Artists cannot complain about marginalization when that is their self-definition. However, many artists do not want to be outsiders, and most of my students certainly do not desire that their work be perceived by the culture as some kind of fatuous lucubration. Therefore, assuming that it is a desirable end that art be integrated, at least in part, into the tissue of a society, and that it function there as an enterprise accorded importance and value, it behooves us to speculate on how such a rehabilitation of art might be accomplished.

A litany of bromides invariably accompanies any discussion of the importance of the arts in our culture. They appear in nearly every NEH or NEA grant proposal, so there is no need to repeat them here. Suffice it to say that they make good catalog copy, but that few people take them seriously. Unfortunately, sincere appeals to the necessity of reserving a central role in our culture for the arts are effective in rallying the converted but have limited impact on the general population, especially on the pockets of economic and political power—our Medici's—whose championing of the arts is a necessary precondition for any aesthetic renaissance. Something is always missing in such arguments, and I believe that what is lacking is a connection between the arts and the sacred. Even a cursory look at history yields the simple conclusion that the cultural currency of art has always been a factor of its relation to the sacred. The quickest way to devalue art is to secularize it. It is no coincidence that the decline of the cultural prestige of art began with the industrialization and consequent desacralization of Western society.

If this premise is accepted, or even provisionally tolerated, then it follows that the way to make art a central cultural concern is to bring it back into the service of the sacred. But which sacred? Judeo-Christianity has lost its cultural mandate and, I suspect, will be seen increasingly as an obsolete cult. The world's other religions, especially Islam, have a devout following, but I believe that they will find it difficult to excite many people as waves of First World information technologies sweep over them (fundamentalist Muslims understand this and have been mounting a reasonable, though I hope ill-fated, campaign against Western values). It is commonly said that science is our new religion. I think that science does indeed fulfill some of the traditional requirements of religion. For the most part, it is the scale against which we measure truth and falsehood, it is where our brightest young people gravitate, and we treat famous scientists with the reverence once reserved for heroes and great artists. And yet, for all this, science is viewed by many people, including many scientists, as a rather sterile affair. Whereas religion has always fired the imagination with its mystery and transcendence, science, especially in its day-to-day, business-as-usual manifestation, is rather tedious and mundane. Religion has always concerned itself with ethical and moral questions, while science is either incapable of dabbling in such matters, or, when it does, is likely to appear awkward, reductive, or downright silly. Furthermore, religion has always responded to the human rage for a coherent cosmology, whereas most scientists are unwilling to look beyond their laboratories. And perhaps most important, religion has always been wed to the intense human need for beauty. The popular image of a computer hacker crunching numbers does little to satisfy the aesthetic hunger inhabiting religion.

Yet, I think that it is precisely in the scientific arena that art must establish itself as a sacred pursuit if it is to rise from its contemporary doldrums. In the belief that a fitting last chapter to this book should continue the tendency toward tentative hypothesis, I would like to suggest a number of ways in which the rehabilitation of art might proceed. Specifically, I will propose a cosmological model in which art plays a primary role. This model incorporates the sacred, because it is organized around a deity, but a deity that, unlike the Judeo-Christian God, or Fredkin's theoprogrammer, does not preexist our universe.

Perhaps the most persuasive of the traditional arguments for the existence of God is the argument by design. It is indeed difficult to imagine that sheer chance has thwarted the great cosmic garbage dump, the second law of thermodynamics. Can survival alone account for the marvelous and intricate structure, complexity, and organization that characterize the natural world, especially that part of it that we are? One example of the mental stretch required to attribute everything to random variation is the incredibly low probability that the two requirements for life, genetic material and proteins, both came into being simultaneously and in such close proximity that they could commence the symbiosis that eventually yielded human beings. Take the room of a typical four-year-old, remove his or her nagging parents, and in short order the entropic ghoul will demonstrate its prowess. The question, then, is whether nature furnishes its own nagging parents, or whether we need to attribute them to supernatural intervention.

In part, traditional religions have sought to account for the order that we can observe and to impose order on that which appears chaotic. Anthropologists McManus, Laughlin, and d'Aquili postulate a "cognitive imperative," a "drive in man, other mammals, and birds to order their world by differentiation of adaptively significant sensory elements and events, and to the unification of these elements into a systemic, cognitive whole" (d'Aquili, Laughlin, and McManus 1979, 10). One of the seminal functions of religion has been to apply the cognitive imperative to the entirety of existence—to differentiate and totalize all of Being under one grand theoretical matrix. That is, the ethical, social, and practical functions of religions are typically a function of a grand narrative whereby the universe's apparent order and organization are explained.

In the future, I fear that bearded Semitic patriarchs speaking to shepherds and fishermen will find it increasingly difficult to capture our imagination. Religions typically embody the natural knowledge of the era in which they developed. One of the problems with Christianity is that it has outlived the currency of its explanations of natural phenomena. In many ways, Christianity is guilty of being out of step with science. Galileo's telescope may have occasioned the last desperate attempt to rehabilitate Christian natural knowledge, creation science, but it will surely lay waste to that too.

In order to work, a religion must be consonant with the best explanatory hypotheses for the natural world available at the time. When Christianity is required to explain the virgin birth, the resurrection of Christ, or transubstantiation as miracles, when it persists in positing a transcendent God the Father who created the universe ex nihilo, an immortal soul, and a rigid eschatology, or worse, when it finds it necessary to claim that none of these bulwarks of the faith need be taken literally but may be understood as symbolic or metaphoric, the whole edifice is bound to crumble sooner or later.

Of course one solution would be to scrap the concept of God altogether. If, however, we wish to retain some of the traditional attributes of God, in particular the relation of the idea of God to the remarkably persistent cross-cultural belief that the universe is in some deep way sacred, then we need a theology that is in fundamental agreement with the most powerful scientific models available to us.

A basic requirement for the new god is that it must be able to account for the universe's apparent passion to violate the second law of thermodynamics. I should hasten to add that such violation has to be paid for by an increase in overall maximum potential entropy. Even the new god must work on borrowed time.

I've speculated wildly and irresponsibly like this for quite a while in my classes, and one of my students, perhaps my best, beamed one day and said that we are clearly addressing the god of self-organizing systems. I like that, except that it is somewhat cumbersome and its acronym sounds like something that swallows up planets in an old "Star Trek" episode. I see no reason to abandon the rather beautiful and terrible word *god,* as long as it is possible to divest it of some of its connotations. This new god cannot be an essence, object, or person. Instead, it must represent the perhaps inexplicable, and certainly mystical, tendency of certain systems to self-organize and increase their own complexity. Specifically, following such theorists as Davies, Fredkin, and Wheeler, I believe that god is simply the becoming-organized, becoming-complex, and becoming-self-conscious of the universe. In other words, the universe *is* god insofar as it is a sublimely complex, self-organizing, dynamical system.

The universe may be, as Fredkin claims, the product of a single recursive algorithm. As farfetched as that may sound, there is a precedent for the idea in the wonderfully detailed Mandelbrot set that anyone can generate using an ordinary computer and a rather simple recursive algorithm. Or the universe might be more of a Prigoginelike far-from-equilibrium self-organizing system. Or it might be, as Ford believes, chaos with feedback. Or, better yet, these ideas may be the descriptions of three blind men confronting the same elephant: an evolving universe whose main fuel is the remarkable propensity of far-from-equilibrium chaotic systems to employ feedback to self-organize spontaneously and globally. I, for one, find that idea as transcendently mysterious and beautiful as any I have encountered in traditional theologies.

If Davies' "cosmic blueprint" can offer some hope for reenchanting the world, then it must allow for a genuinely interdisciplinary dialogue among the arts, the humanities, the social sciences, and the natural sciences. And it must account for their interconnections in a way that is not exclusively wed to the notion of top-down or bottom-up constraint. To pursue this crucial issue, let me return briefly to the question of epistemology. Why, it might be asked, should human beings have knowledge of the natural world?

One explanation, the social constructivist one, maintains that we do not. Our knowledge of the world is simply one of our many social constructions: "Our perceptual categories give the only shape to whatever is called 'real' that it can ever have, and thus response to the real is no different in nature from our response to art" (Merrill 1988, viii). If this highly anthropocentric and ultimately idealistically solipsistic position is wrong, as I am confident it is, then we must be able to account for what Prigogine calls man's dialogue with nature.

Another sort of answer is suggested by the theory of direct and indirect representation. Direct representation is mostly unconscious, so at best allows for only an intuitive sense of commonality with nature. It is important, because it creates a basic, precritical understanding of our belonging to the world, a kind of interdisciplinary mood, but it cannot serve to explain how noo/sociotemporal knowledge can include representations proper to the lower *umwelts*. Indirect representation, on the other hand, suggests that nature's integrative *umwelts* have level-specific languages that can be learned by noo/sociotemporal entities. Thus, mathematics becomes less an interventionist or imperialistic thrust by human beings into the amorphousness of nature than a genuine and caring effort to meet it halfway. If we convince ourselves that nature must be addressed only through natural language, we are reducing the rich hierarchy of the natural world to one of its levels. Well meaning as such gestures may be, they are in essence analogous to screaming English at Mexicans in the belief that their lack of comprehension is stubbornness, stupidity, or deafness. We do not objectify nature by addressing it in mathematics, we acknowledge its ethnicity and temper our anthropo-chauvinism.

Having sounded a warning about the narcissism inherent in reducing nature to an entity that can be addressed exclusively by noo/sociotemporal languages, let me hasten to add that it is still not clear how the languages of the lower *umwelts* can lend themselves to nonmathematical, upper level representations. How can biotemporal trees serve to represent evolution in noo/sociotemporal cosmologies? In other words, how is metaphor possible?

In my view, the important question is not a typological or de- scriptive one, but an ontological and epistemological one: What sort of universe is this that allows for cross-*umwelt* comparison? Or, more simply, why should the world permit, or perhaps even selectively encourage, metaphor?

Popularizations of scientific theory teem with analogies and metaphors to illustrate abstruse mathematical concepts. For example, Davies describes the idea of a wave in quantum mechanics through an analogy to a crime wave (1983), Hofstadter explains the mathemat- ical notion of renormalization by equating it with the way an individ- ual self is constituted by its commerce with other selves (1985), and Hawking explains how the path of bodies in four-dimensional space- time can appear to be curved in our three-dimensional space by sug- gesting that it might be "like watching an airplane flying over hilly ground" (1988, 30). I could go on; the literature is rife with such examples. What interests me is less their accuracy or pedagogical usefulness than their very possibility. Why should a quantum-level phenomenon allow itself to be described in terms of a phenomenon specific to the noo/sociotemporal world?

Since most metaphor is a kind of level violation, describing an event, structure, or object on one level though recourse to a similar event, structure, or object on a another level, it is, in fact, a direct violation of Hofstadter's chunking principle. Metaphor suggests the possibility of isomorphism across evolutionary levels so distant that it would appear that chunking would have erased any similarities based on contiguity.

Constructivists, of course, would maintain that approaching metaphor from such a perspective is nonsense. Since we construct our world, we are perfectly free to construct analogies among its constituent parts. If, however, we reject the creationist implications of radical social constructivism, we are left with the need to account for the possibility of metaphor in a hierarchical universe.

It seems to me that the existence of systematic isomorphisms between upper and lower level languages can only be explained if we assume that the universe tends to be self-similar at different scales. Chaos, self-organization, and Davies' idea of a cosmic blue- print all suggest that the universe creates itself by repeating certain archetypal patterns at different levels of complexity. Going against the grain of almost every significant school of contemporary theory, chaos makes a powerful case for the possibility of resurrecting the concept of the universal. I have already discussed the universality of Feigenbaum's ratios. It is indeed surprising that the road to chaos appears to be quite orderly and to display similar developmental characteristics regardless of the system under consideration. Feigenbaum's interpretation of the regularities he discovered in period-doubling ratios is intriguingly close to Rössler's (discussed in chapter 16, sec 2).

> One has to look for scaling structures—how do details relate to little details. You look at fluid disturbances, complicated structures in which the complexity has come about by a persistent process. At some level they don't care very much what the size of the process is—it could be the size of a pea or the size of a basketball. The process doesn't care where it is, and moreover it doesn't care how long it's been going. The only things that can ever be universal, in a sense, are scaling things. (Gleick 1987, 186)

Feigenbaum concludes with another echo of Rössler: "Somehow the wondrous promise of the earth is that there are things beautiful in it, things wondrous and alluring, and by virtue of your trade you want to understand them" (187). Much like Rössler, Feigenbaum is captivated by the ability of rudimentary recursive processes to create great complexity. Furthermore, he speculates that it is perhaps only in fractal scaling phenomena that universality may be found and that in the pastry chef's filigrees may lie the key to beauty.

Interestingly enough, one of the first formulations of the universality of scaling phenomena comes from a biologist at a time when biology was turning toward more reductionist methodologies. Early in the twentieth century, D'Arcy Thompson, a maverick biologist, zoologist, mathematician, classicist, and philosopher, had a vision of the interconnectedness of things that we are only now rediscovering. Refusing to see biology as an isolated discipline following its own internal laws and axioms, Thompson had the correct, but still controversial, intuition that although biology should, in large part, concern itself with its own level-specific laws, it must nevertheless not violate the lower level regularities of its microstructure. Preferring to see a deep unity in all of nature that cuts across integrative levels,

Thompson was led to develop an early theory of scaling. He saw life as process, and he imagined that certain relations or ratios between processes were such consistently successful evolutionary adaptations that they would be found throughout the hierarchy of natural forms. Thompson's insistence on studying growth, not just taxonomy, led to a theory of universal, almost Platonic, patterns of development. It is as if Plato were right about universality, but that his theory needed rehabilitation. Instead of static eternal forms, Plato's sun consisted of dynamical systemic relations.

> He was enough of a mathematician to know that cataloguing shapes proves nothing. But he was enough of a poet to trust that neither accident nor purpose could explain the striking universality of forms he had assembled in his long years of gazing at nature. Physical laws must explain it, governing force and growth in ways that were just out of understanding's reach. Plato again. Behind the particular, visible shapes of matter must lie ghostly forms serving as invisible templates. Forms in motion. (Gleick 1987, 202)

Although Thompson's integrative vision was acutely prescient of subsequent developments in systems theory, he was nevertheless plagued by the classical presuppositions of his age: he insisted that whatever universal dynamical forms underlay biological processes, they must be continuous, regular, and smooth. In other words, Thompson's Platonic forms were linear. Yet, as physicist Bruce J. West and medical researcher Ary L. Goldberger explain, "Observation and experiment, however, suggest the opposite. Most biological systems, and many physical ones, are discontinuous, inhomogeneous, and irregular. The variable, complicated structure and behavior of living systems seems as likely to be verging on chaos as converging on some regular pattern" (1987, 354). Basing their work on anatomical complexity, West and Goldberger seek to expand Thompson's theories in the light of renormalization group theory, the chaotic dynamics of nonlinear systems, and fractal geometry. Their research demonstrates that fractal structures are not limited to prebiotic phenomena, such as trees, coastlines, and clouds, but that significant physiological structures and systems, such as the lungs, "the bile duct system, the urinary collecting tubes in the kidney, the brain, the lining of the bowel, the neural networks . . . the placenta" (363) and the heart display intriguing self-similarity and scaling. All of these systems share the regular irregularity peculiar to scaling phenomena. In fact, West and Goldberger believe that the sacrifice of linear Platonic forms may yield an unforeseen Platonic profit—the discovery of ubiquitous, dynamical, resilient, and orderly inhomogeneities.

> In applying the new scaling ideas to physiology, we have seen that irregularity, when admitted as fundamental rather than treated as a pathological deviation from some classical ideal, can paradoxically suggest a more powerful unifying theory. (355)

West and Goldberger emphasize two classic scaling patterns, the golden mean and Fibonacci numbers, in an attempt to demonstrate that either such numerical relations are "built into a number of biological structures, or perhaps more appropriately, such structures are constructed in part from a Fibonacci blueprint" (75). Noting Fibonacci scaling in the deployment of leaves on certain plants, in the ratio of total human height to the height from the toes to the navel, and in bronchial trees, West and Goldberger are in agreement with Feigenbaum's belief that scaling phenomena may the only form of universality flexible enough to survive in an evolving universe. There need be nothing metaphysical or mystical in such ideas. They need not imply, for example, a return to Aristotelian final causes. On the contrary, the basic point is that just as the nature of materials when coupled with the needs of human beings seems to favor certain architectural ideas over and over again, so, by analogy, or by scaling, the universe may have chosen certain patterns repeatedly as, in its development and emergence, it faced similar problems at different integrative levels. We need not be surprised that the golden mean appears to describe bronchial architecture as well as it does the proportions of the Parthenon; at least no more surprised than by how the architectural metaphor in the previous sentence seems natural and barely metaphoric at all.

What emerges from this model is a view of the world as an immense Mandelbrot set, but one that goes up, toward the new, not down, toward the already there; that is, the universe is an economy between randomness and order that appears to both imitate and distort itself with every new creation. Davies' cosmic blueprint may be nothing more than that—the tendency of chaotic hierarchical systems to generate scales that display enough similarity so that some universality can be said to exist in our world yet not so much that innovation is precluded. Chaos is universal because dynamical processes incorporating an element of chaos survive better than static ones. Indeed, if there is a cosmic blueprint, it is, as Davies suggests, that self-organizing chaotic systems are preferred whenever nature needs both deep roots and vulnerable flowers.

If Hawking, Hofstadter, and Davies are indeed making coherent metaphors when they compare wildly distant *umwelts*, then it seems to me that the only explanation for the possibility of such tropes is that the universe is sufficiently self-similar across its various levels that patterns in one *umwelt* can be meaningfully compared with patterns in others. In other words, as Gleick puts it, "Of all the possible pathways of disorder, nature favors just a few" (1987, 267), or, to state the matter somewhat differently, nature's solutions to various problems tend to have what Wittgenstein calls a "family resemblance." However, as opposed to Wittgenstein's families, which are all at the linguistic, or noo/sociotemporal, level, the kind of family I am describing has members throughout the universe's integrative levels. I believe that the most awe-inspiring and deeply moving unity it is possible to imagine is that displayed by a chaotic universe whose internal articulations are a hierarchy of level-specific but self-similar dynamical systems. My brain may be the most complex single object in the universe, but it is remarkable that it may share certain formal or dynamical features with a stream. Chaos may be the profound unity of nature that has eluded thinkers convinced that, when they found such unity, it would be an immutable essence.

It is in relation to such a cosmology that I believe art must situate itself if it is to regain the prestige it once enjoyed in our culture. Let me make it clear that I do not mean that painters should devote themselves to painting seahorse tails and writers to writing great evolutionary epics. Actually, the themes that art has treated traditionally are rather limited in number and keep reappearing in different forms. The great aesthetic themes are legitimate cultural attractors, drawing artists to their basins across cultures and through time. There are always, of course, new themes—feminism comes to mind—but they are usually traceable to older ideas (in the case of feminism: freedom, autonomy, dignity, love, etc.). Nor am I arguing that art should sacrifice its historical concerns, such as social confirmation and contestation, experimentation, escape, communication, ritual tuning of the brain's asymmetrical hemispheres, or sensual delight. I am merely suggesting that it is possible to salvage art's traditional concerns while rehabilitating its cultural currency if an aesthetics could be formulated that situates art within a chaotic model of the universe.

In chapter 13, I outlined a theory of art, and in particular literature, that considers literature as an important agent in cultural evolution. By creating a "liminal" space in which new possibilities are tested and old ones reevaluated, literature offers culture the three defining characteristics of evolution: variation, selection, and inheritance. Simply, literature allows human beings an exceedingly swift method of generating cultural variations in the form of counterfactual scenarios, as well as a highly efficient means of transmitting those possibilities that prove most conducive to cultural progress. I think that this noo/sociotemporal-specific theory of art can be extended to the lower *umwelts* in much the same way that, in chapter 17, I suggested that the temporal asymmetry typical of the nootemporal *umwelt* might be conceived of as applying, though at different strengths, to all of nature's integrative levels.

I suspect that in a basically similar way, cosmic evolution as a whole, as well as its component equilibrium *umwelts*, is stretched between a relatively decided and fixed past and a relatively open future. The present, whose unreality has fascinated many philosophers from Aristotle to Derrida, is, as process philosopher David Ray Griffin argues, the time of decision: "The *present* is the realm in which decisions are made: some possibilities are being turned into actualities while other possibilities are being excluded from actualization" (1986, 2).

The concept of temporal asymmetry is the foundation for a theory of the relation between art and science that respects their differences while escaping the trap of simple dualism. I believe that at any given moment in the evolution of the universe, the realm of art can be defined as the indefinite future collapsing into definiteness through present choice, and the realm of science can be defined as the record of previous works of art. Of course, in Fraser's earlier *umwelts*, temporal asymmetry is at best extremely fuzzy, so the difference between art and science is equally ill defined. Yet there must always be one, for it is precisely in the disequilibrium between art and science that the universe finds the force to self-organize and progress. If we assume that, in general, art is the becoming-present of the future and science is the becoming-past of the present, then a beautifully self-similar model of the universe emerges, one that is delicately balanced between freedom and constraint.

At one time, therefore, soon after the big bang, the becoming-chemistry of particle physics was an aesthetic event. Millions of years later, with chemistry a well-defined integrative *umwelt*, the emergence of life was an instance of extraordinary creativity or art. It might be objected that the concept of art is meaningless without the conjoined concept of an artist. Although this is a legitimate objection, it tends to be anthropocentric. Human artists are natural entities doing the work of evolution, so it is reasonable to assume that creativity is an essential feature of the universe, which, in its fractal depth, contains traces of previous, nonhuman "artists." Ultimately, I would argue that it is not human beings who are creative, but that human beings are the most creative expression of the universe's fundamental creativity. Without the artists that came before us, we would be foundering in pure freedom or pure constraint, or, perhaps more accurately, in the strange identity between the two.

If we apply this temporal model to the noo/sociotemporal *umwelt*, then a model of the relation among art, science, and the sacred emerges. According to this model, science is a kind of retrospection, a study of the universe's previous aesthetic decisions. Art, on the other hand, is time travel into the future. In the noo/sociotemporal sense, art is really a version of art in the larger, evolutionary sense. In general, scientists discover past art, whereas artists invent future science using the past as a handrail. Of course, I am not suggesting that all art is a kind of science fiction. Clearly art also allows a culture to assess its present condition. My point is merely that the value of even the most realistic novel is in its ability to present an image of the present that the culture can either affirm or seek to alter. In either case, it is the future that is being served.

Neither do I mean to suggest that art is, or should be, a kind of fetterless invention. The hypothetical nature of art is productively constrained by the history of the universe that constitutes its microstructure and by nature's tendency to create self-similar solutions to problems at different levels. In other words, the kind of self-similarity that accounts for the comprehensibility of metaphors suggests that noo/sociotemporal art is likely to reproduce, in its level-specific language, patterns indigenous to nature's lower *umwelts*. Therefore, we would expect art to bear a family relation to science in the same way that crime waves resemble quantum mechanical wave functions.

Am I, therefore, suggesting a normative aesthetics? In a way, that is indeed the case. For example, the list of human cultural universals offered earlier can be ignored by artists in either their formal or thematic concerns only at the risk of trivializing or marginalizing their work. Such cultural universals are neither eternal nor a closed set. They are, however, the accumulated knowledge of human beings and of the aesthetic events that gave birth to them. Certainly, art is in the business of criticizing, modifying, and replacing the past. But like all good sallies into the unknown, art does its work best when it knows as much about its history as the contemporary state of knowledge allows.

If genuine creativity can only flourish on the soil of the past, then artists need to respect the laws and regularities that eventually gave birth to human art. Such respect would define a broad aesthetics deeply wed to a new sacred vision of the universe. Ultimately, I believe that the most sacred thing imaginable is the proclivity of our universe to self-organize into increasingly complex configurations. Prigogine's championing of the possibility of a new dialogue with nature echoes the beliefs of many traditional people concerning the holiness of natural knowledge. For us, however, such a dialogue, if it is to be authentic, must respect nature's history as revealed by science, as well as its alterity, its mystery, and its creativity. It is only by returning the sacred to science that science can begin to see itself as the history of art. And it is only by seeing art in such a historical perspective that we can reconfirm the wisdom of many of our past experiments and clear the table for new work.

Conclusion

The basic question motivating this book concerns the possibility of change. Can the world be changed? If so, are there any guidelines, no matter how dim, to help us in constructing the future? And is it still conceivable that human beings, both individually and acting in corporate units, will continue to exert effective agency in the postmodern world?

To these questions, this book proposes a cautiously affirmative answer. If the world is a chaotic system, and if culture is self-similar to the complex hierarchy that I have been suggesting best describes both the structure and the dynamics of cosmic evolution, then agency, especially individual agency, may not be an outdated myth associated with bourgeois autonomy. As long as the cultural player understands the rules of the house, then he or she is in a position to play well, to improve the game, or even to create a new game. Chaos offers evolution the stability it needs to be cumulative and the sensitivity to perturbation it requires if it is periodically to reinvent itself.

In the course of this book, I have frequently presented my position by contrasting it to deconstructive, genealogical, and constructivist theories. I wish to emphasize that my criticism of these theoretical schools is predicated on the conviction that not only is change possible, but that it may often be precipitated by individuals. Let me explain. I realize that frequently my rhetoric may have suggested that all the wrong directions in which our culture is being pushed—specifically the desacralization of art, our skepticism about the existence of any foundations to our epistemologies, the recrudescence of Cartesian dualism in the form of a culture/nature or socially constructed reality/natural reality split, the undermining of our culture's belief in the possibility of choice and progress, our loss of confidence in narrative, the sense that any holistic continuum between our various environments has been irreparably shattered by postmodern fragmentation and simulation—have been the result of ignorance or willful fractiousness on the part of our leading theorists and artists. Such is not my intention. In a sense, Derrida and like-minded theorists are correct in describing a world that has been radically transformed due to historical, technological, economic, and sociological pressures, although even these pressures should be understood as the result of cultural decisions in which individuals have played some part. Nevertheless, as I have frequently argued, cultural evolution occurs much faster than biological evolution, thus making it extremely likely that the widespread changes in our cultural environment have created a mismatch with epigenetic rules that had evolved in radically different contexts. It is perfectly possible that contemporary theory and art are simply the result of this incongruity between a rapidly evolving cultural world and our evolutionary heritage.

If I have been petulant at times, it is not because I disagree with the diagnoses issuing from schools such as deconstruction, but because I fear their prescriptions. Although unlike Derrida, I am a champion of the liberal democratic state, like him I am distressed by many of the directions in which our culture is heading. However, rather than calling for endless analysis, resignation, or revolution, I have been arguing that it is always possible to push culture back onto a productive track. I take some solace from the observation that traditional peoples frequently see evil as a lack of balance between the spirit world and the actual world, and understand their art and rituals as the attempt to reestablish harmony. Analogously, I have faith that, if the state of Western culture in the last decade of the twentieth century is, in part, explainable as the disproportion between the exponential growth of sociotemporal technologies and the instructions inscribed in our genes, there are appropriate rituals to be performed in order to reduce the disequilibrium between culture and its evolutionary heritage to productive tolerances.

Of course, it is possible that the historical forces that have directed cultural change are implacable. If that is the case, then it may be that the mismatch between our genes and our social environment is permanent and likely to grow worse. On the other hand, if culture is, in fact, a chaotic system, then there is every reason to hope that slight perturbations issuing from individuals or small collectives can spread throughout the system, bringing it back into a state of chaotic harmony. Of course, as I have argued repeatedly, I do not wish to bring cultural change to a halt. I do not seek a perfect equilibrium between our cultural world and our lower *umwelts*. In fact, I trust that only a lack of proportion between them can foster the far-from-equilibrium conditions that nourish innovation. My point is that when culture and epigenetic rules become incommensurable, then there is a danger that healthy cultural chaos may disintegrate into anarchy.

The normative aspects of this book are all directed against the idea that such disorder is either inevitable or desirable. Instead, I have argued that productive novelty is encouraged, although not guaranteed, by a worldview that sees natural classical categories less as obstacles than as tools in the business of inventing the future. That deconstruction is an expression of the cultural environment of the postwar period is hardly debatable. That this environment is inevitable, inexorable, or inalterable is surely debatable.

Notes

Chapter 1

1. Following Heidegger, I will use Being to designate either the set of all that is or the "is-ness" of things.

Chapter 2

1. It has come to my attention that, in the mid-1970s, Derrida gave a seminar entitled "La Vie/La Mort" in which he considered such works as Jacob's *The Logic of Life* and Monod's *Chance and Necessity*. As far as I know, this material remains unpublished.

Chapter 5

1. The situation in South Africa is changing as this book is going into print. This chapter focuses on apartheid for the contingent reason that, since it is one of the few political issues on which Derrida has written, it can serve as an example of the general political implications of deconstructive intervention. If Pretoria should choose to make this chapter's case study outmoded, my joy would be immense.

Chapter 7

1. There are, of course, many evolutionary models. Some, like that defended by Stephen J. Gould in his recent *Wonderful Life* (1989), eschew the notion of progress that is central to my thesis. Most evolutionary views, however, differ from deconstruction in positing some form of nonconstructivist continuum between the prehuman and human worlds.

Chapter 8

1. My understanding of novelty owes much to Davies (1988), who himself borrows from Denbigh (1975): "Denbigh prefers to think of the com-

ing-into-being of new levels as an 'inventive process', that is, it brings into existence something which is both different and not necessitated: 'for the essence of true novelty is that *it did not have to be that way*'.

Although there are many definitions of hierarchy, in its most general form it is "the principle by which the elements of a whole are ranked in relation to the whole . . ." (Dumont 1970, 66).

2. Although this new model of the cosmos resembles the positivism of Auguste Comte, it differs from it in a number of crucial ways, the most important of which is that, as opposed to the French positivists for whom mind or soul were puerile remnants of the metaphysical or theological period of social and mental development, much current speculation on the evolution of the universe postulates that mind is neither a chimera nor part of a Manichean dualistic struggle with matter, but a real, emergent feature of a resourceful universe.

3. I realize that it is perhaps difficult to cleanse the term *hierarchy* of its unpleasant connotations. For example, Bunge (Whyte 1969, 17) understands hierarchy to mean "an antisymmetric relation of domination or command." In the place of hierarchy, he proposes "level structure," a level being defined as "an assembly of things of a definite kind, e.g., a collection of systems characterized by a definite set of properties and laws, and such that it belongs to an evolutionary line . . ." (20). I persist in using *hierarchy* in this book instead of Bunge's level structure because many of the authors upon whom I focus tend to employ the term, however my understanding of hierarchy is essentially identical to Bunge's notion of an evolutionary level structure.

4. Bunge (1981) criticizes Popper's notion of world 3 on the grounds that it is a new idealism, that is, that it postulates an autonomous nonevolving Platonic realm that is cut off from concrete human beings. My own view is that Popper understands world 3 as a *semi-autonomous* emergent feature of cosmic evolution which, like any evolutionary level, is connected to preceding levels yet able to display novel characteristics of its own. Note how Popper's definition of the relation of world 3 to actual human beings can be applied, mutatis mutandis, to much contemporary speculation on the nature of institutions: "Admittedly, of course, theories are the products of human thought . . . . Nevertheless, they have a certain degree of *autonomy*: they may have, objectively, consequences of which nobody so far has thought, and which may be *discovered*; discovered in the same sense in which an existing but so far unknown plant of animal may be discovered. One may say that world 3 is man-made only in its origin, and that once theories exist, they begin to have a life of their own: they produce previously invisible consequences, they produce new problems." (1977, 40)

Chapter 9

1. Although his interpretation of the phenomenon is radically different from mine, Richard Rorty has discussed the filiation between deconstruction and idealism. For example, he writes, "I hope that these two similarities are

enough to justify an attempt to view textualism as the contemporary counterpart of idealism" (1982, 140).

2. Fraser realizes that very soon after the big bang other forms of energy/matter might have existed. His point is less that photons are the absolute origin of the universe, but that theirs is its most primitive temporality.

3. I wish to emphasize that my model of evolution only holds when sufficiently large time-scales are taken into account. It is indisputable that, on short time-scales, much of what occurs to populations is based on contingency. Passenger pigeons became extinct while more complex humans and less complex crustaceans survived. Surely the fate of the passenger pigeon is not ruled by some evolutionary master plan. My point is simply that, in large time-scales, a pattern of increasing complexation does emerge, although even this pattern is sufficiently muddy to warrant caution. It is only on time scales as large as Fraser's *umwelts* that the pattern becomes clearly apparent and my claims about the increasing complexity, freedom, fragility, and conflict of entities are defensible.

Chapter 11

1. The technical and cultural implications of nanotechnology are explored in Drexler, 1986.

2. Contemporary critical theory deals with many notions of the self, among them the psychological self, the Cartesian self, the gendered self, the semiotic linguistic self, etc. With the possible exception of certain postmodern analyses of the self, for the most part, these are nootemporal ideas. Consequently, the remainder of this chapter will be devoted to an investigation of a nootemporal concept of selfhood.

Chapter 13

1. Although I think that my understanding of sociobiology will become increasingly clear in the course of this book, at the outset I will state that I reject the more reductionist versions of the discipline. If this book has one theme, it is that reductionism is as inadequate a description of our world as constructivism. The radical kind of sociobiology for which all human behavior is determined by our genetic makeup confuses nootemporality with biotemporality. For the purposes of this book, sociobiology simply means a model of human behavior that recognizes the necessary commerce between the genetic level and the cultural level of human existence.

In addition, I would like to alert the reader to the political disputes surrounding the science of sociobiology. In 1975, a number of intellectuals (including Stephen J. Gould) founded Science for the People, a group that proceeded to attack sociobiology by associating it with the extreme political right. Since then, there has been a great deal of controversy surrounding the political and social implications of sociobiology. My own position is that the

picture of sociobiology drawn by the Science of the People group is a caricature enabled by the basically constructivist and dualistic predispositions of
most humanities academics these days. Although a reductive sociobiology
can, in fact, be enlisted in the service of all kinds of heinous political agendas,
I believe that the basic intuition of sociobiology regarding human evolution,
that human beings are, in large measure, the products of the commerce
between their genes and their culture, is a potentially progressive and liberating insight.

2. Ideas, of course, are intricately wed to affect. I am not arguing that
criticism is cut off from those systems of the brain not directly concerned
with the processing of abstract information. In fact, we know that such neural ghettos do not exist; the brain is too interconnected to lend credence to
any such isolationist mental theory. My point is simply one of emphasis.
Whereas literature stimulates a wide range of cognitive and affective responses, criticism focuses on, but does not restrict itself to, the abstract
ideational properties of the neocortex.

Chapter 14

1. For the remainder of this book, unless further qualified, the term
noo/sociotemporal will be used to refer to the commerce between human beings
and their collective institutions. I will reserve the term *sociotemporality* or *time-
compact globe* for those occasions when Fraser's concept of a new integrative
level is an issue.

Chapter 15

1. According to Roger Penrose, quantum mechanics can describe the
macroscopic world as long as different possibilities are separated by very
small energy differences: "Recall, first of all, that the descriptions of quantum
theory appear to apply sensibly (usefully?) only at the so-called *quantum
level*—of molecules, atoms, or subatomic particles, but also at large dimensions, so long as energy differences between alternate possibilities remain
very small" (1989, 296). Of course, at the classical level, energy differences
between alternatives are almost always so large as to preclude the applicability of quantum level, complex-number-weighted superpositions: "Common
sense alone tells us that this is not the way the world actually behaves!
Cricket balls are indeed well approximated by the descriptions of *classical*
physics. They have reasonably well-defined locations, and are not seen to
be in two places at once, as the linear laws of quantum mechanics would
allow them to be" (297–98).

Chapter 16

1. In general, fractals are curves that have no derivative and can therefore be described as possessing fractional dimensions. In addition, they pos-

sess infinite length that is compressed to display infinite detail and are self-similar insofar as they display similar patterns at different scales.

Chapter 19

1. Access to knowledge that is stored extrasomatically involves both mental and institutional processes. Although this chapter deals primarily with the storage, retrieval, and creation of ideas in the mental realm, it is not meant to suggest that the politics of institutional information technologies, that is, the sociotemporality of knowledge, are simply isolable from nootemporal information processing.

2. I am using the terms *idea* and *concept* interchangeably in this chapter. Although I realize that there are important philosophical differences between the two, these differences are not of a nature to affect the argument being developed here.

3. In note 1 in chapter 13, part 2, I defend my use of sociobiological theory by distinguishing reductionist sociobiology, which understands all of human behavior as issuing in a relatively unproblematic way from our genes, from a progressive kind of sociobiology that pays homage to our evolutionary past while respecting the central importance of culture in determining the world of human beings. I wish to alert the reader that my defense of Lumsden and Wilson is only a defense of those aspects of their work that support such a non-reductionist version of sociobiology. Indeed, as Kitcher (1985) argues, it is likely that Lumsden, and especially Wilson, are much more inclined to view sociobiology reductively than many passages in *Promethean Fire* would suggest. My own definition of sociobiology is not substantially different from one that Kitcher himself endorses: "Our actions are not simple reflexes. Nor are they the expressions of desires imposed on us by the surrounding culture. They are determined by the gene-environment interaction" (411).

Chapter 21

1. "It was a splendid mind. For if thought is like the keyboard of a piano, divided into so many notes, or like the alphabet is ranged in twenty-six letters all in order, then his splendid mind had no sort of difficulty in running over those letters one by one, firmly and accurately, until it had reached, say, the letter Q. He reached Q. Very few people in the whole of England ever reach Q" (Woolf 1927, 53).

2. Needless to say, the idea that the universe values chaotic complexity because it fosters the emergence of novelty as well as the conservation of past inventions is controversial. According to Vollmer (Wuketits 1984, 185), "Evolutionary epistemology takes concepts and hypotheses, i.e., descriptive propositions, as cognitive structures, but not values or norms." My own position, as outlined in this chapter and throughout this book, is much closer to Davies' (1988, 203), who argues that an evolutionary value scale may be

discerned in the universe's predisposition to self-organize into increasingly complex structures: "The very fact that the universe *is* creative, and that the laws have permitted complex structures to emerge and develop to the point of consciousness—in other words, that the universe has organized its own self-awareness—is for me powerful evidence that there is 'something going on' behind it all."

References

Abbott, Edwin A. 1952. *Flatland*. New York: Penguin Books.

Aoki, Chiye, and Philip Siekevitz. 1988. "Plasticity in Brain Development." *Scientific American* 259 (6): 56–64.

d'Aquili, Eugene G., Charles D. Laughlin, Jr., and John McManus. 1979. *The Spectrum of Ritual*. New York: Columbia University Press.

Audouze, Jean. 1987. "Is the Universe Changing?" *Diogenes* 138 (Summer): 61–80.

Baudrillard, Jean. 1983. *Simulations*. New York: Semiotext(e).

Berry, M. V., I. C. Percival, and N. O. Weiss. 1987. *Dynamical Chaos*. Port Washington, N.Y.: Scholium International.

Bloom, Harold, et al. 1979. *Deconstruction and Criticism*. New York: Continuum.

Borges, Jorge Luis. 1964. *Labyrinths*. New York: New Directions.

Briggs, John, and David F. Peat. 1989. *Turbulent Mirror*. New York: Harper and Row.

Brooks, Daniel R. and E. O. Wiley. 1988. *Evolution as Entropy*. Chicago: University of Chicago Press.

Bunge, Mario. 1981. *Scientific Materialism*. Dordrecht: D. Reidel Publishing Company.

Butler, Christopher. 1984. *Interpretation, Deconstruction, and Ideology*. Oxford: Clarendon Press.

Chomsky, Noam. 1972. *Language and Mind*. New York: Harcourt Brace Jovanovich.

Cixous, Hélène. 1976. "The Laugh of the Medusa." Trans. Keith Cohen and Paula Cohen. *Signs* (Summer): 875–93.

Crutchfield, James P., J. Doyne Farmer, Norman H. Packard, and Robert S. Shaw. 1986. "Chaos." *Scientific American* 255 (6): 46–57.

Culler, Jonathan D. 1982. *On Deconstruction: Theory and Criticism in the 1970s*. Ithaca, N.Y.: Cornell University Press.

Davies, Paul. 1983. *God and the New Physics*. New York: Touchstone.

———. 1988. *The Cosmic Blueprint*. New York: Simon and Schuster.

Davis, Robert Con, and Ronald Schleifer. 1985. *Rhetoric and Form: Deconstruction at Yale*. Norman: University of Oklahoma Press.

Dawkins, Richard. 1976. *The Selfish Gene.* New York: Oxford University Press.

Denbigh, Kenneth. 1975. *An Inventive Universe.* London: Hutchinson.

Derrida, Jacques. 1973. *Speech and Phenomena.* Trans. David B. Allison. Evanston, Ill.: Northwestern University Press.

―――. 1976. *Of Grammatology.* Trans. Gayatri Spivak. Baltimore, Md.: Johns Hopkins University Press.

―――. 1977. *Edmund Husserl's* The Origin of Geometry: *An Introduction.* Trans. John P. Leavey. Stony Brook: N. Hays.

―――. 1978a. *Spurs: Nietzsche's Styles.* Trans. Barbara Harlow. Chicago: University of Chicago Press.

―――. 1978b. *Writing and Difference.* Trans. Alan Bass. Chicago: University of Chicago Press.

―――. 1981a. *Dissemination.* Trans. Barbara Johnson. Chicago: University of Chicago Press.

―――. 1981b. *Positions.* Trans. Alan Bass. Chicago: University of Chicago Press.

―――. 1982. *Margins of Philosophy.* Trans. Alan Bass. Chicago: University of Chicago Press.

―――. 1985. "Racism's Last Word." Trans. Peggy Kamuf. *Critical Inquiry* 12 (1): 290–99.

―――. 1986a. "But, beyond . . . (Open Letter to Anne McClintock and Rob Nixon)." Trans. Peggy Kamuf. *Critical Inquiry* 13 (1): 155–70.

―――. 1986b. *Glas.* Trans. John P. Leavey, Jr., and Richard Rand. Lincoln: University of Nebraska Press.

―――. 1986c. "Interview." *Art Papers* 10 (1): 31–35.

―――. 1987a. *The Post Card.* Trans. Alan Bass. Chicago: University of Chicago Press.

―――. 1987b. *The Truth in Painting.* Trans. Geoff Bennington and Ian McCleod. Chicago: University of Chicago Press.

―――. 1988a. "Like the Sound of the Sea Deep within a Shell: Paul de Man's War." Trans. Peggy Kamuf. *Critical Inquiry* 14 (3): 590–652.

―――. 1988b. *Limited, Inc..* Trans. Jeffrey Mehlman and Samuel Weber. Evanston, Ill.: Northwestern University Press.

Drexler, K. Erik. 1986. *Engines of Creation: The Coming Era of Nanotechnology.* Garden City, N.Y.: Anchor Press.

Dumont, Louis. 1970. *Homo Hierarchicus.* Chicago: University of Chicago Press.

Eagleton, Terry. 1976. *Criticism and Ideology.* London: Verso.

Fekete, John. 1984. *The Structuralist Allegory: Reconstructive Encounters with the New French Thought.* Minneapolis: University of Minnesota Press.

Flieger, Jerry A., and Alexander Argyros. 1987. "Hartman's Contagious Orbit: Reassessing Aesthetic Criticism." *Diacritics* 17 (1): 52–69.

Foucault, Michel. 1972. *The Archaeology of Knowledge and The Discourse on Language.* Trans. A. M. Sheridan Smith. New York: Harper Colophon.

Fraser, J. T. 1978. *Time as Conflict.* Basel: Birkauser Verlag.

―――. 1987. *Time the Familiar Stranger.* Amherst: University of Massachusetts Press.

Gardner, Martin. 1979. *The Ambidextrous Universe: Mirror Asymmetry and Time-Reversed Worlds*. New York: Scribner's.

Gasché, Rodolphe. 1979. "Deconstruction as Criticism." *Glyph 6:* 177–215.

Gleick, James. 1987. *Chaos*. New York: Viking Penguin.

Gould, Stephen J. 1989. *Wonderful Life: The Burgess Shale and the Nature of History*. New York: W.W. Horton.

Griffin, David Ray. 1986. *Physics and the Ultimate Significance of Time*. Albany: State University of New York Press.

Hartman, Geoffrey. 1980. *Criticism in the Wilderness*. New Haven: Yale University Press.

———. 1981. *Saving the Text*. Baltimore, Md.: Johns Hopkins University Press.

Hawking, Stephen W. 1988. *A Brief History of Time*. New York: Bantam Books.

Hayles, N. Katherine. 1989. "Chaos as Orderly Disorder: Shifting Ground in Contemporary Literature and Science." *New Literary History* 20 (2): 305–22.

———. 1990. *Chaos Bound: Orderly Disorder in Contemporary Literature and Science*. Ithaca: Cornell University Press.

Heidegger, Martin. 1962. *Being and Time*. Trans. John Macquarrie and Edward Robinson. New York: Harper and Row.

———. 1968. *What is Called Thinking*. Trans. J. Glenn Gray and F. Wieck. New York: Harper and Row.

———. 1971. *Poetry, Language, Thought*. Trans. Albert Hofstadter. New York: Harper Colophon.

———. 1974. *An Introduction to Metaphysics*. Trans. Ralph Manheim. New Haven: Yale University Press.

Heisenberg, Werner. 1958. *Physics and Philosophy: The Revolution in Modern Science*. New York: Harper and Row.

Hoffman, Banesh, with Helen Dukas. 1972. *Albert Einstein: Creator and Rebel*. New York: Viking Press.

Hofstadter, Douglas. 1980. *Gödel, Escher, Bach: An Eternal Golden Braid*. New York: Vintage Books.

———. 1985. *Metamagical Themas: Questing for the Essence of Mind and Pattern*. New York: Basic Books.

Husserl, Edmund. 1964. *The Phenomenology of Internal Time-Consciousness*. Trans. James S. Churchill. Bloomington: Indiana University Press.

———. 1969. *Ideas: General Introduction to Pure Phenomenology*. Trans. W. R. Boyce Gibson. New York: Collier.

———. 1973. *Cartesian Meditations*. Trans. Dorion Cairns. The Hague: M. Nijhoff.

Irigaray, Luce. 1977. *Ce sexe qui n'en est pas un*. Paris: Minuit.

James, William. 1890. *Principles of Psychology*. New York: H. Holt.

Jameson, Fredric. 1981. *The Political Unconscious: Narrative as a Socially Symbolic Act*. Ithaca, N.Y.: Cornell University Press.

Kaku, Michio, Jennifer Trainer. 1987. *Beyond Einstein: The Cosmic Quest for the Theory of the Universe*. New York: Bantam Books.

Kitcher, Philip. 1985. *Vaulting Ambition: Sociobiology and the Quest for Human Nature.* Cambridge, Mass.: MIT Press.

Kripke, Saul. 1982. *Wittgenstein on Rules and Private Language: An Elementary Exposition.* Cambridge, Mass.: Harvard University Press.

Kristéva, Julia. 1974. *La révolution du langage poétique.* Paris: Editions du Seuil.

Kuhn, Thomas S. 1970. *The Structure of Scientific Revolutions.* Chicago: University of Chicago Press.

Lakoff, George, and Mark Johnson. 1980. *Metaphors We Live By.* Chicago: University of Chicago Press.

Lentricchia, Frank. 1983. *Criticism and Social Change.* Chicago: University of Chicago Press.

———. 1988. *Ariel and the Police.* Madison: University of Wisconsin Press.

Lieberman, Philip. 1984. *The Biology and Evolution of Language.* Cambridge, Mass.: Harvard University Press.

Livingston, Paisley. 1988. *Literary Knowledge.* Ithaca, N.Y.: Cornell University Press.

Lumsden, Charles J., and Edward O. Wilson. 1983. *Promethean Fire.* Cambridge, Mass.: Harvard University Press.

Lyotard, Jean-François. 1984. *The Postmodern Condition: A Report on Knowledge.* Trans. Geoff Bennington and Brian Massumi. Minneapolis: University of Minnesota Press.

McClintock, Anne, and Rob Nixon. 1986. "No Names Apart: The Separation of Word and History in Derrida's 'Le Dernier Mot du Racisme.'" *Critical Inquiry* 13 (1): 140–54.

Merchant, Carolyn. 1980. *The Death of Nature.* San Francisco: Harper and Row.

Merrell, Floyd. 1985. *Deconstruction Reframed.* West Lafayette, Ind.: Purdue University Press.

Merrill, Robert. 1988. *Ethics/Aesthetics: Post-Modern Positions.* Washington, D.C.: Maisonneuve Press.

Minsky, Marvin. 1986. *The Society of Mind.* New York: Simon and Schuster.

Monod, Jacques. 1971. *Chance and Necessity.* Trans. Austryn Wainhouse. New York: Vintage Books.

Nietzsche aujourd'hui?. 1973. Paris: 10/18.

Penrose, Roger. 1989. *The Emperor's New Mind: Concerning Computers, Minds, and the Laws of Physics.* New York: Oxford University Press.

Popper, Karl R., and John C. Eccles. 1977. *The Self and its Brain.* London: Routledge and Kegan Paul

Prigogine, Ilya, and Isabelle Stengers. 1984. *Order Out of Chaos.* New York: Bantam Books.

Rabinow, Paul, ed. 1984. *The Foucault Reader.* New York: Pantheon.

Rorty, Richard. 1982. *Consequences of Pragmatism.* Minneapolis: University of Minnesota Press.

———. 1984. "Deconstruction and Circumvention." *Critical Inquiry* 11 (1): 1–23.

————. 1989. *Contingency, Irony, and Solidarity*. New York: Cambridge University Press.

Ryan, Michael. 1982. *Marxism and Deconstruction*. Baltimore, Md.: Johns Hopkins University Press.

Scholes, Robert. 1985. *Textual Power*. New Haven: Yale University Press.

Shimony, Abner. 1988. "The Reality of the Quantum World." *Scientific American* 258 (1): 46–53.

Smith, Barbara Hernstein. 1988. *Contingencies of Value: Alternative Perspectives for Critical Theory*. Cambridge, Mass.: Harvard University Press.

Smith, Joseph H., and William Kerrigan. 1984. *Taking Chances: Derrida, Psychoanalysis, and Literature*. Baltimore, Md.: Johns Hopkins University Press.

Teleki, Geza. 1973. *The Predatory Behavior of Wild Chimpanzees*. Lewisburg, Pa.: Bucknell University Press.

Turner, Frederick. 1985. *Natural Classicism*. New York: Paragon House.

Turner, Victor. 1986. *The Anthropology of Performance*. New York: PAJ Publications.

Uexküll, Jakob von. 1957. "A Stroll through the Worlds of Animals and Man." In *Instinctive Behavior*, ed. and trans. C. H. Schiller, 5–80. New York: International Universities Press.

West, Bruce J., and Ary L.Goldberger. 1987. "Physiology in Fractal Dimensions." *American Scientist* 75 (4): 354–65.

Wheeler, John Archibald. 1988. "World as System Self-Synthesized by Quantum Networking." *IBM Journal of Research and Development* 32 (1): 4–15.

Whyte, Lancelot Law, Albert G. Wilson, and Donna Wilson. 1969. *Hierarchical Structures*. New York: American Elsevier Publishing Company.

Wiketits, Franz M., ed. 1984. *Concepts and Approaches in Evolutionary Epistemology: Towards and Evolutionary Theory of Knowledge*. Dordrecht: D. Reidell Publishing Company.

Wilson, Peter J. 1983. *Man the Promising Primate*. New Haven: Yale University Press.

Wittgenstein, Ludwig. 1955. *Tractatus Logico-Philosophicus*. Trans. C. K. Ogden. London: Routledge and Kegan Paul.

————. 1958. *Philosophical Investigations*. Trans. G. E. M. Anscombe. New York: Macmillan.

Woolf, Virginia. 1927. *To The Lighthouse*. New York: Harcourt Brace Jovanovich.

Wright, Robert. 1988. "Did the Universe Just Happen?" *Atlantic Monthly* 261 (4): 29–44.

Index

363